Baseball
UNDER THE PALMS

HISTORY OF MIAMI
MINOR LEAGUE BASEBALL
THE EARLY YEARS 1892 - 1960

SAM ZYGNER
BARBRA CABRERA

SUNBURY
PRESS

Mechanicsburg, PA USA

Published by Sunbury Press, Inc.
Mechanicsburg, Pennsylvania

www.sunburypress.com

For information about special discounts for bulk purchases, please contact Sunbury Press Orders Dept. at (855) 338-8359 or orders@sunburypress.com.

To request one of our authors for speaking engagements or book signings, please contact Sunbury Press Publicity Dept. at publicity@sunburypress.com.

ISBN: 978-1-62006-157-2 (Trade paperback)

Library of Congress Control Number: 2019940155

FIRST SUNBURY PRESS EDITION: April 2019

Product of the United States of America
0 1 1 2 3 5 8 13 21 34 55

Set in Bookman Old Style
Designed by Crystal Devine
Cover by Terry Kennedy
Edited by Lawrence Knorr

Continue the Enlightenment!

In memory of Emilio and Doris Cabrera

Contents

Acknowledgments

We wish to recognize everyone who played a part in bringing *Baseball Under the Palms* to fruition. It is our way of saying "thank you." Our heartfelt appreciation goes out to Larry Knorr, (Founder/ CEO); Crystal Devine (Production Manager); Terry Kennedy (Graphic Artist) and everyone at Sunbury Press for believing in this historic project.

We are grateful to Ashley Trujillo and the staff at HistoryMiami for their research assistance. They are a true credit in helping preserve Miami history. Howard Kleinberg the last editor of the *Miami News* and his perspective on Miami baseball history; Shelly Bender of the East Hillsborough Historical Society; Gilbert Gott from the Plant City Photo Archives and History Center; historian and writer Lamar Garrard; Cuban baseball historian Cesar Lopez; and Stephen Smith for his Florida International League knowledge and input.

One of the many benefits of creating this project is the opportunity to interview players and family members. Thank you to the ballplayers for their memories and anecdotes including: Jim Ackeret, Jim Archer, Bob Bowman, Richard Bunker, Leo Burke, Mel Clark, Angelo Dagres, Billy DeMars, Gerald Didier, Bill Enos, Dave Exter, Humberto "Chico" Fernandez, Dick Getter, Johnny Gray, Dallas Green, Joe Gulvas, Dorrel "Whitey" Herzog, Fred Hopke, Earl Hunsinger, Wilbur Johnson, Steve Korcheck, Bob Kuzava, Joe Kwiatkowski, Ed Little, Stu Locklin, Butch McCord, Richard "Dick" McCoy, Bob "Mickey" Micelotta, Charles "Pete' Morant, Albie Pearson, Tom Qualters, Ron Samford, Ray Semproch, Jerry Snyder, Jack Spring, Carlyle Staab, Ben Tompkins, Robert Tripp, Bob Usher, Fred Valentine, Vito Valentinetti, Fred VanDusen, Raul Villamia, Gale Wade, George Wasconis, Robert Willis, Maury Wills, Gene Zubrinski, and George Zuverink. Special thanks to family members; the Bandrimer family Betty Carr (daughter of Isey), and Robert (son of Isey), Mike Conroy Jr., Elvie Darden (wife of Billy) Anne Enos (daughter of Bill), Terri Fassbender (daughter of Billy Darden), Bill Durney Jr., Nancy Foye-Cox (granddaughter of Joe Ryan) Rocky Knepper (son of Roy), Nancy McKenna (daughter of Jim Ackeret), John Nee (son of Mel), Ryan Rotzell (grandson of Rocky), Thomas Rotzell (son of Rocky), Bill Stammen (son of Pete), Paul Stammen (brother of Pete), the Smith family (Jerry, June, and Reggie), Dan Streza (nephew of John), and Chris Zachritz (son of Robert). Lest we not forget their contribution, former batboy of the original Miami Marlins Tim Anagnost, and former Florida International League umpire, Charlie Albury.

Special thanks to my parents Sam and Pat Zygner, my sister Beth and brother-in-law Frank, my uncle Jack and aunt Jan Zygner, as well as Debbie Pettigrew for her encouragement during the writing process.

Last, but certainly not least, my eternal gratitude to the co-author and the love of my life Barbra whose constant encouragement, patience and dedication to this project were invaluable. I consider myself the luckiest man in the world having a wife that shares with me the love of baseball.

Introduction

I love to talk baseball with anyone who shares the same interest and does not mind my bending his or her ear a little. This comes as no great revelation to anyone who knows me and recognizes the obsession with the game and its history that I hold so near and dear to my heart.

Over the course of time and many conversations with baseball fans, I was struck by their belief that professional baseball sprang forth in Miami only after major league baseball launched a new franchise in 1993. Unbeknownst to a large segment of Miamians is the existence of a rich and illustrious history that has been largely untold. The stories of the men and women who were part of baseball from those bygone days have been largely lost to the passage of time. Our national pastime's roots in southernmost Florida go back as far as 1892. From its pastoral beginnings of contests between hamlets called "town ball," the popularity of the game spread expeditiously, so much so that by 1913 the first professional team was organized, and competed in an "outlaw league" known as the Florida East Coast League.

From 1913 to 1991, minor league baseball thrived off and on in Miami, and for a short time in Miami Beach, bringing enjoyment to legions of fans. Despite being interrupted by two World Wars and the Great Depression, baseball served as the fans' fix in the days before the influence of major league baseball spread to all four corners of the country, and beyond. With the exception of spring training, exposure to big league baseball was limited to newspaper accounts until television and radio entered the scene. Local fandom rooted for their diamond heroes at such venues as Flamingo Park, Miami Stadium, Royal Palm Grounds, and Tatum Park/Field, (later re-named Miami Field) with the same fervor as devotees in Boston, New York, or Philadelphia.

Miami was unique as it had its own Latin flair and was ahead of its time, due to the influx of ballplayers from the Caribbean, mostly Cuba. The formation of the Florida International League in 1946, with the inclusion of Havana, swung the door open wide as Miami and Miami Beach took advantage of the talent pool, signing several players to fill out their rosters with talent from the south. The FIL was truly a league ahead of its time with teams scheduling regularly charted flights to and from the Cuban capital city.

Some of baseballs' most colorful and eccentric front office personnel, owners, managers, and players represented the Magic City. Some names are recognizable and some are not, but to baseball fans that rooted for teams such as the Flamingos, Hustlers, Magicians, Marlins, Seminoles, Sun Sox, Tourists, and Wahoos, they were every bit as beloved as major league stars. In the upcoming pages, you will recognize the names of Gene Bearden, Chico Fernandez, Pancho Herrera, Pepper Martin, Satchel Paige and Maury Wills. While others will be new to you, such as Isey Bandrimer, Labe Dean, Chico Morilla, Melvin Nee, Max Rosenfeld, Joe Ryan, and Woody Smith. Yet, just as each square of fabric is sewn together to form a quilt, so the exploits of these men and many others come together forming Miami's own baseball tapestry.

Two of the oldest players that shared their personal experiences were Bill Enos, a first baseman with the Miami Sun Sox, and Gene Zubrinksi who held down third base for the Miami Beach Flamingos. They shared tales from, not only their hardball careers but also from their personal lives. It was awe-inspiring how they recalled past events with such detail. We are so grateful to have known all these men, if even for a brief time.

Minor league baseball had its own unique flavor, a homespun feel that attracted its many followers. In particular, the players had an up-close and personal interaction with the fans. They knew many on a first name basis and even socialized with them off the field. In general, they were on the same socio-economic level and shared the same interests. The ballplayers were, in general, a hard-bitten and rowdy bunch especially in the early days. It was common for players to engage in brawls with their managers, opponents, umpires, and even people in the stands that provoked them by flinging insults. Ejections and league fines were commonplace. In addition, owners had their own unique set of problems mostly tied to financial concerns. To attract paying customers, owners devised crazy promotions, and stunts to increase attendance.

Alvin Lederer, a south Florida historian, wrote a colorful and fascinating tidbit on a website. His friend, Don Boyd had gathered a vast collection of memorabilia over his lifetime, and as part of his post, he honored his colleague for educating people about local history. His remarks were apropos. Lederer wrote, "He [Don Boyd] told me he started collecting south Florida memorabilia because he got tired of people telling him that Florida didn't have any history and that all we have is the sun and beaches and I told him they're right, we have a lot of son of a bitches coming here telling us we have no history."

Jim Bouton, a former major league pitcher and author of *Ball Four*, eloquently stated, "You spend a good piece of your life gripping a baseball, and it turns out it was the other way around all the time." Our hope is that baseball has the same grip on you. So, join us and go backward in time experiencing the great moments of Miami's baseball past, the thrills, humorous anecdotes, and the heartbreaks. We hope you enjoy learning and gaining insight into the history shared throughout these pages, as much as we reveled in researching, and writing about it.

Let's Play Ball!

CHAPTER ONE

BEGINNINGS

The Miami Miracle and West Palm Beach Expos are playing the second game of a twin bill on August 31, 1991.[1] It is the bottom of the seventh inning, a Saturday game with nothing at stake. The Expos have already qualified for the playoffs and the Miracle are playing out the string.

Each impatient batter's approach at the plate is swinging at anything near the strike zone, especially the Miami contingent, anxious to depart for their offseason destinations. Miami relief pitcher, Joe Klancnik is poised on the mound and delivers the final pitch to retire the last batter that preserves Scott Asche's eighth win of the season. The game reaches its completion in less than two hours, and most of the 4,074 attendees have long since filed out of the West Palm Beach Municipal Stadium; the empty ballpark left only with the echoing sounds of the grounds crew clatter preparing the field for the next day's event.

Unbeknownst to the fans and players that day, they had witnessed the concluding sentence in the last chapter of Miami minor league baseball history. Long before any of the Miracle players were born, hardball evolved in the area and created a vibrant and rich history. Throughout the years, fans lived and breathed to support their local hardball warriors, the same as adherents in major league cities did. What began 80 years earlier with an "outlaw league" club named the Miami Seminoles, had concluded with the Miracle.[2] There was no fanfare, nor were mournful words expressed.

The final refrain had played out two months earlier on June 10, 1991, when baseball commissioner, Fay Vincent announced

Denver (Colorado Rockies) and Miami (Florida Marlins) would be the newest franchises to join the major leagues.[3] Although the Miracle represented Miami as an independent affiliate in the Advanced Class A Florida State League, by 1990 they had relocated to Pompano Beach, 35 miles to the north.

Invariably, time marches on and memories fade with the passing of each generation as they construct their own remembrances. Yet, history is due its rightful attention. Like any story, it has its beginning, middle, and end. This tale commences with the arrival of upstart settlers and the eventual and impressive rise of baseball in a city whose beauty and climate opened its arms to the national pastime.

During the mid to late nineteenth century, Miami was hardly the glitzy modern metropolitan city that most know today. Regarded as little more than a settlement, the untamed land was east of the Everglades bordering Biscayne Bay. It lay close to pristine beaches, stretches of lush mangroves, palm trees with the virgin Miami River running through its center. To the few homesteaders and squatters eking out an existence, the only constant was the monotonous infestation of the ever-present mosquitoes that feasted on them, and the relentless and oppressive humidity.

By 1858, the last of three Seminole Wars had ended. Yet memories of the strife between settlers and the military against the Native Americans still held firm in the recollections of most of the 73 registered Dade County voters dispersed throughout Cocoanut Grove, (its spelling at the time), Cutler and Lemon City in 1876. The location of modern-day downtown Miami consisted of only a few scattered dwellings peppered across the landscape.

Late nineteenth-century South Florida pioneers gave little thought to leisure pursuits. They were busy scratching out a modest living raising a wide range of Caribbean-introduced citrus crops, while others acted as merchants selling goods. Almost all practiced the art of "wrecking," salvaging cargo from ships that ran aground due to the unpredictable weather and seasonal hurricanes.[4]

Meanwhile, across the United States, a new form of recreation known as "Base Ball" swept the nation and gained popularity. Those primarily relocating from eastern parts of the country bring with them a desire to enjoy baseball. The game left its indelible mark in this sparsely populated southeast corner of the U.S.

The first mention in print of "base ball" [*sic*] came in the July 14, 1892 edition of the *Tropical Sun* newspaper. In the article, an unnamed writer painted an idyllic scene in words describing a game pitting Cocoanut Grove against Lemon city, latter prevailing, 18 to 17.

Fourth of July in South Florida! It sounds as if it would be hot and uncomfortable but it is not.

A most perfect day-bright, breezy, and the thermometer only 82 at mid-day.

A charming sail on beautiful Biscayne Bay brought a merry party to Lemon City where the glorious fourth was to be celebrated by a match game of base ball, the first ever played on the Bay.

Less than a month ago the boys began to talk base ball. Each little town organized a club and with little practice, they went at it and played a very good game. But the best part of all was that there was no dissatisfaction. It was agreed that the umpire was just in all of his decisions.

The grounds were a mile and a half out of Lemon City, on the prairie, the scene was very striking-the wide stretch of prairie with pine wood border, the tent for refreshments, the motley collection of carts, wagons, ponies and mules, the pretty dresses of the girls and the natty costumes of the players—then the wonder of all was—where did all the people come from? About two hundred gathered to see the game, and one hundred took supper at the hotel in the evening. Later the club gave a dance at Mrs. McCurry's at which everyone had a good time.

The Lemon City boys won the laurels with becoming modesty and the Cocoanut Grove boys bore defeat with perfect good nature, and all voted the day a success.[5]

Elsewhere in Florida by 1892, the first professional minor league teams were established as part of the newly christened Florida State League. Charter membership included Jacksonville, Ocala, St. Augustine, and Tampa. Jacksonville later moved up in stature becoming a member of the Class C South Atlantic League, better known as the Sally League, from 1904 through 1917. In addition, Pensacola enjoyed a one-year stint in the Southern League in 1893 and later in the Cotton States League in 1913, and Gainesville competed one season in the Class D

Florida-Alabama-Georgia League in 1915.[6][7] Although several barnstorming teams ventured further south, it took twenty years before the first true organized baseball groups started up in southern Florida.

The economic circumstances were rapidly changing and Miami was on the cusp of unprecedented progress, which led to it becoming a trade center. Spurred on by the farsighted vision of Henry Morrison Flagler, (retired co-founder of Standard Oil), his master plan was to modernize the east coast of Florida. He oversaw the construction of a rail line built from Jacksonville to Key West, which included an overseas railway. Wishing to cater to businessmen, tourists, as well as the rich and famous, he also built a system of high-end hotels along the route. Flagler's ambitious dreams brought enormous growth to south Florida in population and pecuniary gains. He launched the region into the twentieth century.

On April 13, 1896, with Flagler in tow, the first train of the East Coast Railroad chugged into Miami. Approximately 300 attendees joined in on the celebration in what proved to be a pivotal moment in Florida history. On July 28, 1896, Miami, with a population of 444 citizens, officially incorporated. Ethan Vernon (E.V.) Blackman, a pioneer journalist, writing for *The Home Seeker*, a Flagler owned magazine, was so enthusiastic about Miami that he christened the new municipality with its popular nickname known to this day. He said, "I got so enthusiastic over the possibilities of the city that bordered on the Gulf stream [*sic*] and faced the broad waters of Biscayne [Bay], that I referred to it as 'the Magic city'."[8]

Not long after that, construction commenced on the majestic Royal Palm Hotel. The resort became a playground for the likes of the Carnegies, Rockefellers, and Vanderbilts. It also served as the cultural center of the community until the 1930s, but for the baseball cranks, the wide-open grass grounds provided the home field for the first professional baseball teams."[9][10]

As Miami reached the 1900s it continued to grow and prosper with people from all over the country migrating there. The newcomers saw unlimited opportunities to succeed, and driven by the restless "American spirit," sought to leave their mark. That competitiveness carried over into their free time as well. Increasingly, town ball games of "base ball" sprouted up, and amateur teams formed. They added to the social life in communities throughout South Florida, most notably in Cocoanut Grove,

Fort Lauderdale, Key West, Miami, Miami Beach, and West Palm Beach. The competition was stiff and teams vied for bragging rights of being the best.

By 1910, almost 5,500 people resided in Miami. That number swelled to 42,753 by 1920.[11] The honorable F.H. "Frank" Wharton (1870–1956) was aggressive in his plans to modernize his fair city. One of the mayor's priorities was to organize an association financing a series of games between fellow cities. According to the *Tampa Tribune*, "Miami has been suffering this summer because it has no baseball. Baseball is a seasonal necessity for every well-regulated town. It stimulates town pride, stirs the sluggishness of the warm period into health action, and keeps men and boys out of mischief by giving them a clean and elevating center of interest."[12] On July 18, 1910, at the packed to capacity Board of Trade Room, (where local business people frequently met), "The Miami Baseball Association" (MBA) was born. Members contributed funds amounting to at least one dollar. The more affluent ones chipped in five dollars for two months of support towards team expenses and brand spanking new white and blue uniforms for the team. At the meeting, Major Harvey J. Payne was selected Vice President, Ed H. Hughes the team's first manager, and Charles "Charlie" Dillon as team captain of the new squad named Miami Seminoles. Excitement in the community was at a fever pitch and some local businesses, like the Marco Theatre and the Lyceum, found themselves so caught up in the hysteria that they offered a percentage of their proceeds to assist the team.[13]

America's pastime in Miami had taken its first baby steps down the path that led it to professional baseball. From 1910 through 1912, a loose confederation of semi-pro teams included Cocoanut Grove, Lemon City, and Miami. The most frequent challengers were organized clubs from Dania, Eau Gallie, Fort Lauderdale, Fort Pierce, Hastings, Key West, Jacksonville, Orlando, Plantation Tee House of Lemon City, Sanford, St. Petersburg and West Palm Beach. Typically, a three-game series schedule format was adhered to, with the highest attended contests held on Saturdays. Game accounts were at the forefront of the local rag, *The Miami Metropolis*, although posted wins and losses, and columns of batting statistics were absent. Nevertheless, it did not stop the various competitors from staking their claim as champions within this loosely organized system of games. Out of the chaos came a more rigid design that determined the true titleholder.

In 1911, Wharton's increasing responsibilities as mayor kept him so busy that he stepped down as President of the MBA. Robert L. Hill, his replacement, took control. Floyd Chaille, one of the early star ballplayers with Miami, became Vice-President; C.H. Ward became Secretary, and E. Bebinger its Treasurer. Ticket sales generated a healthy income, so one of the first acts of the new committee was to raise $500 to build a temporary fence enclosing the outfield of the Royal Palm Grounds. Although there was resistance from the community concerning the construction of an outfield fence due to the commercial nature of the enterprise, the erection of the enclosure ultimately continued and reached its completion just before baseball season began. Funds also afforded a makeshift wood grandstand with a roof, located on the third base infield side of the grounds, which provided an improved level of comfort to the paying patrons.[14]

Throughout the summer, the Seminoles were front-page news. Fans remained eager to see how the hometown boys made out against their rivals. One of its earliest ballplayers was a fair-minded first baseman by the name of Roddy B. Burdine (1888–1936), who later inherited the family business from his father William M. Burdine. He took what started as a dry goods store in Bartow, Florida and a W.M. Burdine & Sons store in fledgling Miami, and made it into one of the most successful department store chains in the history of retail, Burdine's. An avid sportsman, Roddy went on to sponsor several amateur baseball teams representing the family business. However, one of his most lasting accomplishments was away from the baseball diamond. The construction of a football field, christened Burdine Stadium, reached completion in December 1937. It was renamed Miami Orange Bowl Stadium in 1959.[15]

By 1913, their appetites whetted, citizens of Miami were hungry for a higher level of play. Stirrings within the community as far back as March of 1912 resulted in the calling for Miami to join a circuit known as the East Coast League (ECL). The teams under consideration were from Cocoa, Fort Lauderdale, Fort Pierce, Jacksonville, Key West, Lemon City, New Smyrna, St. Augustine, and Titusville.[16] The Miami Seminoles played a loose schedule of games during the summer of 1912 against teams from Dania, Fort Lauderdale, Key West, Sanford and West Palm Beach that set the stage for the ECL. On Saturday, July 12, 1913, at Fort Pierce, under the guidance of Dr. W.E. Van Landingham of Fort

Pierce and Professor W.B. Owens of Miami, they announced a new ten-team league to begin play on July 24, and conclude in September, called the East Coast Baseball Association. Among the teams joining Miami in the infant league were Eau Gallie, Fellsmere, Fort Lauderdale, Fort Pierce, Hastings, Key West, New Smyrna, Palatka, and Palm Beach.[17] The majority of the afore-mentioned teams dropped out of the league before the conclusion of the season because it was cost prohibitive.

Miami commenced their inaugural season at home with great promise defeating Fort Pierce, 15 to 1. The Seminoles banged out fifteen hits and stole twelve bases in the process of a game halted after seven innings. *The Miami Metropolis* raved about the starting pitcher, Frank Brower, a resident of Gainesville, a recent Washington and Lee University student,[18] ". . . he was invincible, indomitable, indubitable, and invulnerable, and with all these ins [sic] he had a few outs too. So many elusive curves of both variet-ies that the Ft. Pierce aggregation was like putty in his hands."[19] Miami remained tied for the league lead as late as September 10 but faded down the stretch. The Seminoles ended their first season with an 18–12 record in second place to the league cham-pion Fort Lauderdale who closed the ledgers at 23–11.[20] Fort Lauderdale's roster boasted a former major leaguer, Orth Collins, an outfielder, who had "cups of coffee" with the 1904 New York Highlanders and 1909 Washington Senators.[21] The "Gate City" squad, also referred to as the "Fort City Boys" proudly hoisted the leagues' first pennant.

The ECL resumed operations for their second season in 1914, but in a much smaller format. Only three teams, Fort Lauderdale, Miami, and West Palm Beach competed for the circuit champi-onship with games scheduled from June 2 through July 4. Two teams played twice a week with the idle club playing scheduled exhibition games on their week off. A fourth team, expected to join the league from Key West, dropped out when it was deter-mined that expenses precluded them from league play.[22] A second half of the season included games for August and September. The leaders of each half would play a best-of-nine game series decid-ing the championship. New manager, William Burdine, replaced Charlie Dillon, who returned to his role as one of the team's out-fielders.[23] Burdine quickly went to work finding players to fill out the squad. Additions included catcher B.E. Chapman[24] and third baseman Fred Davis from the Georgia State League signed to team up with Miami regulars "Piccolo" Robinson, Paul Taylor, Robert Taylor and the Dillon brothers (Charlie and Joe).[25] The remainder of the roster was plucked from local colleges including; first baseman Herman Swink, coming back for his second season with the Seminoles, and a slick-fielding shortstop from Stetson University, Louis F. "Red" Snedigar. The congenial Snedigar played a key role in helping secure the construction in 1916, of Tatum Field, later re-named Miami Field.[26] He also would serve four terms as the mayor of the city of Miami Beach.[27][28]

After a vigorous preseason, the Seminoles opened their regular season on June 4 before an estimated crowd of 600 to 700 loyal followers against the West Palm Beach Beachcombers. Jakie Miller took the mound for the hometown squad and faced off against "Dad" Littrell. Miami's first batsman of the contest, catcher, B.E. Chapman started the game off with a ringing single and promptly stole second base. After Charlie Dillon was retired on strikes, Littrell hit Fred Davis with a pitch followed by a Herman Swink single. "Piccolo" Robinson then hit a hot grounder towards shortstop that was muffed by Williams, and after a series of errors, the hometown team found themselves in the lead, 3 to 0. The Beachcombers combined to commit six errors on the day, and Miller pitched effectively striking out five and walking three, giving Miami their home opening, 6 to 4 triumph.[29]

The Seminoles proved to be the pacesetter in the league the first half of the split season. In a close fought race, they (14–9) edged out Fort Lauderdale (13–11) for the top spot. A great deal of credit for Miami's early success went to their manager Burdine, whose intensive focus on building a winning club, and making upgrades at key positions as the season progressed, kept them on the winning track. In order to strengthen the squad, he made several roster changes. Pitcher Sam Langford was acquired on June 12, the same day that outfielder Robert Taylor returned from college.[30] On June 28, catcher B.E. Chapman's younger brother simply known as "Kid" came aboard[31] and proved his mettle winning his first appearance on the hill, besting Palm Beach, 6 to 2.[32] In a later move, Lawrence Bowdoin who previously played for Columbus of the Sally League, and Brunswick of the Georgia State League, signed on and replaced Fred Davis, as the regular third baseman.[33]

The second half of the split season proved to be more exciting than the first as all three teams held onto the top spot at one time.

Miami got off to a slow start losing five of their first six games. Burdine addressed the team's lagging play by signing Charles Anderson, previously a member of the Waycross Grasshoppers/Moguls of the Georgia State League where he batted .232 in 315 at-bats and inserted him as the starting third sacker.[34] Bowdoin shifted to shortstop and Snedigar to second base.[35] In addition, pitcher Hawkins acquired from the Georgia State League, paid instant dividends winning his first start against Fort Lauderdale on August 21, by the final tally of, 3 to 2.[36]

Hawkins proved to be a lifesaver earning six of Miami's eight wins down the stretch assisting his cohorts to a 10–10 second half finish behind Palm Beach (12–9). All that remained was a best of nine game series pitting the Beachcombers against the Seminoles to decide the East Coast League championship. The first three games took place in West Palm Beach and the remainder in Miami.[37]

The Seminoles got off to an inauspicious start in the opening contest committing ten errors and failed to plate a single run. Hawkins pitched his usual strong game striking out seven and allowing only six hits. It was the poorest defensive outing by his teammates, all season. The final tally showed Palm Beach 5, Miami 0.[38]

Miami evened the series the next day thanks to recently acquired Fort Lauderdale star pitcher Horton (sometimes-spelled Horten in some newspaper accounts) who held Palm Beach to two scores while his mates drove across three.[39] It was common practice at the time to import the best players from other teams for such series' and Burdine did just that to "up" his chances towards gaining a championship.

Jakie Miller came on to hurl the third game but was ineffective as the Beachcombers cruised to their second victory, 5 to 2. Miami tied the series winning the fourth game 9 to 5 behind Hawkins but played poorly the rest of the series losing by scores of 8 to 3, 6 to 0, and 4 to 3 in the final game much to the chagrin of the hometown fans at the Royal Palm Grounds. For the second consecutive year, the Seminoles fell short of grabbing the league crown.

At the conclusion of the 1914 season, the Miami Baseball Association reported losses in excess of $400. Management blamed the cost of signing better players, despite increased revenues, on the deficit.[40] It was determined that overall operations proved too expensive for the ECL to continue and in 1915, the league folded.

The United States citizenry grew increasingly fixated on the war in Europe, and the country entered World War I. On April 6, 1917, President Woodrow Wilson declared war on Germany and men from all corners of the U.S. began to volunteer for service. In May of 1917, 3,800 men in Dade County registered for the draft or enlisted.[41] Because so many were serving in the Armed Forces overseas, baseball was pre-empted in South Florida for the next four years. Nevertheless, with the coming peace and end of hostilities, the public renewed their interest in the national pastime, including Miamians, anxious to put the horrors of war behind them and hear those most cherished of words, "Play ball."

NOTES

1. Otterson, Chuck. Expos split with Miracle, *Palm Beach Post,* 1 September, 1991, p. 12-C.
2. Ibid.
3. Miami.marlins.mlb.com/mia/history/timeline.jsp. Retrieved 23 July, 2017.
4. Parks, Arva Moore. *Miami The Magic City,* Miami, FL: Community Media, 2008.
5. *Tropical Sun,* 14 July, 1892, p. 1.
6. Baseball-reference.com.
7. Johnson, Lloyd & Wolff, Miles. *Encyclopedia of Minor League Baseball, Third Edition* (Durham, NC: Baseball America, 2007).
8. Woodruff, Helen. How Blackman Put Magic Into The Name Of Miami, *Miami Daily News,* June 14, 1925.
9. Parks, Arva Moore. *Miami The Magic City,* Miami, FL: Community Media, 2008.
10. George, Paul. *South Florida History,* Volume 24, No 2, Summer 1996, Miami: One Hundred Years of History.
11. Florida Census 1920. http://fcit.coedu.usf.edu/florida/docs/c/census/1920.htm.
12. *Daily Metropolis,* Miami Baseball Association, 18 July, 1910, p. 4.
13. *Daily Metropolis,* Citizens Back Up Baseball Assn With Liberal Assistance, 19 July, 1910, p. 1.
14. *Daily Metropolis,* Fort Pierce Will Give Seminoles Game On Fourth, 4 May, 1911, p. 1.
15. Salo, Jackie. Sports stadiums have a long complicated history in South Florida, retrieved 14 August, 2017 from http://www.miamiherald.com/news/local/community/miami-dade/coral-gables/article1977041.html.
16. *Miami Daily Metropolis,* The Sporting World Is Waking Up, 16 March, 1912, p. 3.
17. *Miami Daily Metropolis,* East Coast Baseball League Organized On Saturday At Fort Pierce, 14 July, 1913, p. 8.
18. *Miami Daily Metropolis,* Miami In Paragraph, 16 September, 1913, p. 5.
19. *Miami Daily Metropolis,* First Game Of League Was Something Awful; Better Game Promised, 25 July, 1913, p. 8.
20. *Miami Daily Metropolis,* Miami Wins Last Two Games; Fans Hope To Keep The Team, 22 September, 1913, p. 8.

21. Baseball-reference.com. Collins also pitched in one inning for the Washington Senators in 1909. His total major league career consisted of 24 at-bats finishing with a .250 lifetime average.

22. *Miami Daily Metropolis*, East Coast League Is Formed With 3 Clubs And Month's Schedule, 20 May, 1914, p. 6.

23. *Miami Daily Metropolis*, Wm. Burdine Elected Manager Of Seminoles For 1914 Season, 14 May, 1914, p. 6.

24. *Miami Daily Metropolis*, Reorganized Seminole Team Will Play First Game With Lauderdale, 26 May, 1914, p. 6.

25. *Miami Daily Metropolis*, Games Next Week Being Booked For Local Fans, 23 May,1914, p. 3.

26. Tatum Field was located at Northwest 3rd Street and 16th Avenue next to the Orange Bowl.

27. *Miami News*, Snedigar Career Closed By Death, 10 December, 1951, p. 7-A.

28. Miamibeachfl.gov/. Snedigar served as Mayor: 1922–1926, 1928–1930, 1934–1937.

29. *Miami Daily Metropolis*, Seminoles Win First League Game Cheered By Big Crowd Of Fans, 5 June, 1914, p. 6.

30. *Miami Daily Metropolis,* Miami Won Third Game Yesterday From Ft. L, 13 June,1914, p. 4.

31. *Miami Daily Metropolis*, Seminoles Will Play Away From Home This Week Until Saturday, 29 June, 1914, p. 8.

32. *Miami Daily Metropolis*, Miami Is Again Victor Over West Palm Beach, 4 July, 1914, p. 10.

33. Baseball-reference.com. Batted (22 games, 76 at-bats, .184) at Columbus of the South Atlantic League, and (63 at-bats, .317) at Brunswick of the Georgia State League.

34. Baseball-reference.com.

35. *Miami Daily Metropolis*, 13 August, 1914, p. 6.

36. *Miami Daily Metropolis*, Lauderdalites Met A Second Defeat At The Hands Of The Seminoles, 3 To 2, Yesterday, 22 August, 1914, p. 8.

37. *Miami Daily Metropolis*, East Coast Post Season Baseball Series To Be Started Next Tuesday, 28 September, 1914, p. 6.

38. *Miami Daily Metropolis*, Errors Lost Yesterday's Game To The Seminoles, Second Game On Today, 30 September, 1914, p. 6.

39. *Miami Daily Metropolis*, Seminoles Take Beachcombers Into Camp In Second Game of Serious, 1 October, 1914, p. 6.

40. *Miami Daily Metropolis*, Baseball Association Over $400 To The Bad And Is Wanting Help, 13 October, 1914, p. 3.

41. Parks, Arva Moore. *Miami The Magic City*, Miami, FL: Community Media, 2008, p. 136.

CHAPTER TWO

ROARING INTO THE 1920s

World War I ended with the signing of the armistice, and with it, a halt to the hostilities between opposing nations. It was a time for rebuilding, and with this new peace came many social and economic changes. A new era of hope and prosperity followed known as, "The Roaring Twenties." It was a period marked by hyper-industrial growth, leaps in technology, and the shedding of Victorian norms allowing women to express themselves and enjoy more freedoms. The ratifying of the 19th Amendment assured that they would be able to cast their votes in elections. Larger than life sports and entertainment icons such as Jack Dempsey, Red Grange, and Babe Ruth, and movie stars Charlie Chaplin, Greta Garbo, and Buster Keaton, defined the era.

Meanwhile, south Florida was amid an unprecedented land boom. Speculators made fortunes overnight and aggressive developers were increasing Miami's boundaries as small municipalities like Coconut (the "a" was dropped in 1919) Grove,[1] Lemon City and other communities were absorbed into Miami. Furthermore, entrepreneurs and business leaders capitalized on the ever-expanding tourist trade. The lure of swaying majestic palms, sun and surf enticed people to the "Magic City" from all corners of the U.S. and beyond, to live in paradise.

Miami shed its small-town persona and propelled forward as a major economic center in the southeast U.S. It developed relationships with its neighbors to the south in the Caribbean, Central America, and South America. By the end of the 1920s, the population ballooned to over 140,000.[2]

Corruption accompanied Miami's newfound prosperity. The city gained a new reputation as a lawless town, which took root during the Prohibition era, a stigma it carries to the present day. Hardscrabble bootleggers, who slipped past law enforcement authorities and delivered illegal alcohol from the Bahamas to black market dealers, and owners of speakeasies, generated most of the trouble.[3]

1915–1919

Miami was proud to host their opponents. Through the efforts of the land developer Smiley Tatum, the conception of a new ballpark took root. He recognized the need for a better playing facility than the Royal Palm Grounds. His idea would attract a higher quality level of baseball, enrich the community, and provide financial rewards. His initial goal was to lure a major league team to Miami to train in the spring, followed by the establishment of minor league baseball for the delectation of fans throughout the remainder of the year.

Smiley Mosteller Tatum (1870–1935) was one of a quartet of brothers including Bethel Blanton (1864–1943), Johnson Reid (1866–1938) and Judson H. (1859–1923) that arrived in south Florida during the 1890s from Dawson, Georgia. Together they had visions of developing commercial ventures and buying land to sell for profit. Thirty-five-year-old B.B. was the first brother to invest in the area when he purchased the local *Miami Metropolis* newspaper in 1899. He sold the publication on April 20, 1909. He joined his brother in purchasing and developing real estate from Biscayne Bay south to Florida City and west to the Everglades.[4] They quickly began draining and filling thousands of acres of swamp they owned, which expanded farming, and spurred the growth of new residential areas. The first trolley system debuted in the city in July 1906.[5]

In early 1915, in preparation for a new ballyard, Smiley had a parcel of land cleared on the corner of Northwest 3rd Street and 16th Avenue, (an area known as Lawrence Estates). He proudly declared that it would be the finest ballpark that money could afford. On May 19, 1915, twenty laborers began working to level the uneven lot and clear out the occupying Palmetto trees and low-lying scrub brush that covered the property.[6] Coincidentally, the site's location is where Marlins Park, home of major league baseball's Miami Marlins, currently resides.

By the summer of 1915, the construction of Tatum Field (sometimes referred to as Tatum Park) was in full swing. The infield dirt was in place and fresh sod laid down. The wooden grandstands and roof soon followed. With the new ballpark in place, Smiley, and his brother J.H., (who were at the forefront of promoting baseball), remained confident in their vision of Miami being a viable location for major league baseball during the spring, and top-flight minor league baseball through the summer.[7]

Smiley courted several teams including the National League's Boston Braves, and the American League's Chicago White Sox, Detroit Tigers, New York Highlanders (forerunners of the Yankees), and the St. Louis Browns. All these teams were involved in negotiations at various levels with Tatum.[8] Colonel Robert L. Hedges, the owner of the Browns, visited the new field personally and stated, "Miami is a fine place for a training camp."[9] It looked as though early discussions favored St. Louis. However, on September 21, 1915, G. Collins, a business partner of Boston Braves' team owner James E. Gaffney, and a consortium of club representatives signed the initial contract to bring their club to Miami to train. With an agreement in hand, Smiley left for New York on the first train to meet with Gaffney and put the finishing touches on what would become a finalized deal on the use of Tatum Field.[10] For the next three seasons (1916–1918), the Boston Braves called Miami their springtime home.[11]

By 1916, most of the land holdings controlled by the Tatum brothers were subdivided; the land sold to investors and speculators amounted to approximately $200 million.[12] At the forefront of several of those deals was Smiley.

1920

Interest in our national pastime was at its peak. The East Coast League had provided Miamians with a degree of professional baseball, albeit, an "outlaw" league. At the time, most circuits were independent, or considered "outlaw," and did not respect the contracts of other leagues. Although not recognized by the National Association, (the governing body of minor league baseball), the rosters of several teams within the ECL had players from other leagues with professional experience including, Cotton States League, Florida-Alabama-Georgia League, Georgia-Alabama

League, Georgia State League, and South Atlantic League. As Miami increasingly became more metropolitan, so too did the desire for the brand of baseball that highlighted a growing municipality.

With a renewed enthusiasm for baseball's return, 75 community leaders gathered to re-form the Miami Baseball Association (MBA). The meeting held on April 27, 1920, resulted in the organization of the group's leadership. They elected Ben Shepard as Chairman, and he proposed a plan to sell $10 shares of stock in the club to raise the $1,000 entry fee to join the newly organized Florida East Coast League (FECL).[13]

After official acceptance by the FECL, practices for the recently formed Miami Magicians began in early May at Tatum Field. All home games took place at the new ballpark. Instead of passing around the hat to cover expenses, as was the custom at the Royal Palm Grounds, fans now had to pay an admission fee.[14] Early participants looking for roster spots were locally familiar names, Earl Horton, J.R. Murphy, Judge T. E. "Tubby" Price, W. Whaley, and the Van Landingham brothers, (Louie and Ray).[15] As part of the preparation for the upcoming season, warm-up scrimmages against local High School squads from the Miami area were scheduled.[16]

The Van Landingham's were the most recognizable and prominent family on the local baseball scene. Four of seven brothers, Louie, Ralph, Ray, and W.E. (or William) either played or managed in South Florida. William, the oldest brother served as FECL president in 1920 until June 1921 and managed the Palm Beach club in that same year. Both Ralph (a catcher), and Ray, (second and third baseman) played for the Miami Seminoles in 1916 and 1917. Ray had also toiled in the Georgia State League. He returned to Miami in 1920 for two more seasons. Still another brother, Louie made the grade with West Palm Beach in 1920, playing all positions, except catcher at different junctures of his career. He stayed through 1922. Louie, Ralph, and Ray continued to play semi-pro and amateur hardball around south Florida until 1930.[17]

Springtime baseball increased interest in more hardball, which was exactly what Smiley had envisioned. The return of organized baseball following spring camps soon followed and came to fruition on May 17, 1920, when the newly formed FECL officially announced a four-team league consisting of teams representing,

Fort Lauderdale (Tarpons), Fort Pierce (Commercials), Miami (Magicians), and West Palm Beach (Invincibles). All four of the club's representatives agreed to a fifty-fifty divide when it came to league finances. This included all gate receipts no matter where teams played.[18] East Coast Baseball Association's President H. B. Martin announced that all scheduled league games were to be played on Thursdays and Sundays running from June 3 through October 3, with a split season format highlighted by first-half champions taking on the second half champs for the league title.[19] In addition, fifteen players per team was the allowed limit. Due to the size of the roster, managers were also required to field a position.

Baseball was a much different game in the past. Although it would be recognizable to fans today, there were some marked differences. Instead of form-fitting lightweight moisture wicking uniforms, men of this era wore baggy heavy wool togs that were especially uncomfortable during the humid summer months. Leather fielding gloves were barely larger than a hand. They resembled an overgrown mushroom crown and had almost no webbing versus the high-tech large traps that are in use in the 21st century.

The conditions of the playing fields were rough at best. Manicured grass and smooth playing infields were non-existent. When looking at photographs from this era, playing fields had burned out patches of sward within the infield and throughout the outfield. Moreover, the infield had more than its share of pebbles, and its hard-baked surface made it an adventure for infielders on any hard hit ground ball.

The strategy employed by managers was as different as the appearance of the diamond. Noticeably absent was the reliance on the home run for offensive production. The ability to manufacture runs through sacrifice bunting, stealing a base, and the use of the hit-and-run were in vogue. Expectations for pitchers were to start and finish a game, and pitchouts were unheard of. Relief pitchers' usage was only in case of a complete meltdown, or injury. It is interesting to note that the Magicians did not hit their first home run during their inaugural season until their seventh game when first baseman Murray Beard went deep.[20]

Miami kicked off their season at home against the team that proved to be their stiffest competition, West Palm Beach. The contest proved to be a foreshadowing of the forthcoming campaign, as the outcome was close, and with Miami coming out on the short end. Sloppy defense marked play (4 errors by Miami, 5 by West Palm Beach), as the Invincibles got the best of the Magicians' starter Bob Hathaway, 3 to 2. In the eleventh inning, "Tubby" Price misplayed a fly ball to center field allowing the visitors to reach scoring position. West Palm Beach pitcher Bob Mooty then followed with a single, driving in the go-ahead run that proved the game-winner. There was no official attendance given, but the total receipts amounted to $700. With the price of tickets ranging from 25 to 50 cents, by calculating the gate take that day, it was safe to say the crowd was in excess of 1,500.[21]

To address some of the early deficiencies in the Magicians' offense and defense, J.R. Murphy signed what would prove to be one of the most colorful players to ever grace Tatum Field, infielder Isey Bandrimer (or as he was sometimes referred to by sportswriters, "Izzy").

Bandrimer exemplified the kind of rough and rowdy ballplayer that populated the FECL. Although short of height compared to his teammates, he was a fellow with a big heart. His spirited play and congeniality would soon make him a fan favorite wherever he traveled. He was born on Christmas Day, 1900 in the Bronx, New York, but raised in Jacksonville, Florida. As a young man, he quickly earned his reputation as a scrapper. He began a short-lived pugilistic career in the boxing ring at a local establishment called Guy's Pool Hall. "We'd get a dollar for a four-rounder, two bucks for a six-rounder. Some of the fans would throw silver dollars into the ring if they liked our fight," remembered Bandrimer in a 1985 *Miami News* interview. Although the money was good, a split tongue gave the brash youngster reason to reconsider his stock and trade. The sixteen-year-old had a seemingly strong craving for adventure, and too young for military service, hooked up with the Second Florida Infantry as the company mascot. Shortly after arriving at their camp, the youngster found himself whisked off to Laredo, Texas. From there, he participated in the U.S. Army's Punitive Mexican Expedition in pursuit of the revolutionary bandit, Pancho Villa. He then joined the United States Merchant Marines where he worked as a coal-passer on Atlantic sailing wooden ships. In 1919, Isey arrived in Miami and followed his dream of becoming a professional baseball player. His career carried him to such locales as St. Petersburg, Florida (1920), Raleigh, North Carolina (1922), Little Rock, Arkansas (1923), Galveston, Texas (1924), Chattanooga, Tennessee (1924–1925),

Springfield, Massachusetts (1926), Portsmouth, Virginia ((1927), Terre Haute, Indiana (1928), Wilkes-Barre, Pennsylvania (1929), Bloomington, Illinois (1930), and Danville, Illinois (1931). After leaving organized baseball, he continued playing for the famous all bewhiskered barnstorming House of David club into the 1930s.[22][23]

The first half race proved as close as two kittens in a bed. The Invincibles (14–5) edged out Miami (13–7) by a game and a half. Miami vowed to take the second stanza and bolstered their pitching staff by signing a couple of promising hurlers, Davenport and southpaw Oran "Squirrelly" Swearingen. [24][25]

FECL executives revised the second half season schedule to adapt to three games a week played on Wednesdays, Thursdays, and Sundays. Because of several players' inability to get away from other responsibilities away from the field, there were no longer Saturday games.[26] However, Sunday baseball would eventually prove to be problematic. In 1921, challenges to "Blue Laws" would take the forefront. These laws, designed to enforce religious standards, included the banning of Sunday sports activities and sale of alcohol.

With the new schedule in place, the coming second half of the season proved to be another hard-fought race between Miami and West Palm Beach. After jumping out of the gate and winning four of their first five games, Miami began to struggle. Throughout the summer, competitiveness between league combatants had frequently led to several profanity-laced exchanges that would make a sailor blush, as well as physical altercations on and off the field. On August 26 when the Magicians traveled to West Palm Beach, matters really heated up. A bang-bang call by the umpire that ruled Bandrimer out at second base began a chain of events that led to fisticuffs. As the scrappy Isey left the field and walked past the grandstand, the wife of patron L. Sperry called out the impetuous Miamian for his aggressive behavior and started banging a soda bottle on the metal rail. Bandrimer misinterpreted the action of the woman and surmised they were preparing to launch a bottle at him. After threatening Mrs. Sperry, her husband called Bandrimer out and the two men got into it; the melee was on. Bandrimer received a quick ejection from the game. "Poker" Barnes and Police Commissioner J. K. Fink helped to separate the two men, and placed them under arrest. The inspired Invincibles pulled out a come from behind, 7–5 victory.[27]

Vexations continued as the summer closed. Miami (11–10) struggled to keep their heads above the .500 mark. Cellar-dwelling Fort Pierce faced a doubleheader against West Palm Beach (12–7), the latter two games in front of the pack. With only eight games left to play, and facing the Tarpons' best starter Les "Sugar" Sweetland, the hometown Miami club faced a near must-win situation.

The 5'11" slender southpaw, who later pitched in the major leagues for five years with the Philadelphia Phillies and Chicago Cubs, was a formidable opponent known for his devastating sinker and biting fastball.[28] [29] He became famous, or infamous, depending on your point of view, for holding the unenviable re-cord of the highest earned run average in a major league season by a qualifying pitcher at 7.71 in 1930.[30]

The largest crowd of the season crammed into Tatum Field. According to *The Miami News,* the club failed to report the number of fans in attendance. What started out as a calm Sunday after-noon soon turned into a calamity. The Fort Lauderdale Tarpons jumped out to a quick three-run lead before Miami rallied against Sweetland in the eighth inning. The first batter up was George Braun who smacked a double, followed by Louis MacReynolds who drilled a single down the third base line, which plated his teammate and cut the Fort Lauderdale lead to 5–3. Bandrimer followed by cueing a soft groundball to Callahan that looked like a sure infield base hit. On the bang-bang play at first base, umpire Monahan yelled, "He's out." The fiery Bandrimer was livid at the perceived bad call. He felt he had legged out the tapper and the ensuing shouting match soon escalated. In a fit of frustration, Isey threw a handful of pebbles at Monahan. It was not long be-fore the situation got uncontrollable and angry home fans, sens-ing an injustice, swarmed the playing field. Local police quickly rushed onto the diamond to quell the dispute and maintain order, saving Monahan from imminent bodily harm. Officers escorted Bandrimer from the field due to his ejection, and MacReynolds took his place at second base.[31]

The altercation seemed to have rattled the Tarpons. The next batter, Pettit, reached first base on an error by Meyers. Fort Lauderdale manager, W.E. Van Landingham, seeing that his ace was flustered, pulled Sweetland and called on Monty Priest to extinguish the fire.[32] Pinch-hitter Beard then reached on a second miscue. MacReynolds promptly stole third base and scored when

Grantham overthrew the ball to the third baseman. Ray Van Landingham and Harbison drew free passes and Pettit crossed the plate with the tying score. Priest coaxed a grounder out of Purcell and Beard raced across the home slab on the fielder's choice giving Miami a 6 to 5 win.[33] Meanwhile, the Invincibles were splitting a doubleheader with Fort Pierce losing the first game 4 to 2, but bounced back to win the second game, 6 to 0.

The Magicians' victory was a springboard for the rest of the season as they won six of their final seven games passing West Palm Beach (16–13) for the second half title. Miami's success set the stage for a showdown in a best of seven-game series between the Invincibles and Magicians to compete for the championship.[34]

As was the league custom, and player movements being fluid, the Magicians recruited the league's top hurler Sweetland from Fort Lauderdale to represent them in the finals.[35] Both West Palm Beach and Miami had significant injuries as the Invincibles were without their best starting pitcher Mooty, and the Magicians were minus one of their most feared sluggers MacReynolds. Both were out with undisclosed physical ailments. Nonetheless, Magicians skipper Ben Willard, who had taken over managing chores halfway through the season from J. R. Murphy, chose Arthur "Emory" Johnston[36] from Spartanburg to pitch the opener of the series at West Palm Beach's Poinciana Park (located on the grounds of the Hotel Royal Poinciana), against "Red" Stewart, who the Invincibles had acquired from the Sally League.[37]

The series got off to a dubious start as Miami won the first game 9 to 1. Following the game, manager Van Landingham filed a formal protest with the league accusing Magicians' Johnston of using a foreign substance to doctor the baseball, either emery or resin, that he hid inside his cap while pitching. During a special meeting held by league directors, and West Palm Beach representative, Otto Carmichael, and president, H. B. Martin ruled in favor of Miami. A second vote taken resulted in a tie. League officials then asked Martin to resign, and after he refused, resulting in his ousting. W. Quince Bryan of Dania named to take his place reversed the decision and awarded West Palm Beach the win.[38 39 40]

Despite much grief over the fact that the first game was a loss, the Magicians came back with a vengeance winning game two, 1 to 0, in ten innings, behind the top-notch twirling of Sweetland. Van Landingham once again protested the game as the previous day's Miami starter Johnston also served as a pinch-hitter in the tenth inning. Sweetland was not only the pitching hero but also the hitting star by driving in the game's only run, which plated Bandrimer, the recipient of an Invincibles' error.

The series then shifted to Tatum Field where Miami won, 4 to 1, behind Davenport who outperformed his former teammate Swearingen. The Magicians, holding a 2–1 edge in the series played to a 4 to 4 tie in game four despite the strong effort by pitchers Lefty Fussell and Johnston who both worked out of several jams and scattered ten hits. With the onset of darkness, the umpires called the game.[41]

In the final game of the series, Sweetland came back to pitch another gem. Miami scored two runs in the third inning on one hit and three errors. It proved to be all the offense the Magicians needed to win, 3 to 1. Following the game, President Bryan changed the previous ruling and disallowed West Palm Beach's protest on the first game stating it was contrary to baseball law, which prohibits protests on postseason games. The decision awarded Miami a victory, and the championship. It was one of the strangest twists ever for a league title, and Miami hoisted the league crown as 1920 FECL champions.[42]

1921

The league returned with the same teams for the 1921 season with the Fort Lauderdale (Tarpons), Fort Pierce (Commercials), Miami (Magicians) and West Palm Beach (Gators). Although there was no expansion in the league, there was an answer to a call from fans for more games. Sunday baseball was still on the slate to help maintain team attendance. However, for the first time, local clubs faced challenges by the state of Florida and its "Blue Laws" that prohibited Sunday baseball games. According to the Florida State Legislature, conditions had changed since the law's enactment in 1905. An old-timer in baseball proclaimed, "That because games were backed by liquor interest, and most of the contests were followed by big drunks, and there were other related expenses, the element in control of baseball then made the game more or less obnoxious in their opinion." Ultimately, the edict prohibiting games on the Sabbath day was enforced.[43]

Ballplayers challenged this law by playing Sunday baseball. This brought on a rapid response by law enforcement. On May 1, a Sunday, Miami opened their season at Tatum Field defeating Fort Lauderdale, 20 to 3 behind the crafty pitching of Jack Sewell, while Fort Pierce upended West Palm Beach, 4 to 2 at Poinciana Park. Sheriffs assigned to all of the games immediately detained all league players and managers for the violation of Sunday laws at the conclusion of their contests. Total arrests numbered 107, among them, amateur players from Homestead, Miami Beach, and the Miami Beach Fire Department.[44]

Baptist Pastor, Reverend J.L. White, a major proponent against Sunday baseball, came out strongly in support of "Blue Laws." Not mincing words, he said, "Sunday baseball not only endangers the sanctity of the Sabbath, the one day in the week set aside for the worship of God and for the rest of man but is a thrust at the Christian religion, for an open Sunday is no Sunday at all, and the community, state or nation which has no Sunday is not Christian even in name."[45]

On Friday, May 6, the honorable Judge Tom Norfleet presided over the case in front of a packed room. Sensing a strong reaction from the audience, and the accused, Norfleet warned against outbursts regardless of whatever verdict returned. Ordered to attend the proceedings, were many of the Miami and Homestead ballplayers. Judge T.E. "Tubby" Price was among the charged as a member of the Magicians. After both sides presented arguments, Norfleet cited the state statute concerning law prohibiting Sunday baseball. He then instructed the jury based on the evidence presented, if they believed the defendants were guilty of playing baseball on Sunday, they should return a guilty verdict.

After an hour of deliberation, all eyes remained fixed on the six jurors that nervously returned to their seats. The atmosphere brought on by the anticipation of the moment was thick as the summer humidity in the Everglades. The foreperson stood and read the verdict. The words rang out, "Not Guilty." The players and their supporters, exhaled in relief. Judging by the separation of the jury into two parties of three prior to the decision it was deduced that there must have been a split jury.[46] With that, at least until pro-Blue Law supporters could regroup, Sunday baseball games continued.

Now free from their previous peripheral distractions, Miami reeled off an impressive start to the season winning 13 of their first 14 games. Led by returnees Bandrimer, Beard, MacReynolds,

Price, and Ray Van Landingham, the Magicians quickly forged a 4½ game lead in the standings over second place Fort Pierce.

Nonetheless, Miami's success was short-lived and began to show signs that winning the first half was not going to be as easy as anticipated. The FECL announced that for the remainder of the season, the two-day-a-week policy would change to a six-day-a-week schedule. This particularly had an adverse effect on the Magicians, as their first baseman Beard, outfielder-pitcher Price, outfielder H.M. Purcell, and infielder Ray Van Landingham, all held down regular jobs, and were not available to play daily. As word spread of the forthcoming roster openings, the reaction to the news was immediate. Miami received applications from fifty players seeking a spot on the club; the first infielder being "Red" Craig from Central Florida, and right-handed pitcher Technor (later newspaper accounts spelled it as Ticknor).[47]

After dropping a series finale against Fort Pierce, the Magicians, taken to task twice by last-place Fort Lauderdale, fell by scores of 3 to 1, and 6 to 3. The remainder of the month of June proved disastrous as Miami dropped 14 of 21 games. The departure of slugging outfielder MacReynolds, to a wrist injury, was a major blow to the club. Without their star player, Miami had their worst outing on June 29, when Fort Pierce thrashed them 17 to 1; relinquishing first place to the Commercials. *The Miami Daily Metropolis* reported, "The visitors circled the bases until they were out of breath . . ."[48] Miami's record dropped to 20 wins and 15 losses.

Their struggles were not limited to the playing field; they were also disappointing at the ticket office where attendance was down to an average of 496 per game. In order to sustain the Magicians, the MBA launched a fundraising drive to obtain $5,000 to pay off current debts and cover forthcoming expenses that would enable the Magicians to finish the season.[49] In fact, the FECL was having economic difficulties league-wide, most notably in West Palm Beach where the club came very close to folding. Only a financial commitment by county sheriff, R.C. "Bob" Baker and Carl Kettler president of the Bijou Amusu Company kept the team alive.[50] [51] Miami continued on the edge of insolvency all season.

Miami improved their play and regained first place on July 6 when they out-hit Fort Lauderdale in a slugfest 15 to 10. In the seven-inning affair, Ticknor went the route and received plenty of support by his teammates that had everyone in the lineup collect at least one base knock including three each by Bandrimer, Beard, and Price.[52] The first half race remained heated between Fort Pierce and Miami as they jockeyed for the top spot throughout the summer.

With the end of July's approach, the Magicians made several moves in their quest to win the first half title. Benny White, a shortstop out of Atlanta, joined the team. He was welcomed to the club by MacReynolds who was returning to active duty after a more than month-long hiatus.[53] One of the team's leading hitters, Arthur Quinn took over managerial duties on July 28, in time to see new recruits, infielders Butteroff, and Mike Sieglitch, from Daytona Beach, take starting slots.[54] The most impactful acquisition came with the arrival of outfielder Gene Gaffney, from the Class C Florida State League's Orlando Tigers, considered one the best players in the state after hitting an impressive .335.[55]

On July 28, Miami (35–26) moved into a first-place tie with Fort Pierce after defeating Fort Lauderdale at Tatum Field 4 to 2, while the Commercials fell to West Palm Beach, 3 to 1.[56] With only four games left to play in the first half of the season, Miami had two games each at West Palm Beach, and at Fort Lauderdale, while Fort Pierce traveled to Fort Lauderdale for a pair before finishing at home against West Palm Beach for another two.

The next day's game was rained out in Palm Beach. This forced a rescheduling of a doubleheader for July 31. Miami easily won the first game 6 to 2. The second game proved a different story as the Gators bounced back to take a close contest, 2 to 1 in seven innings. West Palm Beach's last victory proved to be the dagger in the heart of the Magicians' hopes. Fort Pierce went on to win their last four games to clinch the first half title.[57]

First Half Standings

TEAM	W	L	GB
Fort Pierce	39	26	–
Miami	38	27	1
West Palm Beach	35	30	4
Fort Lauderdale	18	47	21

Miami started the second half promisingly enough when their newest pitching acquisition from St. Augustine, Hernandez, shutout Fort Pierce on their home turf, 10 to 0 allowing only six base hits.[58] The Magicians continued their winning ways nabbing their first six games. In order to make room for the newest hurler, Ticknor was dispatched to Fort Lauderdale and Davenport drew his release.

Still dogged by financial woes, the team remained focused. They were not alone as the FECL was operating under a black cloud and swimming in red ink. On August 30, Carl Kettler and R.C. Baker announced that the West Palm Beach club was $864 in arrears.[59] On September 2, at a meeting of league members at the Tamiami Hotel, Miami formerly withdrew from the FECL over a dispute regarding reapportioning of gate receipts and revision of scheduling. League rules stated that each visiting team be given $60 for each game. Whenever $120 (or more) was taken in at the gate, the clubs designated surplus funds as divided equally. Miami complained that when teams visited their home park, teams regularly walked away with more than $60, while they had yet to receive more than the minimum from the other clubs. The repercussion was an abrupt ending to the 1921 season.

In order to generate additional income, and in an effort to keep the team afloat, the Magicians played a series of exhibition games against the Class C Florida State League's Daytona Beach Islanders (55–60) and Tampa Smokers (64–50). The FSL concluded their season on September 6 and both their clubs were anxious to see how they would fare against their neighbor to the south.

The FSL had established itself as the premier minor league in Florida. The league started out as a Class D in 1919 but moved up to Class C by 1921. Initially, teams were from cities primarily in north and central Florida, although that would eventually change. They would continue operations up to the present day with exception of interruptions from 1929–1935 as a result of the Depression, and 1942 through 1945 due to World War II. As of present, the rating for the league is Class A+.[60]

The Islanders, a fourth-place finisher in the six-team FSL, proved a worthy opponent to the Magicians taking the opening game of the six-game set by a score of, 9 to 2.[61] It appeared as if the Miami squad was outclassed, but the results from the series lid-lifter proved to be deceiving. Miami came back to win three of the next five contests earning a split in the series. The Magicians most impressive wins came in games four and five. In the former,

Frank Riel pitched a valiant six-hitter, stranding nine enemy base runners and did not allow an extra-base hit during a 3 to 1 win.[62] Tampa, impressed by Riel's mastery on the mound, signed him for the 1922 season. He later won 16 games and lost 18 while leading the club in innings pitched toiling for 285 innings for the Smokers. Over the course of his nine-year minor league career, he won 79 and lost 77. Among his highlights, he was a 20-game winner twice. First in 1923 splitting time with the Tampa Smokers and Raleigh Capitals of the Class C Piedmont League, and again in 1927 with the Wilson Bugs of the Class B Virginia League.[63]

The next day, Magicians' starter A. R. Thomas, who pitched poorly during his first appearance, came back with sweet retribution. The erstwhile Miami hurler had previously pitched for Detroit of the Michigan-Ontario League. Prior to World War I, he missed a couple of seasons due to eye problems because of exposure to poison gas released by the Germans while fighting during the conflict. He seemed to have regained his full visional capacities.[64] His second go-around against the Islanders' batters must have left them wondering if they were facing an evil twin as they were held hitless in the course of 3 to 0 whitewashing.[65] The result was the wily Thomas made history producing the first no-hitter at Tatum Field.

The Magicians felt good about their efforts. They proved they could compete against superior competition and were anxious to take on their next opponent, Tampa. However, the Smokers proved to be up to the task and took all four games from the Magicians. The only highlight for Miami was Riel's near no-hitter in the opening game. With the score knotted at zeroes going into the ninth inning, Riel walked Nelson Leach on four pitches, retired Reed, and then gave up the only hit of the game, a double by Hines Vaughn that scored Leach. Despite six Miami hits against Craig, they were unable to string together a rally and Tampa prevailed, 1 to 0.[66]

For the subsequent two years, Miamians rooted for local city leagues and semi-pro teams. FECL league officials were unable, due to financial reasons mostly due to poor attendance, to put together enough stable teams to re-organize the league. They remained dormant until their re-launch in 1926, although informal leagues were organized from 1923 to 1925 consisting of a shuffling roster of teams from Coconut Grove, Fort Lauderdale, Homestead, Little River, Lake Worth, Miami, Stuart, Vero Beach, and West Palm Beach. Following the previously formatted schedule, the various clubs played a first and second half schedule consisting of 42 games total, followed by exhibition games against barnstorming and traveling clubs. It took another six years before Miami gained official recognition as an official minor league team.

NOTES

1.   *The History of Coconut Grove*, retrieved August 16, 2017 from www.coconutgrove. com/history.
2.   Florida Census 1930. http://fcit.coedu.usf.edu/florida/docs/c/census/1930. htm.
3.   George, Paul. *Miami: One Hundred Years of History*, South Florida History, Vol. 24, No. 2, Summer 1996.
4.   Blakley, Jeff. *The Tatum Brothers*, Retrieved 18 August, 2017 from townhallmuseum.org.
5.   Parks, Arva Moore. *Miami The Magic City*, (Miami, FL: Community Media, 2008), p. 109.
6.   Clearing Tatum Park For Baseball Grounds, *Miami Daily Metropolis*, 20 May, 1915, p. 6.
7.   Kleinberg, Howard. Boston Braves trained here in 16, *Miami News*, 13 February, 1982, p. 15-A.
8.   Ibid.
9.   Good Town For Training Camp, That Is What Colonel Hedges Thinks Of The City Of Miami, *Miami Daily Metropolis*, 10 June, 1915, p. 1.
10.   Sign Contract Today With Boston Braves for a Training Camp, *Miami Daily Metropolis*, September 21, 1915, p. 1.
11.   Baseball-reference.com.
12.   Parks, Arva Moore. *Miami The Magic City*, (Miami, FL: Community Media, 2008), p. 109.
13.   Shepard Chairman Of Baseball Association, *Miami Daily Metropolis*, 28 March, 1920, p. 4.
14.   All Ball Games To Be Played At Tatum Park, *Miami Daily Metropolis*, 4 May, 1920, p. 10.
15.   Ibid.
16.   New Miami Teams Plays High School Tomorrow, *Miami Daily Metropolis*, May 5, 1920, p. 10.
17.   Miami Team, *Miami Daily Metropolis*, 4 June, 1920, p. 1.
18.   Fort Pierce Joins The East Coast Ball League, *Miami Daily Metropolis*, 17 May, 1920, p. 8.
19.   Official East Coast League Season Opens Here June 3, *Miami Daily Metropolis*, 29 May, 1920, p. 7.
20.   Miami Is Again Victor Over The Invincibles, *Miami Daily Metropolis*, 25 June, 1920, p. 12.
21.   West Palm Beach Wins First Game Of Season, *Miami Daily Metropolis*, 4 June, 1920, p. 14.
22.   Archdeacon, Tom. Isey's First Love, *Miami News*, 5 April, 1985, p. 1-B, and 3-B.
23.   Baseball-reference.com.
24.   Standings, *Miami Daily Metropolis*, 2 August, 1920.
25.   Exhibition Ball Game Magicians-Invincibles, *Miami Daily Metropolis*, 23 October, 1920, p. 7. Article indicates nickname for Swearingen.
26.   Revised Schedule Of East Coast League, *Palm Beach Post*, 9 August, 1920, p. 6.

27. Shortstop Bandrimer And Spectator In Fight, *Miami Daily Metropolis*, 27 August, 1920, p. 10.

28. Neyer, Rob & James, Bill. *The Neyer/James Guide to Pitchers*, (New York, NY: Fireside Books, Simon & Schuster), p. 399.

29. Baseball-reference.com. Born Lester Leo Sweetland pitched four years for the Philadelphia Phillies (1927–1930), and one year for the Chicago Cubs (1931) compiling a lifetime record of 33 wins and 58 losses to go along with a 6.10 ERA. He also accumulated a 76–61, 3.17 ERA during his eight years in the minor leagues.

30. Spatz, Lyle. *The SABR Baseball List & Record Book*, (New York Scribner a Division of Simon & Schuster: 2007), p. 264.

31. Police Rescue Umpire As Magicians Win, *Miami Daily Metropolis*, 20 September, 1920, p. 7.

32. West Palm Beach Takes Second Game By 3 To 2, *Miami Daily Metropolis,* 18 September, 1920, p. 7. List pitcher Priest's first name as Monty from Mobile.

33. Police Rescue Umpire As Magicians Win, *Miami Daily Metropolis*, 20 September, 1920, p. 7.

34. Ibid.

35. Magicians Win Again But First Thrown Out, *Miami Daily Metropolis*, 9 October, 1920, p. 8.

36. Some newspaper accounts in the *Miami Daily Metropolis* and *Palm Beach Post* listed Johnston as Johnson. According to baseball-reference.com, a pitcher named Art Johnson pitched for the 1920 Spartanburg Pioneers of the South Atlantic League.

37. League Game Today On Poinciana Field, *Palm Beach Post*, 7 October, 1920, p. 6.

38. Baseball Season Nears Its Close, *Palm Beach Post*, 29 September, 1920, p. 6. Martin blamed abuse and fault finding as his reasons for stepping down as president of the league.

39. Magicians Win Again But First Thrown Out, *Miami Daily Metropolis*, 9 October, 1920, p. 8.

40. Martin Ousted As Head Of East Coast League, *Miami Daily Metropolis*, 27 September, 1920, p. 6.

41. Magicians Take Third Game; Fourth Is A Tie, *Miami Daily Metropolis*, 11 October, 1920, p. 11.

42. East Coast Pennant Won By Magicians, *Palm Beach Post*, 12 October, 1920, p. 6.

43. Lauderdale In Magic City As Scheduled, *Miami Daily Metropolis*, 30 April, 1921, p. 11.

44. Season Opens In The East Coast League, *Miami Daily Metropolis*, 2 May, 1921, p. 6.

45. Sunday Baseball Is Discussed By the Reverend Dr. White, *Miami Daily Metropolis,* 2 May, 1921, p. 6.

46. Jury Returns A Verdict Of "Not Guilty," *Miami Daily Metropolis*, 7 May, 1921, p. 9.

47. Magicians In To Lose Several Players By Change To Six-Day-A-Week Schedule, *Miami Daily Metropolis,* 27 May, 1921, p. 11.

48. Miami Team Swamped By Ft. Pierce Attack, *Miami Daily Metropolis*, 30 June, 1921, p. 3.

49. Baseball Association Asking For $5,000, *Miami Daily Metropolis Baseball Extra*, 13 July, p. 1.

50. County Sheriff And Movie Manager Take Over Club, *Miami Daily Metropolis*, 19 July, 1921, p. 6.

51. R.C. Baker and Carl Kettler New Combination To Manage Destinies Of Baseball Club, *Palm Beach Post*, 19 July, 1921, p. 5.

52. Miami Outdoes Ft. Lauderdale In Tally Fest, *Palm Beach Post*, 6 July, 1921, p. 5.

53. Gators Win The Last Game Of Series Here, *Miami Daily Metropolis*, 25 July, 1921, p. 6.

54. Pests Weak But Will Have a Fighting Team; Egan Heads Them Now, *Reading Times*, 11 April, 1922, p. 10. According to the article Seiglitch played for Daytona Beach of the Florida State League in 1921. He is also listed in baseball-reference. com on the aforementioned team's roster appearing in 6 games with 20 at-bats.

55. New Manager Is Named By Miami Club, *Miami Daily Metropolis*, 28 July, 1921, p. 9.

56. Miami Victorious Over Lauderdale Thursday, Miami Daily Metropolis, 29 July, 1921, p. 9.

57. Miami And W.P. Beach Divide Double Header, *Miami Daily Metropolis Baseball Extra*, 1 August, 1921, p. 1.

58. Miami Hands Ft. Pierce A Terrible Drubbing, *Miami Daily Metropolis*, 6 August, 1921, p. 6.

59. West Palm Beach Still Farther In The Hole, *Miami Daily Metropolis,* August 30, p. 8.

60. Milb.com. *Florida State League History.* Retrieved May 13, 2015.

61. Miami Is Walloped By Daytona Ball Players, *Miami Daily Metropolis*, September 9, 1921, p. 12.

62. Miami Again Victor Over Daytona Team, *Miami Daily Metropolis*, 12 September, 1921, p. 8.

63. Baseball-refence.com. Raleigh was a member of the Class C Piedmont League in 1923, and Wilson was in the Class B Virginia League in 1927.

64. Thomas To Play With Southern League Team, *Miami Daily Metropolis*, 6 March, 1922, p. 6.

65. Shut-out For Daytona Club By Magicians, *Miami Daily Metropolis*, 14 September, 1921, p. 6.

66. Tampa Gets Winning Run In Ninth Inning, *Miami Daily Metropolis*, 16 September, 1921, p. 11.

CHAPTER THREE

THE HUSTLERS

Nineteen twenty-seven was a magic year for sports. Gene Tunney defended his heavyweight boxing crown in a rematch against Jack Dempsey in the controversial fight known as, "The Battle of the Long Count," Bobby Jones and Walter Hagen were tearing up the links, and the National Football League's New York Giants win their first title. In the world of baseball, front-page headlines in newspapers across the country heralded the accomplishments of the larger than life slugger, George Herman "Babe" Ruth set a major league record hitting 60 home runs. The New York Yankees were the darlings of the baseball world. The team that Jacob Ruppert and general manager Ed Barrow constructed was so powerful that, the press bestowed upon them the apt name of, "Murderer's Row." Many baseball historians and fans consider them the greatest team ever assembled. The roster was comprised of seven future Hall-of-Famers including, manager Miller Huggins, and players Earl Combs, Lou Gehrig, Waite Hoyt, Tony Lazzeri, Herb Pennock, and Ruth. The Yanks lay to waste the American League winning 110 games, 19 games ahead of the runner-up Philadelphia Athletics and swept the Pittsburgh Pirates in the World Series.

1927

Miami was a long way from the bright lights of Broadway, but its fan interest in the national pastime was equal to that of any major league city, including New York. A six-year absence by the Magicians, dating back to the last full season of the Florida East Coast League, had ended. On April 6, Florida State Baseball

League President, J.B. Asher sent a telegram to former Magician, Louis K. MacReynolds. Acting as representative for the city, Louis accepted the invitation that succinctly stated that the Magic City join the league, and in order to jumpstart the team in time for the upcoming season, $5,000 needed to be raised by the ownership.[1]

Asher, in his second year as President of the FSL, was interested in stretching the league boundaries further south. Miami with a first-class playing field and swelling population looked like just the cure the league needed to boost attendance and strengthen the FSL that was losing the Bradenton, Fort Myers and Lakeland franchises. On April 11, Board of Director's members, MacReynolds, Executive Secretary, Charles W. Helser, City Manager, Joe Wilcox, and community leaders met at the Miami Chamber of Commerce building to make the formal announcement that for the first time in the history of Miami it would have its officially recognized minor league franchise.[2] Another condition of acceptance into the FSL, was that the Bradenton Growers, a charter member of the league, transfer to Miami under the direction of former Bradenton club President W. B. Kirby.[3] It must have been gratifying for the former Miami Magicians outfielder, MacReynolds to play such a vital role in negotiating the deal, and helping to lay the groundwork for the establishment of an FSL franchise in his beloved city. A natural born glad-hander, Louie as his friends called him, was just beginning to learn the art of deal-making. He was the first Commissioner of the Miami Boxing Commission in the mid-1920s.[4] He later gained nationwide recognition playing a significant role in organizing the famous March 1, 1934, heavyweight boxing match between Primo Carnera and Tommy Loughran in Miami.[5] The match took place at the Madison Square Garden stadium located on NW 25 Street and 8th Avenue. MacReynolds stayed in his post until 1937 when ousted.

With everything in place, the last order of business was determining Miami's new moniker. The choice was Hustlers. Today, the nickname would carry a somewhat negative connotation, and might more closely resemble the name of a strip club's city league sponsored softball team, but at the time, it was more an apt description of the energetic efforts of the players on the diamond. Tryouts began the next day and 50 players turned out for drills under the watchful eye of William "Bill" Holloway the newly named player-manager. Holloway began his ball career as an outfielder with Bloomington (1922) and Rockford (1923) of the Class

B III-League.[6] He first arrived in Florida in 1924 and earned a roster spot with the independent club Daytona Beach that later relocated to Clearwater before he ventured to Miami.[7]

On top of his duties as the skipper, he inherited the starting first base position. Holloway's most immediate challenge was picking a 14-man squad. The feelings of club organizers were that homegrown talent should fill out their roster. Nevertheless, a few carryovers did make the initial squad including pitcher Dick Peel, backstop Herman Matzet, and shortstop Rip Turner from the previous year's Bradenton club. Although a delightful sentiment in theory to bring in local talent, the decision would prove to be the clubs undoing during the first half of the season.[8] By the end of the year, only two players chosen by Holloway survived until the end of the year.

Due to Miami's late entry into the league, the roster was hastily constructed. Workers rushed to prepare the home diamond; Tatum Park, renamed Miami Field, for the April 21 season debut against the Sarasota Tarpons. "The club has gotten a late start, we began practice when other members of the league were nearly in condition to start the season," said Holloway. Players came to tryouts with their own gear, and the team uniforms did not arrive until just a few days before the opening game.[9]

Fervor throughout the community was reflected in the anticipation and excitement generated in preparation for opening day. An estimated crowd of 5,000 fans squeezed into the 3,400 capacity Miami Field. It was the largest crowd to date to witness a baseball game in the Magic City. Several local businesses ran ads in the local newspapers congratulating the team and offered their best wishes for the upcoming season. Many establishments closed their doors early, encouraged by the local Chamber of Commerce, in an effort to support the hometown boys. Commencing the day's activities was a parade that began at the central firehouse on Flagler Street. The Fireman's Band played their most enthusiastic refrains as they wound their way through the streets. The ballplayers and team personnel followed behind, waving as they passed by, expressing their gratitude vocally, before arriving at the ballpark.[10]

Elbow to elbow the fans packed the wooden ballpark like sardines in a can. Former city of Miami mayor, and current city manager, Frank Wharton joined in on the festivities. Wharton, a heavyset figure with his prominent cigar held between his teeth, threw out the first ball signaling the official beginning of the season. Taking the mound for Miami was chunky Cuban left-hander Joe Domingo assigned to square off against the Tarpon's ace Dudley Bonner. Sloppy defensive play proved the Hustlers' undoing when they committed four errors, two miscues by short-stop Rip Turner. Sarasota tallied four runs in the first two in-nings and chased Domingo with no one out in the second frame. Peel entered the game in relief and held the Tarpons to three runs over the remainder of the game, but the Miami offense fell short in scoring enough runs to overcome the early deficit and the Tarpons prevailed, 7 to 5.[11]

The Hustlers' opening day performance was a harbinger of things to come. Poor pitching, a porous defense, and a lackluster offense plagued the club early on. Other than their first series against Sarasota when Miami took two out of three games, there-after, they failed to take another series for the remainder of the first half season.

By mid-May, the Hustlers had lost 16 of their first 22 games, which left them mired in the league basement. At one point from May 30 through June 19, the club lost 18 consecutive games before finally beating St. Petersburg, 5 to 2 on June 20. Despite making wholesale changes to the roster during the opening weeks, none of the new faces performed any better than the old ones. The fortunes of the Hustlers (16–42), a whopping 18 games behind first-place Tampa in the standings were bleak. Under mount-ing pressure to win, club president, W.B. Kirby, and Holloway resigned, which resulted in Smiley Tatum taking control of the club. Tatum made an immediate change and named 38-year-old Henry "Cotton" Knaupp as his new player-manager.[12]

The flaxen-haired Texan brought with him a wealth of experi-ence as a player and reputation as a natural born leader of men. At the tender age of 20 years old, the Victoria Rosebuds of the Class D Southwest Texas League in 1910 signed him. Although not impressive with the stick, he flashed enough leather to catch the eye of the Cleveland Indians. He signed that same year to serve as a reserve shortstop with the Tribe. He spent two seasons in Cleveland appearing in 31 games while batting .184 before return-ing to the minor leagues. He went on to a lengthy career mostly spent with the Southern Association's New Orleans Pelicans, twelve seasons in "The Big Easy" where he established himself as a local diamond legend. He holds the distinction of completing the only unassisted triple play in Southern Association history.[13]

Knaupp faced two daunting tasks, those being changing the pessimistic attitude in the clubhouse and rebuilding the roster. His first transaction was responsible for him earning his first win as skipper. The *Miami News* reported an upstart pitcher from the far west named, Lefty Wetsell arrived. Later accounts stated he was from the Pacific Coast League. His debut victory came on June 20 an impressive performance at that.[14] He kept St. Petersburg batters in check during his debut a 5 to 2 win dazzling the enemy hitters with his blazing fastball.[15] Wetsell (sometimes spelled Wetzel in game accounts), would later cause quite a stir in the FSL.[16]

Four days later, the Hustlers' ambitious manager continued making moves by releasing infielders, Eddie Dean and C.E. "Slick" Vincent, pitcher Elmer "Heinie" Hymel, and outfielder J.W. Richards. New arrival Benjamin Keyes from the Cotton States League moved the former Cincinnati Red prospect Walter "Babe" Bennin[17] from behind the plate to the outfield, and Knaupp took over regular duties at second base.[18]

First Half Standings

TEAM	W	L	GB
Orlando	38	26	–
Sarasota	36	29	2.5
Tampa	35	29	3
Sanford	33	30	4.5
St. Petersburg	32	30	5
Miami	18	48	21

With an almost completely re-worked roster, the Hustlers launched the second half of the season with new vigor and fire against the first half champions, the Orlando Colts. Pitcher, Hy (sometimes listed as "Hi" in newspaper accounts) Meyer, recently recruited, was chosen to face-off against the opposition's workhorse Minor Formby. Both teams failed to score through the first three innings. Spurred on by their new leadership and displaying a newfound attitude, the Hustlers were determined not to be the "whipping boys" anymore. Shortstop Clem Foss, a member of the Colts the previous season, "got hot under the collar" in the third inning when he disagreed with what he perceived to be a questionable strike call. After a ferociously heated exchange with umpire Raphon, Foss was tossed from the game. It was one of only two punch-outs that afternoon by Formby. Both team's bats seemed to have wilted under the stifling humidity that day. The Hustlers showed off their newfound intestinal fortitude and scored the only run of the game during the top of the fifth frame when Holloway hustled around the bases and scored on a Frank "Lefty" or "Big Boy" Barron's single.[19] Miami had sent a clear message that they were no longer doormats.

Knaupp continued fine-tuning his roster throughout the month of July. The first announcement came at the beginning of the month when he accepted the resignation of team captain, and former skipper, Holloway. After being relieved of his managerial duties, Holloway stayed on as a player but later revealed that he was taking a job managing a club in Gary, West Virginia. On July 7, the team announced three new player additions, shortstop Clint Bingham, outfielder Cotton Tatum, and first baseman Matt Hinkle.[20] The regular shortstop Foss shifted over to third base dictating the release of short-time infielder Mike Maloney.

The new arrivals paid instant dividends against their next opponent Tampa when all three new recruits garnered key base hits in the 6 to 3 win over the Smokers. Bingham drew lauds for his spectacular defensive prowess robbing Tampa of a possible run-scoring double on a sharply hit line drive. Backed by a Fausto "Cas" Casares home run, and excellent mound work by Chad "Georgia" Davis who held the Smokers to seven hits, Miami prevailed and improved their record to (5–2). It was good enough for second place in the standings behind the Sanford Celeryfeds (6 to 1); one of the more interesting names in minor league history, a reference to the cities designation as the celery capital of the world.[21]

Throughout the remainder of July, Miami's position in the standings vacillated between second and third place, as they were unable to wrest the league lead from Sanford. First-half league-leader Orlando was ostensibly resting on their first-half laurels and playing under .500. With playoff implications for the second half championship hanging over the competing clubs, tempers were bound to explode again and with vehement passion, they did. Increasingly, league wide the quality of umpiring was coming under question by fans, managers, players, and by FSL officials. Matters came to a head during the July 18 game between Orlando and Miami. The match that sparked the flame occurred in the fourth inning when Colts third baseman C. Lehrmann, came in with his spikes high, sliding and cutting the second baseman so severely that Bingham was forced to leave the game, due to the injury. Words exchanged by the opponents included some choice expletives from Knaupp directed at the arbiters. It took a while before the umpiring crew restored order.[22] In the eighth frame, facing former Miami pitcher "Big Boy" Barron, Knaupp went down on called strikes. Many in the stands protested the questionable call. The prickly pilot soon got into another heated discussion this time with the umpire Joe Leichich. Knaupp's patience reached its end, and the Louisianan in his rage slapped Leichich across the face. The brutal action resulted in both benches clearing and Knaupp's ejection. Adding insult to injury was the fact that Barron held off the Hustlers and earned the victory by the final of 6 to 5. The *Miami Metropolis* opined, "the quality of umpiring, barring the usual allowance for rabid fans' enthusiasm, has been very mediocre; in fact, laughable at times."[23] Repercussions followed, and in a surprising decision by league president, Asher, he ruled that Leichich was negligent in his duties and relieved of his position.[24] To Knaupp's amazement, the expected fine or suspension was not forthcoming and he received no reprimand.

With the matter resolved the Hustlers' manager went back to seeking new avenues of opportunities to improve his Hustlers. A major part of Miami's turnaround was the positive contribution of their re-built pitching staff. The Hustlers' four-man rotation of Meyer, "Georgia" Davis, Wetsell and Peel had quickly established itself as the best mound corps in the league; Peel being the only holdover twirler from the opening day roster. The Hustlers appeared ready to make a run when they received a stroke of bad luck. Peel injured his leg during warm-ups prior to their July 26 contest with St. Petersburg. It proved to be his last appearance of the year. In his stead, Meyer took his place, but on short rest was ineffective against the Saints. Although Miami took the loss, 9 to 4 at Miami Field, once again, Knaupp proved his value as an excellent evaluator of talent by introducing his latest newcomer Buster "Lefty" Brown who pitched two scoreless innings to end the game. Brown would aptly fill Peel's rotation spot for the rest of the season.[25]

Miami remained close on the heels of front-running Sanford into mid-August before finally snatching first place. On August 17, the Hustlers leap-frogged the Celeryfeds when they easily bested

St. Petersburg, 7 to 2, and Sanford fell to Tampa, 10 to 4. Bennin was the hitting start of the day with three base knocks, and the Miami staff continued to impress thanks to some fine twirling by Davis, and two scoreless innings of relief work by Meyer.

From August 13 to September 4, the Hustlers went on a tear winning 16 of 20 games. During the stretch run, Knaupp continued to fortify his club. The crafty skipper acquired two of St. Petersburg's best players by claiming Jose "Joe" Hernandez, after his release,[26][27] and nine-year minor league veteran outfielder Bill Brazier.[28] In addition, the Hustlers' signed a highly touted 26-year-old Oklahoman, veteran southpaw hurler, Pryor "Chief" McBee, formerly with Jacksonville of the Class B Southeastern League.[29] McBee, who enjoyed "a cup of coffee" in the American League with the Chicago White Sox the year before, also brought with him five years of minor league experience.[30]

The investment in Hernandez, who had previously starred in the Cuban winter leagues and Negro leagues, paid instant dividends when the ex-Saint shutout Sarasota, 5 to 0 on September 4. The victory clinched the second half championship for Miami. It was the greatest turnaround in the short history of the FSL when Miami more than doubled their first-half win total. The Hustlers were set to play Orlando for the championship.[31]

No one expected Miami's successful run the second half of the season. Their "Cinderella story" was lost on Sanford who was smarting from their second place finish and inability to defend their title. Sanford management filed a formal protest with league officials pointing out a rule that in short stated, "only up to three players with higher level professional experience were allowed per team." The claim centered on Miami's hurler Wetsell, who they felt qualified as a fourth player on the Miami roster with previous higher level experience, thus disqualifying Miami from participating in the league championship." Upon further review by Asher, the protest was overturned, clearing Miami's way to play for the league pennant.[32] Either the *Miami Daily News and Metropolis* reported Wetsell's background inaccurately, or he misrepresented himself to Hustlers' officials. There is also the possibility that he played under an assumed name since there is no record of him ever having been with the Pacific Coast League, or participating at any level of professional baseball after 1928.

It was an unexpected and incredible turnaround, nothing short of miraculous. Accolades flowed from the Miami fandom and Knaupp received a great deal of credit for spurring his club's accomplishments. Team management was ecstatic and they promised their players a trip to Cuba if they brought home the league pennant.

Second Half Standings

TEAM	W	L	GB
Miami	38	19	-
Sanford	34	21	3
Orlando	31	25	6.5
Sarasota	25	32	13
Tampa	21	34	16
St. Petersburg	18	36	18.5

The September 7 championship series curtain-raiser met with a relentless downpour that dampened the crowd's spirits and led to its cancellation at Orlando's Tinker Field. The next day was, as the *Miami Daily News and Metropolis* reported, "A bitterly fought game." McBee started against the Colts 11-game winner "Red" Sweeney. Orlando scored a pair of runs in the first inning and looked to add onto their lead in the third inning. Paul Kirby, hoping to tag up from second base on Casares' long fly ball to center field, dashed for third. The play turned out to be an inning killer. To the runner's dismay, the umpire ruled him out because he left his bag early while tagging up. This set off Colts' manager-catcher Phil Wells who erupted in a rage as he flew from the bench. The ensuing argument led to a few choice words between umpire Moore and Wells. The Colt's manager-catcher found himself tossed from the game contributing to hard feelings between the two clubs.

Emotions remained high in the seventh inning, and it was Miami's turn to lose their cool. On a close play at third base, Rollie Tinker the son of baseball Hall of Famer Joe Tinker received a safe ruling on a bang-bang play on the bases causing Foss to jump into hysterics. An intense argument followed with umpire Fredericks and fisticuffs ensued. It took a few policemen and several players to separate the two combatants. Foss was given the heave-ho. His ejection had a far-reaching effect on the outcome of the series.[33] The Hustlers only tally on the day came in the fifth frame when Bingham scored on a slowly-hit tapper in the infield by a later to be expelled Foss. Orlando added a single run in the seventh and garnered the lid-lifter win by the final of 3 to 1.[34]

Following the game, FSL officials came down hard on Foss and handed him a 90-day suspension that included all of the remaining games of the championship series. Joe Hernandez filled in at third base for the remainder of the series. The Hustlers were shocked at losing their teammate and came out flatter than a two dollar bill the next day as Orlando took the second game by the score of 1 to 0.[35]

The Hustlers bounced back on July 12 in what was technically the fourth game, since the third game had ended in a 2 to 2 tie after 13 innings; the game called because of darkness. Georgia Davis, in his finest performance of the year, threw a masterful one-hitter shutting out the visiting Colts at Miami Field, 2 to 0, earning the home team their first win of the series.[36] Prior to the game, Hustlers' fans showed their appreciation for the team by naming center fielder Cas Casares as the most popular player and awarding him a wristwatch. Bennin, shared in the bounty, voted as the most valuable player. The big catcher-outfielder received a suit of fine clothes from the Dempsey Haberdashery Company.[37]

The Hustlers looked to capitalize on the shift of momentum. Lefty Wetsell and Red Sweeney locked horns in a game five classic pitcher's duel. Through the regulation nine innings, neither team tallied a run. In the top of the tenth inning, Rollie Tinker and Tausy Abrams hit back-to-back singles. Wetsell then retired Sweeney on a ground ball to Hernandez at third base for the force. The next batter, Kirby promptly hit a sharp hit grounder to shortstop Bingham who misplayed the ball giving Abrams just enough time to race home with the deciding run. The final on the scoreboard showed Orlando 1 Miami 0.[38]

With a day off to catch their collective breaths, the Hustlers' squad seem-re-energized taking the following two games from Orlando at Miami Field, the last game of the home set being the strangest game to date. The Colts' taken to task by the Hustlers lost by a final of 12 to 4.[39] Miami looked to tie the series at three apiece the following day. Once again, Sweeney and Davis found themselves in a duel. Orlando scored first in the top of the third inning when catcher, J. Lee tagged up from third on Tinker's sacrifice fly. The game went into the bottom of the ninth with Miami trailing 1 to 0 and then the proceedings got bizarre. With one out and Casares taking a lead off third base, Keyes hit a low liner between first and second base that appeared like Tinker had caught the ball an inch above the ground. Tinker was so confident of snagging the ball that he failed to make the cautionary throw to his first baseman Abrams to get Keyes dashing down the first base line. To Tinker's astonishment, umpire Fredericks ruled the ball as trapped and Keyes safe. This drew the ire of Colts skipper, Wells. A riotous argument soon followed as players from both benches stormed the field egged on by 2,000 vocal fans. Keyes joined in on the fray and further argued that whether or not Tinker caught the ball before it hit the ground that Colts backstop Lee had interfered with his swing and that Keyes should have been awarded first base on the catcher's interference regardless. With league president, Asher on hand, both clubs referred to him for a ruling. After several tense moments, the verdict came down and the umpires' decision upheld. Wells was hysterical and refused to allow his charges to take the field. After the third request by officials was ignored, it resulted in Miami being awarded the game and win by forfeit, thus evening the series and setting up a one-game take all championship game.[40]

What should have been a dream finale turned into a nightmare. Joe Fernández was Knaupp's choice against their mainstay, Minor Formby. Miami got off to a shaky start and allowed the Colts to tally a pair of runs in the top of the first inning. Trailing 2 to 0 going into the fifth inning, the usually effective Hernandez faltered and allowed the Colts six straight hits, which plated five runs, and Orlando increased their lead to 7–0. Despite nine Hustler hits the Miamians were unable to string them together as Orlando cruised to an easy 12 to 1 victory leaving the once enthusiastic crowd at Miami Field stunned. The *Miami Daily News and Metropolis* called it one of the poorest performances of the year. Orlando had earned their second league championship and left Miami and its followers to mournfully weep, "Wait 'til next year."

1928

With an eye towards the upcoming season, Miami ownership received an unexpected offer to leave the FSL in February of 1928 and join the Class B South Atlantic League. It was announced that the Augusta Tygers (the name derived from Ty Cobb who began his pro career in Augusta in 1904) franchise was up for sale and that Sally League officials were courting Miami as a replacement. The Sally League also listed Tampa as a possible location for expansion. The FSL was in flux since Tampa had withdrawn from the league, and Sanford threatened to depart as well. It would have left the league with four teams. Miami awaited word from FSL officials before they made their decision on the league's future.[41]

In the days before airline travel, Miami's biggest obstacle, or any clubs, was the expense of travel posed by the distance between playing venues. Sally League teams spread out between Georgia, North Carolina, South Carolina, and Tennessee already required long trips. Any team traveling to or from the Sunshine State would require an extra day off, which "opened up a "whole can of worms" as far as game schedules and expenses.

Ultimately, Miami officials felt secure to stay within the FSL and agreed to a six-team arrangement for the upcoming season. Daytona Beach, Fort Lauderdale, and West Palm Beach replaced Sarasota, St. Petersburg, and Tampa who had agreed to drop out of the league. In addition, Orlando, and Sanford settled their differences with FSL officials and agreed to return for one more season.[42]

One can only speculate how Miami would have fared in the other league. Hindsight is a wonderful thing if one possesses such a skill. Despite what appeared to be a sound move by president Asher to stabilize the FSL, instead financial difficulties crept up and marred the 1928 season. The first sign of trouble came at the end of May when Fort Lauderdale, because of lack of attendance, relocated to St. Petersburg. By June 30, owners met in Melbourne, Florida to talk over the future of the league. The first order of business discussed whether Sanford and West Palm Beach should shut down before season's end. The agenda focused on the issue concerning the players from Fort Lauderdale who had not received their paychecks and were threatening to strike hoping to recover some of their back wages.[43] Ultimately, these issues were resolved before the close of the season. Both Sanford and West Palm Beach completed their schedules and the ex-Tarpons acquired the pay that was due them.

On July 4, Miami split a doubleheader against the Palm Beach Sheriffs. It was the last game of the season as the league formally disbanded. The Hustlers finished a disappointing fourth place at the close of the abbreviated season.[44]

Final Standings

TEAM	W	L	GB
Fort Lauderdale / St. Petersburg	38	23	-
Orlando	37	23	.5
West Palm Beach	31	32	8
Miami	29	35	10.5
Daytona Beach	26	36	12.5
Sanford	25	37	13.5

It would not be long before baseball would take a back seat to hard economic times. The result of the severe curtailment of money and credit led to Florida's economic bubble bursting by 1926. Investors lost confidence in so-called "paper" millionaires.[45] Two more severe setbacks were yet to come. The first blow came on September of 1928 with the Great Okeechobee Hurricane that caused an estimated $16 billion (in today's dollars) of damages. When it struck land in Palm Beach estimates put the death toll between 1,770 to 3,000 people with consequences felt throughout the state.[46][47] Shortly thereafter, the Mediterranean fruit fly infestation began in the spring of 1929 and it wiped out the Florida citrus crop.[48] These two disasters combined, along with nationwide financial difficulties, delivered a knockout punch that plummeted Florida into an economic depression. The rest of the nation and the world joined in the miseries. Scores of people migrated to urban areas including rural farmers looking for a prosperous life, lured to jobs in industry. This, in turn, led to declining agriculture production that triggered an economic collapse. An era of excess and increasing wealth known as "The Roaring Twenties" built on a house of cards had imploded on itself and by 1929, the Stock Market crashed.

Essentially professional baseball in Miami went into hibernation during the 1930s. The only respite for hardball enthusiasts was during the three springs when the Brooklyn Dodgers returned to Miami in 1933, and the New York Giants came to Miami Beach in 1934 and 1935. During these depressed times, only amateur baseball survived to entertain the locals. For Miamians who attended these rough and tumble semi-pro and amateur baseball games, occasionally they discovered a familiar face in the lineup from the bygone days. Names like Murray Beard and Clint Bingham, heroes from the past, were now playing at the neighborhood diamond. The appearance of these vestiges from yesteryear served as reminders of happier days. It would not be until 1940 that professional baseball would return.

NOTES

1. Miami Offered League Berth, *Miami Daily News and Metropolis*, 7 April, 1927, p. 11.
2. State League Team For City Will Be Urged, *Miami Daily News and Metropolis*, 11 April, 1927, p. A-12.
3. Fifty Players Seeking Berths In Miami Team, *Miami Daily News and Metropolis*, 13 April, 1927, p. 11.
4. Bell, Jack. "O'er the Sports Desk," *Miami Daily News*, 30 May, 1937, p. 1-D.
5. Referee Big Problem For Title Fight, *Reading Eagle*, 22 February, 1934, p. 16.
6. Baseball-reference.com.
7. Minorleaguebaseballplayer.blogspot.com. Retrieved, 23 August, 2017 from https://minorleaguebaseballplayer.blogspot.com/2016/09/pre-war-minor-league-baseball-player.html.
8. 120 Game Play Opening Is Set For April 21, *Miami Daily News and Metropolis*, 12 April, 1927, p. A-13.
9. Miami Starts Diamond Tilts Here Thursday, *Miami Daily News and Metropolis*, 17 April, 1927, p. 14.
10. Street Parade Will Precede Opening Game, *Miami Daily News and Metropolis*, 21 April, 1927, p. 12.
11. Opening Game Offered Fans Run For Money, *Miami Daily News and Metropolis*, 22 April, 1927, p. A-23.
12. S.M. Tatum Is New President Of The Miami Baseball Club, *Miami Daily News and Metropolis*, 16 June, 1927, p. 10.
13. Milb.com. *New Orleans Baseball History*, Knaupp turned the unassisted triple play on 8 August, 1916.
14. Lefty Wetsell Pitches Great Ball In Game, *Miami Daily News and Metropolis*, 24 July, 1927, p. 14. There is no record of anyone by the name of Wetsell ever playing in the Pacific Coast League.
15. Cotton Knaupp Boost Spirits of "Jinx Boys," *Miami Daily News and Metropolis*, 21 June, 1927, p. 14.
16. League Moguls Find Against Sanford's Club, *Evening Independent* [St. Petersburg, FL], 7 September, 1927, p. 8.
17. Locked Gates To Speed Work Holloway Says, *Miami Daily News and Metropolis*, 15 September, 1927, p. A-16.
18. Sanford Plays Here Saturday With Hustlers, *Miami Daily News and Metropolis*, 25 June, 1927, p. 9.
19. Miami Hurler Bests Formby In Mound Due, *Miami Daily News and Metropolis*, 1 July, 1927, p. 13.
20. Hustlers Play Tampa Thursday At Miami Field, *Miami Daily News and Metropolis*, 7 July, 1927, p. 7.

21. Clint Bingham Makes Record Catch In Game, *Miami Daily News and Metropolis,* 8 July, 1927, p. 13.
22. Knaupp Slaps Umps In Face, *Sarasota Herald-Tribune*, 19 July, 1927, p. 3.
23. State League Official Has Plenty Of Action, *Miami Daily News and Metropolis*, 19 July, 1927, p.10.
24. Lefty Wetsell Pitches Great Ball In Game, *Miami Daily News and Metropolis*, 24 July, 1927, p. 14.
25. Visitors Have Another Field Day In Battle, *Miami Daily News and Metropolis*, 27 July, 1927, p. 9.
26. Saints Release Cuban Hurler, *Evening Independent* [St. Petersburg, FL], 8 July, 1927, p. 2.
27. Baseball-reference.com. Pitched 1922–24 and 1927 for St. Petersburg, and 1927 Miami (Florida State League)
28. Baseball-reference.com. Brazier career stops: 1913 Cordele (Class-D Empire State League), 1915 Griffin (Class-D Georgia-Alabama League), 1916–17 Augusta (Class-C South Atlantic League), 1919 Greenville (Class-C South Atlantic League), 1919–1920 Columbia (Class-C South Atlantic League), 1920 Charleston (Class-C South Atlantic League), 1923–24 Lakeland (Class-C Florida State League), 1927 St. Petersburg (Class-D Florida State League), and 1927 Miami (Class-D Florida State League).
29. Double Iron Man Stunt May Be Offered—Local Pilot to Use Southpaw, *Evening Independent* [St. Petersburg, FL], 16 August, 1927, p. 8.
30. Baseball-reference.com. McBee made his major league debut for the Chicago White Sox on May 22, 1926 and pitched 1.1 innings walking three batters, striking out one and allowing one base hit. It was his only major league appearance.
31. Double Header Monday Closes League Series, *Miami Daily News and Metropolis*, 5 September, 1927, p. 5.
32. League Moguls Find Against Sanford's Club, *Evening Independent* [St. Petersburg, FL], 7 August, 1927, p. 8.
33. Orlando Wins Series Opener, *Sarasota Herald-Tribune*, 9 September, 1927, p. 3.
34. Two Players Are Banished For Talking, *Miami Daily News and Metropolis*, 9 September, 1927, p. 8.
35. Hustlers Need Victory Badly In Flag Race, *Miami Daily News and Metropolis*, 10 September, 1927, p. 10.
36. Davis Pitches One Hit Game For Knauppmen, *Miami Daily News and Metropolis*, 12 September, 1927, p. 6.
37. Players Are Given Awards, *Miami Daily News and Metropolis,* 12 September, 1927, p. 6.
38. Bingham Lets Orlando Score In The Tenth, *Miami Daily News and Metropolis*, 13 September, 1927, p. 15.
39. Orlando Loses Hectic 12 To 4 Tilt Wednesday, *Miami Daily News and Metropolis*, 15 September, 1927, p. 8.
40. Colts Forfeit Thursday Game In The Ninth, *Miami Daily News and Metropolis*, 16 September, 1927, p. 16.
41. Franchise At Augusta Open For Purchase, *Miami Daily News and Metropolis*, 16 February, 1928, p. 10.
42. Ibid.
43. Moguls To Meet And Settle Fate Of Clubs Sunday, *Evening Independent*, [St. Petersburg, FL] 30 June, 1928, p. 30.
44. State League Baseball Teams Play Final Games On Fourth, *Miami Daily News and Metropolis*, 5 July, 1928, p. 9.
45. Publication of Archival Library and Museum Material. *Florida History Timeline, 1919–1929*. Retrieved 4 June, 2015 from palm.fcla.edu.
46. Hurricanescience.org/history/storms/1920s/Okeechobee/, Retrieved 4 June, 2015.

47.   Brochu, Nicole. *"Florida's forgotten storm: The Hurricane of 1928,"* 14 September, 2003. Retrieved 4 June, 2015 from sunsentinel.com/fsl-hurricane14sep14-story.html#page=1.

48.   Florida Agriculture, *"The Saga of the Mediterranean Fruit Fly, Part I, 1929–1950,"* Retrieved on 4 June, 2015 from https://fldpi.wordpress.com/2013/03/19/the-saga-of-the-mediterranean-fruit-fly-part-i-1928–1930.

CHAPTER FOUR

THE RETURN OF THE FLORIDA EAST COAST LEAGUE

The Great Depression of the 1930s severely tested the mettle of the people of the United States. Following the stock market crash of 1929, millions found themselves out of work and losing their homes. Miami was not immune to hard times. Rampant unemployment, brought on by the economic crash, coupled with a screeching halt to the local land boom of the late 1920s further depressed the area. The terrible hurricane of 1926 destroyed much of the infrastructure and facilities in the community. Together all these factors negatively affected the Miami area until the mid-century.

It was not until 1933, following the election of Franklin Delano Roosevelt to the presidency, that the launching of his "New Deal," allowed many to return to gainful employment. The Depression left its indelible mark on Miami, yet the population suffered less than most areas of the U.S. Normalcy returned by the mid-1930s. The arrival of Eastern Airlines and Pan American Airways (who established headquarters in the city), was enhanced by a burgeoning tourist industry. The new jobs created, softened the blow of the otherwise bleak prospects. The local citizenry began to see the light at the end of the tunnel, and by 1940 recovered from over ten years of financially trying times.[1]

1940

Nationwide, the minor leagues were experiencing a resurgence spurred on by consumers with increased discretionary income to spend on leisure activities. Attendance at ballparks climbed and from a low of 14 loops in 1933, the number exploded to 44 by 1940. After more than a decade, professional baseball was again making its debut in Miami. It had been 12 years since the breakup of the last FECL in 1928. The formation of two new clubs triggered excitement throughout the community. One launched in Miami, and the other in Miami Beach as members of the reincarnated Class D Florida East Coast League (FECL).

Judge Gordon Lynn of Palm Beach, president of the brand spanking new six-team league, announced that each team would play a 120-game schedule, with a playoff held at the conclusion of the season to determine a champion. The Shaughnessy playoff format pitted the top four teams in the league (first and second place to play third and fourth respectively), and the winners to meet for the championship.[2] Roster limitations allowed three veterans (players who had major or high-class minor-league experience), three limited-class men (players with Class D experience), and eight rookies with less than 45 days experience in organized baseball. Rounding out the circuit were four clubs, Fort Lauderdale (Tarpons), Fort Pierce (Bombers), Hollywood (Chiefs) and West Palm Beach (Indians).[3] The Tarpons were the only team affiliated with a major league club, the Pittsburgh Pirates.

Miami officials selected their moniker as the Wahoos. The name derived from the high-speed sporting game fish that populates the waters of the Caribbean, and coast of Florida. Miami Beach fans took a more standard approach. Several of the entries submitted suggested Flamingos as their preference. The winning entry chosen came from local resident Sheldon Schreiber that possessed the earliest postmark. It earned him the grand prize of season tickets to all home games at Flamingo Park.[4] Schreiber's experience proved the old adage of the "early bird gets the worm" being true.

Separate consortiums of investors backed the Miami and Miami Beach clubs. The Miami Beach group was among the first of the owners to gain membership in the FECL. Naturally, the Flamingos played their home games at Flamingo Park, on the corner of Michigan and 15th Street. Constructed in 1925, the ball grounds experienced several improvements over the years. Most notably, the addition of grandstands to accommodate the New York Giants, who used it as their spring training site in 1934 and 1935, and the Philadelphia Phillies beginning in 1940.[5][6] Instrumental in the development of the Flamingo Park, dating back to the 1920s was J.B. Lemon; Director of the city recreation department was instrumental in the development of the park dating back to its birth. A tremendous supporter of all sports, he was offered and accepted the position of Flamingos team president.

One of Lemon's first official moves was to hire Freddy "Lefty" Heimach as his field manager. The new president did not have to look far to find him because he was working as a Miami Beach police officer.[7] Lefty's resumé included big league experience. His last appearance in the majors was in 1933, after which he relocated to south Florida. He toiled, as a pitcher, during his 13-year major-league career with the Boston Red Sox, Brooklyn Dodgers, New York Yankees, and Philadelphia Athletics compiling a 62–69 record.[8]

Across the bay, another ownership group secured their place in the FECL. The last organization to throw their cap into the ring was Miami, spearheaded by ten local executives acting as stockholders under the familiar masthead, the Miami Baseball Association. Their first course of action was to elect Charles "Jack" Baldwin, Chairman of the local Orange Bowl committee, as the team president.[9]

Baldwin's first task was finding a new manager to head up the Wahoos. He, like Lemon, did not have to trek far to find his new field boss. His choice was baseball legend, Max "Scoops" Carey (given name was Maximillian Carnarius). A broad-shouldered and square-jawed descendent of German heritage, the former National League star outfielder with the Pittsburgh Pirates (16 seasons) and the Brooklyn Dodgers (4 seasons), was residing in the area running his Persian lime growing business. Since retiring from the major leagues in 1929, Carey had been involved in a number of activities. Following the stock market crash, when he lost over $100,000 in investments in Florida real estate and stocks, he returned to Pittsburgh as a coach for one season in 1930. He then took a year off from the grand old game after discovering a cream called "Minit-Rub" that a country druggist in Illinois had invented for aches and pains. In an interview with Tommy Fitzgerald of the *Miami News*, Carey recounted, "I stayed out of baseball in 1931 after a year as a coach to put it on the market and develop it. We later sold it to Bristol-Meyer [sic]." Carey returned to baseball in 1932 as manager of the Brooklyn Dodgers and held the position for two seasons, only later replaced by Casey Stengel in 1934.[10] Soon thereafter, he returned to Florida, where he seemed to have settled into a life outside of baseball, yet the itch to be back in the game persisted. When Baldwin approached Carey with an offer to manage again, he jumped at the opportunity and took the position along with the role of vice-president and general manager.[11]

The two new skippers each took a different tact putting their squads' together. Although the league rules precluded the use of many players with experience, Heimach was more comfortable with the few veterans he could sign. For example, the Flamingos starting lineup featured battle-hardened ex-major leaguer 37-year-old, Max Rosenfeld, and 26-year-old George Pratt with three prior seasons at the Class D level. Carey, on the other hand, went with younger players with limited experience to mix with his rookies. The only player on the roster over 24 years old was pitcher Stanley Todd, who became a fixture in South Florida baseball.[12] However, because of Miami's late entry into the circuit, they had less opportunity than their competition to sign veteran players, and for the most part, recruited within the area. In a further effort to attract talent, they ran an advertisement in the Sporting News that read as follows:[13]

Max Carey at Magical Miami
Class "D" East Coast League
Don't Come Unless
You Can Run, Hit, Throw or Pitch
We'll teach you the rest-Opening May 3-Low
fare by bus or coach-Fare and board refunded if
you make good-Bring equipment
Wire Max Carey, Manager, Report Immediately
Miami Baseball Club

The Flamingos' reliance on a more veteran-laden roster, with Miami's insistence of building a youthful squad, was a pattern that repeated itself over the years until 1954.

On May 3, Miami and Miami Beach kicked off their season at Flamingo Park. League President Judge Gordon Lynn threw out the first ball, followed by the introduction of the players.[14] The Wahoos wore their road grays, and the Flamingos, their home white togs trimmed in orange and green. Following the festivities, umpire, Frank DeHaney bellowed, "Play ball."[15]

Taking the hill for the Wahoos was right-hander Robert Franks, a local product out of Miami Edison High School. For the Flamingos, the Philadelphia Phillies dispatched Bill "Red" Brydges, a slender right-hander to Miami Beach for seasoning. Both hurlers were making their professional debuts.[16]

The first meeting between the two teams was a stage-setter for one of the all-time great minor-league rivalries. In a high scoring and sloppily played game, highlighted by eight errors, the Flamingos came out ahead by a tally of 12 to 10. Miami Beach's more experienced lineup led by the old-timer Rosenfeld, proved to be the difference, as the ex-Brooklyn Robins/Dodgers outfielder poked two hits and drove in a pair of runs.[17]

On May 5, the series shifted to Miami Field for the Wahoos' opening night. Considered a unique scheduling arrangement when the two teams were in town, they exchanged venues on alternating days. A generous gathering of 1,370 paying customers inside, and another 400 outside of the wire fencing, watched hometown product, Fay "Red" Bohn work his magic. Bohn, who also worked as a clerk at Miami's Biltmore Hotel, earned the first victory besting Pat Berry and the Flamingos, by a score of 5 to 4.[18]

Miami Beach performed well early on, while the Wahoos struggled to stay above the .500 mark. On May 25, the Beachites (12–7) resided in first place, a game and a half ahead of second place Hollywood, while Miami remained competitive with a 10–9 record.[19]

Frequent roster changes were common at this point in the season as both teams tinkered with their personnel. Arguably, Miami Beach's most important acquisition was Phillies prospect Henry "Gene" Bearden. The nineteen-year-old left-hander Bearden had pitched unimpressively the year before with the Class D Moultrie Packers of the Georgia-Florida League[20] compiling a 5–11 record.[21] However, having learned his lessons well, and with a year of experience under his belt, he later proved to be the Flamingo's chief stopper on the mound. He was also a capable batsman with a respectable .247 average. Bearden's first start against West Palm Beach on May 14 was a disappointing 6 to 5 loss,[22] but he followed that up with an 11-inning complete game win by the same score against Fort Lauderdale, twice stroking base hits, the latter proving to be the game winner.[23]

An eagle-eyed Carey spotted a talented prospect performing on local diamonds, who like Bearden, would go on to a successful major league career. He convinced, and then signed, highly regarded pitching phenomenon Robert "Bobby" Hogue. The son of a well-known boxing trainer Oakley Hogue, and Miami High School graduate, Bobby was also a fighter who won 36 of 39 decisions inside the ring.[24] At 5'9" and 190 pounds, the youngster possessed nothing more than a blazing fastball and good control. Carey, impressed by the stocky, right-hander, baptized him by allowing two innings of relief work against Fort Pierce on May 20. Unfortunately, Miami spoiled his debut by losing to the Bombers, 6 to 0. Nevertheless, the stocky right-hander fared well working both frames without giving up a run or base on balls.[25]

Signed only a few days apart Bearden and Hogue were two of four ballplayers from the 1940 FECL season that would rise to the major leagues. Hogue was one of the first native and high school players from Miami and made it to the big leagues in 1948. He recalled what it was like his first year, and the toughness of his fellow ballplayers, "I was in my share of fistfights. Ballplayers were a bunch of nasty old men back then."[26] The other two players who later saw action in the majors were Chester ("Chesty Chet" or "Lefty") Covington of Hollywood who spent time with the Philadelphia Phillies in 1944, and Mike Schultz of Fort Lauderdale who appeared in one game for the Cincinnati Reds in 1947.[27]

In many ways, the fortunes of Bearden and Hogue mirrored the success of their teams. Hogue made seven starts for the Wahoos and earned a solitary win. Carey became so frustrated that he released the youngster halfway through the season. Hollywood immediately picked up Hogue.[28] Conversely, Bearden carried on through the season as one of the FECL's best twirlers and finished leading the league with a glossy 1.68 ERA, accrued the most shutouts with five, and tied Tarpons Al Reitz for second in the league in wins with 18.[29]

On June 13, Miami stood at 17–14 and Miami Beach at 14–17 trailing first-place Hollywood (19–11). The two rivals soon took diametric paths. Miami plagued by poor pitching, and numerous injuries found themselves by August 26 with an undistinguished 34–61 won-loss record. At one point in August, they lost 19 of 21 games. Meanwhile, their rival across Biscayne Bay remained a respectable 50–45. It was not enough to catch front-running Fort Lauderdale who staked their claim to first place on August 25; clinching first place on September 17.[30] The Tarpons had a collection of graybeards including 38-year-old player-manager, Herb Thomas who previously enjoyed a brief major league career with the Boston Braves and New York Giants, finished the year batting .352. Five-year minor-leaguer 27-year-old Guilford "Buster" Kinard, topped the club with a .353 average. Moreover, the mound duo of 36-year-old ace ironman Reitz (18–10, 3.06) in his fourteenth season of minor-league ball, and ex-major leaguer George Hockette (13–6, 3.18) who spent parts of two seasons with the Boston Red Sox in 1934 and 1935 anchored the league's most experienced staff.[31]

Miami, burdened with an injury list that resembled a war casualty count, found some on the roster playing out of position, hurt, or just outright released. The Wahoos leading power hitter, Oliver Kelly started the season at third base but developed a sore arm that left him unable to throw a ball across the diamond. Despite his "bad wing," Carey switched him to left field keeping his potent bat in the lineup. Fred Brunle started the season at shortstop, before wrenching his leg, and subsequently drew his "walking papers." Tom Cornish, a natural shortstop, forced to play in the outfield, never adjusted. Third sacker Johnny Adz came down with an illness, and "fly chaser" Jesse Bressie asked for his release because his leg injury would not heal. If that was not bad enough, nearly every starting pitcher came up with a sore arm.[32] Greenville of the Class B Sally League recalled of the few healthy limbed hurlers, Louis "Slick" Brittain in July. This after he had previously strung together six straight wins.[33] Particularly disturbing was the "revolving door" of nine catchers, none of which had a modicum of success.

Although the season was a disappointment, the Wahoos did have some encouraging highlights. Fast as lightning, Billy Watts stole 45 bags by season's end. He pilfered second, third and home in the same inning twice. A proud Carey could relate, having led the NL in steals 10 times, and in 1922, stole 51 bases in 53 attempts.[34] Oliver Kelly finished tied with Miami Beach's Dale Lynch for the league lead in homers (11).[35] Pitcher Franks struck out 13 Indians on June 20, during a 9–2 victory[36] and finished the season with a 13–13 record.

In contrast, the Flamingos fared much better finishing in third place. The one-two punch of Bearden (18–10, 1.68) and Jim Glover (16–11, 240 IP, 2.81) provided the pitching staff with a two-headed monster that kept Miami Beach in first division the majority of the season. The Flamingos were able to avoid the injury bug and kept five of their eight regulars on the field in 100 or more games. The list included center fielder Rex Gardecki

(107), second baseman Dale Lynch (109), catcher George Pratt (101), first baseman Bill Tustin (107) and outfielder-third baseman John Zulberti (105). Rosenfeld finished as the team's top slugger appearing in 89 games, driving in 52 runs and batting .341, which was third best in the league.

On September 22, Heimach's charges opened the Shaughnessy playoffs against Hollywood in a best-of-five showdown. Game one at Dowdy Field incorporated the most bizarre dimensions of any ballpark in minors. It was a pitcher's paradise and a long ball hitter's nightmare; 363 feet to right field, 431 to left field, and 600 to straightaway center field, which nearly precluded any home runs.

Miami Beach called on their ace Bearden to face Chet Covington. The 29-year-old late bloomer was in his second year of organized baseball, but on his way to a storied minor-league career mostly spent in Florida. A tough as nails competitor, he started at the age of 13 by earning a living as a prizefighter. He retired from the ring at age 22 with a 187–19–10 record.[37] [38] Chesty Chet found himself on the winning side of most of his appearances, but on this day, Bearden proved superior by handcuffing the Chiefs and limiting them to four base hits. The Flamingos glided to a 6 to 1 win.

Game two pitted Glover against ex-Wahoos Hogue (8–11, 4.15),[39] who had resuscitated his season under the guidance of his new skipper Edward "Jiggs" Donahue. Since arriving in Hollywood, he increased his total with seven more victories and played an integral part in the Chiefs' second-place finish. Both pitchers posted goose eggs until the bottom of the ninth. With one out, Rosenfeld singled and then young Bobby walked the next two batters. Donahue, seeing that Hogue had tired, called on Sam Langford to stem the tide, but instead Langford was unable to find the strike zone, and issued a base on balls allowing the winning and only run of the game. Miami Beach now had a commanding two games to none lead.

The Flamingos completed the sweep in the third game in a real nail-biter. Heimach called on Coral Gables' own Bill "Slim" Salokar (10–10, 3.31) to go up against 15-game winner Earl Lurtz. Miami Beach got off to a running start scoring four runs in the top of the second inning. Salokar (sometimes spelled "Solokar" in newspaper accounts), experienced control problems and by the third inning, he walked four Chiefs, prompting Heimach to make a trip to the mound. Only two nights before Bearden pitched a gem, but on short rest, his manager signaled for the lefty to take the hill. Bearden escaped the inning but ran into trouble in the fifth frame giving up three runs on three hits. The Flamingos scored a run in the seventh only to have it negated in the bottom of the same inning. Daring base running by shortstop Billy Miller scored from third when catcher Pratt made a throw to first base on a dropped third strike. The Chiefs threatened in the bottom of the ninth, but a slick fielding play by Zulberti thwarted the rally when he started a snappy 5-4-3 double play. The final score was 5 to 4.[40]

Miami Beach moved on to Fort Lauderdale for the championship series-opening game at West Side Park against the Tarpons who had taken their series from West Palm Beach in four games. The Flamingos' winning momentum carried over as they won the lid-lifter, 6 to 5. A home run and double by Lynch, and a strong combined pitching effort by starter, Harry Dunlevy (4–5, 3.22), Salokar, and Bearden held the Tarpons to six hits.[41]

On September 29, game two shifted to Flamingo Park. In a unique arrangement, FECL officials agreed that each team would play alternate days on their home fields, instead of playing blocks of games to save on travel expenses. Due to the short distance between both cities, this did not prove difficult for the ballplayers.

Local fandom sponsored game two in recognition of a pair of hometown heroes. "Gene Bearden Night" honored the Flamingos most valuable player and most popular player. In a pre-game ceremony, Judge Gordon Lynn presented, Bearden, with a gold wristwatch, courtesy of the fans, as the Flamingos MVP. In addition, Lynch, voted as "the most popular player," accepted a portable radio.[42]

The festivities turned to disappointment later when the Beachites finally stumbled, dropping their first game of the postseason 6 to 2 with Bearden absorbing the loss. The Flamingos' feathers ruffled when they committed five errors, negating any chance of taking a commanding two-game lead in the series. Bearden, once again, worked on short rest and it showed, lacking his usual sharpness allowing the enemy to reap eleven base hits.[43]

Fort Lauderdale made short work of the Flamingos snatching the next two games winning by the scores of 6 to 4, and 11 to 1. Although Miami Beach made a valiant effort in the fifth game, Bearden in his fourth appearance of the series was not up to par. The Tarpons squeezed by the Flamingos, 4 to 2 at West Side Park to bring home the championship in front of their hometown fans. The hope for better results next year was all that remained.[44]

Final Standings

TEAM	W	L	GB
Fort Lauderdale	69	40	–
Hollywood	62	47	7
Miami Beach	60	51	10
West Palm Beach	52	60	18.5
Fort Pierce	49	65	22.5
Miami	42	71	29

1941

Nineteen-forty-one was a year of change, not only for the Miami Wahoos and for the Miami Beach Flamingos, but the FECL as well. After guiding the league through its initial season, Judge Gordon W. Lynn relinquished his position as league president. J. B. Lemon took his place, on January 18, at the league meetings in Palm Beach. Lemon announced that the FECL would expand its schedule to 140-games while maintaining its membership at six teams.[45] The only change in team representation came when Hollywood forfeited its franchise because of its poor performance at the box office. Cocoa filled the vacancy and adopted their new nickname, Fliers.[46]

There were also changes in leadership in both Miami and Miami Beach's front offices, under different circumstances. Max Carey was under scrutiny, along with Hollywood's "Jiggs" Donahue and three ballplayers from the FECL. Together they drew the ire of the National Association's minor-league offices for working at Florida horse and dog tracks during the offseason. During the previous winter, Judge W.G. Bramham ruled that any ballplayer connected with racing should have no place in baseball. J. B. Lemon informed Carey, who had worked as a judge at the Biscayne Kennel Club during the offseason, of the possible consequences. Bramham later changed course and stated, "East Coast league ballplayers who worked at Florida horse and dog tracks during the offseason, will not be barred from participating in the national pastime." He added, "They must find other means of livelihood in future years, however, to stay in good graces." Although the original decision was overruled, Carey remained a stockholder with the Wahoos but stepped aside as the club's manager.[47] Later, Archie Martin, a local strawberry farmer, a 5-year minor-league veteran, and one-time House of David outfielder became the player-manager taking Carey's place.[48]

The Flamingos made changes of their own by selling the club to famous nightclub owner Robert "Mother" Kelly and one of his three sons, Gerald.[49] The elder Kelly, a white-haired and rotund jovial sort, of Russian descent, owned the famous Miami Beach nightspot Mother Kelly's (on Dade Boulevard and Bay Road) that bore his name and featured many popular and varied entertainers of the day. On any given night, you might see anyone from Billie Holiday to Kalan, "Man with the x-ray eyes," while enjoying a Ronrico Rum daiquiri cocktail.

One of Kelly's first orders of business was naming Max Rosenfeld as player-manager. Since Max had overseen Miami Beach clubs prior to the war, it was an easy choice based on his wealth of experience.

With all of their off-season issues rectified, both teams prepared for the upcoming season. There were only a few carryovers from the previous season. Miami welcomed back pitchers Red Bohn, Kirby Hayes, Chet Saunders, infielder Howard "Skinny" McGinness, and outfielder Jack Troupe. Miami Beach saw the return of pitcher Jim Glover, infielder Harold Rubin, and of course Rosenfeld.

Although the Wahoos and Flamingos had no affiliation with major league clubs, they did have ties to organizations that provided them with some of their talent. In Miami's case, they had a close working relationship with Washington Senators scout Joe Cambria and a wealth of local talent to draw from.[50] Miami did not look far for its most significant acquisition. He turned out to be a 6'2" strapping 22-year-old former University of Miami football star, Johnny Douglas.

The Flamingos also benefited from local talent. More importantly, they had ties to the Atlanta Crackers, an independent minor-league team in the Class 1-A Southern Association. The year prior, the Crackers purchased Gene Bearden for $1,000. Atlanta re-assigned him to Savannah and through the efforts of a persuasive Rosenfeld; the Flamingos reacquired their star lefty on option.[51] During the season, this was one of his creative orchestrated moves, which paid huge dividends.

The regular season started inauspiciously for Miami Beach. Miami and Fort Pierce swept them before they won their sixth game of the season, harpooning the Fort Lauderdale Tarpons, 13 to 8. Not coincidentally, on the same day that Bearden returned to town, the pink birds' fortunes took a turn for the better.[52] He not only handled pitching chores but also played regularly in right field between mound assignments. Still not done dealing, the Flamingos further strengthened their roster and acquired right-handed pitcher Jack Embler who had won 18 and lost 9 the previous year with the Waycross Bears of the Class D Georgia-Florida League, along with outfielder Jimmy Milner from Fort Pierce.

On the other hand, Miami got off to a good start by winning six of their first ten games. Southpaw Kirby Hayes won his first three starts.[53] Heavy hitting by Douglas included a seven-ribbie outburst and two home runs against Fort Lauderdale on April 22 during the 20 to 5 romp. Early indications seemed brighter for the boys from Miami Field.[54] Local attorney Robert "Bob" Lane supplanted Jack Baldwin as head of the Miami Baseball Association.[55]

Slowly, Miami Beach turned things around and climbed up the standings. By May 8, they reached the .500 mark courtesy of a 15 to 4 thumping of Fort Lauderdale. They followed the next evening with another one-sided victory, this time gutting the Tarpons, 21 to 7. Bearden coasted to the win and from that point on the Flamingos never looked back. Although the recent offensive outburst was impressive, excellent defense and outstanding pitching including rookie newcomer Milt "Rosey" Rosenstein contributed to their success.

Rosenfeld discovered the twenty-year-old son of immigrant parents from Russia, during a chance encounter.[56] Prior to arriving in Miami during the winter of 1939, "Rosey" had pitched semi-pro ball for three years in New York with the Hunter Indians. He later moved up to the renowned amateur club, Saugerties A. C. (NY), where he lost only five of thirty games that he appeared in. His most noted triumph was against the infamous Sing Sing prison team, one of the top amateur teams in unorganized baseball. He allowed four hits and struck out 13 during the 2 to 1 victory.[57]

Anxious to further his pro career, he made a decision to trek to Miami hoping to catch the eye of a major league team. The enterprising young man approached both the Giants and Phillies, who were in spring training for tryouts, but went away disappointed rebuffed by both teams. One day, while walking to the ballpark with glove in hand, he stopped by Rosenfeld's garage to purchase a cold drink and that is where he caught the Flamingos player-manager's eye. Rosenfeld sensed the kid had talent and began to work with him. Initially, he hoped to make a first baseman out of the young man but soon discovered that Rosenstein was better suited for mound work. The decision to stay with Rosey as a pitcher proved to be a fortuitous choice.[58]

Three solid starters at the top of the Miami Beach rotation consisted of Bearden, Embler, and Rosenstein. Along with solid hitting from right fielder Jack Howard, Milner, and Rosenfeld, the Flamingos began to climb upward in the standings. Further fortifying the offense, the pink birds purchased the contract of last year's FECL batting champion, first baseman Jack Westley, from Harrisburg of the Class B Interstate League.[59] On June 17, following a doubleheader split against Fort Pierce, Miami Beach (30–28) stood 8½ games behind the front-running Bombers (41–22).[60] From June 18 through July 6, the Flamingos reeled off 17 wins in their next 22 games tying Fort Pierce for the league lead.[61]

Miami Beach's numerous transactions were paying dividends; the results were quite different for the Wahoos. After peaking on April 25 with an 8–5 record, Martin's charges went into a tailspin losing 25 of their next 34 games. Miami had plummeted into the cellar by the end of May.

In reaction to their poor play, management made a flurry of moves attempting to right their ship. The roster changed more often than the tides in Key Biscayne. In total, Miami made ten player moves during the month of May, including the signing and releasing of John Kurucza, a teammate and backfield mate of Douglas at the University of Miami.[62] After batting only .211 in five games he drew his walking papers after only a week.[63]

One of the more disappointing Wahoos' acquisitions was that of highly touted right-hander Pete Wojey (shortened from his real last name Wojciechowski) from Olean of the Class D Pennsylvania-Ontario-New York League. Expected to take a significant role in the starting rotation, instead, he went on to appear in twelve games, winning only twice and losing six with an inflated 7.33 ERA in his first start against Miami Beach on May 26.[64] He gave up five runs in two-and-one-third innings of work in the 8 to 4 loss to the Flamingos. Despite his poor showing in Miami, he went on to pitch 14 games for the Brooklyn Dodgers in 1954 and had "cups of coffee" with the Detroit Tigers in 1956 and 1957.[65]

Fort Pierce continued to be the pacesetter through June. Practically carrying the Bombers single-handedly on his back was Covington. A winner of 14 straight games, his streak ended on June 9 when West Palm Beach, won an 11-inning thriller 3 to 2.[66] Not all of the outstanding performances were reserved for Covington. Rosenstein nearly equaled Chet's current league record of 19 strikeouts, set during a game on May 21, 1940, against West Palm Beach fanning fifteen Miami batters.[67] Despite staked to an early five-run lead, his efforts went for naught as the Flamingos fell by the final tally of 6 to 5.[68]

With the halfway point of the campaign just around the corner, the FECL chose Wright Field in West Palm Beach as the site for their annual All-star game. The June 11 contest pitted the league-leading Fort Pierce Bombers against the All-Stars, a contingent of the best players from other teams. Four players from Miami Beach; outfielder Jack Howard, shortstop Billy Miller, second baseman Ken Nordstrom, and pitcher Milton Rosenstein were named to the team joining Miami outfielder Jack Troupe and pitcher Kirby Hayes. A small crowd of 1,130 witnessed a close game featuring a two-run home run by Fort Pierce rookie, Harris Lowery that proved to be the difference-maker in the 7 to 5 win, over the All-star team.[69]

While Miami was seemingly fading out of playoff contention, the pennant race narrowed down to a three-team foot sprint between Fort Pierce, Miami Beach, and West Palm Beach. Not all of the action was taking place on the field. Matters heated up in the FECL offices when league owners tossed aspersions at J.B. Lemon involving his alleged financial interest ties to the Flamingos, which presented a conflict of interest. The accusations started when Lemon forfeited a postponed July 4 game to Miami Beach that Miami leadership claimed was not regularly scheduled. The Flamingos and Wahoos were supposed to play the previously postponed game as ordered by Lemon, but manager Martin and team president Lane refused to take the field and later that same day departed for their road trip against Cocoa.[70] Lane commented, "We had to be consulted and we decided we couldn't play it." Lemon retorted by stating that W.G. Bramham, who was the ultimate authority, backed his decision.[71] The ruling stood, resulting in the replay. The outcome was not what Miami had hoped. Miami Beach tagged

Wahoos' pitchers, Darden Archer and Larry "Speedy" Baldwin for 13 runs and cruised to an easy 13 to 1 win. The old workhorse, Rosenfeld did the most damage driving in five runs, and Bearden tossed a 7-hitter hardly breaking a sweat while earning the win.[72]

Under Rosenfeld's adept direction, the Flamingos continued to play well and closed in on the top spot. On June 18, Miami Beach took both ends of a doubleheader from Fort Pierce as Embler picked up the win in the opener, while Bearden captured the nightcap. Almost unnoticed was the fact that starter Embler had put together an impressive streak of victories. After a disappointing start to the season in which he lost his first three decisions, his fortunes turned for the better winning ten straight. Columnist Guy Butler of the *Miami News* described him as a "Carl Hubbell look-alike" without the screwball. Butler wrote that Embler claimed he did not pick up a baseball while in high school. He added that while hanging out at local sandlots in Charleston, South Carolina, he felt drawn to the game, and soon was hurling the horsehide sphere with great success.[73]

On June 26, the Charleston phenomenon stretched his win streak to twelve by handcuffing Fort Lauderdale, 2 to 1. The tobacco chewing right-sider scattered eight hits while striking out four and walking two batters. Combined with West Palm Beach's 7 to 3 loss to Cocoa, the Flamingos pulled to within 1½ games of first place.[74] Embler further extended his winning skein to thirteen on June 30, seizing the second game of a doubleheader against West Palm Beach, a 9 to 3 victory. The Hubbell dead-ringer was one game short of tying Covington's FECL record of fourteen.[75]

The stage was set for the next day's double-dip against Cocoa as the Flamingos jumped into a tie for first place with Fort Pierce taking both games. On the same day Joe DiMaggio tied Willie Keeler's 1897 record of 44 consecutive games with a base hit, recently signed Billy Morgan was impressive shutting out the Fliers, 2 to 0. Bearden took the second game, 3 to 1. Amazingly, the two games combined took 2 hours and 51 minutes.[76]

All good things come to their end. On July 9, Embler's attempt at the coveted fourteenth successive win came to an abrupt halt during the first game of a doubleheader in Fort Lauderdale. The Tarpons banged out fifteen hits during the 13 to 0 whitewashing. Skipper Rosenfeld, seemingly capitulating defeat, refused to go to his bullpen and left his starter out on the mound to endure the vicious beating. It proved to be a seminal moment in the campaign for Embler as he never regained the form he enjoyed during his successful run. He finished the season with only three more wins against eight losses. The Flamingos followed up by dropping the nightcap 1 to 0 despite Rosenstein's five-hitter, as Fort Pierce regained the league lead, and their ace Covington took a sigh of relief knowing his win streak record was still intact.[77]

Embler was not alone enjoying impressive achievements. The Wahoos' Johnny Douglas put together one of his own streaks, albeit with the bat, beginning on July 20. The first game of a twin bill against Fort Pierce, he singled three times. He followed that with 26 consecutive games; reaching by way of a base hit. On August 10, Miami edged West Palm Beach in the first game of the doubleheader, 8 to 7, aided by three hits and two RBIs by Douglas. The subsequent game found the Wahoos facing an ex-teammate, Chet Saunders; Traded in July to the Indians in exchange for Darden Archer,[78] earlier in the season he put the brakes on Douglas' 16-game hitting streak. Once again, he hand-cuffed the big first baseman in his three at-bats and earned a shutout by the final score of 4 to 0 putting the "kibosh" on the hottest hitter in the FECL.[79] During the former U of M's star's hit-ting skein Miami won 14 of 26 games, and in a large part thanks to his efforts, managed to escape the league basement.

The Wahoos improved play in August, spurred new hopes, and the possibility of finishing in fourth place for the final post-season berth. Miami engineered their first winning month compiling an 18–15 record. August 25 was "Johnny Douglas Night," honoring their most recognizable star.[80] Fan-favorite Douglas went on to win the FECL batting crown and lead the league in runs scored.[81] Heading up the Wahoos' late charge were two midseason acquisi-tions; Archer who had started the season with West Palm Beach and Alex McCaskill, a former three-sport athletic star from the University of Georgia. McCaskill was coaching football at Athens High School before signing with the Wahoos.[82] Combined with Douglas and Troupe's hot bats Miami (63–75) found themselves only two games behind Fort Lauderdale (65–73). Despite the surge, Miami fell short in their quest to secure the final post-season spot.

Although Miami Beach (80–58) was still in the hunt for the top spot, West Palm Beach (84–54) set a torrid pace in August, win-ning 20 of 30 games. Led by a balanced offense that featured five regulars with .290 or better batting averages, and two workhorse hurlers who finished the season with over twenty wins; Len Bullis (21–10, 254 IP) and Al Reitz (22–15, 310 IP),[83] the Indians crossed the finish line three games ahead of Miami Beach.

Going into the Shaughnessy championship series, the opening round best-of-five format matched Fort Lauderdale, who had held off Miami for fourth place, against league-leading West Palm Beach. In other action, second place Miami Beach's opponent was third-place Fort Pierce.

Going into the playoffs, the Flamingos suffered two severe blows when they lost the services of their best hitter, outfielder-first baseman, Jim Milner (.340, 5 HR's) who accepted a job in the war defense industry.[84] [85] Rosenfeld improvised and used Bearden in right field, between pitching assignments, and starting shortstop Billy Miller. Bob Jordan, a shortstop acquired from the Waycross Bears of the Class D Georgia-Florida League,[86] replaced Miller, who suffered a fractured left arm, due to an errant pitch.[87] He later took over at the hot corner position. Rosenfeld in left and Howard in center staffed the outfield, while Westley held down first base.

Although Rosenstein had been the team's best starter during the season, Rosenfeld opted for the more experienced Bearden to pitch the opener at Flamingo Park. Miami Beach then received a huge break. According to the *Sporting News,*

> Lefty Covington was sold to Jacksonville of the Sally League on a conditional basis, was back with the Fort Pierce Bombers for the last week of the season, the sale being canceled. He was prevented from going to work immediately, however, by a ruling made by League President J.B. Lemon who held he was ineligible because he was not on the Fort Pierce roster 20 days before the season closed. Covington insists he is either a free agent or a member of the Bombers and has appealed to President W. G. Bramham of the National Association.[88]

J.K. Walker, president of the Fort Pierce club pointed out that Miami had used pitcher Ray Ashton, although he signed during the last 20 days of the season. The difference was that Covington did not return to the Bombers during the time limit, and so the final ruling against him stood, much to the dismay of Bombers' fans.[89]

In a hard-fought opener played under protest by Fort Pierce, the Flamingos went into the bottom of the ninth inning tied at two apiece. With a tiring Ross Beatty on the mound, and pinch runner Billy Morgan in scoring position, Jordan stroked the game-winning walk-off single sending the Bombers home with a 3 to 2 defeat.[90]

Lady luck's gaze shifted toward Fort Pierce in the second game. In the bottom of the eleventh inning with the score tied at two, Rosenstein and Bombers' Bit Beebe stayed engaged in a heated duel. Bill Hansen, who earlier in the game scored on a triple, stroked his second extra-base hit of the night. Rosenstein lost his cool and committed a balk allowing Hansen to advance to third base. Jim Poole then lofted a long fly ball to Morgan who was unable to cut down Hansen at the plate as Fort Pierce outlasted the Flamingos, 3 to 2.[91]

Game three proved to be another thriller. In a second extra-inning marathon, the results were another 3 to 2 final decision. Back at Flamingo Park, Bombers' manager Jim Poole called upon Beatty on two days' rest, to win the pivotal third game. For fourteen innings, Miami Beach starter Dave Keyser matched his opponent. With one out in the bottom of the inning and the score tied at two each, once again Jordan came through in the clutch with a key single. After Howard was retired, Westley followed with a single advancing Jordan to third. Beatty then tossed up a tantalizing offering to George "Spec" Dozier who drove the ball through the middle; a game-winning run batted in. A dejected Covington who remained on the bench throughout the series commented, "This fight is between my owners and the rest of the league and I'm out of it. He added, "I've got a plumbing job down there when this series is over. Sure I'd like to pitch, but I'm not as good as the rest of the league seems to think."[92] Although trying to remain detached from his situation, there is no doubt the ultra-competitive Covington was chomping at the bit to take the mound for at least one crack at Miami Beach.

In game four, Bearden took the bump against Beebe. For the first time, the result was one-sided as the masterful pitcher shut out the Bombers, 7 to 0. The future Cleveland Indians' star struck out five and scattered five hits. Both Howard and Westley provided a pair of runs batted in as icing on the cake.

Fort Lauderdale had unexpectedly taken a 2–1 series edge against West Palm Beach. After losing the first game 7 to 3, the Tarpons bounced back winning the next two contests, 3 to 2 in

11 innings, and 9 to 0. The Indians tied their series against Fort Lauderdale thanks to two ribbies by nineteen-year-old leadoff hitter Elmer Kirchoff, a 3 to 1 final.[93] West Palm Beach went on to take the series the next night defeating the Tarpons in an 11-inning white-knuckler, 2 to 1 setting the stage for the top two teams to play in a best-of-seven finale.[94]

The next day, heavy rains suspended the opening game of the championship series scheduled at Wright Field (West Palm Beach), but play resumed September 10. The day off seemed to benefit the Indians more than the Flamingos as West Palm Beach came out with more fire in their bellies. Keyser gave up six runs in the first four frames. Morgan and Embler followed and did not fare any better, as the pink birds "had their wings clipped" in the 13 to 3 loss. Although Miami Beach knocked out 12 hits against Indians' starter, Hubert "Big Train" Brown (16–9, 3.33) the rotund hurler was resilient and earned the victory.[95]

The Flamingos rebounded taking the next two contests. Twenty-game winner Rosenstein held the Indians to three hits as the Birds glided to a 5 to 0 win.[96] The subsequent night, they returned to Wright Field where Bearden bested 6'6", Len Bullis, 6 to 5. Big Len exited after only one inning giving up four tallies after Bearden was touched for a couple of runs in the bottom of the ninth inning cutting the Beach lead to one.[97] Rosenstein retired the last two batters to seal the deal.

Manager Harry Hughes came back with Bullis against Keyser in game four with better results. The towering right-hander helped out his cause driving in a pair of runs as the Indians prevailed 4 to 3 to even the series at two apiece.[98]

Rosenstein struggled early and after five innings, the Flamingos trailed 4 to 2. Rosenfeld pulled his star pitcher after the fifth frame because he was looking to rest Bearden for a possible deciding sixth game. In a surprise move, and faced with the dilemma of whether or not to use Bearden on short rest or going to the bullpen, he turned to Embler. He performed admirably holding West Palm Beach to one run over the next six innings of work. Jordan's timely hitting again proved the difference. With two outs in the bottom of the eleventh, he stroked a single, scoring Eddie Arthur, securing Miami Beach's 6 to 5 victory.[99]

Due to a rainout on September 16, working on five days' rest, a fresh-armed Bearden took the hill to face the ancient mariner Reitz at Wright Field. Trailing by one and going into the eighth inning, Miami Beach exploded for five runs. No stranger to game-winning RBIs, Jordan drove in the fourth and fifth runs with a key single that proved to be the game winner. The Indians mounted a two-run rally in the bottom of the ninth, but with runners on base, Bearden struck out LeRoy Melvin to end the game setting off a celebration scrum in front of home plate. The victory gave the Flamingos their first championship by a final score of 5 to 3. The celebration continued throughout the night at Mother Kelly's nightclub.[100]

Final Standings

TEAM	W	L	GB
West Palm Beach	84	55	–
Miami Beach	81	58	3
Fort Pierce	75	64	9
Fort Lauderdale	66	73	18
Miami	63	76	21
Cocoa	48	91	36

1942

FECL directors held their annual meeting on November 30, 1941, and announced they were seeking approval from the National Association to upgrade the league's classification to Class C or Class B, with the possible inclusions of Lakeland, Orlando, St. Petersburg and Tampa, thus increasing the circuit to eight teams.[101] In addition, league officials agreed that a number of limited service players were to be available to each team; roster sizes increased.[102]

The bombing of Pearl Harbor by the Japanese on December 7, 1941, plunged the United States of America into the Second World War. Although most Americans supported neutrality after that day's tragic events, the public consciousness shifted overnight. A wave of patriotism swept the nation and focus turned to a successful war effort in the Pacific arena, and in the European conflict.

FDR initiated the Selective Training and Service Act on September 16, 1940, calling for men between 21 and 36 years of age to serve for one year in the military. When the draft began, few major or minor-league ballplayers saw themselves affected. The events on December 7, and Germany and Italy's declaration of war against the United States changed circumstances drastically. Waves of draft age men either volunteered or conscripted into the military.[103] Minor-league teams throughout the country soon found themselves with few able-bodied players. Draft eligible men called to duty left a workforce shortage that had a profound impact on professional baseball's future.

Major league baseball came close to having play suspended for the duration of the war. Nevertheless, a plea from baseball executives and a handwritten letter to President Franklin Delano Roosevelt (FDR), sent by Commissioner Kennesaw Mountain Landis, respectfully inquired whether they should continue for the duration of the war. Known as "the green light letter," it received a positive response. FDR, a known fan of our national pastime, stated in his reply, "I honestly feel it would be best for the country to keep baseball going."[104]

Although baseball persevered through the war years, most of the minor leagues suspended play for the duration of the conflict. By 1943, and continuing into 1944, only 10 leagues were in operation. FECL officials had hoped to continue play. Both Miami and Miami Beach began spring training at their home fields on March 31. Players arrived to damp and messy fields, apprehensive about what the future held. The most notable change was the suspension of night games, due to the war, which was part of a blackout effort in response to fears of possible German attacks on the Florida east coast. Game times shifted from the regular 8:15 P.M. to 5:45 P.M., which had a negative impact on attendance.[105]

The FECL planned to maintain the 140-game schedule even with the addition of two new affiliates, the DeLand Red Hats and Orlando Senators. A major concern for the owners was the loss of nighttime play. Gameday attendance always lagged behind evening affairs usually drawing half as many fans. Only DeLand avoided the blackout since it was further inland.[106]

As was customary, Miami and Miami Beach kicked-off the season squaring off against each other. A scheduled doubleheader split between Flamingo Park and Miami Field accommodated both fan bases. Patriotic music greeted the scant crowd of 350 courtesy of the Miami Beach High School band. The Miami Seminoles, under a new name and the new leadership of player-manager Harry

Hughes, fired the first salvo of the season in the opening frame when Hughes smacked a base hit plating "Truck" Melvin. In a sloppily performed game, the Seminoles committed four errors on the day. The multiple miscues opened the door to the Flamingos', 6 to 4 win. Because of the length of the game, the newly instituted blackout forced the cancellation of the Miami Field curtain raiser much to the disappointment of the much larger crowd at Miami.[107]

The early season hampered by unusually heavy rains caused cancellations of several games around the league. On April 21, J.B. Lemon announced that Cocoa dropped out of the circuit due to team owner Burl Munsell's failure to post a $600 forfeit fee.[108] Soon after, FECL stalwart Fort Lauderdale disbanded.

With attendance sagging due to nighttime restrictions, and newly placed gas-rationing quotas, it made it difficult for the remaining teams to travel. On May 14, the remaining owners voted whether to carry on with the season. By a vote of 4 to 2, only Miami and Miami Beach advocated to continue, the FECL officially disbanded. Due to the suspended season, and based on having the best record, Orlando, a Washington Nationals/Senators farm team, was declared champion.[109]

Final Standings

TEAM	W	L	GB
Orlando	19	9	–
Miami Beach	17	10	1.5
DeLand	13	13	5
Fort Pierce	12	14	6
Miami	12	15	6.5
West Palm Beach	9	18	9.5
Fort Lauderdale*	4	3	NA
Cocoa**	0	4	NA

* Fort Lauderdale disbanded on April 25.
** Cocoa disbanded April 21.

The majority of ballplayers served in the armed forces or were employed in war-related jobs. The military found Miami and Miami Beach an excellent area for training personnel, due to its vast amount of vacant land and warm climate. The face of both cities changed drastically as both municipalities took on a more military base-like atmosphere. Hotels and apartment buildings became armed forces hospitals, training facilities, and personnel housing. Between 1942 and 1945, nearly half a million soldiers passed through Miami Beach alone. Many of these men found Miami to their liking and after the war, relocated to south Florida.[110]

Most of minor league baseball went into hibernation until the war's conclusion. From the remnants of the FECL, a new and better league would rise. Fueled by returning service members, young prospects, and a healthy dose of talent from the Caribbean, they formed one of the most interesting loops ever to grace our national pastime.

NOTES

1. George, Paul. *South Florida History*, Volume 24, No. 2, Summer 1996, Miami: One Hundred Years of History.
2. Two Games Scheduled At Night, *Miami Daily News*, 2 May, 1940, p. 2-B.
3. One Night, Two 3 P.M. Games In East Coast Loop Opener, *Miami Daily News*, 1 May, p. 2-B.
4. Miami Beach Selects Flamingos As Nickname For Baseball Club, *Miami Daily News*, May 2, 1940, 2-B.
5. Floridamemory.com/items/show/144428. Retrieved 11 September, 2015.
6. Baseball-almanac.com/teams/springtrainingsites-nl.shtml.
7. Former Big-Timers Pilot Florida Clubs, *Portsmouth Daily Times*, 18 May, 1940, p. 5.
8. Baseball-reference.com. Heimach compiled a (62–69, 4.46) record over the course of his 13 year big league career that lasted from 1920 through 1933. He also hurled in the minor leagues for six seasons winning 80 games and losing 56. His last appearance was with the St. Paul Saints of the American Association in 1934.
9. Max Carey Selected As Manager, *Miami Daily News*, 3 April, 1940, p. 2-B.
10. Fitzgerald, Tommy. Dream Comes True, Carey Reaches 'Hall', *Miami News*, 30 January, 1961, p. 1-C.
11. Max Carey Selected As Manager, *Miami Daily News*, 3 April, 1940, p. 2-B.
12. Baseball-reference.com.
13. *Sporting News*, 11 April, 1940, p. 12.
14. Bell, Jack. Wahoos Never Catch Flamingos, *Miami Daily News*, 4 May, 1940, p. 1-B.
15. Florida East Coast on Mark; Staff of Six Umpires Signed, *Sporting News*, 2 May, 1940, p. 13. Lists umpire DeHaney's first name as Frank.
16. Bell, Jack. Here We Go—Florida's East Coast Baseball Season Is On, *Miami Daily News*, 3 May, 1940, p. 2-B.
17. Bell, Jack. Wahoos Never Catch Flamingos, *Miami Daily News*, 4 May, 1940, p. 1-B.
18. *Sporting News*, Florida East Coast, 16 May, 1940, p. 11.
19. *Sporting News*, 30 May, 1940, p. 7.
20. Gene Bearden Signed By Phillies Team, *Pottstown Mercury*, 1 March, 1939, p. 7. Bearden was signed by Philadelphia Phillies scout Doc Prothro.

21. Berger, Ralph. *Gene Bearden,* 2015, www.bioproj.sabr.org/bioproj/person/ffc84797.

22. Balfe, Bob. Large Crowd Sees Exciting Contest, *Palm Beach Post,* 15 May, 1940, p. 8.

23. Beardon's Hit Beats Tarpons In 11 Innings, *Miami Daily News,* 21 May, 1940, p. 3-B.

24. MacLennan, Diane, Bill Nowlin, and Saul Wisnia. B*obby Hogue,* http://sabr.org/bioproj/person/ bfadc5b3.

25. Bombers And Wahoos Battle Tonight; Ladies Get In Free, *Miami Daily News,* 21 May, 1940, p. 3-B.

26. Levine, Al. Hogue Just Left With Memories, But No Bitterness, *Miami* News, 27 March, 1969, p. 1-D.

27. Baseball-reference.com.

28. *Sporting News,* Florida East Coast, 8 August, 1940, p. 8.

29. Spalding-Reach Official Base Ball Guide 1941 (American Sports Publishing Company: New York), 363–364.

30. *Sporting News,* Florida East Coast, 26 September, 1940, p. 11.

31. Baseball-reference.com. Herb Thomas (74 games, .221 1 HR, 15 RBIs) played with the Boston Braves (1924, 1925 and 1927), and the New York Giants 1927 at second base, shortstop and the outfield. Al Reitz spent 21 seasons in the minor leagues as a pitcher winning 201 games and losing 199. He also managed 6 seasons at the Class-D level (complete record is not available).

32. Bell, Jack. Sports Desk, *Miami Daily News,* 18 August, 1940, p. C-1.

33. *Sporting News,* Florida East Coast, 25 July, 1940, p. 8.

34. *Sporting News,* Florida East Coast, 23 May, 1940, p. 9.

35. Baseball-reference.com/bullpen/Florida_East_Coast_League.

36. *Sporting News,* Florida East Coast, 26 September, 1940, p. 11.

37. *Miami Herald,* 16 July, 1997, p. 1-C.

38. Smith, Steve. "*Chet Covington,*" sabr.org/bioproj/person/21dbe265

39. Baseball-reference.com.

40. Flamingos Tarps Set For Series, *Miami Daily News,* 25 September, 1940, p. 3-B.

41. Flamingos Take First From Tarps, *Miami Daily News,* 26 September, 1940, p. 2-B.

42. Lauderdale Evens Series for Coast League Crown, *Miami Daily News,* 30 September, 1940, p. 2-B.

43. *Sporting News,* Fla. East Coast Playoff, p. 11.

44. Ibid.

45. *Sporting News,* J.B. Lemon New President of Florida East Coast League, 23 January, 1941, p. 1.

46. *Sporting News,* Hollywood, Fla Deals Under Fire, 6 March, 1941, p. 10.

47. Judge Bramham Clears Players On Track Jobs, *Miami Daily News,* 28 March, 1941, p. 2-B.

48. Butler, Guy. No More Whiskers For Archie, *Miami Daily News,* 9 March, 1941, p. 1-C.

49. Simmonds, Leslie. Rosenfeld Sends Miami Beach Squad of 30 Through Paces, *Sporting News,* p. 12.

50. Springfield To Send Aid To Wahoo Nine, *Miami Daily News,* 30 March, 1941, p. 2-C.

51. *Sporting News,* Florida East Coast, 24 April, 1941, p. 15.

52. Flamingos Finally Win, Play Indians, *Miami Daily News,* 18 April, 1940, p. 3-B.

53. *Sporting News,* Florida East Coast, 1 May, 1841, p. 12.

54. Kelley, Whitey. Wahoos Seek Second, Honor Women Fans, *Miami Daily News,* 23 April, 1941, p. 3-B.

55. Bob Lane Elected Head Of Wahoos, *Miami Daily News,* 23 April, 1941, p. 3-B.

56. Bedingfield, Gary. *Baseball's Dead of World War II: A Roster of Professional Players Who Died in Service* (McFarland & Company, Inc. Publishers: Jefferson, North Carolina & London) p. 90–91.
57. McMullan, John. 'Hughes Better Hitter Than Kinard'-Rosenstein, *Miami Daily News*, 27 July, 1941, p. 3-C.
58. Ibid.
59. Flamingos Buy Jack Westley, *Miami Daily News*, 15 June, 1941, p. 1-C.
60. Kelley, Whitey. Improved Flamingos Battle Bombers Twice, *Miami Daily News*, 18 June, 1941, p. 3-B.
61. In Tie For Lead, Beach Seeks Sweep, *Miami Daily News*, 7 July, 1941, p. 2-B.
62. Wojey Reports, Faces Flamingos in First, *Miami Daily News*, 25 May, 1941, p. 3-B.
63. Mike Kurucza was signed on May 1 and was released on May 7. Roland "Babe" Cagni was suspended and was later re-instated by the team, Terry Shrader was signed. Catcher, Bob Suarez was released. Mark Flythe was acquired. Catcher Ed McCorkle was signed. Peter Wojey (real name Wojciehowski) was signed. Ed Welsh was released. Pitchers, Larry Baldwin and Gene Colaw were signed on May 29.
64. Baldwin Joins Wahoos, Beach Again Is Foe, *Miami Daily News*, 26 May, 1941, p. 2-B.
65. Baseball-reference.com. Wojey's major league totals were 18 games, 1–1 win-loss record, and 3.00 ERA in 33 innings of work.
66. *Sporting News*, Florida East Coast, 19 June, 1941, p. 9.
67. Chiefs' Hurler Whiffs Indians, *Palm Beach Post*, 22 May, 1940, p. 8.
68. *Sporting News*, Florida East Coast, 19 June, 1941, p. 9.
69. Butler, Guy. Bombers Show Why They Lead; Blast All-Stars For 7–5 Victory, *Miami Daily News*, 12 June, 1941, p. 2-B.
70. Butler, Guy. Wahoos Refuse To Play, Tilt Forfeited, *Miami Daily News*, 5 July, 1941, p. 9.
71. *Sporting News*, Florida East Coast, 10 July, 1941, p. 7.
72. Max Rosenfeld Drives In Five Runs, *Miami Daily News*, 27 July, 1941, p. 1-C.
73. Butler, Guy. Embler Threatens Covington Streak, *Miami Daily News*, 20 June, 1941, p. 2-B.
74. Beach Ties For Second After Embler Cops 12th, *Miami Daily News*, 27 June, 1941, p. 3-B.
75. Flamingos After Dual Victory Over Fliers, *Miami Daily News*, 1 July, 1941, p. 3-B.
76. Flamingos Deadlock Bombers For Top, *Miami Daily News*, 2 July, 1941, p. 2-B.
77. Flamingos Grapple Bombers For Lead, *Miami Daily News*, 10 July, 1941, p. 2-B.
78. *Sporting News*, Florida E. Coast League, 17 July, 1941, p. 8.
79. Kelley, Whitey. Leading Indians In Final Game Here, *Miami Daily News*, 11 August, 1941, p. 2-B.
80. Bombers Shift To Beach For Series, *Miami Daily News*, 26 August, 1941, p. 3-B.
81. Baseball-reference.com.
82. Onlineathens.com/stories/100808/oth_341466874.shtml#.VhgNAitBQrk. Retrieved online Athens Banner-Herald, 8 October, 2008. Kenneth Alexander McCaskill played football at the University of Georgia (1938–1939), basketball (1940) and was an all SEC forward, and baseball (1938–1940). He also coached Athens High School (1940–1941) and won a state championship there in 1941. McCaskill was elected to the Georgia Sports Hall of Fame in 1997.
83. Baseball-reference.com.
84. *Sporting News*, Florida E. Coast League, 14 August, 1941, p. 13.
85. Kelley, Whitey. Leading Palm Beach Battles Miami Twice, *Miami Daily News*, 10 August, 1941, p. 2-C.

86. Hayes To Face Beach In Second Of Series, *Miami Daily News*, 6 August, 1941, p. 3-B.

87. *Sporting News,* Florida E. Coast League, 14 August, 1941, p. 13.

88. *Sporting News*, Florida E. Coast League, 4 September, 1941, p. 11.

89. Kelley, Whitey. Fort Pierce Opens At Flamingo Park, *Miami Daily News*, 2 September, 1941, p. 2-B.

90. McMullan, John. Bombers Ask 'Probe' Of Playoff Series, *Miami Daily News*, 4 September, 1941, p. 3-B.

91. Birds And Bombers Renew Fight Here, *Miami Daily News*, 5 September, 1941, p. 3-B.

92. McMullan, John. Flamingos, Tarpons Hold 2 To 1 Edges, *Miami Daily News*, 6 September, 1941, p. 9.

93. McMullan, John. Beach Waiting Tarpon-Indian Series Result, *Miami Daily News*, 8 September, 1941, p. 2-B.

94. McMullan, John. Flamingos Open Final Play-off With Indians, *Miami Daily News*, 9 September, 1941, p. 3-B.

95. *Local Club In Lead In Playoff Series*, *Palm Beach Post*, 11 September, 1941, 7 and Birds Pick Bearden To Even Tribe Series, *Miami Daily News*, 11 September, 1941, p. 3-B.

96. Flamingos Invade Wigwam Of Indians, *Miami Daily News*, 12 September, 1941, p. 3-B.

97. Butler, Guy. Flamingos Lead, 2 To 1; Play Tonight On Beach, *Miami Daily News*, 13 September, 1941, p. 9, and Indians Defeated In Third Game, 6–5, *Palm Beach Post*, 13 September, 1941, p. 5.

98. Len Bullis Stars In Tribe's Victory, *Palm Beach Post-Times*, 14 September, 1941, p. 15.

99. Birds Need One More; Bearden Faces Reitz, *Miami Daily News*, 15 September, 1941, p. 2-B.

100. Dillon, Carl. Flamingos Play-Off Champs of League, *Miami Daily News*, 18 September, 1941, p. 2-B.

101. Butler, Guy. East Coast League To Seek 8 Clubs And Higher Rating, *Miami Daily News*, 2 September, 1941, 2-B and *Sporting News*, Florida East Coast Playoff, 18 September, 1941, p. 11.

102. Faster Ball Seen For Class D Loop, *Palm Beach Post Times*, 30 November, 1941.

103. Bedingfield, Gary. *Baseball's Dead of World War II: A Roster of Professional Players Who Died in Service* (McFarland & Company, Inc. Publishers: Jefferson, North Carolina & London), p. 3–7.

104. Bazer, Gerald, and Culbertson Steve. When FDR Said "Play Ball," *Prologue Magazine*, Spring 2002, Vol. 34, No. 1, retrieved on 14 October, 2015 from https://www.archives.gov/publications/prologue/2002/spring/greenlight. html.

105. Dillon, Carl. Screen-Out Test Unfavorable, Flamingos Bank On Twi-Light, *Miami Daily News*, 31 March, 1942, p. 2-B.

106. McMullan, John. Seminoles And Flamingos Finish, Practice For Opening Game, *Miami Daily News*, 14 April, 1942, p. 2-B.

107. Butler, Guy. Flamingos Win First, Second Game Called, *Miami Daily News*, 16 April, 1942, p. 2-B.

108. FEC Directors Hear Thomas' Plan For Eight-Team League, *Miami Daily News*, 22 April, 1942, p. 2-B.

109. Kelley, Whitey. Gas Rationing Chief Reason For East Coast Loop Quitting, *Sporting News*, 21 May, 1942, p. 5.

110. Parks, Arva Moore. *Miami The Magic City*, Miami, FL: Community Media, 2008. Retrieved 16 October, 2015 from www.miamibeachvets.com.

CHAPTER FIVE

THE FLORIDA INTERNATIONAL LEAGUE 1946–1948

On September 2, 1945, the Empire of Japan, the last Axis power standing, laid down their arms and unconditionally surrendered, ending World War II. It had been almost four years since the United States had entered the war and the price to preserve freedom came at a terrible cost. Of the 1.6 million Americans who served in the military, 405,000 gave their lives.[1] Countless others returned home maimed, some missing limbs, or bearing the psychological scars from their experiences in combat.

From 1939 until 1945 over 500 major leaguers and more than 4,000 minor league ballplayers had traded in their wool togs for military uniforms. Of those that served, and made it to the big leagues, Elmer Gedeon and Harry O'Neill lost their lives along with 137 minor league players never to return to ply their trade on the field again. Among those with Miami ties were John J. Zulberti, a third baseman for the Miami Beach Flamingos in 1940, and pitcher Milton "Rosey" Rosenstein, a twenty-game winner for the same club in 1941. On the morning of January 20, 1944, at the Battle of Bloody River (on the Italian Peninsula), Zulberti, a commissioned second lieutenant, was killed in heavy fighting. He posthumously received the Purple Heart for his valor on the field of battle. Rosenstein also paid the ultimate price. He obtained the rank of Staff Sergeant and took part in the landing of Leyte in an effort to recapture the Philippines in the Pacific Theater. On November 28, he sustained wounds in combat and died. For his bravery, he received both a Silver Star and Purple Heart.[2] We are left to speculate how far these two brave men would have advanced in their baseball careers.

One courageous man, a teammate of Rosenstein's, returned home; not unscathed. Gene "Lefty" Bearden made it to the majors against all odds overcoming injuries that would have stopped most other men in their tracks. After winning 18 and 17 games for the Flamingos in 1940 and 1941 respectively, he signed with the Philadelphia Phillies and was assigned to Savannah of the Class B Sally League. That same season, he went to the New York Yankees organization. Like many of his contemporaries, Bearden felt it was his patriotic duty to enlist in the Navy, and he left baseball behind." He soon found himself going through basic training at the Great Lakes Naval Training Center near Chicago. His first assignment took him to the *Helena* where he worked in the bowels of the ship in the engine room. On July 6, 1943, while the cruiser was patrolling in the South Pacific at Kula Gulf, during the course of the ferocious battle, three Japanese torpedoes struck its hull. One hundred sixty-eight men died that day, and several others wounded. One of the severely injured was Bearden who suffered deep lacerations on his head, a skull fracture, and mangled knee. Doctors placed a metal plate in his skull, and allowing for mobility, they inserted a hinge into his knee. Two plus years of painful rehabilitation followed, and doctors advised him that his chances of playing baseball again were slim. For the rest of his life, "Lefty" would take painkillers and struggle with poor eyesight.[3]

After the Navy discharged him in 1945, he refused to accept his plight by hanging up his cleats. He returned to the Yankees farm Club in Binghamton with renewed focus, (Eastern League) surprising his naysayers. He defied the odds by finishing the season with a 15–6 slate, and a 2.41 ERA.

A promotion in 1946 to the Oakland Oaks of the Pacific Coast League followed, and he won 15 games and did even better the next season collecting 16 victories. More importantly, under his manager Casey Stengel's tutelage, he learned to throw and soon perfected an effective knuckleball, which he added to his repertoire of pitches. The effective use of the floater ultimately proved to be his ticket to the majors. In 1948, the Cleveland Indians signed him and he stunned the baseball world by winning 20 games, helping lead the Tribe to their first World Series crown since 1920. Although he never repeated the success of his magical rookie season, he went on to win 45 games over the course of a seven-year big league career, and prove the cynical doctors and his many detractors wrong.[4]

A sense of elation and new hope swept the U.S. as service members like Bearden and scores of others began their slow transformation back to civilian life. Many of the veterans that had played ball before and during the war hoped to rekindle their dream of returning to their diamond careers. Some would realize their aspirations, while others would not. With an optimistic look to the future, minor league baseball was on the cusp of what many baseball historians considered its "Golden Age."

1946

On September 23, 1945, representatives from the cities of Fort Lauderdale, Fort Myers, Lakeland, Miami, Miami Beach, West Palm Beach, and Havana gathered to resurrect the Florida East Coast League. Under the watchful eye of interim Chairman Max Rosenfeld, along with the new owners of the teams, as a group, they reached an agreement that finalized the formation of a new loop known as the Florida International League. The most tantalizing aspect of the new circuit was the inclusion of a team from outside the U.S. borders, thus how the league derived its name. Owner's expectations for the success of the league ran high based on the projected lofty attendance numbers forecasted for the baseball-crazed city of Havana. However, several teams were concerned about their costs to travel to the Cuban capital. In order to make it worth their while, Baldomero Pedro (Fernandez) "Merito" Acosta, President of the Cuban's ball club, agreed to pay visiting clubs 25 percent of total receipts, or pay the expenses for 17 men to and from Havana in addition to ten percent of receipts when the Cubans were the visiting team.[5] This was Cuba's first step into organized minor league baseball, leaving them with one last obstacle, the approval of the National Association and acceptance into the league.[6]

The formation of the FIL was not without its pitfalls. Robert C. Lane, former president of the FECL representing Miami, was insisting that a clause be included in the agreement, which stated they be allowed to withdraw from the FIL to join the Class AA-Southern Association (SA) if invited. Miami had courted the

SA in the past, but the biggest impediments were financial and time concerns tied to long-distance travel that teams would face trekking from Atlanta, Birmingham, Chattanooga, Little Rock, Memphis, Mobile, Nashville and New Orleans to south Florida. It was also generally perceived that Miami's inability to support a higher level of baseball precluded any chance that Lane had in negotiating a deal to move up to a higher classification no matter how enthusiastic he was.[7] The proposal put before the seven FIL delegates at the September 23 meeting received a 5 to 2 nay vote.[8] Miami reluctantly agreed to the terms without the stipulation. One of largest markets in the FIL would now be ready to play on opening day, April 17.

Another issue on the plate for the FIL was the goal of rounding out the league to an eight-team circuit. Chief on the agenda of newly elected league President, Judge Wayne Allen was bringing in ownership groups from Tampa, and a possible Sarasota-Bradenton combine. The biggest obstacle to acquiring Tampa was their insistence on their entry into the FIL being contingent upon Havana securing a franchise.[9] Since Tampa had a large Cuban population, many of whom were avid baseball fans, the consensus was that the natural rivalry between the two cities was the perfect match for ensuring high attendance figures. With that in mind, the other persuasive club owners could convince G.C. "Tom" Spicola Jr., a Tampa attorney, that Havana be awarded entry into the league, thus guaranteeing his success. Spicola, a well-known baseball enthusiast, was won over and put down the $50 "binder's fee" tossing Tampa's hat into the league's ring.[10] On December 6, after much debate, the executive committee of the National Association qualified and approved Havana's membership. This overturned a previous ruling disallowing teams from Mexico and Cuba to participate.[11] Fort Lauderdale and Fort Myers failed to organize clubs due to financial concerns, and the Sarasota-Bradenton combine dissolved. Yet, plans to open the season carried on. Notwithstanding, the new Class C FIL launched their inaugural season on April 17 with six teams consisting of the Havana Cubans, Lakeland Pilots, Miami Sun Sox, Miami Beach Flamingos, Tampa Smokers, and West Palm Beach Indians.

In preparation for opening day, both Miami and Miami Beach began "beating the bushes" looking for the best available talent. League rules stated that each club could carry 22 players on their roster until May 7, thereafter reducing the number to 18. By June 15, further downsizing would leave each team with fifteen. In addition, the maximum limit for veteran players (higher level or major league experience) was three, limited service players (players with one year of equivalent level experience) four, and the remaining would be rookies (no minor league experience) eight. These player statuses would later come into question and have repercussions on the league standings.[12]

Although both Miami and Miami Beach sought to entice major league teams to act as their affiliates, in the end only "Beach," as they were sometimes referred to, would be successful in acquiring an attachment. For many minor league owners, a relationship with a major league club was a guaranteed source of talented players resulting in more wins, which produced better attendance and increased revenues. The other club that enjoyed a relationship with a big league team was Havana. Although not officially recognized, the Cuban capital city already had strong ties to Washington of the American League thanks to the efforts of their super scout Joe "Papa Joe" Cambria that recruited scores of Latin American ballplayers, especially from Cuba. By July 1946 Senators' owner Clark Griffith, purchased 20,000 shares of the Havana club from George Foster, one of the Cubans' owners, thus binding the team to a working agreement.[13]

On January 13, the Miami Beach Exposition Company, a group of leading citizens from the Beach, named Carl Gardner as President of the Flamingos. Handed a laundry list of tasks to jump on post-haste he put his nose to the grindstone.[14] One of Gardner's highest priorities and most important decisions came two days later when he secured the services of Max Rosenfeld as the team's field manager. The ink was barely dry on Max's contract when the announcement that a working agreement with the Boston Braves was completed. The Beantowners' agreed to supply all 15 players needed to fill the roster. The Flamingos also reserved the right to sign their own players.[15]

Trying to follow Miami Beach's lead by finding an affiliation with a major league club, Miami's brass sought an agreement with Larry McPhail of the New York Yankees but failed in their effort to make a similar connection. Club president Lane, who had played some baseball himself while attending Mercer College in Macon, Georgia, went to work recruiting players.[16][17] Searching for talent, he turned to one of his own recent signees, 28-year-old Charles

"Chuck" Henderson, a member of the 1942 Miami club. The first order of business was rounding up ex-servicemen with playing experience and offering them a tryout. Unfortunately, Henderson had little success, and of the fifteen players recruited, only one found his way onto the opening day roster; Russell Mayhugh, a hometown boy, that resided in Coral Gables.[18]

Lane's efforts towards finding and signing a manager had also been plagued with difficulties. His initial plan to ink Harry Hughes, the ex-manager of the 1942 Seminoles, who was serving in the Marines in the South Pacific, would soon hit a wall. Lane had great difficulty in reaching the erstwhile ex-manager and by the time February rolled around, he found out that Hughes had already signed on with West Palm Beach as their pilot.[19]

A bevy of names was thrown around for the skipper vacancy including ex-major leaguers John "Stuffy" Stewart, Hugh Wise, and Freddie Frink, acting business manager of the club, and a former Wahoo.[20] Ultimately, the newly named Sun Sox surprised everyone on February 22, by landing a big fish for the job of player-manager, Paul "Big Poison" Waner.[21] Waner, the elder of two future Hall of Fame brothers, reportedly contacted Miami Wahoo's Board of Director member, Van Kussrow expressing interest in buying stock in the organization.[22] This triggered Lane to jump into action and seek the native Oklahoman as their club's skipper. It was a real coup for Miami as the former three-time batting champion came only one year removed from his final season in the majors. During his 20-year big league career as an outfielder, he produced a .333 lifetime batting average and 3,152 base hits.[23] The Sun Sox also expected him to provide a productive bat to the lineup.

With both managers in place, and major league baseball teams already doing workouts and playing exhibition games at their own spring training camps, the two new field generals Rosenfeld and Waner started workouts drills to determine their rosters; Miami in Fort Lauderdale and Miami Beach at their home base at Flamingo Park. Players arriving at camp were a mix of returning servicemen, 4-F's (men rejected for military service because of a physical defect), fresh-faced high school and college grads, and even a few fellows with major league experience. Many returning veterans had participated on service teams during the war and those that had played came into camp in better physical shape. Others had been less active in their athletic pursuits and were looking to knock off some of the "rust" they had accumulated from the prior months and years of athletic neglect. Some would regain their skills and others discovered they had lost a step. Unable to recapture their proficiencies on the field, meant giving up on their dream of making the major leagues altogether.

One example of an older player was a veteran of 12 big league campaigns, Sun Sox's Lloyd "Gimpy" Brown, his nickname acquired due to a leg injury that kept him from serving in World War II.[24] Brown, a 5'9" lefty originally from Beeville, Texas broke in with the Brooklyn Robins in 1925 after coming up from Ardmore of the Class C Western Association when he went 17–1 with a 2.45 ERA. Although his debut was less than impressive (17 g, 0–3, 4.12) with the Robins, he had a great deal more success his second tour to the show when he landed on the Washington Senators and went on to win 58 and lose 49 games between 1928 and 1932. He later pitched (in order) for the St. Louis Browns, Boston Red Sox, Cleveland Indians and Philadelphia Phillies finishing his career with 91 wins.[25]

One of the young service members returning from the war with aspirations of a professional baseball career was Eugene "Gene" Zubrinski; a determined third baseman by trade from Cambridge, Massachusetts. He was one of several prospects who reported to Miami Beach in the spring of 1946. Just like scores of other hopefuls, the war interrupted Gene's baseball career, where he served on a Navy tanker. His big break came in 1943 prior to joining the Navy. It eventually paved his way back to the minor leagues.

> I was 17 years old my junior year. I had a tryout with the Boston Braves. I was friendly with Joe Cashman who was a sportswriter for the Boston Herald American and talked with him. And I said, "Can you get me a tryout with the Boston Braves?" Now, this was 1943 and I am 17 years old. So he said, Yeah, I'll get you a tryout. So I get a tryout with the Braves . . . Casey Stengel was the manager and they wanted to send me away . . . They wanted to send me away to the PONY League, a D league. I said, "I got one more year of high school. I want to play hockey. If I sign a contract I couldn't play hockey and so forth in my senior year."
>
> What they did, they gave me $25 a week and I would go to Braves Field when they were home. Okay, they played day games. They didn't play at night and I'd take infield practice

with them and throw batting practice. I almost got my head taken off by a line drive from Clyde Kluttz, the catcher in 1943.

After his honorable discharge, Zubrinski was anxious to resume his career on the diamond. He recalls how he returned to the sport he loved, "I came back after the war, April of '46 . . . I went to Braves Field and talked to Bob Quinn, the General Manager, and you know, told him I was available to play. And he sent me to the Miami Beach Flamingos. So I played for the Miami Beach Flamingos in '46."[26]

With the end of spring training, roster sizes reached their minimums. Increasingly, anticipation for the upcoming campaign focused on the Flamingos' opening game in the Cuban capital city. Local newspapers in both cities gave the game top billing in their sports pages. The historic event marked the beginning of Havana's entrance into organized baseball. Although teams from Canada participated in various other leagues dating back to 1877 with the formation of the International Association,[27] it was the first time that a predominately-foreign speaking country had competed against U.S. teams in an officially sanctioned league. It also marked the first time that an entire minor league would use regularly scheduled passenger airliners for travel to scheduled games.[28]

Estimated crowds at the contests were from 16,000 to 20,000 for the season lid-lifter at Stadium Cerveza Tropical.[29] To put this in perspective on just how important Havana's entry into the league was, Miami had the second largest opening day crowd of just over 2,500, although the paid count was 1,798.[30]

When the Miami Beach club arrived in Havana, the most rabid fans they had ever seen greeted them. Gene Zubrinski reminisced about his own baptism to the Cuban baseball fandom and their loyalty to their team. It was something he had never experienced.

> I remember it was a great place to play. It was my first experience in pro ball and we stayed at a nice hotel. And I remember we were flying over to Havana on an airplane. Boy, oh boy, that was big stuff . . . God, they had good pitching and we would go over there and what I remember, we'd either be coming in our bus, or leaving on a bus, and the Cubans would come up to the bus and yell, "Americanos, malo, malo." In other words,

you were lousy. We couldn't beat em' . . . They were good. I
mean they had good pitching and defense![31]

There was plenty of pomp and circumstance surrounding the
gala opening game. Several dignitaries were present including,
Havana mayor, Francisco Batista, (brother of the former Cuban
president), and Miami Beach mayor Herman Frink. In addition,
Bill Klem, the famous arbiter elected into the Baseball Hall of
Fame in 1953, was bestowed the honor of umpiring the first inning, and President Baldomero Pedro "Merito" Acosta Fernández
of the Havana club threw out the first ball.[32]

To visitors, the atmosphere at the ballpark resembled more
of a Mardi gras celebration than a ball game. Throughout the
contest, the raucous Havana crowd banged on drums, sang
songs, cheered incessantly for their hometown heroes as rum
flowed freely throughout the grandstand, and cigar smoke hung
heavy in the air. The Cubans grabbed an early 5–0 lead as left-
hander Rafael Rivas, who won 27 games that season, stymied
Miami Beach holding them to two hits. In the sixth inning, the
Flamingos offense came to life. After Ed Maslauskas reached on
an error by the pitcher followed by singles from Buck Rogers and
Deo Grose, who drove in the first run for the Flamingos in a three-
run frame. Richard "Dick" Henton replaced struggling starting
pitcher Roger Hunt in the fourth inning. The right-hander kept
the Cubans in check the rest of the way without giving up a run.
In the top of the ninth, the pink birds rallied when Bill McDowell
singled with one out. Rivas followed by issuing a free pass to Joe
Lynn and allowed Joe Vaughan to scratch out a single. Roger La
France then bunted and Rivas misplayed the slow rolling ball
allowing McDowell to score. Cuban manager, Oscar Rodriguez
was steadfast in his belief of sticking with his starting pitchers
to finish what they started, and it paid dividends when the confident Rivas, with bases loaded, retired the last two batters on
strikes to end the game. The final tally showed Havana 5 Miami
Beach 4.[33]

Compared to their counterparts to the south, the atmosphere
was considerably more subdued within the confines of Miami
Field on opening night against Lakeland. The late arrival of tickets and lack of ticket-sellers caused a 30-minute delay of game
drawing the ire of fans. An irksome crowd was further annoyed
when parts of the park were left unlit.[34]

During opening night festivities, Mayor Perrine Palmer tossed the opening ball to FIL President, Judge Wayne Allen. Miami spotted the Pilots a pair of runs in the first inning, aggravated by some poor fielding. Waner delighted the crowd by smashing a double in the second frame as part of a two-run rally that tied the game. Veteran hurler Larry Baldwin, returning for his third campaign in a Miami uniform, settled down after some early jitters, and gave up 11 hits to Lakeland, and held the opponents to five runs as his teammates accounted for seven, earning the Sun Sox the victory. Waner, who removed himself after the third inning, finished the game guiding his club from the dugout. Overall, he must have been well pleased with his managerial debut.[35]

On April 24, Flamingo Park hosted the first appearance of a team from a foreign-language speaking country in organized baseball. In a pre-game ceremony in front of 1,963, Flamingos' team owner, Carl Gardner received a scroll delivered by Cubans team President Acosta to commemorate the event. There was a whirlwind of excitement swirling around the Havana club.

The Flamingos, behind the flawless hurling of Bill Wixted, held a 4–0 lead going into the eighth frame, the imposing 6'4" right-hander surrendered three runs and another run in the ninth, forcing extra innings. The Cubans offense came to life and exploded for an eight-run tenth inning putting the Flamingos away to roost by the final tally of 12 to 4.[36]

Both Miami and Miami Beach came out of the gate to start the season slower than a farmer's nag. Both teams' early struggles were a result of their poor performances against the talent-laden Cuban team. By mid-May, the Flamingos (11–12) had lost all six of their games against Havana whilst being outscored 69 to 26. Meanwhile, Miami (9–19) had performed even worse losing all eight of their contests against their neighbors to the south. Their only consolation was the fact that at least three of the games were closely contested, having been decided by two runs or less.

Havana opened the season with a 13-game win skein. They so dominated the competition that league owners expressed concerns that Merito Acosta was stocking his roster with an excess amount of players with professional experience; a violation of FIL rules. The first two teams that came to the forefront and reported suspected irregularities were a pair of the Cubans' earliest victims, Miami Beach and West Palm Beach. Officials with both organizations made it known that the Havana club may have had as many as six ineligibles, over the limit, on their roster.[37] FIL rules allowed for three high level or class men, four limited service players, and the remainder as rookies.

Judge Allen notified all club owners by telegram to meet at the Monterrey hotel in West Palm Beach on April 28 to discuss the Havana issue.[38] Representing Havana's interest was the dynamic Acosta. In his own defense, he stated that his interpretation of the rookie rule was, "if a player who had not played pro baseball, or has never been signed to a pro contract for as long as 45 days was considered a rookie." He added, "If we used any ineligible players it was through a misinterpretation of the rules. If they take anything away from us that we have won you can see what effect that would have. I'm afraid our customers would boycott the league."[39]

Following the summit, Acosta was using the attendance and money it brought into the FIL as leverage. Allen announced a compromise; he would liberalize the player rules admitting that carrying eight rookies on a roster was a Class D standard. By reducing the number of rookies, and allowing for more experienced players, this would strengthen the league and its other teams.[40] This was subject to a final decision from the National Association. In essence, Allen was admitting that Havana had broken the rules, but because the Cubans' were such a powerful drawing card in the league, he was hesitant to rule against them fearing a backlash from the fans in Havana who had been coming out in record numbers; an average of 5,438 per game. In comparison, both Miami and Miami Beach were averaging just over 1,100 per game.[41]

By the first part of June, directors of the league amended their rules reducing the number of rookies to six, and allowing for four-limited experience and eight veteran players per club by June 16 when rosters were to be pared to 18.[42]

The Cubans' domination of their opponents continued to be a concern. The disparity between teams in the league was even more evident on May 12 in front of 2,225 at Miami Field, when Havana's Alberto Matos and Fernando Rodriguez stymied Miami hitters and shutout their opponents by scores of 7–0 and 4–0. Although Matos was impressive in the first game hurling a five-hitter, the second game was historic in the fact that 22-year-old rookie right-hander Rodriguez topped his teammate by handcuffing the Sun Sox and throwing FIL's first no-hitter in the seven-inning second game of the twin bill. Only four Miami batters reached base, two on free passes, and a pair on errors. Two double plays and an attempted steal erased three of the base runners.[43]

By June 3, Havana was running away with the league having posted a 37–7 record. The Cubans' closest competitors were Tampa 23–20, and Miami Beach, a distant third place at 19–21. Allen ruled on June 23, via an edict passed down by Judge W. G. Bramham of the National Association, concerning Havana's player eligibility situation. Much to the disappointment of Cubans' fans, it was decided that a 17-game deduction be applied to Havana's win total, because of the use of 14 limited-service players who performed during games played from April 28 through May 7. In addition, the same aforementioned games subtracted from the losing columns of West Palm Beach (7), Miami Beach (6), Lakeland (2), and Miami (2) figured in their records. Tampa was the only member not benefitting from the violation. It was further determined that the 1946 season would be split into two halves with the four teams with the greatest combined winning percentages for the first and second halves playing off for the league championship. This system replaced the first and second half champions meeting to decide the throne and holder of the newly minted International Cup.[44] Although Miami Beach and West Palm Beach officials argued that 17 losses should add to Havana's loss column, their complaint was to no avail. Miami's Lane later joined the other dissenters and strongly declared, "The case of Havana's ineligibility isn't closed. I'm backing Miami Beach in its request to Judge W. G. Bramham for his ruling on what the penalty should be." He added, "Those games should be forfeited. I'm glad to see the Beach has asked for clarification." Nevertheless, despite all the bluster, Bramham's final determination stood.[45]

First Half Standings

TEAM	W	L	GB
Havana*	33	14	–
Miami Beach	33	26	6
Tampa	31	31	9.5
West Palm Beach	26	28	10.5
Lakeland	26	35	14
Miami	25	40	17

* By the direction of League President Allen, 17 victories were taken away from Havana. They were found guilty of using an excessive number of classmen. The 17 aforementioned games were not included in all of the official averages.

By virtue of the six wins added to their win column, the Flamingos, leapfrogged into second place and were flying high going into the second half the season. The pink birds relied on the second-best scoring offense (315 runs second behind Tampa with 343), in a pitching dominated league, to climb into the first division. So moribund were hitters league-wide that at the mid-point only seven batters, who had enough bats to qualify for a batting title, were carrying a plus .300 average. Furthermore, the league's leading slugger, Bill Baker of Miami had a mere four homers. The solitary Miami Beach regular with a plus .300 average was first baseman Deo Grose (240 at-bats, .320). Reinforcing the attack were semi-regular third baseman Zubrinski (61 at-bats, .361), and recently acquired catcher Jack Sweeting (75 at-bats, .307).[46]

On the other hand, the Sun Sox had the most offensively challenged group having tallied only 238 runs. Two of the few bright spots were shortstop Howard "Red" Ermisch (.305 0, 29), a 28-year-old Army veteran, who like many, had lost four of his prime athletic years (1941–45) while serving his country,[47] and 21-year-old former member of the Army Air Corps and ball-hawking outfielder Roy Knepper (.281, 32 runs).[48]

Undoubtedly, the most proficient Miami hitter was Paul Waner (50 at-bats, .380). Bill Enos, who joined the club on June 21, remembered that although 43-year-old Waner was a small frail looking person, he still had excellent coordination. "He'd pitch hit once in a while. I'll tell ya, he used to say before he'd get up to bat. 'I'll take that pitcher's cap button off.' And he would do it too. He'd hit a line drive every time."[49]

Many in the Miami front office began to question Waner's decision of spending more time in the dugout than on the field of play. Based upon the team's tail-end position in the standings, their assessment was justified. The ongoing frictional relationship would rear its ugly head before the year's end.

Nevertheless, Lane was not ready to give up on the season. One of the Sun Sox's most interesting signings was that of Enos. A defensive specialist who would soon be christened by the Miami press corps as "The Ballerina" for his gracefulness around the first base bag, made fast friends with Miami fans not only for his adept skills in the field, but also his personable nature. Enos also recalled what minor league life was like in 1946 and how upon arrival in Miami his new skipper put him to work before he was barely able to catch his breath.

> I remember going from Asheville to down there. [Miami] They picked me up at the airport, some guy did, and I put the uniform on, on the way to the ballpark, because we were playing that night . . . And I walk in and I didn't know anybody or anything. Paul Waner said, "You're pinch-hitting for a guy." For some reason, or other, they pinch hit me right away. But anyway, that's how I broke in with the Miami club and I enjoyed playing in Miami.[50]

Enos went one for two in his debut with a single and a stolen base. Despite his efforts, the Sun Sox fell to Havana 3 to 2 in eleven innings. The following day club officials, in haste, found housing for their new acquisition and referred to him as, "the surest fielding first baseman in the Tri-State League."[51] With a chuckle, he exclaimed. "I lived across the street from the ballpark. Yeah, I could walk right out my door to the ballpark."[52]

Although Miami acquired quality talent like Enos from Asheville of the Class B Tri-State League, and fellow infielder, Joe Bodner from St. Augustine of the Class D Florida State League,[53] the Sun Sox could not escape the cellar. Their lack of success was the result of not pursuing players from the well-stocked talent pool just over 100 miles to the south in Cuba. Teams like Tampa with first sacker Benny Fernandez (118 g, 4, 79, .288) and Felipe Jimenez (178 IP, 11–11, 3.03), and West Palm Beach with receiver Emilio Cabrera (86 games, 1, 39, .308) and Octavio Rubert (167 IP, 13–6, 1.72), all found key contributors that upgraded their roster. Even Miami Beach enjoyed the services of outfielder Oscar Garmendia (86 g, .239, 1, 39) and during the course of the season acquired shortstop Omar Blanco (105 g, 0, 25, .241), and outfielders' Fernando Solis (109 g, 4, 51, .257) and Armando Valdes (121 g, 7, 69, .240). Miami and Lakeland were the only two clubs not to ink Cuban players. Not coincidentally, they were both at the tail end of the standings. In the coming years, all FIL teams took a more aggressive approach to sign Cubans. Notwithstanding, the Sun Sox, with newfound enthusiasm, kicked off the second half schedule beginning on June 26 on "Baseball Night" by drawing 2,216 which was up to that point their biggest crowd of the season.[54] With a sense of eagerness, they won five of their first six games. First, sweeping a trio of contests against Lakeland at Miami Field, and then taking two of three in Tampa. Leading the charge was one of the few bright lights in the otherwise dim landscape, Ermisch. In his fifth season of pro ball the rubicund pate shortstop, born in Philadelphia, Pennsylvania was not only turning the heads of opponents, and major league scouts with his proficiency with the war club and competence with the leather. Predominant among those "ivory hunters" were representatives of the New York Giants that offered $5,000 for his services.[55]

John McMullan of the *Miami News* reported there was also keen interest by scouts towards purchasing pitcher Gene Elliott and outfielder Knepper. The Sun Sox were struggling at the box office, and an injection of cash would have been a welcome deposit into the club's coffer, Resisting temptation, President Lane refused to concede the season by selling off the little quality talent he had. He stated, "But we're not wrecking this team until the end of the season."[56] Even Lane had limits to his patience and his sunny outlook on reaching the playoffs.

Lane's optimism turned to disappointment. On July 6, Miami knocked off Havana 6 to 2, while the Smokers edged the Flamingos 7 to 6, dropping the Cubans out of first place for the first time. Despite starter Mel Fisher's inability to punch out a single Havana batter, the Sun Sox prevailed. Fisher, described as a husky curveball artist, received some welcome aid from light-hitting second baseman; John "Jackie" Meyer and catcher, Bill Lewis both driving in a pair of runs each helping Fisher earn the win.[57] It was one of the few highlights during the Sun Sox second semester as they proceeded to lose 38 of their last 60 games cementing their hold on last place.

Miami Beach fared better than their cross-town rival, but not by much. The Flamingos limped through the second half seven games below .500. General Manager Joe Ryan, restricted by payroll constraints, found it difficult to improve his roster and failed to add a much-needed bat to bolster the lineup. The inability to make moves was evident by the fact that 34 different men made at least one appearance for the Flamingos, the lowest in the league; the league average was 44. The next closest team was Havana with 38. West Palm Beach had the most active revolving door with 52.[58]

Rosenfeld relied heavily on his four starters, Harold "Zeke" Graham (31 g, 13–12, 2.80), Henton (30 g, 8–11, 2.71), Frank Matthews (34 g, 13–11, 3.00) and Wixted (37 g, 14–14, 312), while occasionally throwing in Jim McGuire (13 g, 3–3, 2.81). The staff's impressive stats were indicative of the FIL's quality pitching. Ten hurlers, with 45 or more innings compiled, sub 2.50 ERA's including Tampa's Chet Covington (28–8, 1.66), and Havana's Rivas (27–4, 2.03).[59]

Second Half Standings

TEAM	W	L	GB
Tampa	45	24	–
Havana	43	27	2.5
West Palm Beach	32	36	12.5
Miami Beach	31	38	14
Lakeland	27	39	16.5
Miami	28	42	17.5

A great deal of interest surrounded the championship match-up between the first half leader, Havana and second half front-runner, Tampa. Fans around the league accepted it as a foregone conclusion that the two top finishers would meet to decide the FIL crown based upon their decidedly better records. FIL officials projected that attendance averaging 6,000 at Tampa, and 10,000 at Havana per game resulting in $25,000 of additional gate receipts.[60]

Rosenfeld's charges staggered into the playoffs like an ibis with a clipped wing. Their sub .500 logs during the second semester was a portent of things to come. The third-seeded Flamingos were up against FIL runner-up Tampa; while pennant-winning and heavily favored Havana was to oppose fourth-place West Palm Beach.

The Smokers overmatched the Flamingos, in large part due to the pitching performance of Covington who won games two and three, the latter in a relief effort. Tampa completed a three-game sweep sending the pink birds back to their nest. Miami Beach pushed across a paltry three runs in the games against a trio of Tampa pitchers, Chesty Chet, Charlie Cuellar, and Hal Johnson.

The real shock came on September 10; West Palm Beach stunned the Cubans in their deciding fifth game, 2 to 1 in a fourteen innings marathon. In a series highlighted by top-notch mound work and airtight defense, the boys from Havana came up short. With the troublesome Cubans out of the way, Tampa took down the Indians in six games in the best-of-seven series and claimed the International Cup as FIL champions.

The curtain closed on the 1946 season, as did the managing careers of baseball legend, and Miami Beach icon, Max Rosenfeld. Although the steely-eyed Paul Waner was harangued by the Wahoos' team directors, and by club President Lane who commented to the *Miami Daily News* that, "Waner's a grand fellow personally, but I signed him with the understanding he would get us ballplayers through his major league connections and that he would play. Well, he didn't get the players and he hasn't played a full game this season."[61] Despite Lane's criticism at the year-end meeting in October, Waner was given a show of support and encouraged to return for the subsequent season. Four of the five directors voted to renew his contract as manager, but Waner a twenty percent stockholder in the club posted his own dissenting vote and opted not to come back as the club's field boss; it was the only season Waner served as manager.[62] He went on to become a successful hitting coach working with several teams. He also wrote a book about his craft entitled, *Paul Waner's Batting Secrets*, which is still in use today. His greatest honor was his induction into the Hall of Fame in 1952. He died on August 29, 1965, from pneumonia in Sarasota, Florida. The Veterans Committee inducted his younger brother Lloyd into the same hallowed halls, two years later.[63] [64]

Like Waner, Rosenfeld stepped down. He never returned to managing a baseball team again. He remained active in the Miami Beach area later serving as president of the Miami Beach Anglers and Boating Club, as well as the Director of the Miami Beach Fishing tournament.[65] Even so, the call of the diamond never left Max and he remained active in the Old Timers Professional Baseball Association of Greater Miami. He sometimes crossed paths with his friend Isey Bandrimer and shared tales from the old days. Rosenfeld even participated in a gathering of old teammates and former big leaguers for an exhibition game at Miami Stadium on July 18, 1957.[66] Sadly, Max passed away on March 10, 1969, one of the most influential forces in bringing minor league baseball back to Miami and the Beaches.[67]

Final Standings

TEAM	W	L	GB
Havana	76	41	–
Tampa	76	55	7
Miami Beach	64	64	17.5
West Palm Beach	58	64	20.5
Lakeland	53	74	28
Miami	53	82	32

1947

The inaugural season for the FIL was a smashing success. One of the few disappointments was the league officials hoping to swell the circuit's coffers failure of Havana to advance in the playoffs for a highly anticipated championship. According to the *Sporting News*, the six-team league attracted 548,843 fans through the turnstiles; bolstered significantly by Havana's 202,873 (average of 5,063 per game) figures.[68] Miami finished third in the league having drawn 76,282 while their cross-town rivals Miami Beach lagged behind with 63,958 finishing ahead of only Lakeland in the turnstile count.[69]

Buoyed by the enthusiastic response by fans from Havana to Tampa, at the October 1946 league meetings, six confident owners unanimously voted to expand the league to eight teams accepting applications from the Fort Lauderdale Braves, and St. Petersburg Saints. Despite the success of Havana's entry, Merito Acosta discounted a bid by Matanzas feeling it was an infringement on his territory. His complaint denied the league a second admittance from Cuba. With the addition of new blood, the season schedule expanded to 154 games, a reaction to the possibility of increased gate receipts.[70]

Seizing upon the opportunity, and with great enthusiasm, George L. "Tiny" Parker, a former National League umpire and current umpire chief of the FIL, made a successful bid to purchase controlling interest in the Sun Sox for $15,000, a 60% share of the club's stock leaving the remaining cut of the pie to Paul Waner and Miami attorney William Pruitt.[71] Parker, of small stature, ruddy-faced with red hair, made up for his size by gaining a reputation as a man with unquestionable integrity. Parker began his career in baseball as an arbiter in the New York-Penn League where he served from 1925–1927. He received a promotion to the International League in 1928 and stayed until 1936, reaching the highest classification in the minor leagues.[72] Parker was so highly regarded by his peers that he was called upon as one of three umpires to participate in the 1936 summer Olympics held in Berlin, Germany.[73] The same games made famous by the outstanding performance of track star Jesse Owens, who earned four gold medals in track and field. His performance countered Hitler's propaganda machine of Aryan racial superiority.

Parker eventually got his shot at the majors and umpired in the National League from 1936–1938. He resigned in 1939, advising he would be running for a city commissioner job in Miami. His bid was unsuccessful, which led him back to his previous career, before returning to the Magic City again prior to his successful attempt to become majority owner of the Sun Sox.[74]

Across town, with almost no fanfare, one of the most important figures in the history of Miami baseball entered the stage. Edward Joseph Ryan was the son of baseball lifer Ray Ryan. The father spent over 50 years in the game as a league president, manager, minor league player, scout, and team owner. He must have been proud when his son arrived in Miami Beach to interview for a position in the Flamingos front office.[75] The younger Ryan, known as Joe, had the love of the game in his DNA and his devotion to the national pastime coursing through his veins. Just like his father, he too would spend his entire adult life in and around baseball.

In December of 1946, Joe Ryan accepted a position with the Flamingos to serve as the team's business manager.[76] It is the beginning of an eight-year relationship with the team and an even longer relationship with Miami baseball. The 30-year-old Ryan, donning his characteristic coke-bottle glasses, had an outgoing demeanor, and strong desire to succeed. A pitcher by trade in high school, he had given up his dream to play professional baseball due to weak eyesight and instead focused on working in an administrative capacity. He began his journey as a concession manager working for the Jeannette Reds of the Class D Pennsylvania Association where he steadily climbed to positions of more responsibility. His on-the-job training prepared him for his position with the Flamingos.

Going into the season Ryan had his work cut out for him. The Flamingos, now an independent club, no longer depended on the Boston Braves to deliver talent, having broken off their affiliation. It was up to Ryan to scout and find players to fill the roster, not a small task considering the competition was the talent-laden Havana and Tampa squads.

One of Ryan's first orders of business was choosing a successor for the wildly popular Rosenfeld. After a series of interviews, his choice was minor league veteran backstop, Albert "Al" Leitz. At 5'7", but full of piss and vinegar, Al, known as a fiery and smart manager, concentrated on "hustle." He was a fan favorite that was good for the box office.[77] Leitz broke into professional baseball in 1935 with the Minneapolis Millers of the American Association as their backup catcher batting .249 in 69 games. Ironically, it was the highest level he would reach. The Millers, seeing that the rookie needed more seasoning demoted him to Jacksonville of the Class B Sally League the next season. Leitz never returned to Minneapolis and played mostly in the lower levels of the minor leagues for the rest of his 12-year career. However, he proved a strong leader, motivator and teacher, and by the time he arrived in south Florida, he brought with him a wealth of experience as a manager after previously serving as a player-manager for the Waycross Bears of the Class D Georgia-Florida League from 1939–1942, the Atlanta Crackers in 1943, and the Macon Peaches in 1946.[78] [79]

Leitz and Ryan immediately swung into action to build their club for the upcoming season. One of the most highly heralded signings was the inking of 27-year-old Johnny "Big John" Streza, an imposing 6'3" and 220 lbs. from Alliance, Ohio. The local press dubbed him the "poor man's Hank Greenberg." The mighty Streza had been a force at every stop along the trail of his minor league career. He drove in over 100 runs with the Williamson Red Birds (1939), Mobile Shippers (1940), Columbus Red Birds (1941), and Durham Bulls (1946). He served in the U.S. Army from 1942 to 1945.[80] Team president Gardner enthusiastically proclaimed, ". . . and we're expecting him to hit at least 30 homers." Gardner added, "that just like the Pittsburgh Pirates had shortened the cavernous left field for pull-hitting Greenberg, that they would propose to FIL allow them to reduce the dimensions at Flamingo Park to increase their new slugger's probability of poking a few out of their own park."[81]

In addition, joining the pink birds' flock were two Cubans, returnee outfielder Oscar Garmendia, and 21-year-old right-handed pitcher Ernesto "Chico" Morilla. Both proved to be impactful during the upcoming season. Garmendia, in particular, had sharpened his skills with Camagüey in the Cuban Winter League during the offseason. He was ready for a breakout year.[82]

On the other hand, Morilla was an untapped talent. At the conclusion of spring training, Havana cut and exposed him to any team to sign. Ryan wasted no time in bringing him into the flock. The rookie would soon leave his mark and reward his GM with the best season of his career. Morilla described as diminutive by various sources had a listed height from 5'3" to 5'8", and weighing from 135 to 160 pounds. The wiry and long-necked hurler was far from intimidating standing on the sidelines, but enemy batters soon learned to respect him after flailing at his assortment of effective pitches.[83]

Joining Morilla on Beach's mound staff was another returnee, Zeke Graham. The 28-year-old righty relied on his control, lacking overpowering stuff. Together they would form one of the best one-two pitching duos in the history of the FIL.

Across town, Miami named David Coble to lead their charges as player-manager. Like Leitz, Coble was a catcher. Like many others, he lost a substantial chunk of his playing career due to his military service (1942–45). Originally signed by the Columbia Sandlappers, who moved to Asheville later in the season, he appeared in 33 games and batted .224. After stops in Moultrie (Georgia), Columbia, (South Carolina), and Little Rock, he earned a spot on the Philadelphia Phillies roster early in 1939. Although he only appeared in 15 games, mostly as a pinch-hitter, batting .280, he made quite an impression on local fans, and with his catcher's mitt.[84] Coble participated in a Phillies' publicity stunt to stimulate attendance. It involved Coble and fellow Phillies teammates Gil Brack, Del Young, Walter Milles, who were called on to catch a ball dropped from the 521-foot-high William Penn Tower. Coble efficaciously held onto a ball that nearly broke the bones in his hand. Of all the participants in the group of four, he was the only one to achieve the feat during his turn.[85] [86]

Coble had long since recovered from the force of the plummeting sphere, by the time he arrived in Miami. He was familiar with south Florida having served a previous assignment with the Army Air Forces Officer Candidate School in Miami Beach during the spring of 1943 that lasted until the expiration of his service obligation in 1946. He then signed on with the Gadsden Pilots of Class B Southeastern League as player-manager before accepting his new position in Miami.[87][88]

With spring training scheduled to begin on March 10 in Key West, Coble was looking forward to another crack at serving the dual role as player and skipper. Arriving in camp were bevies of new young hopefuls looking to don the uniform of not the Sun Sox, but the newly named Tourists. In order to create interest, a team-sponsored contest encouraged fans to select a new moniker. The winner turned out to be a room clerk from a local hotel named G.E. List who submitted the entry and gleefully received his reward; a pair of season passes.[89]

Coble counted on a loose affiliation with the New York Yankees, to supply some of their lower level minor league players so that they would receive more playing time. He also depended on a working agreement with the Palatka Azaleas of the Class D Florida State League, to bolster the existing roster that included returnee frontline pitchers Gene Elliott and Mel Fisher. Most of the new arrivals were more suspect than prospect as the new field general soon found out. One of the more interesting players in camp was a local named Seward S. Lee. He was the proprietor of the Pilot House Bar and Restaurant located on the corner of Northwest 36th Street and 49th Avenue near the Miami airport. His net worth believed to be $300,000; he offered his playing services free of charge to the Tourists. Ultimately, they cut him before the season began.[90]

Two assignees on option from the Yanks farm system who were about to make a significant impact for Miami were a 22-year-old right-handed pitcher from Bedford Valley, Pennsylvania, Melvin Edgar Nee, and 26-year-old outfielder William Dempsey "Jack" Bearden (no relation to Gene Bearden) from Augusta, Georgia. Nee originally signed with the Pittsburgh Pirates in 1942, only to have his contract sold to the Washington Senators affiliate, Kingsport Cherokees of the Class D Appalachian League in 1943. That same year the Army called him to service and after his honorable discharge, he reported to Kingsport in 1946 going 14–14 with a 3.53 ERA.[91] Known for his sunny disposition and hustling play, he soon won over the hearts of the local fans. Minor league legend, Muscle Shoals, who usually drew the most recognition wherever he played was a teammate of Nee's, reflected with a tinge of disappointment in George Stone's book "Muscle," "They had a vote for the team MVP and Melvin Nee . . . got the award and I was second.[92]

Upon arriving in Miami, Nee joined his new teammate Bearden. The Georgia native previously served his country as a member of the Third Army in Europe.[93] He began his ball-hawking career in 1939 with his hometown Augusta Tigers of the Sally League. Following a successful debut when he collected 15 hits in 35 at-bats. He then began his journey through the lower rungs of the minor leagues at Easton (Yankees), Butler (Yankees), Amsterdam (Rugmakers), and Norfolk (Tars). He ultimately forged a 12-year career in the bush leagues.[94]

With everyone's rosters in place, the FIL kicked off the season on April 9 with Miami squaring off against Miami Beach at Miami Field. Two-thousand-nine hundred-fifty-three rooters squeezed into the rickety wood grandstands and witnessed their home team outhit the Flamingos 16 to 12, but come out on the short end of the stick 8 to 4. Tourists' starter Elliott took a beating only lasting four innings. The Beach's choice of hurlers Curtis Mitchell did not fare much better, he was able to scatter the Tourist hits, and earn the "W". It would be his only win of the season before his release.[95]

One of the highlights of the season came at Flamingo Park when the city honored baseball legend, George Herman Ruth by bestowing upon him "Babe Ruth Day." The Babe and his wife, who both had a long affinity for Florida, hoped that the sunny weather and fresh air would help the former big slugger's battle with cancer. A record crowd of 2,805 paying customers and an estimated 1,000 children who were admitted free paid tribute to the convalescing Babe by greeting him with wild applause. Team president Carl Gardner presented the once mighty slugger with a scroll in appreciation of his service to the sport of baseball. Rather embarrassed and obviously much thinner and with his graying hair, the humble Babe accepted the accolades handed out and watched from the grandstands as Havana's ace Connie Marrero handcuffed the Flamingo hitters. After five innings the "Sultan of Swat," obviously tired, waved goodbye to the throng of men, women, and children and retired for the night. Little could anyone have imagined that in just over a year, on August 16, 1948, he would succumb to cancer. The hometown fandom hoped their embrace of the Ruth might bring them good luck against the visiting Cubans, but instead, Havana's ace Marrero spun a gem holding the Flamingos to a half a dozen hits and no runs as his Cubans shut out the home team 5 to 0.[96][97]

Miami Beach struggled losing 12 of their first 17 contests and shared the basement with the St. Petersburg Saints. Meanwhile, across town, Miami came out running by winning 11 of their first 17 games. On April 27, the Flamingos hit their lowest point against Mel Nee in what turned out to be his most magical night as a pro.

The 6'1", 190-pound right-hander Nee, acquired only a few days before from the Class B Pensacola Fliers, made his debut as a Tourist. He had more than a few butterflies as he toed the rubber (at Flamingo Park on April 27), in front of 1,600 spectators. After taking a few deep breaths, he gained his poise and proceeded to retire the first three batters in order. Each inning followed with Nee continuing the same script of, three batters up and three batters down. "It was about the fifth that I realized I hadn't allowed a man to reach first safely," said Nee. Aided by defensive gems by Miami second baseman Skeeter Webb in the second inning, and shortstop Dan O'Connell in the sixth, the partisan crowd sensed they were witnessing history and gradually switched allegiance rooting for Miami as each Flamingo batter went down. By the eighth inning, the Miami Beach fans were holding their collective breaths and cheering as each successive batter turned back to the bench empty-handed. It almost ended in the eighth frame when center fielder, Jack Chandler began his pursuit of a solidly hit ball to deep center field. What looked like extra bases instead turned into a sensational catch that was the play of the evening. Going into the top of ninth Nee quickly dispatched both Harold Kase and Leitz in short order before pinch-hitter Eddie Wayne stepped to the plate batting for Graham. Just like the script of a Hollywood movie, the dangerous hitter Wayne went down on strikes and the local throng went wild. Nee's teammates rushed to the mound to congratulate him as his catcher Bill Lewis handed him the prize ball. "I'm saving this one for Johnny," Nee proclaimed. He added, "Johnny's my four-month-old son and I knew he'd like to have it when he gets older." In the course of a conversation on July 13, 2016, Nee's 69-year-old son revealed with great pride that he still had that ball in his possession; a wonderful memory from his dad's baseball career.[98]

Nee's performance ranks as the top pitching debut in Miami history and one of the greatest performances ever in the Magic

City. To his credit, his command of pitches allowed only four batted balls to leave the infield while striking out four. He tossed the first perfect game in the short history of the FIL, the first perfecto at Flamingo Park, and the first no-hitter by a Miami hurler since the Magicians' A. R. Thomas did the trick in 1921. The humble and convivial Nee shared platitudes for his catcher by saying, "Give Lewis a lot of credit. He caught a splendid game. After all, I'm new here and you know a catcher has a hard time doing the receiving for a pitcher he isn't used to."[99]

Four days after his perfect performance, Nee made a run at duplicating his feat, before giving up three hits and losing a heartbreaker, 1 to 0 to Octavio Rubert at Wright Field in West Palm Beach.[100] All of the Tribes' hits came by way of former Sun Sox, Knepper with two, and Enos with one. Knepper's single in the sixth frame scored Rubert, Nee's first free pass, and the only tally of the evening in a game that lasted a mere one hour and 40 minutes.[101]

By popular demand, Miamians honored Nee with his own night. On May 7, 3,065 enthusiastic fans, the largest turnout ever at Miami Field for a FIL game, turned out on "Mel Nee Night." The happy pitcher received several gifts during the pre-game ceremony; for which he expressed his sincere appreciation to all in attendance.[102]

With the festivities concluded, leadoff hitter Skeeter Webb got the contest started by tripling in the first frame. After Mario Fajo was retired, Dave Stokes doubled and plated Webb. After Bearden drew a free pass, Aurelio Fernandez hit the second three-bagger of the inning adding two more runs and giving the Tourists an early 3–0 lead. Nee battled early with his control, and unharacteristically gave up six free passes, yet he worked out of several jams and held the visiting St. Petersburg Saints scoreless for the first six innings. Nee allowed a couple of unearned runs in the seventh frame, and after a scoreless eighth, allowed two more runs in the ninth. An errant throw to the plate by shortstop Webb should have ended the game. Coble sensed Nee's exhaustion. He strolled to the mound to remove Nee, and signaled to the bullpen for recently acquired Julian "Yuyo" Acosta to extinguish the threat. The fresh-armed Acosta promptly coaxed Oscar Del Calvo to fly out to the center fielder Bruce Ware, who squeezed the ball for the final out. Nee had twirled his second victory of the season; defeating the Saints by the final of 5 to 4.[103]

The outlook was not rosy for the Tourists. By the beginning of July, they found themselves barely clinging to fourth place in the FIL with a 37–43 slate, 26½ games behind the front-running Havana Cubans.

Across town, the Flamingos had righted their early-season woes and after a slow start climbed to third place with a 46–33 record. Much of the teams' success centered on their three best starting pitchers, rookie Morilla, Graham and 36-year-old veteran Stanley "Red" Todd. He pitched for Miami in 1940 (5–13, 3.39, 146 IP).

Over the course of a professional ballplayer's career, it is a rarity that he will enjoy his best season during his freshmen season. Nevertheless, Morilla proved to be the exception. In what would be his most iconic run, the undersized curveball specialist clicked off a skein of 42 consecutive scoreless frames. He began his streak pitching the final four innings of scoreless relief against West Palm Beach on July 21. He followed that performance pitching a 2-hit shutout against Fort Lauderdale on July 24. On July 27, he blanked Tampa in an 11-inning affair described by *The Sporting News* as grueling, before the skein stopped during his next start. The Smokers game was not his only marathon whitewashing; on June 25, he took the Lakeland Pilots to task in 16-innings, earning the win during a 1 to 0 affair. His best performance came against Havana, and the FIL's best mound man Marrero, earning yet another hard-fought victory, 3 to 0. It was the second time he beat the Cubans' best who went on to win 25 and lose only six times that year.[104]

Ironically, Morilla's streak would have never happened if he had followed up on his earlier threats to quit the team when he declared he was homesick and expressed his strong desire to return to his native Cuba. His teammates and manager convinced him to stay. He finished the campaign with a 23–9 record.[105]

Miami Beach continued to play consistent winning baseball, while their counterparts to the west remained on the road to mediocrity. It is unknown whether the Tourists' skipper Coble, was under pressure by the front office, or just disappointed by his team's performance. On July 1, he announced that due to ill health, and worry over failure to develop the Tourists into a winner, that he was stepping aside as manager of the team. Jay Cone, Miami's team business manager promptly found a replacement, Charles Baron. The 33-year-old career minor leaguer previously managed in the St. Louis Cardinals farm system (Class C at Fresno California League 1947) before obtaining his release. The parent club ultimately dismissed him because they were displeased with their skipper when they discovered he had released players without consulting the main office.[106]

Baron inherited a fourth-place team with an unimpressive 37–43 record, barely holding onto fourth place a half-game ahead of West Palm Beach. On July 2, he made his debut against archrival Miami Beach at Miami Field. A sparse crowd of 924 greeted the new manager with a round of applause. The ebullient atmosphere did not last long. A commotion started in the third inning when Ralph Franck went on a mad dash to score when pitcher Elliott's relay toss went awry. Catcher Mickey O'Brien hastily retrieved the ball and threw to the pitcher Elliott covering the plate, the tag catching Franck. Wayne, who was batting, thought that Franck had beat the throw and launched into a verbal fracas with the home plate umpire. Leitz soon joined in the heated exchange, which in turn led to the tossing of both from the game. In the bottom half of the same inning, Morilla faced Elliott and fired several bean balls aimed at his head causing words to be exchanged between the opposing benches. Morilla let his temper get the best of him and in his frustration, allowed a Bob Morem double that plated a pair of runners, Walter "Mousie" Halsall, and Tom Mahon, during the three-run inning. The final tally showed Miami 5 Miami Beach 2.[107]

The mercurial Leitz's behavior towards umpires continued to be a problem. On July 5, the night designated as "Eddie Wayne Night," the skipper's temper flared again.[108] With the score knotted at nine in the bottom of the tenth, the Flamingos appeared to have scored the winning run only to have it ruled a putout at home plate by umpire Bob Preddy. Leitz protested vehemently with the arbiter before the heated exchange escalated to the point the umpire gave him the thumb. He angrily stomped off the diamond and refused to let the Flamingos take the field in the eleventh, and announced the game was under protest. Despite orders from the umpiring crew, he would not yield to their instructions. Arbiter Preddy made the decision to forfeit the game and award the win to the visiting Smokers. Although Leitz filed a formal protest with the league office, Judge Allen ruled in favor of Tampa, fining the Flamingos $100, and slapped Leitz with a $25 fine, and a three-game suspension. Fortunately, for the tempestuous skipper, the suspension did not affect his status as manager for the upcoming FIL All-star game.[109]

In pre-game festivities, Miami Beach Mayor, Marcie Lieberman presented Eddie Wayne with the A. G. Spalding Bat Award honoring the previous years' minor league rookie with the highest batting average. He hit a glossy .403 with Lenoir of the Class D Blue Ridge League.[110]

It was not the last time Leitz received fines and suspensions before the close of the season. On August 18, he once again drew the displeasure of league officials and issued another $25 penalty and a five-day suspension. His use of profanity while arguing with umpires during an August 15 contest against St. Petersburg brought down the ire of the league offices.[111]

Summer was especially long and humid for the players and coaches who were looking forward to the anticipated four-day layoff marked by the second annual FIL All-Star game. Once again, league leader Havana challenged a showcase of All-stars from the other clubs at El Gran Estadio del Cerro (sometimes called Gran Stadium). Three Flamingos including, outfielder Garmendia, and pitchers Graham and Morilla appeared, led by their skipper Leitz. The sole representative from the Tourists was "No-hitter" Nee. Garmendia was the most interesting choice as offensive numbers usually trumped defensive competency. Although steady with the war club, he shined brightest when he displayed his defensive prowess. Incredibly, he had gathered 16 assists in his teams' first 31 games. Enemy base runners soon learned that discretion was the better part of valor when contemplating taking an extra base on the rifle-armed center fielder.[112]

On July 10, heavy rains postponed the highly anticipated night of stars. Not dissuaded by a downpour, the local fanatics witnessed a memorable match-up the next day. Both teams battled to a 1–1 tie through regulation. Finally, in the tenth inning, a circuit blast by Tampa's Lamar Murphy was the difference maker. The FIL stars edged the Cubans 2 to 1. Four pitchers, Octavio Rubert (West Palm Beach), Milford "Punchy" Howard (Lakeland), Morilla and Nee, combined to thwart the Cubans, overshadowing Fernando Rodriguez's brilliant performance with a three-hitter. Nee, who entered the game in the eighth, chalked up the "W".[113]

With the second half in full swing, teams all around the league made a flurry of moves to bolster their roster. Traditionally, a tight budget limited Ryan's ability to engage in transactions. One player grabbed the Flamingos' attention. Thanks to his rival

Tourists' inability to close a deal, Ryan was able to purchase a local legend.

Mike "Lefty" Schemer was available and Ryan convinced ownership to loosen their purse strings and sign the local star. A natural born athlete, the former Miami High School graduate, and University of Miami football star excelled in multiple sports but found his niche on the diamond. Originally, signed by the New York Giants, he broke in with the Salisbury Giants of the Class D North Carolina State League batting .365 in 110 games. He steadily climbed up the ladder, served in the Army, and upon his return to the states in 1945, started out the season with New Jersey of the International League before receiving a call to the majors. On August 8, Lefty made his debut with the Giants collecting two singles in four at-bats and garnered the distinction of being the first Miamian to reach the big leagues. The agile first baseman went on to appear in 31 games that year while batting .333. Most impressively, in his 114 plate appearances, he struck out only once. By 1946, he was a candidate to make the Giants as a regular. He failed to impress his superiors despite hitting the ball well for average because he failed to hit the well-coveted long ball. After a solitary pinch-hitting appearance, he found himself dealt to the Sacramento Solons of the Pacific Coast League.[114] By 1947, although still productive, he was yielding playing time to Rip Russell and John Zipay, and so Solons' management deemed him expendable and made it known they were accepting offers for Schemer's services.

Cone, the Tourists' vigilante business manager, saw an opportunity, to not only strengthen his club but also bring in Lefty as a gate attraction. Despite an offer to purchase his contract from the Solons for $2,000, Schemer demanded his release by the close of the season to pursue other opportunities. A flabbergasted Cone assessed the asking price as being double what he would pay any FIL player, to "fly the coup" in October. He passed on the deal.[115]

Ryan felt handcuffed trying to sign players in the past. He did not hold back this time and jumped on the deal by agreeing to Sacramento's terms and purchasing Schemer at the same price the Tourists had passed on. Hearing of the news, and now given the chance to play every day, Lefty wasted no time boarding a plane for Havana to hook up with his new teammates.[116]

Despite the acquisition of Schemer, who went on to hit .303 in 39 games and drive in 15 runs, the remainder of the campaign,

Miami Beach stayed entrenched in third place looking up at Havana and Tampa who continued to dominate the league in a two-team race for the pennant eventually won by the Cubans. Meanwhile, Miami held off threats by St. Petersburg and West Palm Beach for fourth place and the final playoff spot. Two milestones were reached when Nee bested Fort Lauderdale 3 to 1 on September, 9,[117] and Graham topped Miami 4 to 1 on September, 16,[118] both earning their coveted twentieth wins of the season.

While players and personnel nervously readied for the best-of-five playoff series, Hurricane George (also known as the Fort Lauderdale hurricane), moved at a steady and threatening pace towards South Florida. Both Miami at Havana and Miami Beach at Tampa were feeling the effects, both physically and psychologically, from the approaching storm that would eventually reach a "Category 4." Its full force unleashed its destruction from Palm Beach to Miami.[119]

Miami players seemed especially distracted, most not familiar with what the weather had in store. They dropped their opener to the Cubans. Marrero allowed six scattered hits, shutting out the Tourists, 4 to zip. That same day in Tampa, 1,800 spectators watched the Smokers dominate the Flamingos behind the masterful hurling of Octavio Rubert, who struck out 13 batters. The only Miami Beach run came in the second inning when Streza scored ahead of a Garmendia triple. The final tally showed Tampa 5 Miami Beach 1.[120]

By the afternoon of September 17, the early impacts of the "big blow" slammed into Florida. Heavy rains forced cancellations of games for the next three days in Tampa. Havana cruised to an easy 12 to 0 victory in their second game. With all the major newswires knocked out of service, due to the hurricane, the gory details of the defeat went unannounced to Miamians.

The storm left in its wake 11 dead and $31 million dollars in property damage.[121] The devastation at Flamingo Park left the ball field unplayable leaving the pink flock to play the remainder of their series on the road. It was not ready for play until the spring of 1948. Miami Field suffered $7,000 in damages. If not for the efforts of workers to patch up the field and structure, they would have experienced the same fate as their cross-town rivals.[122]

Play resumed on September 21, as Miami edged Havana, 4 to 3. In the bottom of the tenth inning, big Ed Bass hit a ringing single off reliever Daniel Parra that scored Candido "Candy" Mendizabal for the walk-off winner.[123] Miami Beach's fate was different as their ace Morilla failed in his bid to win his first play-off game. The Flamingos were "lit up" by the Smokers by a 4 to 3 score.[124] The next night Miami Beach went down without much of a fight, as Oscar Del Calvo held the pink birds to four hits and coasted to a 10 to 4 win at Plant Field completing the sweep.[125]

In game four, Miami put a scare into the Cubans. A clutch Bob Morem solo blast in the eighth inning broke up a 1 to 1 tie and another brilliant effort by Nee forced a deciding fifth game. It was déjà vu for the Cubans, memories still fresh from the previous years' upset at the hands of West Palm Beach. Determined not to repeat, Havana sent Julio "Jiqui" Moreno (19–4, 2.13) to the mound against Walt Wilson (10–3, 2.25), the Cubans second appearance in the series. The Cubans were spotted a 5–0 lead before the Tourists rallied and chased Moreno from the game. Skipper Oscar Rodriguez not taking any chances called on Marrero to silence the enemy bats, but instead, he gave his manager a fright, coughing up three runs. Unfortunately, the trio of runs fell short for the 729 fans peppered amongst the grand-stands as they watched their hometown heroes go down valiantly. Miami's downfall was their inability to hit with runners on base stranding 14. It was now the Cubans' turn to shine and take their first championship. As a consolation, Miamians divvied up $400 into 20 shares as a reward for being semi-finalists in the playoff series.[126]

Havana bolstered by the league's best pitching staff that featured four future major leaguers; Marrero (25–6, 1.66), Rogelio Martinez (9–4, 1.90), Moreno (19–4, 2.13) and Fernando Rodriguez (6–6, 3.62) went on to overwhelm Tampa in the finals taking all four games in the best-of-seven series.[127]

Final Standings

TEAM	W	L	GB
Havana	105	45	–
Tampa	104	48	2
Miami Beach	88	65	18.5
Miami	74	77	31.5
St. Petersburg	71	80	34.5
West Palm Beach	68	86	39
Lakeland	50	101	55.5
Fort Lauderdale	48	106	59

1948

The last time a Miami franchise experienced a winning record was in the second half of the 1927 season when the Miami Hustlers went from a last-place club in the first half of a split season and nearly winning the championship. Hopes were running high in 1948 that the Tourists would finally turn it around. There were strong indications to justify the positive mood of fans since the club had signed perennial FIL star pitcher Chet Covington a five time 20-game winner, a past minor league player of the year in 1943. In addition, Sanford's Bill Stanton (19–7, 2.46) who was third the year before in the Class D Florida State League in wins came on board, to go along with returning fan favorite starter Mel Nee.[128]

Chosen to lead Miami to the "promised land" was new player-manager Howard "Red" Ermisch. Already a fan favorite with the locals, he hit .314 in 1946 while a member of the Sun Sox. Sensing his chances of making the big leagues unattainable, he accepted a position in 1947 at La Grange of the Class D Georgia-Alabama League where he first learned the ropes as a rookie player-manager. Ermisch declared he was ready to take the reins of a veteran team that averaged age 27.4 years.[129]

Conversely, Miami Beach experienced better results than their cross-town foes having made the playoffs every year dating back to the inception of the Florida East Coast League in 1940; including the league title in 1941. The *Sporting News* glowingly predicted, "Miami Beach threatens to field the heaviest hitting team in the loop."[130] Four returning position players included, outfielder Wilmer Chappell (.291, 3, 68), second sacker Russ Nelson, third in the league with 25 stolen bases,[131] (.277, 1, 43), first baseman Mike Schemer for a full season (.303), and outfielder Eddie Wayne, who showed great promise (.314, 9, 84).[132] With the return of Todd and Morilla and the signing of 35-year-old Cuban Winter League star Juan Montero, it afforded the Flamingos' the most experienced staff in the league. The club seemed poised to knock Havana off its perch.

Joe Ryan's choice to lead his club was 33-year-old Harry Chozen. A catcher by trade, the trusty backstop had toiled in the minor leagues since 1935. Other than a one-game appearance with the Cincinnati Reds on September 21, 1937, a game in which he garnered his only major league hit in four at-bats, he never rose above Class AA. Although never regarded as a great hitter, ironically he received national attention in 1945 when he strung together a 49-game hit streak while playing for the Mobile Bears of the Class A-1 Southern Association. An article in the 1978 *Anniston Star*, Chozen recalled the attention he received from his monumental accomplishment.

> We were sitting on the bench before a game and a Memphis sportswriter came up and asked us if we realized one of the Memphis players had an 11-game hit streak going. Chozen added, "I told him that's nothing. I had a 27-game streak alive." The guy went off and researched it and the next day it was in the papers. I began getting all types of publicity with sports writers and radio announcers wanting interviews . . . I enjoyed all the attention. It was like playing with someone else's money.[133]

While the sunny Chozen was optimistic about his team's prospects and a steady-handed Ermisch prepared his squad for the upcoming season, Tourists' President, George "Tiny" Parker, was busy working behind the scenes planning Miami's baseball future. He formed the Sportsman's Holding Company to garner financial support for a new ballpark. The architectural firm of Marr and Holman, known for their art deco style and functional designs, created plans that ultimately featured a stadium with a cantilever roof. The unique configuration was a one-of-a-kind structure.[134]

Together with the newly formed Miami Chamber of Commerce sports committee, Dr. Ralph Ferguson, who was supportive of backing Parker's proposals, felt a new facility would be more conducive to a major league team to conduct spring training. This allowed the local team to expand its fan base,[135] Ferguson declared, "I believe that the city would appropriate money to obtain a major league baseball team for spring training same as they would appropriate funds for golf tournaments and thereby obtain more publicity." Despite his outlook, Ferguson felt more confident that a campaign amongst the citizens would be easier to raise funds than negotiating with the city of Miami.[136]

The Tourists continued playing their home games in cozy, but dilapidated Miami Field. In mid-August 1947, neighboring

Burdine Stadium began expanding its new upper deck in preparation of its rechristening of the "Orange Bowl."[137] Much like the class bully pushing the skinny weakling with the horned rim glasses aside, it was abundantly clear that the old ballpark's days were numbered.

In what was becoming an all too familiar script, Havana got off to another fast start maintaining a hold on first place; while Miami and Miami Beach struggled, both entrenched in the second division. The Tourists opened by losing seven of their first ten games, while the Flamingos fared worse dropping eight of ten. The biggest surprise was the quick start by perennial tail-enders, the Lakeland Pilots led by future major leaguer Chuck Aleno and two hurlers, Antonio Garcia and Bernard Winkler that would go on to 20-win seasons.[138]

Havana's continuing domination caused concern amongst the other league owners. They again proposed that the number of rookies on each roster be reduced, and allow clubs to carry as many as ten veterans in the hopes it would level the playing field. The accusation was that Cuban rookies were on par with limited service and veteran players.[139] Although the proposal failed to get the required two-thirds vote, it did pass the next season.

Despite coming out of the gate sluggishly, the Tourists and Flamingos began to climb back to respectability. Miami (11–11) reached the .500 mark on April 26, when Bill Stanton held Havana to five hits in a 5 to 0 whitewashing on the road.[140] On May 18, Miami Beach balanced their ledger, pummeling West Palm Beach, 12 to 6.[141]

The Tourists seemed to have jelled as a unit, ready to make a run at a first division spot then a distraction rocked the team. On April 28, Miami took a 1 to 0 loss to Havana. The same day a petulant Covington decided he was more comfortable elsewhere besides the dugout. After the morning workout, he dressed in his civilian skivvies and watched the game from the grandstands. He had also been indifferent to fielding a ground ball in his most recent start. Chesty Chet's actions drew the ire of his skipper Ermisch who handed down a swift one-week suspension.[142]

The portly Covington, probably the most colorful, zany, and eccentric player to grace a Miami ball field. His multitude of insubordinate acts ran parallel with an exceptional amount of great moments he experienced on the diamond. Most ballplayers began their professional careers in their late teens, but "Chesty Chet,"

"Chester the Great," or "Lefty," as he was known at different times, entered organized baseball at 28 years old. Born November 6, 1910, in Cairo, Illinois, his father, a stern disciplinarian and an official with the Pullman Company, doled out a fair amount of physical abuse on young Chet.[143] This may explain his rebellious nature and blunt outspokenness that he later became known for in adulthood. After his family relocated to Jackson, Tennessee, the ambitious Chester launched into his first vocation as a pugilist. As a teen, he competed professionally winning 187 of 216 bouts over a nine-year period. It was only after his nose was broken, and some stern convincing from his wife that he decided to hang up his boxing gloves and change occupations.[144]

After leaving the ring, Covington turned to his next favorite sport, baseball, and decided to give it his all. "I debated quite a while, but once I decided to go into the game professionally, I was determined to see it through," he asserted in a 1943 *Sporting News* feature story conducted by Chic Feldman. After starring in the amateur Dade County League, he signed with the Philadelphia Phillies and reported to Portsmouth, Virginia of the Class B Piedmont League. He later was reassigned to the Goldsboro Goldbugs of the Class D Coastal Plain League.[145] So began a 15-year career that included, twenty-one minor league stops, and a three-month stay in the big leagues with the Philadelphia Blue Jays/Phillies in 1944. Before hanging up his glove and cleats, Chet collected 220 wins in the minors, and one victory in the majors over 15 years.[146] His most recognized accomplishment was when he was awarded the Outstanding Minor League player of 1943. It was the same season he pitched the Eastern League's first perfect game during in the middle of a 45 inning scoreless skein.[147]

The other side of his complicated personality, despite being an extremely talented pitcher demanding of perfection, was his belligerence. He seemed always in conflict with his teammates, managers, and employers. He could not stand the lack of hustle on the playing field. He had the nerve to ask for a demotion from Philadelphia when he said, "These Phillies had a defeatist attitude." Yet, he was known to shun fielding bunts believing that was the infielder's or catcher's job, but fans and teammates blamed it more on his wide girth that grew more pronounced with advanced age.[148]

Nevertheless, he was also a showman and like a moth to a lighted lamp, the fans could not stay away from him. The "local bugs" loved his antics including the time when he warmed up for a game in Miami. He placed the baseball on the pitching rubber, removed a yo-yo from his rear pocket, and began yo-yoing for five minutes expressing his insouciance towards the opponents. *Baseball Magazine's* spring 1953 issue may have summarized it best when they referred to Covington as, "a bush league Dizzy Dean."[149]

Covington's life off the field was just as interesting as his exploits on the diamond. His resumé was an index of careers. Not only was he a prizefighter, but he also performed as a black-face minstrel song-and-dance man, hosted his own hillbilly band show for two years in Fort Lauderdale, and worked as a radio announcer. There was no end to his chosen professions. He also served as a deputy sheriff at a Tampa dog track, sold pots and pans, worked and played baseball for Eastern Airlines, and even drove the team bus during a short stint in Palatka, Florida because he was the only member on the team with a chauffeurs license.[150] [151]

Covington served his sentence and returned to action on May 6, against Miami Beach at Flamingo Park. With the game tied at two apiece in the fifth inning a scorching line drive, back to the box, had eyes for Chet. Not known as the most adept fielder, he strained a kidney muscle trying to snag the ball and was forced to leave the game in favor of Charlie Bowles. Bowles would earn the decision when the Tourists rallied in the ninth frame plating a couple of tallies, gaining their first win in four tries against the Flamingos.[152] Not discouraged by any physical maladies, Covington did not miss his next start against Havana.

Covington's suspension was not an isolated incident in the "rowdy, wild and wooly" league. President Allen was lowering the boom on many of its players and managers for bad behavior around the entire circuit. Miami Beach personnel were not exempt from his harsh punishment. Their ace, Morilla was handed a five-day suspension and $50 fine for abusing an umpire. Flamingos manager Chozen, and shortstop Sindu Valle were assessed $10 and $5 fines for using profanity during games.[153]

As both Miami and Miami Beach continued to struggle on the field there would be several instances of punishments doled out to offenders. In June, Tourists' infielder Antonio "Chico" Rodriguez received a suspension for 15 days for bumping umpire James Drury. The ultimate sentence was given to outfielder Ed Bass: banishment from the league, along with a $100 fine for wrestling an umpire to the ground during a game with Miami Beach on June 24.

Both Miami and Miami Beach's continued struggles brought about some changes on the field, including managerial changes. The biggest surprise came on May 22 when the Palm Beach Indians announced they had purchased the contract of local hero Mike Schemer from Miami Beach.[154] One of the most productive hitters for the pink birds, who had been batting at a .290 clip, Schemer was reluctant to take the helm at first, but finally reported on May 24. On a promising note, Schemer guided West Palm Beach to a 2 to 1 victory over front-running Havana in his debut.[155] Although fans felt perplexed by the move, they did receive some positive affirmation when their local hero's replacement Roy Vinbladh (obtained from Omaha of the Western League) blasted a 345-foot homer at his coming out party during a 7–6 triumph over St. Petersburg. Ultimately, the move proved beneficial to the Flamingos as the former Western Leaguer provided the power punch that Joe Ryan was looking for smashing, 15 homers and driving in 53 runs in just 109 games. Schemer, in turn, brought his average up to .324 but had only two long-range balls to show for his efforts.[156]

On June 1, the continuing saga of Chesty Chet continued. Miami brass had just about enough of the obstinate left-hander and announced his sale to Port Chester of the Class B Colonial League. Despite his 9–5 record, it was felt that his distractions outweighed his productivity.[157]

On June 20, former Lakeland manager Bill Perrin took over the managerial reins from Ermisch, who resigned after his team went into a slump losing sixteen of eighteen games the same month. However, Ermisch (.290, 1, 70) stayed on as a player to complete the season.[158] Ryan fired Chozen on August 21, following a dropped doubleheader to the Tourists, which amounted to the Flamingos' fifteenth and sixteenth consecutive defeats. It was the longest skein in their history and was the dagger that ended any hope of their making the playoffs. The most humiliating game during the streak occurred on August 11, when Miami Beach was no-hit by Lakeland's Bill Tutka. The only hard hit ball of the day came off the bat of "Chappy" Chappell who sent a scorching liner that found first baseman John Greenwald's glove during the 7 to 0 loss.[159] It marked the first time since the formation of the FECL that either Miami team would reach the preseason.

In the aftermath of a disappointing season for the two south-ernmost Florida clubs, Havana swept Lakeland in the semi-finals in three games, while Tampa overcame their cross-town rival St. Petersburg in five games. The Cubans in due course reigned as champions taking a hard-fought series from Tampa in seven games.[160]

Miami finished with the second highest scoring in the offense in the league led by William Copcheck (.301, 20, 108), Morem (.308, 10, 90), and Barney Bridgers (.283, 119 runs), but their downfall proved to be their pitching. Although Stanton recorded a 20–12 re-cord, the only other Tourists starter to record double-digits in wins was Nee and Frank Tincup both with ten. Covington gutted out nineteen wins on the season, unfortunately, ten of those W's came during his time in Portsmouth after his release from Miami.[161]

Miami Beach's troubles were polar opposite from the Tourists'. An offense that preseason prognosticators were picking as one of the elite instead produced only the seventh best in the league scoring 629 runs; only Fort Lauderdale was worse with 602. Eddie Wayne (.353, 10, 76) and the mid-season acquisition of Vinbladh proved to be the only productive hitters. Nevertheless, the Cuban combination of Morilla (20–18, 3.34), and Montero (17–14, 3.69) teamed up to win over half of the clubs games. Together they combined to hurl 577 innings as Morilla eclipsed the 300 mark.[162]

Despite the lack of success on the field, happier days were ahead with the anticipation of news for a new state of the art baseball-only stadium's location would soon be revealed, but not without a surprising twist of events. On October 9, Judge Allen announced that Tiny Parker, so committed to bringing the new stadium to Miami, sold the club to a consortium known as the Magic City Baseball Club, Inc. (MCBC). Parker's effort to pur-chase a land tract that failed, played a role in his decision to sell. The MCBC backed by a then unnamed wealthy Cuban who owned real estate investments in Miami, paid the healthy sum of between $45,000 and $50,000 (the actual final figure coming out to be as much as $64,000) for the financially strapped Tourists. The group also agreed to provide the funds to build the new sta-dium that was more than appealing to the city of Miami.[163][164]

The man at the forefront of the MCBC was 33-year-old Harry B. Taber. Within a month of the purchase of the Miami team, he an-nounced that the new site for the stadium would be located on the corner of Northwest 10th Avenue and 23rd street in the Allapattah section of Miami where the old circus grounds were located. He proudly proclaimed, "We will spare no expense in giving Miami a winning team. We are amply financed and are not interested in making money."[165] The latter part of the quote would prove a prophetic commentary in regards to money, and down the road have an impact on the stadium and baseball in the Magic City.

On December 14, groundbreaking ceremonies, which included several dignitaries, went off without a hitch. Within short order, tractor operators began to clear the land and construction workers started the initial phase of what would become Miami Stadium.[166]

Optimism and curiosity hung heavy in the air as Miamians anxiously viewed the rise of their new diamond facility. With high hopes towards the future that the fortunes of the Tourists, would soon turn the corner, the new baseball playground was beginning to take shape. With the progress came the increasing inquisitiveness by the community on who was financially backing this impressive stadium in the making. The name of a then 17-year-old youngster became exposed. He would be the one leaving his long-lasting mark on Miami. It was a point in time when the future looked so bright and it marked the peak of Miami's dalliance with the FIL.

Final Standings

TEAM	W	L	GB
Havana	97	57	–
Tampa	84	67	11.5
Lakeland	82	72	15
St. Petersburg	78	73	17.5
Miami	75	78	21.5
West Palm Beach	70	83	26.5
Miami Beach	69	82	26.5
Fort Lauderdale	55	98	41.5

NOTES

1. World War II Foundation, retrieved 20 October, 2015 from www.wwiifoundation.org/students/wwii-facts-figures/.
2. Bedingfield, Gary. Baseball's Dead of World War II: A Roster of Professional Players Who Died in Service, (McFarland & Company, Inc. Publishers: Jefferson, North Carolina & London), p. 3–4, 90–91, 121–123.

3. Berger, Ralph. Gene Bearden, 2015, www.bioproj.sabr.org/bioproj/person/ffc84797.

4. Ibid and baseball-reference.com. In 1946 pitched 167 innings and posted a 15–4 record with a 3.13 ERA. In 1947 pitched 198 inning and posted a 16–7 record with a 2.86 ERA. He finished his major league career with a record of 45–38, 3.96 ERA hurling for the Cleveland Indians, Chicago White Sox, Detroit Tigers, St. Louis Browns and Washington Senators.

5. Florida International League, *Sporting News*, 23 May, 1946, p. 25.

6. Butler, Guy. Florida International Loop Born, *Miami Daily News*, 24 September, 1945, p. 2-B.

7. Butler, Guy. BB League Meetings Scheduled, *Miami Daily News*, 23 September, 1945, p. 7-B.

8. Butler, Guy. Florida International Loop Born, *Miami Daily News*, 24 September, 1945, p. 2-B.

9. Ibid.

10. Butler, Guy. Tampa Eighth City To Post Fee, Judge Allen Boomed As President, *Miami Daily News*, 6 November, 1945, p. 2-B.

11. Kachline, Clifford. "Shift to AAA for Big Three; Texas Now AA." *Sporting News*, 13 December, 1945, p. 7.

12. F-I Rosters Must Be Cut By June 15, *Miami Daily News*, 7 April, 1946, p. 2-C.

13. Washington Buys Control of Class C Havana Club, *Sporting News*, 31 July, 1946, p. 33.

14. Beach Team Produces Check; Officers Elected, Gardner Prexy, *Miami Daily News*, 14 January, 1946, p. 2-B.

15. Butler, Guy. Rosenfeld Is Beach Pilot; Braves Supply Full Roster, *Miami Daily News*, 16 January, 1946, p. 7-B.

16. Balfe, Bob. "It's Post Time With," *Palm Beach Post*, 21 April, 1946, p. 13.

17. Compton, Allen. Florida International Called 'Strange' League, *Miami Daily News*, 24 January, 1946, p. 4-B.

18. McMullan, John. 15 Players Corralled By Miami Baseballers, *Miami Daily News*, 4 February, 1946, p. 2-B.

19. Hughes Signed By Palm Beach, *Miami Daily News*, 9 February, 1946, p. 1-B.

20. Ibid. Frink was an outfielder who appeared in two games with the Philadelphia Phillies in 1934 without a plate appearance. Stewart, a second baseman, third baseman and outfielder, had an 8-year big league career spent with the St. Louis Cardinals (1916–17), Pittsburgh Pirates (1922), Brooklyn Robins (1923), Washington Senators (1925–27, and 1929). Hugh Wise appeared in two games at the catcher position for the 1930 Detroit Tigers.

21. Waner Is Diamond Chief, *Miami Daily News*, 23 February, 1946, p. 8.

22. Paul Waner Wired Offer To Pilot Miami Club, *Miami Daily News*, 20 February, 1946, p. 9-B.

23. Baseball-reference.com.

24. Nowlin, Bill. "Lloyd Brown," acquired 13 April, 2016 from SABR Bio Project at http://sabr.org/biopro.

25. Ibid. Brown's major league lifetime record is 91–105, 4.20, 1693 IP. He pitched with Brooklyn (NL) 1925, Washington (AL) 1928–32, St. Louis (AL) 1933, Boston (AL) 1933, Cleveland (AL) 1934–37, and Philadelphia (NL) 1940.

26. Zubrinski, Eugene. Phone interview with the author, 18 July, 2014.

27. Baseball-reference.com. Canadian teams in the league were Guelph Maple Leafs, and London Tecumsehs. The Tecumsehs defeated the Pittsburgh Alleghanies for the league championship.

28. Three F-I Loop Openers Expected To Draw 25,000, *Miami News,* 14 April, 1946, p. 2-C.

29. Florida International League, *Sporting News*, 25 April, 1946, p. 28.

30. McMullan, John. Miami Seeks Second Win; Havana Tops Beach, 5–4, *Miami Daily News*, 18 April, 1946, p. 2-B.
31. Zubrinski, Eugene. Phone interview with the author, 18 July, 2014.
32. Butler, Guy. Flamingo Rally In 9th Falls One Run Short, *Miami Daily News*, 18 April, 1946, p. 2-B.
33. Ibid.
34. McMullan, John. Miami Seeks Second Win; Havana Tops Beach, 5–4, *Miami Daily News*, (Main Edition), 18 April, 1946, p. 2-B.
35. Ibid.
36. Havana Trims Miami Beach, *Sarasota-Herald Tribune (AP)*, April 25, 1946, p. 7.
37. Butler, Guy. F-I League Calls Meeting To Probe Cubans' Roster, *Miami Daily News*, 25 April, 1946, p. 2-B.
38. Ibid.
39. Butler, Guy. Topics of the Tropics Column, *Miami Daily News*, 13 May, 1946, p. 2-B.
40. Florida Ints May Reduce Rookie Number, *Miami Daily News*, 26 April, 1946, p. 4-B.
41. Havana May Break All Records, *Sporting News*, 19 June, 1946, p. 30.
42. Granell Quits Tampa Helm, *Sporting News*, 12 June, 1946, p. 29.
43. McMullan, John. Rodriguez Baffles Sox With No-Hitter, *Miami Daily News*, 13 May, 1946, p. 2-B.
44. Second Half Race Starts Wednesday, *Palm Beach Post*, 24 June, 1946, p. 3.
45. Kinnamon Slated For Mound Role, *Palm Beach Post*, 3 July, 1946, p. 9.
46. Florida International Averages, *Palm Beach Post*, 30 June, 1946, p. 14.
47. 1946 Miami Sun Sox Baseball Program, p. 15. Information acquired from player biography.
48. https://veteransfuneralcare.com/obituary/Roy-Allen-Knepper.
49. Enos, Bill. Phone interview with the author, 6 September, 2014.
50. Ibid.
51. McMullan, John. Sox Get 3 New Men For Havana Finale, *Miami Daily News*, 21 June, 1946, p. 3-B.
52. Ibid.
53. McMullan, John. Sox Get 3 New Men for Havana Finale, *Miami Daily News*, 21 June, 1946, p. 3-B.
54. Matthews, Matty. Sox Get Off To Winning Start, *Miami Daily News*, 27 June, 1946, p. 3-B.
55. McMullan, John. Miami Awaits Giants Reply' On $5,000 Asking Price Asked For Ermisch, Miami Daily News, 2 July, 1946, p. 2-B.
56. Ibid.
57. Matthews, Matty. Mel Fisher Stops Cubans, Sox Win, 6–2, *Miami Daily News*, 7 July, 1946, p. 2-C.
58. Baseball-reference.com. Numbers based upon team roster figures given on website.
59. Sporting News Baseball Guide and Record Book 1947, Charles C. Spink & Son: St. Louis, Missouri, p. 391.
60. Havana Upset in Synthetic Playoff Muddles Florida-Int Title Picture, *Sporting News*, 25 September, 1946, p. 34.
61. Waner's Sun Sets In Miami, *Sporting News*, 4 September, 1946, p. 31.
62. Paul Waner Loses Miami Pilot Job, *Akron Beacon Journal*, 18 October, 1946, p. 37.
63. Waner, Neal A. Paul and Lloyd Waner Big Poison and Little Poison, retrieved on May 19, 2015 from www.redlandsfortnightly.org.
64. Baseball-reference.com.
65. Horvitz, Peter S. and Horvitz, Joachim. *The Big Book of Jewish Baseball, 151–152*, (S.P.I. Books: New York, New York, 2001), p. 151–152.
66. Oldsters Stay Up Late to Play for Crowd at Miami and TV, *Sporting News*, 13 July, 1957, p. 19.

67. Ancestry.com.

68. *Sporting News*, 18 September, 1946, p. 34.

69. League Attendance Tops Half-Million, *Palm Beach Post*, 5 September, 1946, p. 9.

70. Balfe, Bob. 154-Game Schedule Adopted For 1947, *Palm Beach Post* via *Post-Times*, 21 October, 1946, p. 10.

71. Parker Buys Miami Club, *Sporting News*, 27 November, 1946, p. 23.

72. Retrosheet.org/TSNUmpireCards/Parker-George.jpgv, retrieved on 28 May, 2016.

73. Baseballrevisited.wordpress.com/2012/07/28/baseball-in-the-1936-olympics, retrieved on 28 May, 2016.

74. With The Cameraman . . . On Winter Baseball Trail, *Pittsburgh Press*, 22 January, 1939, p. 19.

75. Baseball-reference.com. Ray Ryan biography retrieved 27 May, 2016.

76. *Sporting News*, 11 December, 1946, p. 25.

77. Al Leitz Is Selected To Pilot Crackers, *Herald Journal* [Spartanburg, SC], 13 December, 1942, p. 26.

78. *Sporting News*, 27 November, 1946, p. 23.

79. Baseball-reference.com.

80. www.tributes.com. Retrieved 26 August, 2017.

81. Beach Signs 'Poor Man's Greenberg'; 14 Report for First Official Workout. From newspaper clipping, provided by John Streza's nephew Dan Streza, through a personal correspondence dated 23 June, 2016.

82. Figueredo, Jorge. *Who's Who in Cuban Baseball, 1878–1961*, (McFarland & Co., Inc., Publishers: Jefferson, North Carolina and London), p. 155.

83. Morilla, Tiny Hurler In 42 Zero Frames, *Sporting News*, 13 August, 1947, 35. Morilla is listed as 5'3", 135 pounds. According to baseball-reference.com Morilla, 5'8", 160 pounds.

84. Ibid.

85. Bedingfield, Gary. "Dave Coble," Retrieved from www.baseballinwartime.com/player_biographies/coble_dave.htm. The ball was reported at an estimated speed of 125 miles an hour when it hit Coble's glove.

86. "Phillies' Catcher Snares "High" One," *Shamokin News-Dispatch*, 11 May, 1939, p. 13. A reported crowd of 15,000 saw the event at a party to honor the Newspaper Guild of Philadelphia and Camden.

87. Ibid.

88. Baseball-reference.com.

89. Miami Club Named Tourists, *Sporting News*, 12 March, 1947, p. 20.

90. *Sporting News*, 2 April, 1947, p. 24.

91. Bedfordcountysportshalloffame.com, "Melvin Mel Nee," retrieved on 19 June, 2016 from bedfordcountysportshalloffame.com/class_2006/melnee.html.

92. Stone, George. *"Muscle" A Minor League Legend* (Infinity Publishing: Haverford, PA, 2003), p. 111–112.

93. Garrard, Lamar. "Baseball's Best: Adversity Produced Successful Players," *The News Reporter*, [Washington Ga], Retrieved 18 June, 2016 from http://www.news-reporter.com/news/2015-04-16/Sports/BASEBALLS_BEST.html.

94. Baseball-reference.com.

95. *St. Petersburg Times (AP)*, 10 April, 1947, p. 13.

96. McMullan, John. Babe Proves He's Still BB's Top Attraction, *Miami Herald*, 15 April, 1947, p. 2-B.

97. Babe Ruth Night, *Sporting News*, 23 April, 1947, p. 36.

98. Nee, John. Phone interview with author, 13 July, 2016.

99. 95 Matthews, Matty. Perfect Game Rookie Lauds Miami Support, *Miami Herald*, 28 April, 1947, p. 2-B.

100. Melvin Nee Pitches Perfect Game In Florida International League, *Kingsport News*, 8 May, 1947, p. 12.

101. Rubert Blanks Tourists, 1–0. *Palm Beach Post*, 3 May, 1947, p. 5.

102. Miami Honors County Hurler For No-Hit Game, *Bedford Gazette*, 15 May, 1947, p. 4.
103. Burns, Jimmy. "'Nee' Night A Success As Saints Bow, *Miami Herald*, 8 May, 1947, p. 15-A.
104. Johnson, C.H. Morilla, Tiny Hurler, in 42 Zero Frames, *The Sporting News*, 13 August, 1947, p. 35.
105. Ibid.
106. Charles Baron Named Manager of Tourists, *Miami Herald*, July 2, 1947, p. 4-B.
107. Kelley, Whitey. Managerial Bow Made By Baron, *Miami Herald*, July 3, 1947, p. 14-A.
108. Eddie Wayne Gets Trophy as Leading '46 Rookie Hitter, *Sporting News*, 16 July, 1947, p. 17.
109. Argument Costs Game, $125 And Manager's Suspension, *Palm Beach Post*, 7 July, 1947, p. 5.
110. Matthews, Matty. Beach In Row, Forfeits Game, *Miami Daily News*, 6 July, 1947, p. 3-C.
111. *Sporting News*, 27 August, 1947, p. 36.
112. *Sporting News*, May 28, 1947, p. 33.
113. Stars Cop Fla. Int. Classic, *Sporting News*, 23 July, 1947, p. 33.
114. Horvitz, Peter S. and Joachim Horvitz. *The Big Book of Jewish Baseball*, (S.P.I. Books, Publishers: New York, New York), p. 167–168.
115. Tourists Lose Hope For Landing Schemer, *Palm Beach Post*, 20 July, 1947, p. 15.
116. *Palm Beach Post*, 28 July, 1947, p. 5.
117. *Palm Beach Post*, 10 September, 1947, p. 8.
118. *Palm Beach Post*, 17 September, 1947, p. 33.
119. wikipedia.org/wiki/1947_Atlantic_hurricane_season.
120. Associated Press, *Miami Herald*, 17 September, 1947, p. 8-A.
121. Sumner, H.C., *North Atlantic Hurricanes and Tropical Disturbances of 1947, Monthly Weather Review,* December 1947, p. 252.
122. Walt Wilson Will Face Cuban Rivals Today At 4, *Miami Herald*, 20 September, 1947, p. D-1.
123. Burns, Jimmy. Clubs Meet In Fourth Tilt Today, *Miami Herald*, 21 September, 1947, p. 6-D.
124. *Miami Herald (AP)*, 21 September, 1947, p. 6-D.
125. Smokers Eliminate Beach, *Miami Herald*, 22 September, 1947, p. 12-A.
126. Burns, Jimmy *Miami Leaves 14 On Base, Miami Herald*, September 24, 1947, 4-B.
127. Spink, J.G. Taylor, Lanigan, Ernest J., Rickart, Paul A. and Kachline, Clifford. *Sporting News Baseball Guide and Record Book 1948* (Charles C. Spink & Son: St. Louis, MO), p. 389–395.
128. Ibid.
129. Baseball-reference.com.
130. Havana Cubans Stand Pat, *Sporting News*, 14 September, 1948, p. 29.
131. *Sporting News*, 5 May, 1948, p. 35.
132. Spink, J.G. Taylor, Lanigan, Ernest J., Rickart, Paul A., Kachline, Clifford. *Sporting News Baseball Guide and Record Book 1948* (Charles C. Spink & Son: St. Louis, MO), p. 389–391.
133. Pete Rose five short of SL's Harry Chozen, *Anniston Star*, 3 August, 1978, p. 6-C.
134. Evans, Luther. Commission To Reconsider Bid For Baseball Park Site, *Miami Herald*, 14 October, 1947.
135. Burns, Jimmy. South Florida Wooing Clubs, *Sporting News*, 31 March, 1948, p. 1, 6.
136. Ferguson Gets Jaycee Sports Position Again, *Miami Herald*, 28 March, 1948, p. 4-D.
137. Yarborough Sees Need For New Ballpark, *Miami Herald*, 23 March, 1947.

138. Baseball-reference.com.

139. Worried By Havana's Strength, *Sporting News*, 28 April,1948, p. 30.

140. Stanton Stops Havana, 3–0, On Five Hits, *Miami Herald*, 27 April, 1948, p. 2-D.

141. McMullan, John. Beach At .500 Goes For No. 3, *Miami Daily News*, 19 May, 1948, p. 2-B.

142. Minor League Highlights, *Sporting News*, 12 May, 1948, p. 34.

143. Cote, Greg. Forever In Her Hall of Flame Widow's Only Wish: Don't Forget My Chet, *Miami Herald*, 16 July, 1997, p. 1-C.

144. Feldman, Chic. Biff on Beezer Checked Chet Covington as Boxer, Now He's Stopping Baseball Biffers as Boxman, *Sporting News*, 10 June, 1943, p. 5.

145. Ibid.

146. Baseball-reference.com. Covington's lifetime mark during 15 minor league seasons was (220–126, 3.41, 2,912 IP).

147. Burns, Jimmy. Covington's Rambles Make Bobo Just a Stay-at-Home, *Sporting News*, 22 February, 1950, p. 16.

148. Cote, Greg. Forever In Her Hall of Flame Widow's Only Wish: Don't Forget My Chet, *Miami Herald*, 16 July, 1997, p. 1-C.

149. Ibid.

150. Ibid.

151. Feldman, Chic. Biff on Beezer Checked Chet Covington as Boxer, Now He's Stopping Baseball Biffers as Boxman, *Sporting News*, 10 June, 1943, p. 5.

152. *Sporting News*, 19 May, 1948, p. 33.

153 Ibid.

154 Flamingo Due In City Today, *Palm Beach Post-Times*, 23 May, 1948, p. 17.

155 Balfe, Bob. Tribe Wins 2–1 In 10 Innings, *Palm Beach Post-Times*, 25 May, 1948, p. 8.

156 Spink, J.G. Taylor, Lanigan, Ernest J., Rickart, Paul A., Kachline, Clifford. *Sporting News Baseball Guide and Record Book 1949* (Charles C. Spink & Son: St. Louis, MO), p. 312–314.

157 Chet Covington Sold, *Palm Beach Post*, 1 June, 1948, p. 7.

158 Perrin Takes Miami Helm, *Sporting News*, 30 June, 1948, p. 34.

159 Bill Tutka Hurls First Florida Int No-Hit Tilt, *Sporting News*, 28 August, 1948, p. 35.

160 Spink, J.G. Taylor, Lanigan, Ernest J., Rickart, Paul A., Kachline, Clifford, *Sporting News Baseball Guide and Record Book 1949* (Charles C. Spink & Son: St. Louis, MO), 312.

161 J.G. Taylor Spink, Ernest J. Lanigan, Paul A. Rickart, Cliff Kachline. *Sporting News Baseball Guide and Record Book 1949* (Charles C. Spink & Son: St. Louis, MO), 312, 313, 319.

162 Ibid.

163 Evans, Luther. 6-Man Group Buys Tourist Franchise, 10 October, 1948, p. 1-D, 4-D.

164 Llanes, Rolando. *White Elephant: The Rise and Fall of Miami Baseball Stadium*, (Blurb Inc., 2010), p. 46–54.

165 Evans, Luther. 6-Man Group Buys Tourist Franchise, *Miami Herald*, 10 October, 1948, p. 1-D, 4-D.

166 Ceremonies Mark New Park's Start, *Miami Herald*, 15 December, 1948.

CHAPTER SIX

THE FLORIDA INTERNATIONAL LEAGUE 1949–1951

Hope, prosperity, and paranoia were the words defining the 1940s as it ended, and the 1950s lay beckoning just over the horizon. After suffering through a depression and World War II, the days of shortages, rationing and recycling drives ended. It is the beginning of an era of lofty expectations reflected by the larger size of new model cars, televisions becoming commonplace, and working wages on the rise. Yet, the indubitable American optimistic spirit is jaded by the threat of new enemies; the Russians and their acquisition of the atomic bomb, the Chinese aggressiveness which leads to a police action in Korea, and the threat of communism lurking around every corner of America's consciousness.

Miami is transforming as well. Newcomers to South Florida, arriving from all corners of the U.S., are purchasing new homes resulting in expanding subdivisions around the city that are built at a record pace. Reflected in this growth is the change of Miami's skyline as new commercial buildings rise and downtown commerce booms. Meanwhile, construction workers hurriedly labored on a new state of the art baseball stadium that will define Miami baseball for the next 40 years. As the ballpark began to take shape, curious neighbors follow its progress with a watchful eye.

The Florida International League had progressed too. No longer classified as C level, the National Association granted an upgrade of status to the league, advancing it to Class B. The two most notable changes were team's ability to carry more veteran players and an increased salary limit.

Another major change came in leadership. Judge Wayne Allen, tired of bickering owners and ongoing quarrels within the FIL, stepped down from his post. Allen, so fed up with the FIL that when offered a lifetime membership to the league he declared, "I might not want to accept it." Several names were bantered about to replace the good judge including; Tiny Parker, Max Rosenfeld, former major league pitcher and Clearwater oilman, Jack Russell, Miami Judge Ben Willard, and boxing commission member Bob Williams. In the end, team owners decided on an alternate choice: Palm Beach State attorney Phil O'Connell. He was reluctant to accept the job, (due to the amount of time it required). Several phone calls from encouraging fans around the league convinced him to accept the position of league president.[1][2]

1949

Changes in leadership also came on the field when both Miami and Miami Beach named new managers to guide their respective teams. Two teammates from the 1930s famed St. Louis "Gas House Gang," John Leonard Roosevelt "Pepper" Martin (Miami) and Joe "Ducky" Medwick (Miami Beach) made headlines that promised to take the inner-city rivalry to new heights.

Eighteen years before, Martin came to the nationwide public eye fostering the image of the lovable county bumpkin who played the game with reckless abandon and all-out hustle. He led the Cardinals to an upset victory over the Philadelphia Athletics in the 1931 World Series and it forever earned him the devotion of St. Louis and baseball fans everywhere. "The Wild Horse of the Osage," a nickname bestowed upon him by sportswriters, characterized by his nose that resembled a beak of an eagle, red-sun-burned neck, and a perpetually soiled uniform that came from diving for ground balls and sliding into bases head first, encompassed the spirit of this "blue collar" working man. Always cordial with fans to a fault, an avid outdoorsman, a religious "teetotaler" who let a curse word fly now and again, he loved his family, shotguns, welding, and racing midget automobiles. His passion to win at all costs attitude, that sometimes boiled over with aggressiveness endeared him to his admirers even more.

Gale Wade, who went on to a major league career, and spent parts of two seasons with the Chicago Cubs in 1955 and 1956, remembered his fiery spirited manager fondly from his time with the Sun Sox. His teammate, Robert Tripp saw Martin and Wade as kindred spirits. Tripp declared, "In fact, if anybody was ever a clone of Pepper it was Gale."[3] Wade exclaimed, "Well, I'll tell you. Pepper believed in going full bore. Just give it all you got. And that's why I thought the world of old Pepper Martin." He added, "Oh gosh, he was just a wonderful man and I never seen anybody, like I said, that was more driven than him."[4]

Coming to Miami represented a demotion for Martin, but one handled with his usual positive attitude. His previous managing jobs were at a higher level, Sacramento (1941–42) and San Diego (1945–46) of the Pacific Coast League, Rochester (1943) of the International League, and Greenville (1947) of the Sally League.[5] What intrigued Martin the most was the idea of playing in a large city like Miami for a Brooklyn Dodger affiliate overseen by Branch Rickey. With the new stadium on the horizon, Martin saw it as an opportunity that he did not want to pass up. When he arrived in March of 1949, waiting to greet the club's new skipper was president, H. B. Taber.[6] He was instrumental in negotiating and bringing the new stadium to Miami and was anxious to make Martin feel at home in his new digs.

Miami Beach's ownership group had also been aggressive in securing a manager (albeit one with a personality), very much opposite the Sun Sox's choice. Whereas Martin was more flamboyantly happy in his own rural way, 37-year-old Medwick, who earned the nickname "Ducky" because his walk resembled the strut of a duck, sometimes seemed standoffish. Some of his teammates regarded him as selfish, and he had earned a reputation for being less than cordial with fans and the press. His twenty-year wait after retiring as a player to be inducted to the baseball Hall of Fame can most likely be traced to his prickly relationship with reporters who covered him during his playing career. He despised his given nickname acquired while playing in the minor leagues for the Houston Buffaloes of the Class A Texas League. He preferred his second most used nickname "Muscles." He later learned to accept "Ducky."[7]

Having hung up his glove and put away his cleats the year before, Medwick began putting his feelers out for a managerial position. During the minor league's winter-meetings in Minneapolis, Flamingos owners Sid Gans, Carl Gardner and Sam Shapiro approached him about a managerial opening. The Miami

Beach trio was so impressed with Medwick, despite no previous managerial experience, that they made an offer that Ducky accepted on the spot. Undoubtedly, the Miami Beach brain trust regarded Medwick as a gate attraction able to boost their sagging attendance numbers. When asked why he picked Miami Beach, he stated, "I liked the club executives who talked with me." He added, "I feel that I am lucky to get a nice club in Class B. I didn't want to start too high." Medwick weighed several other offers in higher classification leagues but chose the Flamingos.[8] Medwick, an avid golfer and frequent participant in ballplayer sponsored golf tournaments, could not resist the temptation of the quality of golf courses that Florida offered.

Despite his reputation, Medwick appeared to have mellowed. Shortly after arriving in Miami Beach, he exhibited a smile on his face, smoked a big black stogie and enjoyed an ice-cold beer.[9] As he prepared his team for the upcoming campaign, the trials of management would soon become apparent and test the patience of "Muscles."

Both managers jumped into preparations for the season with determined fervor. Travis Jackson the new skipper of the Tampa Smokers and former New York Giants shortstop who played for John McGraw during the 1920s and 1930s assessed the upcoming campaign, "You Miami people are going to have a lot of fun this summer with Martin and Medwick separated only by the bay which lies between Miami and Miami Beach. Pepper will go after Ducky and there'll be a lot of excitement."[10]

The biggest change for Miami came during the offseason when Brooklyn Dodgers GM Rickey signed a working agreement with the club to serve as an affiliate. The Dodgers deep farm system had an instant positive impact. Rickey supplied Martin's newly re-named Miami Sun Sox with a roster filled with experienced players. Among them were 25-year-old second sacker August "Knobby" Rosa (115 games, .256) from Class B Danville, Illinois of the Three-I League, outfielder Dick Haviland (.341 5, 57) and slick-fielding shortstop Chris Kitsos (.253 5, 82) from Class C Johnstown, Pennsylvania of the Middle Atlantic League, as well as steady pitch-caller with a rifle arm, Pete Stammen (.323 2, 77) from Class D Valdosta, Georgia of the Georgia-Florida League.[11]

To bolster Martin's mound corps, the Dodgers also recruited two hurlers with experience from the Cuban Winter Leagues, Vicente Lopez and Rene "Tata" Solis. Lopez, a slender righty known for his knee-buckling curveball, came to the Dodgers after their scouts had spied him pitching in the Cuban amateur league for Club Hershey where he was instrumental in leading the team to a championship.[12] Later, pitching for Almendares in 1948–49 he appeared in five games with a less than impressive 0–1 record and 7.94 ERA. Nonetheless, he redeemed himself well in the inaugural Caribbean Series that same year pitching six and two-thirds innings, giving up only four hits while striking out three, and not allowing a base on balls against Panama.[13] [14]

Solis, a teammate of Lopez's on the Almendares team, came off his rookie season in the states having risen as high as Class AA Mobile of the Southern Association. During that same winter with Almendares, he compiled an impressive (7–4, 2.36) mark, and matched Lopez for wins while striking out five, walking one with a 3.00 ERA in nine innings in his sole Caribbean series appearance. "Tata," as his teammates liked to call him, and Lopez would soon leave their marks on Miami and their FIL opponents.[15]

In contrast, the Flamingos' being an independent minor league team with no affiliation depended on scouting, referrals, and recommendations. Two men who would play a key role for Miami Beach came from the St. Louis Cardinals organization. Outfielder Mike Conroy spent most of 1948 with Omaha of the Class A Western League where he hit .311 in 119 games and had a short stint with Houston of the Class AA Texas League. He was joined by first sacker Ed Lewinski who batted .308 in limited action for Omaha of the Class A Western League.[16] The two former Redbird prospects joined returnee "pasture worker" Charles "Rocky" Rotzell (.314 2, 44, 70 runs), and Medwick as the key offensive threats.[17]

Anchoring the Flamingos' pitching staff again were Chico Morilla (20–12, 3.40) and compatriot Juan Montero (17–14, 3.69). Together they teamed up with 38-year-old Stanley "Red" Todd (10–18, 3.16), Cuban Gaspar Del Monte (6–8, 4.31) acquired from the Gadsden Pilots of the Southeastern League and 5'9" right-hander Andrew Daly who chucked for Springfield and Elmira of the St. Louis Browns organization the previous year. Brought on board to handle the staff was veteran backstop Emilio "Cabby" Cabrera, participating in his third FIL campaign. The reliable game-caller was an All-Star with both West Palm Beach in 1946, and Tampa in 1948. His steadying influence provided invaluable aid to the top-flight Flamingos' staff.[18]

The regular season kicked off on April 4 with differing results. The Sun Sox opened at Miami Field against West Palm Beach. New league president, O'Connell tossed out the traditional first ball to Miami city manager, O.P. Hartley to start the festivities in front of 3,460 attendees. Martin's choice for the opening day starter, Solis, responded well to his skipper's confidence scattering eight hits and striking out seven in a 7 to 1 victory over the Indians. Martin's philosophy of aggressive play was evident as his team took the extra base at every opportunity. Haviland and catcher Ramirez each stole a base, and the offense took advantage of six base on balls and three errors by West Palm Beach while collecting eight hits to the Indians' seven.[19]

A rookie pilot wants nothing more than to start out on the right foot, but Medwick's coming out party had a disappointing result. Both teams battled for nine innings to a 6 to 6 tie. Rotzell and Lewinski each hit home runs matching their opponent's player-manager Chuck Aleno's own output on the day. Uncharacteristically, for an FIL game, it was a slugfest with five circuit blasts. The deciding solo blast coming in the tenth inning off the bat of catcher Armando Valdes, a walk-off winner as the Braves triumphed 7 to 6 spoiling the rookie manager's debut.

Since its inception, the FIL had gained the reputation as one of the most colorful leagues in the minors: known more for the raucous behavior of its managers, players, and fans than its quality of play. The 1949 season was no exception. Around the FIL, O'Connell had been handing out fines like a vendor handing out bags of peanuts. The numerous indiscretions involving players and managers including verbal abuse, cursing, and fighting were increasingly becoming a problem. Among the wrongdoers were members of the Flamingos and Sun Sox. One of the chief early offenders was Martin who during an April 12 game between Lakeland cursed, laid his hands on an umpire and failed to control his players; a game that, despite his theatrics, Miami went on to win, 13 to 6. The only thing that saved Martin from suspension was his quick apology to the league. He still received a $25 fine.[20]

Early season results had Miami quickly out of the gate grabbing first place winning eight of their first ten games. Tampa (7–4) and Miami Beach (6–5) were close behind. "Martin has his Sun Sox running hard and taking chances. That upsets the opposition . . .," said Miami Herald's Jimmy Burns.[21] The much-anticipated three-game series that pitted Martin versus Medwick finally came on April 16 at Miami Field. As expected, the game lived up to all the hype. The meeting between the two clubs was like a powder keg just waiting for the spark to set it off.

The fireworks started in the third inning when Miami found themselves trailing by four runs. Miami Beach's Daly's control went south walking three of the first four batters he faced only retiring one batter on a pop out. Haviland followed with a base hit driving in a couple of runs but was gunned down at second base trying to stretch it into a double.[22] The next batter Tripp, walked. Medwick immediately tapped his right arm, removing the starter. The Flamingos' skipper then called on Del Monte. Bob Morem greeted the new replacement with a hot shot to third baseman, Ed Dickerman who promptly threw high and over the head of first baseman Lewinksi. It appeared he caught the ball for the final out, but in reality, the ball rolled past the first base coaching box before Sun Sox coach, Bill Cates picked it up. Both Rosa and Tripp crossed the plate, but since umpire Lew Payor had called Morem out at first, the side was retired negating the two scores.[23]

As the Flamingos exited the field, the Sun Sox bench cleared. The sharp-tongued Sun Sox fiercely aimed their acidic tongues at Payor for his obvious oversight. Cates even showed the errant ball to Payor who refused to overturn his call. During the melee, home plate umpire Joe Arian corrected Payor because he saw the ball clearly sail over the head of Lewinski and ruled Morem safe. He then ordered the Flamingos back to the field and ruled that both runs counted.[24]

Medwick exploded out of his dugout, and not so kindly advised the umpiring crew that he was playing the game under protest. Trying to appease the situation the umpires huddled and decided to allow only one run, and ordered Tripp to return to third base. Adding more confusion to the proceedings, both arbiters stated that Tripp would have to return to second base as Cates had interfered with the play because he picked up the loose ball. Martin then went into a second diatribe and argued that the ball was already dead and that the runs should count. Pepper then informed the umpiring crew that he was also playing the game under protest. the Flamingos ended up winning handily, 11 to 4, and ultimately the matter dropped.[25] Nonetheless, the stage was set for some of the fiercest competition between the two rivals, and the bad blood between the combatants would carry on through the rest of the season.

The teams exchanged profanity-laced insults on the night of April 22, a game that Miami won 8 to 5. Tempers again erupted when the rivals met again on April 23 at Flamingo Park. The building tension came to a boil in the seventh inning after pinch-hitter Bill Burda doubled, Conroy followed with an RBI single. Jim Long then stroked another base hit and Conroy advanced to third. Pitcher Lopez, seeing Conroy taking a generous lead at third, tried a pick-off throw, but instead threw wild. Rather than retrieving the ball, Hyman Prosk the Miami third baseman fell on Conroy impeding his efforts to go home. During the ensuing struggle, Conroy injured his left shoulder and the umpire ruled interference allowing Conroy to score. This, of course, stoked the fires of discontent.[26]

In the eighth frame, Frank Brown scored on an errant throw by Medwick from the outfield. The ball bounded into the Miami dugout and when third baseman Long tried to retrieve the ball from the dugout, he found himself confronted by Brown. Soon the two traded punches, which started the melee that cleared both benches. It took five minutes to restore order and in the end, Brown, his teammate George Boston, and Long, all received the heave-ho for fighting. Rosa joined them for good measure for his use of abusive language.[27] The Flamingos came out on top in 11 innings, 5 to 4.

Martin and his Sun Sox were gaining quite a reputation around the league for their aggressive attitude and play. Martin and his charges' tirades continued as the season wore on. Not lost on Miami fandom was the effect Pepper's leadership had on his club. It showed positive results as the Sun Sox battled Tampa and Havana for the league's top spot.

On May 14 at Gran Stadium, Miami came off an especially frustrating defeat the night before as Mel Nee lost his decision to the Cuban's Julio "Jiquí" Moreno, 2 to 1. In the second inning, sure-handed shortstop Kitsos took exception to a called third strike, which quickly drew "old Pep" out of the dugout resulting in a red-hot exchange of words and then the heave-ho. Catcher Armando Valdes continued where his teammate Kitsos left off and, in short order, was escorted off the field. Despite all of the bluster, Havana won a ninth consecutive game, and third in a row against the visitors, the final result was 6 to 0.[28]

Opponents and umpires felt Martin's wrath when it came to his desire to win ballgames. Gale Wade remembers an incident in Miami Field when his fiercely passionate skipper set one of his young teammates straight for lack of hustle.

> And I remember one story there in that old ballpark next to the Orange Bowl. I don't remember who we were playing, but I believe we had a shortstop and I think his name was Chris Kitsos . . . Anyway, a guy hit a ground ball between second and where the shortstop was and he was to the left of second base. And of course, I'm coming in to field, naturally. But Chris should've got it, but he short-legged it.
>
> When he did, Pep was sitting in our dugout over on the third base side and it had a little wooden post or steel post in front of it, and Pep he came off the bench and wham! He went head first into one of those posts. He was heading out to get Kitsos. God yeah, he was going out after him, no question, but it hit him and it knocked him down and so he didn't get out there and we were all concerned about it.
>
> Anyway, we lost the game and after the game, we were taking our showers . . . Pep, his little office was on the back end of our clubhouse there, and he had to walk through there to go down to the showers. Well, now we have little old benches, little old long benches in front of our lockers . . . and Pep he comes a walking and he was a physical specimen . . . here he comes walking down with no clothes on going to the shower and he's still mad at Kitsos see. And he gets close to the bench and where Chris is at, and Chris was talking to someone and kinda laughed. When he did, Pep grabbed him, and jerked him off the bench and right down on the floor he took him. Then, oh God, four or five of us got down there and we pulled him off him. He would've killed him I swear.
>
> Oh my gosh! So, we pulled him off of him and I'm telling you one thing. Chris, he never laughed or made anymore remarks, but Pep wouldn't put up with anybody that didn't hustle.[29]

By May 31, a mere four games separated front-running Havana (35–21) from fourth place Miami Beach (31–25); Tampa (33–23) trailed by two games and Miami (32–23) was 2½ in the arrears.[30] Driving the Flamingos' success were pitchers Del Monte (5–1) and Montero (7–4), together they accounted for nearly 40 percent of the team's wins. Miami Beach's offense was led by Medwick (.372, 17 RBIs), and Rotzell (.362, 30 RBIs), second and third in the league trailing Havana's Frank Campos. Also, emerging star Conroy was turning heads gathering 25 base knocks in his first 52 at-bats.[31] Yet, despite the trio's success the rest of the Flamingos offense was a moribund bunch and the team was next to last in the FIL in runs scored per game (4.12) ahead of only Lakeland (4.07).[32] Nevertheless, obtaining Medwick as player-manager proved a masterstroke by Joe Ryan and team ownership. Without Ducky's contribution offensively, and as a manager, it is safe to say that the team would have been a second division club.

In an effort to bolster his club offensively and defensively, Flamingos GM Ryan acquired 25-year-old shortstop Armando Gallart from Lakeland. Originally signed by Washington of the American League in 1945, Gallart was a fixture in the FIL having played for Miami and Tampa in 1947, and Lakeland from 1947 through June of 1949. He was also the veteran of four seasons in the Cuban Winter Leagues with Cienfuegos (1945–46, 1947–48, 1948–49), and Matanzas (1946–47).[33] The 6'2" rail thin Cuban native had seen his batting average slip close to the .200 mark with the Pilots after hitting .295 the year before. Ryan banked on the chance that a change of scenery would snap the slumping infielder out of his funk and provide a suitable replacement for Don Server and Bill Chandler who had both struggled in their roles at the shortstop position.

Miami Beach continued to play just over .500 ball throughout the summer. After a slow start losing 14 of their first 27 games, Havana re-established itself as the top team. Miami and Tampa fought hard to keep pace.

Even in the most testosterone competitively fueled season, important human events take a front seat and remind us of the beauty of life. Prior to the June 23 doubleheader with the Sun Sox at Flamingo Park, pitcher Ernesto Morilla met Nora Gonzalez at home plate to exchange the vows of marriage. The teammates, team personnel and FIL president O'Connell greeted the couple prior to the game. In a non-traditional, but time-honored ceremony, the bride and groom vowed to share their lives together. Owners Gans, Gardner, and Shapiro presented the new couple with a gift check of $250, and O'Connell touched by the moment got into the act by rescinding a $10 fine that he had levied against Morilla just days prior to the game for improper use of language. Although Miami swept the double dip winning 3 to 2 and 5 to 1, it was Morilla and his new wife that were the big winners of the day.[34][35]

Across town, the Sun Sox were winning more frequently than their cross-town rivals. As the dog days of summer progressed, both Miami Beach and Tampa slowly faded from contention leaving only Miami within striking distance of front-running Havana.

The Sun Sox (81–55) arrived in Havana on August 25 only 4½ games behind the Cubans (87–52). With only two weeks until the season's conclusion, for Miami every game was a must win. Martin especially was in a foul mood coming off the series at Miami Field in which his club dropped two of the three games to seventh place Lakeland. The most frustrating defeat came in the series-ender when the Pilots scored four unanswered runs in the ninth to come back and win 5 to 4 against Solis.

The opener of the three-game series favored Havana as the Cubans' ace Connie Marrero matched up against Earl Gray a 25-year-old southpaw jettisoned by Lakeland halfway through the season.

Miami struck first in the sixth inning when Bridgers singled with the first base knock of the night off Marrero. Rosa reached on Gil Torres' throwing error, and Frank Brown walked. Haviland then hit into what looked like an inning-ending double play, but shortstop Chino Hidalgo overthrew his peg to first base allowing Bridgers to score. The Sun Sox added to their lead in the eighth frame when Stammen trucked home on Rosa's triple to right center field. Gray danced around several Havana threats and scattered nine hits without allowing a run as Miami shut out the Cubans, 2 to 0.[36]

With an impending hurricane closing in on the east coast of Florida, which would eventually force the cancellation of the final games of the series, the teams took the field at Gran Stadium for the second contest. Both teams had no idea of the storm that was about to hit, but not of the meteorological kind.

Miami got the upper hand early gaining a 2 -1 lead going into the bottom of the fifth inning. Despite the advantage, throughout the game, Havana had been benefitting from close calls that caused Martin's blood pressure to rise. Gil "Chino" Valdivia reached base on a wild throw by shortstop John Jeandron and when Valdivia advanced to second safely on a close play, Rosa protested the call. Jiqui Moreno followed drawing a free pass. With Valdivia on second and Moreno on first, Cuban manager Oscar Rodriguez ordered a double steal that both players executed to perfection. However, Rosa, who was covering second base, exploded when he heard the call. The fiery second baseman vehemently argued that the tag beat the runner. Rosa chucked the baseball into right field and then threw his cap at the umpire, W.E. Williams. The umpiring crew ordered Rosa off the field, which drew the further ire of first baseman Tripp who began kicking dirt on the umpires. He was summarily ejected, and Martin was warned to get his team on the field. After a fifteen-minute delay, Martin refused to comply and the umpiring crew huddled before ordering the game forfeited to Havana. At that point, Martin had seen enough. To everyone's surprise "The Wild Horse of the Osage" approached umpire Clem Camia and then he grabbed him by the neck choking him. It took a contingent of police officers to get the red-faced Martin off the shocked arbiter and restore order to the field.[37][38]

Martin recalled the incident in a 1959 article in Rochester, New York's *Democrat Chronicle,* "I grabbed the umpire by the throat and started to squeeze. For a minute, I was going to kill the --- -- - -----. Then I said to myself, 'Lord, what am I doing?' and I let the --- -- - ----- go."[39]

Tripp who was ejected and later fined for the incident shared his memory of the unfortunate confrontation between his skipper and Camia.

> It was a shame because Pepper was a born-again Christian thirty years ahead of his time. But, he wouldn't swear, and he is standing there literally choking the umpire to death. And all he is saying is, "You insidious rat." You know he wouldn't violate that commandment, but thou shalt not kill was in jeopardy.[40]

For all intents and purposes, the Sun Sox's chances of ending Havana's drive for their fifth straight pennant ended that evening. On September 1, O'Connell suspended Martin for the remainder of the regular season and handed him a $100 fine. "Pep" as his players called him, would later admit that his conduct was unacceptable, recognized the error of his ways, and apologized for his indiscretions. His assistant coach and right-hand man Bill Cates took over the reins and guided the team through to the conclusion of the regular season. Miraculously, Martin received permission to return and manage his team for the playoffs. O'Connell fined Rosa $25 and Tripp $10 for their actions.[41]

Although there would be no pennant-winning celebration, the Sun Sox and the city of Miami had much to revel in. The completion of the much-anticipated opening of the state-of-the-art Miami Stadium had finally arrived.

On a seasonably pleasant warm August 31 evening, on the corner of Northwest 10th Avenue and 23rd Street in Allapattah, the neighborhood was abuzz with excitement. A brand new baseball palace (reported to have cost $1.4 million) had finally come to fruition. Regular folks and dignitaries filed through the shiny new turnstiles to see their Sun Sox take on the Havana Cubans.

As the crowd approached the stadium, directly over the main entrance, twelve 20-foot tall blaring orange neon letters greeted them, spelling out M-I-A-M-I S-T-A-D-I-U-M. Passing through the gates the sounds of the greater Miami Boys' Drum and Bugle Corps serenaded the incoming ticket holders as they viewed a bountiful assortment of potted plants and flowers beautifying the corridors, and an expansive mural depicting various athletic endeavors with a baseball contest highlighting its focal point.[42]

Once inside, walking up through the ramparts into the grandstand, uniformed ushers welcomed the patrons. The burst of emerald green field grass and brownish-orange tinted infield dirt that shaped the familiar dimensions of the playing field beckoned the eyes, as did the modern electric scoreboard in the outfield outlined by swaying palm trees. Looking up the distinctive 83-foot-high cantilever roof that wrapped itself around the first and third base sides offered no sight blocking girders and allowed for an unobstructed view for the 9,500 paying customers lucky enough to have purchased ducats for that location. Unique for its time, the roof design was the one and only of its kind in the United States.

Along both outfield foul lines were the open-air bleachers built to seat an additional 5,000. Notable features of the new ballpark reportedly included 137 rooms strategically placed throughout the stadium to accommodate front office personnel and special guests (some of the rooms featured shower stalls). There were lounges for the players, and their families, a well-stocked cocktail bar for patrons to purchase adult beverages, an elevator that transported the press from ground level up to the well-appointed press box, and oversized dugouts that featured tunnel access to locker rooms where each player had his own assigned, personal steel locker.[43] It was a stark contrast from Miami Field, where players dressed in a neighboring locker room away from the ball-park before traipsing to the field with its cramped dugout and austere wood benches protected by what resembled chicken wire.

Tripp recalled Miami Field and its eccentricities.

> The old one [Miami Field] was only 315 feet to center field be-cause it was adjacent to the Orange Bowl. When they expanded the Orange Bowl, the ramp cut into center field. In fact, our dressing room was in the Orange Bowl. Yeah, there was a gate and the fence was only five or six feet tall. There was a gate we walked through to get to the ball field.[44]

With the exception of a few unfinished seats, two non-operational tower lights flanking the press box, and approximately a third of the synchronized light bulbs not working, the opening went off without a hitch.[45]

Several dignitaries and notables had toured the ballpark before game time. Prominent among the attendees were MLB Commissioner A. B. "Happy" Chandler, dean of umpires Bill Klem, Fresco Thompson, head of the Brooklyn Dodger farm system, FIL president Phil O'Connell, city of Miami Mayor Robert "Bob" Floyd, Mayor W. Keith Phillips of Coral Gables, Dade County Commissioner Hugh Peters, and Florida Congressman George Smathers. Also, Cuba sent its own contingent of 300 people to en-joy the festivities that included, Cuban Consul to Miami, Manuel Velasquez, Senator Carlos Prío-Socarrás, Cuban Winter League President, Antonio Mesa, and Havana Cubans' team president, Merito Acosta.[46][47]

Over the course of the night where so many shone brightly, the most dazzling star of the evening was young Jose Aleman Jr., the majority stockholder of Miami's new stadium and con-trolling interest holder in the Sun Sox. The 17-year-old, son of Jose Manuel Aleman, the former minister of education in Cuba, was gifted the stadium by his father. The young man expressed his intentions of attracting big-time baseball to Miami.[48] It must have been a bittersweet evening for the young Aleman, whose father was battling a terminal illness while at the same time being dogged by the Cuban government for misappropriation of $174 million in funds.[49]

As the scheduled game time of 8:30 approached the introduction of the luminaries in their prime seats proceeded. Caught up in the excitement of the evening's events, Chandler told the crowd, "I know no more beautiful baseball park in the whole country."[50] With all eyes glued on the playing field, the Drum and Bugle Corps played, "To the Colors," followed by Indian Princess Wah Nese Red Rock singing her rendition of the National Anthem, and concluding with the organist's offering of the Cuban National Anthem.

Slated by skipper Martin to face Havana's 30-year-old veteran Rogelio "Limonar" Martinez (his nickname acquired from the town he was from) was twenty-year-old, right-hander Vicente Lopez, a fellow countryman who was no stranger to the opposition having faced most of them during the winter chucking in the Cuban Winter Leagues. Martinez was in the prime of his career and only one year away from making his major league debut with the Washington Senators.[51]

With all the official pleasantries out of the way, the home plate umpire bellowed, "Let's play ball," and the public address announcer blared out the name of the first official batter to appear in Miami Stadium-"Now batting, Jose Zardon." The first pitch, a ball, christened the first game.[52] The offering was one of the few errant tosses the youthful Lopez threw all evening.

The Sun Sox came out fired up in their half of the first inning. Bridgers led off the inning by grounding sharply to the Cubans' shortstop Hidalgo. The usually sure-handed infielder misplayed the ball allowing Bridgers to reach first base. Martin ordered the next hitter, Rosa to lay down a sacrifice bunt, no doubt impatient to score the first run in the new park. Rosa delivered. First Baseman Justo Azpiazu fielded the ball cleanly, but while running over to cover first base, Martinez collided with second baseman Frank Gallardo and dropped the ball allowing Rosa to reach safely. The usually stalwart Cubans resembled the Keystone Cops more than the veteran club they were. Switch-hitting Frank Brown continued the assault drilling a single to left field as Bridgers rushed home with the game's first run. Martinez retired Haviland on a groundout, but Brown moved up to second while Rosa clung to third. The next hitter, Benny Moore singled to right field just in front of Hiram Gonzalez plating two more runs. Martin, sensing an early kill ordered Moore to steal, which he promptly did. After Martinez induced Tripp to pop out, Jeandron connected for

another single allowing Moore to cross the plate increasing the
lead to 4 to 0. Jeandron advanced to second base when Hidalgo
let the relay throw get past him, his second miscue of the evening.
Stammen followed and intentionally walked to get to Lopez the
ninth batter of the inning who then lined out to Hidalgo to close
the books on the initial frame."[53]

The Sox built on their lead in the second inning. Following
singles by Rosa and Haviland, Moore doubled past Zardon in center field, plating two tallies and giving him his third and fourth ribbies of the night. Rodriguez had seen enough and pulled Martinez
handing the ball to 38-year-old Izzy Leon.[54]

The Cubans' troubles continued as Lopez escaped jams in almost every inning. Thanks to three double plays and outstanding
efforts by his outfield trio of Brown, Haviland, and Moore who
handled six chances in the new and more spacious outfield, despite nine hits by Havana, they managed only one run in the
ninth inning. Lopez went the route without any relief help and
garnered the complete game win and honor of being the first
winning pitcher in Miami Stadium. The final score showed the
Sun Sox the victors, 6 to 1.[55] Cuban manager Oscar Rodriguez
commented to a reporter whether his team was nervous playing in front of 13,007 fans. He pooh-poohed the thought saying,
"Nervous? We play before 25,000 sometimes in Havana."[56]

By all accounts, the grand opening of the new ballpark was a
smash hit. *The Miami News* described the stadium as "colossal"
and "stupendous." Several players chimed in with their own accolades. "I've been in quite a few parks," said right fielder Benny
Moore, "but this easily the finest. Geez, this is great." His fellow
fly-chaser Haviland went so far as to say, "Listen, what's the use
of going higher. You got it right here."[57]

Although the official attendance announced was 13,007, the
actual count was closer to 14,000. Overflow crowds gathered in
the not-yet-completed bleacher sections. According to the *Miami
News*, "fully 750 passed in free to swell the crowd . . ." This count
included Commissioner Chandler, dignitaries, club presidents,
press and radio, etc.[58]

One sad fact that tarnished an otherwise perfect evening was
that African-American fans attending the game felt the sting of
denying them access to many of the creature comforts inside
Miami Stadium. In 1949, Miami had a much different demo-
graphic than today. The population was predominately white

and many were still attached to the old southern ways of thinking, including the enforcement of Jim Crow laws. As an example, separate parking two blocks from the entrance, and only seating along the right-field foul line designated with "For Colored Only" signs.[59] Regrettably, it would not be until the 1960s, the Civil Rights Act of 1964 that public consciousness and change of attitudes changed the circumstances. The city that currently prides itself on the appreciation of diversity with large populations of people of various colors, creeds, cultures, and nationalities in 1949 excluded a large part of the black community from participating in that historical day.

Team owners in the FIL had up to that moment, not made any efforts toward the integration of black ballplayers. Although many Cuban players were of the light-skinned variety, even they felt the occasional sting of taunts and racial comments directed by mean-spirited fans. Nevertheless, change would eventually come.

With the stadium grand opening now behind them, the second place Sun Sox looked forward to trying to wrest the league crown from the Cubans. Across town, Miami Beach (80–71) limped into the Shaughnessy playoffs just edging out Tampa (81–72), taking third place. In an unusual setup by league officials, they decided that the first and third place and second and fourth place teams meet in the initial round of playoffs in a best-of-five series with the winners squaring off in a best-of-seven series to decide the championship. The Flamingos would take on Havana, while Miami would matchup against Tampa.

Returning to the helm, following his garroting incident, Martin was ready and eager to guide his Sun Sox into the playoffs. Having played just over .500 since July 4, the Smokers looked like easy pickings. Tampa's banishment of their ace Covington to Class D Palatka after reports of dissension in the clubhouse left the Smokers' staff as thin as lathe shavings.[60] With ace Vicente Lopez, taking the mound the betting odds favored the hometown club. Miami matched Tampa hit for hit, but their inability to string consecutive base knocks together cost them dearly. Bob Swanson (18–10, 2.24)[61] was masterful and limited Miami to six singles and a pair of doubles while striking out five during the 4 to 1 win.[62]

Game two, the Sun Sox evened the series thanks to a brilliantly pitched performance by Tata Solis. The crafty Cuban spun a three-hitter and struck out six. Miami broke out of a seventeen-inning scoreless streak in the ninth inning when Rosa reached on a base on balls, advanced to second on Frank Brown's sacrifice, and then raced home on Haviland's single. The final tally showed Miami on the positive side, 1 to 0.[63]

Games three and four moved to Tampa. The Sun Sox offense exploded for ten runs at Plant Field in the road opener, but regrettably, four Miami pitchers could not contain the Smokers as they outscored the visitors, earning a hard-fought 13 to 10 victory.[64] The Sun Sox's offense reverted to their previous hitting struggles in game four. Miami was throttled in the finale by Smokers' diminutive right-hander Oscar Del Calvo (13–11, 3.26) who held the Sun Sox to four hits in the 15 to 0 thrashing.[65] [66]

Miami Beach was involved in their own tense playoff confrontation. Marrero (25–8, 1.53)[67] was coming off a magical season for which if the FIL had a Cy Young Award he would have been the runaway winner. Opening up at Gran Stadium it was almost a guarantee that the Cubans ace would win the lid-lifter. His opponent on the mound was Andy Daly (10–6, 2.74) a 25-year-old right-sider who had faced the Havana club before with success.[68] Daly was up to the task and pitched his best game of the season. Despite walking five hitters and allowing six hits, he was magic in the clutch and smothered every rally when it counted. A key Medwick double and a couple of clutch base hits from Emilio Cabrera led the attack as the Flamingos stunned their neighbors to the south, 4 to 1.[69]

Havana bounced back to win the second game. Sandalio "Sandy" Consuegra,[70] who later went on to an eight-year major league career, persevered for eleven innings against Morilla before Hidalgo stroked a bases-loaded single in the bottom of the same frame to hand the Cubans the win. The Flamingos only managed four hits including a triple by Lewinski and a double by Server.[71]

The Cubans split the next two games in Miami Beach, winning game three 4 to 1, then losing the fourth 2 to 1 thanks to a fourth-inning Mike Milosevich blast over the left field fence following a Rotzell triple. Del Monte earned the win stingily giving up only six hits to his fellow compatriots.[72]

After a September 10 rainout, the deciding game the following day in Havana proved to be a nail-biter. Marrero and Daly renewed their match and true to form, both battled to a hard-fought conclusion. The Flamingos and Cubans matched each other for the first six innings both scoring a couple of runs. In the bottom of the seventh frame, Hidalgo safely bunted and advanced to second base on Lewinski's misplay at first. Daly then fanned Alejandro "Alex" Montesino with a third strike, but backup catcher Leonilo Marrero, who had replaced the sure-handed Cabrera, let the ball pass and in his confusion looking for the ball allowed Hidalgo enough time to come around and score what was ultimately the winning run.[73][74]

It seemed as if destiny was in the back pocket of Havana, but fate has a way of altering history. In stunning fashion, the Smokers swept the heavily favored Cubans in four straight games, denying them their third title. It was Tampa's second championship since the inception of the league, and the most unlikely one in the short history of the FIL.

Although Miami and Miami Beach fell short in their quest for the title of FIL champs, there were accomplishments and accolades handed out to the local boys. Mike Conroy proved to be a hitting machine. The Quincy, Massachusetts native was the first to win a batting title by a Flamingo; he finished the campaign with a .359 average edging out Miami's Rosa by .002, and earned himself a trophy for his efforts.[75] While across the bay in Miami, although there were no individual league leaders in any offensive or pitching categories from the Sun Sox roster, East Lansing native speedy Dick Haviland batted a steady .288 and was second in the league in outfield assists (23),[76] a tribute to defensive prowess. In a close voting race, Haviland edged out Rosa as the team's most popular player. Jimmy Burns of the *Miami Herald* described Haviland as one of the best players in the FIL and added, "Haviland has a great arm as he's demonstrated on more than one occasion . . . Dick patrols his territory with the keen-eyed agility of a hawk seeking prey."[77] His reward for his all-out hustle and exemplary play earned him a brand new wristwatch.[78]

The future of minor league baseball in Miami looked bright. Leading the way, a wealthy, albeit, youthful owner had ample resources at his disposal. His solid affiliation with the Dodgers offered the Sun Sox a steady stream of excellent young talent. Coupled with arguably the best facility in the minors, positioned the Sun Sox to knock Havana off their throne. Yet, what was possibly the most important acquisition during the offseason was not a player, but the re-signing of manager, Pepper Martin. For the first time, Miami had a manager returning for a second season to his post.[79] The decision to bring back the fiery Martin would prove to be a fortuitous choice reaping positive results.

Miami Beach's ownership future seemed less sunny. Although GM Ryan, an eternal optimist, felt he could compete with the Sun Sox, and the Cubans', it was clear that he had a much tougher row to hoe without ties to a major league team. Ryan's success in signing quality players rested on the ability to draw fans into the seats to create revenues. Regrettably, since the league's inception, the Flamingos had failed to draw over 100,000 fans during a season, which would have allowed the financial leverage to ink better talent.

Although the Flamingos attendance increased from 78,742 to 90,682,[80] Ryan felt that it did not warrant bringing back their biggest gate attraction. Following the unsuccessful playoff performance, with accusations by fans and a local scribe of suspect managerial decisions during the postseason, Medwick was handed his release.[81] The perennial search for a new skipper was on Ryan's full list of things to do in what would prove to be a busy winter.

Final Standings

TEAM	W	L	GB
Havana	95	57	–
Miami	87	62	6.5
Miami Beach	81	70	13.5
Tampa	81	72	14.5
West Palm Beach	74	78	21
Fort Lauderdale	65	88	30.5
St. Petersburg	62	86	31
Lakeland	60	92	35

1950

Miami's state-of-the-art stadium was the talk of the baseball world. According to *The Miami News*, the facility cost $2 million, $600,000 more than they had reported. At the same time, the Flamingos were entrenched as the poor stepchild that struggled to keep their heads above troubled financial waters.

The usual talk about both team's chances for a pennant seemed subdued as attention was increasingly focused on Miami

Stadium and its beautiful accommodations. Jose Aleman Jr. had entrusted his right-hand men Harry B. Taber Sr., as club president, and John W. Hamill, secretary-treasurer, with the task of ensuring the Sun Sox and the new ballpark be an immediate success. Judging by the early results of increased attendance during spring training games the future looked bright.

Two exhibition games were staged in the spring between the Brooklyn Dodgers and the Boston Braves, which drew an aggregate crowd of 25,498. The most impressive number came soon afterward when on March 17, a Dodgers versus Yankees match drew an overflow throng of 17,554 patrons; exceeding the stadium's capacity by over 500. At this point, Aleman's goal of bringing top flight, if not major league baseball to Miami, and strengthening its place as an attractive spring training site, seemed an attainable dream.[82]

Despite the fact that construction kinks existed prior to the 1949 grand opening, Miami Stadium drew rave reviews. Some of the most interesting amenities were the lavish press box complete with modern divans, tiled floor to ceiling restrooms throughout the structure, parquet wood floors in the locker rooms surrounded with floor to ceiling tiles, and comfortable home, visitor, and umpire lounges to kick back and relax in. Upon seeing the ballyard for the first time Yankees manager Casey Stengel glowingly expressed, "Considering the excellence of the playing field and the magnificence of the stands I have never seen anything like this." Bobby Hogue of the Boston Braves, who started his professional career in 1940 with the Miami Wahoos and could still remember the stark conditions of Miami Field, jokingly raved after touring the various conveniences, "We Boston players are going to strike until they give us a Class B clubhouse."[83]

Almost lost in the optimism of the time was the passing of the senior Jose Aleman on March 25. His massive fortune, an inheritance bequeathed to his son, had made it possible for the marvelous Miami Stadium to be constructed. The elder Aleman left his son an estimated $70,000,000 to $200,000,000; including $20,000,000 of property in the Miami area. His rise to power from an obscure clerical position to Head of Cuba's Ministry of Education was checkered with accusations of misappropriating government funds. He was also accused of taking part in an attempt to overthrow the government of the Dominican Republic, and organizing the successful campaign that brought Carlos

Prío-Socarrás to power as president of Cuba. He owned the Marianao baseball team, an airline, and a sugar mill. Aleman died from a blood ailment related to pseudo-leukemia at the age of 44.[84]

It must have been an emotional roller coaster ride for the younger Aleman. In a span of just over six months, he saw his dream for a palatial stadium come to fruition only to lose his precious father. Still, life went on for the ambitious teenager who continued attending the University of Miami seeking a degree in Business Administration. He had even tried out for the university's baseball team exhibiting some skills that he acquired while playing at Worcester (Massachusetts) Academy.[85]

Aleman took a great deal of consolation in his relationships with the Cuban ballplayers on the Sun Sox. Known as being quite generous with all of his players, especially his fellow compatriots, Aleman supplied the living arrangements for several players at the Iroquois Apartments, one of many which he owned. Even Pepper Martin had his own place at a nearby location, which worked out quite well because Martin was notorious for enlisting his players to join him on one of his many after-game and early morning fishing jaunts.[86]

Dick McCoy, one of the star pitchers for the Miami club, was familiar with Martin who was instrumental in his signing a contract to play professional baseball. He shared one of his favorite fishing outing stories with Pepper.

> They had two or three different apartment houses in that area and Pepper comes up one day with a frame of a Plymouth; just a frame with headlights and no fenders. "What are you going to do with that," I said. He (Martin) says, "We'll fix it up and then we go fishing." There was no windshield, no nothing, no gauges, and so he kept coming over to our apartment in the parking lot and we built a little box on the back where somebody could ride. In addition, off we would go at 4 o'clock in the morning down the Tamiami Trail going fishing in that car. And we had goggles and bandanas on because of the bugs, and one thing and the other . . . We made many a trip in that old car.[87]

Jim Ackeret, who joined the club early in the season, received a quick baptism into Martin's exploits into the pursuit of game fish. He vividly recalled his most memorable excursion with his adventurous skipper.

> Oh yeah, I remember one time he went fishing up around Lake Okeechobee. And he had a trailer. And he had a flat tire on the trailer and he unhitched it and came back to Miami. And he picked me up, and another ballplayer; I don't remember his name. But he said, "Let's go out and get that trailer and find it." So we went out around Lake Okeechobee and we never did find it. I think some farmer picked it up and hooked it up and took it home . . . He had a lot of fishing really nice guy, Pepper Martin.[88]

Teammate Gale Wade recalled one of his own fishing experiences with Martin, who he fondly called "Pep." Martin so loved to fish that he had to be reminded he had a job back as a manager of his club.

> Oh, he was tied up in fishing . . . Pep liked to fish. And we'd go out, you know the old road from Miami across to Naples; the old Tamiami Trail. That used to be the road you know, the main road, and on each side of the road, there was these canals. And Pep, he would want me to go fishing with him. And I didn't care too much about fishing, but he wanted me to go and so I went with him. And we went out there and we'd fish and catch these fish. And finally, it got along late in the evening; you know late in the afternoon and finally I told him, I says, "Pep, we got a game." [laughing heartily] He just about forgot we got a ballgame to play.[89]

Martin grew comfortable with his surroundings and was overjoyed when the Brooklyn Dodgers brass re-assigned him to manage the Sun Sox for a second season. Between angling, working on cars, and welding, Martin was finding time to build the Sun Sox into a team that would finally knock Havana off its perch.

A cache of returning veterans including pitchers; Vicente Lopez, Mickey Mihalik, Arturo Seijas, infielder Barney Bridgers, Knobby Rosa, and outfielder John Walker solidified the club that also featured a group of experienced minor leaguers including pitchers. Prominent amongst the staff were Laban "Labe" Dean (8–14, 4.14), an Arkansas native, unrelated to his famous counterpart

Dizzy Dean, came from Newport News of the Piedmont League, and Billy "Buck" Darden (15–6, 3.56) from Asheville of the Tri-State League. The remainder of the roster featured three highly rated prospects, third baseman Jim Ackeret (.282 in 98 games), catcher Warren Patterson (.300, 7, 73) from Newport News, and first sacker Milt Ticco from the Cincinnati Reds affiliate Sunbury of the Class B Interstate League. Ackeret, known for his steady glove work at the hot corner received high marks with offense and defense after sharing time with Hartford of the Class A Eastern League, and St. Petersburg of the FIL previous season.[90] Ticco gained prior fame for his exploits on the hardwood, rather than on the infield dirt. The former All-American forward from the University of Kentucky surprised his critics when he traded in his canvas Converse sneakers for cleats in 1946. He quickly developed the agility to handle first base duties while yielding an effective war club. During his fourth season with Sunbury of the Class B Interstate League, he batted a steady .274 while clubbing nine home runs and driving in 74.[91][92]

Under newly named player-manager Jerry Crosby, the Flamingos brought back its own familiar cast. Chico Morilla returned for an unprecedented fourth season. Upon arriving in Miami Beach for spring training the diminutive Cuban ace was greeted by Juan Montero, in his third season with the club, and second-year returnees, catcher Emilio Cabrera, FIL batting champ Mike Conroy, first baseman Ed Lewinski, as well as pitchers Andy Daly and Gaspar Del Monte.

Crosby was coming off his tenth season in the minors having finished his first season as a player-manager for the Anniston Rams of the Class B Southeastern League.[93] Crosby took over the Aniston club on May 11 from Charles Baron, who had served as Miami's manager during part of the 1947 season, and despite being unable to get the club out of second division, he stayed focused and hit an impressive .289 while belting 14 home runs in 95 games.[94]

One new pink bird prospect grabbing the most attention in camp was an ebullient trumpet player from Brockton, Massachusetts, Lou Colombo. Colombo enlisted in the Army in 1944 and exhibited his talent by playing his instrument in the military band. Shortly after his honorable discharge, he was signed by the Brooklyn Dodgers in 1945, before being acquired by the St. Louis Cardinals organization prior to the 1949 season. In order to acquire the

sweet-swinging outfielder, Colombo hit .282 and clubbed ten homers the year before, GM Ryan traded veteran shortstop Gallart to
Columbus of the Sally League.[95] The trade would prove to be fortuitous. The talented Brocktonite would bring sweet music to the
fans and his teammates in Miami Beach not only with his bat but
with his horn. Later, when he hung up his cleats Colombo made
the scene as a jazz legend, and one of the worlds' great trumpet players playing with the likes of Benny Goodman, Gillespie
Damaso Perez Prado, and the Artie Shaw Orchestra.[96]

Colombo rapidly made his presence known teaming up with
a fearsome threesome of hitters including Rotzell and Lewinski.
Together the threesome fueled Miami Beach's quick start out
of the gate. At one point the club won nine consecutive games.
Combined, the trio accounted for 46 RBIs in the first 19 games;
Rotzell leading the way with 16 and Lewinski and Colombo with
15 apiece, they were playing all the right notes. Seven regulars in
the lineup were hitting over .280 including Ray Sowins leading
the club with a .346 batting mark.[97] On April 23, the Flamingos
(14–5) were tied with Tampa at the top of the FIL. Havana was
only a half game to the rear, and Miami (12–7) had their sights set
on the top spot only two games off the pace.[98]

However, Miami Beach's stay on the top would be short-lived.
The next day, Havana again established their dominance moving
back into the top spot when Rogelio Martinez earned his fourth
straight win holding the Flamingos to five hits during the 8–2
victory.[99] Havana would not relegate the league lead the rest of
the season. Miami Beach went into a slump dropping five of six
games sending them into a tie with Miami for fourth place.

Miami had expectations of competing, but instead were struggling to find their rhythm. After a 6 to 1, May 11 loss to Havana
at Miami Stadium the Sun Sox record dipped to 17–20 tied with
Lakeland for fifth place. Martin previously stated in spring training that he did not have as strong a team as in 1949, and so far,
the results were in keeping with his opinion. Nonetheless, Pepper
and Sun Sox management knew that Brooklyn would supply reinforcements and they would spend the money if it meant W's.
Ultimately, this proved true and the Sun Sox made moves that
bolstered their club.

Arguably, the best transaction made by Miami was the purchase of outfielder, Paul Armstrong. Standing a modest 5'9" and
just a shade over 150 pounds, the speedy outfielder had spent

the previous four campaigns with the Memphis Chicks of the Class AA Southern Association. A two-time all-star, he batted a cumulative .305 during his time in the "Bluff City."[100] His steadying veteran's presence and consistent hitting proved invaluable the remainder for the Sox.

Miami Beach was experiencing their own troubles not only in the win column but attracting fans. According to the *Sporting News*, Syd Gans said that he might confer with H. B. Taber Sr. of Miami to see about shifting some of their home games from Flamingo Park to Miami Stadium to bolster sagging attendance.[101] Many Flamingos home games drew less than 1,000 and reflected the overall league situation that included six of the eight clubs reporting a cumulative decline of 76,116 for the first month of the season. Lakeland and St. Petersburg were the two cities in the plus column.[102] By the season's end, the overall number of tickets sales at Flamingo Park would drop from 90,682 to 47,278.[103]

Oddly, the reason why several of the owners in the FIL felt they were experiencing a decline in attendance centered on Havana's domination of the league. Butch Henline, a former National League umpire working in the league assessed, "The Cubans could hold their own in a Class A league."[104] Indeed, eleven players on the Havana roster had major league experience or later went on to play in the big leagues.[105]

The only dissenters were Tom Spicola of Tampa, who benefited from rivalry based on the large Cuban population in Tampa, and Miami's H. B. Taber who originally supported expelling Havana. Taber later softened his stance but oddly stated, "It would be suicide to put Havana out of the league." After reviewing that 28% of their attendance was when the Cubans came to town, he added, "But it would be suicide to keep them." Havana had won every league title since its inception and two outright championships. The Cubans were well on their way to a fifth title. President O'Connell's response was to put the matter off until the winter meetings.[106]

In the continuing saga of troubles in Miami Beach, Jerry Crosby resigned as manager of the Flamingos on May 28 and was replaced by former Detroit Tiger Jimmy Outlaw. Speculation was that the former Bengal, who had been signed by the club 11 days before, had been brought in to replace Crosby. Reports were denied by team officials and Crosby said the decision was made on his own and came without any pressure from club officials.

Crosby had also been struggling with injuries and his .188 batting average was the lowest in his 10-year career. He took much of the blame for the team's struggles based on his lackluster performance.[107] Regardless of the reasons, Outlaw took over the reins of the club for the remainder of the season.

For Martin and his Sun Sox, their fortunes began to change for the better. Miami won 12 out of 17 games to close out May and by June 30 were solidly in third place with a 47–38 record, six games behind Tampa (53–32) for second place, and fifteen games in arrears to Havana (62–23).

The super-competitive Martin was tough on his players and demanding that they play with the same spirit that he had so exemplified during his playing days. Yet, at the same time, he instilled in his men that they should also love and respect the game and play with joy. McCoy recalled how Pepper schooled him, and several of his teammates in the clubhouse, on the finer art of winning, not on the field, but on a ping-pong table.

> He was so competitive sometimes instead of going out and having batting practice and stuff (pauses) Miami had a brand new stadium. It was state of the art. They had parquet floors and everything. And they had ping-pong tables. He [Martin] was the only one that played ping-pong. He was good at it and he liked to beat ya. Instead of having batting practice he would have ping-pong games.[108]

One of the strangest sights of the season came on June 10 when management decided to dress Martin and his assistant Bill Cates in something new, striking white baseball shorts and rayon jerseys. Earlier that year, on April Fools' day, the Hollywood Stars of the Pacific Coast League donned short togs against the Portland Beavers.[109] Seeing the knock-kneed Wild Horse was worth the price of admission. Although Martin was embarrassed by the stunt, he agreed to participate if it helped to bring extra fans into the stands.[110]

From July 1 to the end of the season, the Sun Sox went on a tear by winning 22 of 31 games in July. Leading the way on the mound was the workhorse Dean (12–7), and McCoy (9–3). Lurking in the wings was Vicente Lopez (6–6) who was about to put together a run that would spark the team even further. Miami's biggest problem was its anemic offense, which ranked fifth in the league and had by June 25 accounted for 324 runs well behind league leader Tampa with 465 tallies. Not one of the Sun Sox regulars was over .300; the highest average being Warren Patterson with a .293 average.

Not shy to improve their team, Miami made another move that would have positive repercussions on their fortunes. For several weeks' the Sun Sox made inquiries about purchasing Miami Beach's Rocky Rotzell but had been unable to make a deal with their rivals, even offering $4,000 for the Flamingos star. Then on July 28 financial concerns got the better of Miami Beach, and they agreed to sell Rotzell for the sum of $5,000 to Miami. "The sale was forced upon us by poor attendance," said Sam Shapiro club president. He added, "We had to salvage something some- place." Sadly, the sale came on the heels of a six-game winning streak that would prove to be a last gasp effort to catch Miami and Tampa in the standings.[111]

The Rotzell deal was the second major move based on cash concerns that the Flamingos had made having previously on June 22, traded Lewinski to the Asheville Tourists for Walter "Mouse" Halsall and an unknown disclosed amount of cash.[112]

With Rotzell and Armstrong now sparking the offense, the Sun Sox set their sights on Havana and grabbing the top spot. Dean had been the club's mainstay and ace, but emerging after a so-so start was Vicente Lopez. On June 26, Lopez was knocked out of the box by Tampa in the eighth inning before surrendering the mound to Mihalik.[113] It was a tough 6–3 loss for the tempera- mental Cuban and his sixth of the year, but it would be his last. In his next start on June 29, in front of 3,754 at Miami Stadium, Lopez allowed nine scattered hits, but stingily did not give up a run as the Sun Sox triumphed, 4 to 0. The usually light-hitting shortstop Gus Montalbano coaxed three hits, an RBI and scored a run in support of his teammate[114] He would go on to win the next fourteen games in a row achieving what turned out to be his only 20 win season in his career.

Miami had been planted in third place most of the season. Finally, on August 7, the Sun Sox leap-frogged Tampa into sec- ond place; it did not come easy. While Tampa was losing to Miami Beach at Flamingo Park 5 to 3, their fourth straight loss, the Sun Sox were going into extra innings at St. Petersburg. After nine frames both clubs stood at five runs apiece, the Sun Sox were the recipients of three gift unearned runs thanks to two Saints' errors.[115]

In the top of the seventeenth, Armstrong started with a double to left field. Rotzell then popped up, but Don Siegert followed with a single to break the tie score. With one out Ackeret flied out. With Siegert running on the pitch Ticco singled to right field. Ticco in his attempt to stretch his base hit into a double was caught between first and second thanks to Roxie Humberson's perfect throw to the infield. Ticco masterfully stayed in the rundown until Siegert could score giving the Sun Sox an insurance run.[116]

Vicente Lopez, who had relieved Jack Gutierrez after the fourth, retired the first batter in the bottom half of the seventeenth, but then gave up a single to Humberson and double to Don Pope putting runners on second and third base. Martin had seen enough of the weary Lopez and called on Dean to squelch the rally and end the night. Dean was up to the task and fanned John Sinnott, then coaxed Bob Jarmon into a groundout to end the game. The result was the longest contest at Al Lang Field since the Saints joined the FIL.[117] Miami (76–48) stood only 6½ games behind Havana (81–40) for top honors.

Miami continued on a torrid pace to season's end, but was unable to catch a talented Havana club that nearly matched them game for game; the Sun Sox won 22 of their last 29 games, while the Cubans won 20 of their last 29. During the closing weeks of the season, Dean won his twentieth of the season against Havana on August 5, out-dueling the league leaders for the 3 to 1 victory. Dean eventually closed out the season ledger with 24 W's winning his last game in relief during the opening game of the two-game set against the Cubans.[118]

On the last day of August, Vicente Lopez set a new league record by winning his 14th straight game, breaking Tony Lorenzo's record of 13, as he out-dueled Havana and Lorenzo, 2 to 0. The victory was especially sweet since it came versus his fellow countrymen and was the Sun Sox fire-baller's twentieth of the season. Lopez's shutout pulled Miami within three games of the top spot and left them with a chance, albeit a long shot, to wrestle the pennant from Havana.[119] Miami still had five games to play while Havana had only three contests left on their schedule.

Arturo Seijas kept the Sox's hopes alive the next day by mirroring Lopez's performance and whitewashing West Palm Beach, 6 to 0 in front of a scant crowd of 399 at Wright Field. Six Indian errors were the main culprit and welcome gift to Miami whose joy was soon dampened when Havana edged St. Petersburg, 1–0 to clinch at least a tie for the top spot.[120]

Finally, Havana clinched the top spot, and their fifth straight pennant, on September 2 when they swept both games of a doubleheader from the hapless Saints. While Miami fought to the end and behind McCoy, who finished the season with his sixteenth win, he went the route as the Sun Sox edged the Indians again on the road, 7 to 6. Upon finding out the results in Havana, the Sun Sox's mood turned darker than a stormy Miami night. But better days were to come.

Down the stretch, Tampa dropped out of the race finishing in third place dropping 14 of their last 27 games. Miami owed much of their success to St. Petersburg's ineptness as they swept them during the season taking all 22 games and thus setting a FIL record for perfection. In turn, Miami Beach limped through the finishing line at 77–72, looking forward and hoping for better results in the upcoming championship series.

Once again, the FIL continued the odd practice of matching the first place finishers against the third place team and the second place club against the fourth seed for the upcoming Shaughnessy playoffs. The first round series was best of five, followed by the championship best of seven. In this case, it pitted hated rivals against each other; Miami versus Miami Beach and Tampa against Havana.

The September 5 opener at Miami Stadium featured 24-game winner Labe Dean against a lanky southpaw from Puerto Rico, Adolfo "Bin" Torres (6–10, 3.08). Dean got off to an uncharacteristic slow start giving up a pair of runs in the first frame. The Miami batters finally warmed up in the fourth inning, the second go around with Torres, and knocked him out of the game by plating a trio of runs. A dejected Bin handed the ball over to Del Monte who fared none the better yielding another pair of tallies; one in the fifth and one in the eighth. Alternatively, after gathering himself from a tough first frame and giving up six hits in the first three innings, Dean dominated the rest of the way allowing only two hits in the last six innings and earning the win; the final being 5 to 2.[121]

The next day, Lopez continued his mastery over opponents by pitching a one-hitter in a hard-fought duel against Morilla. The Sun Sox broke through in the fourth inning getting back-to-back doubles by Armstrong and Rotzell. It would prove to be all the offense the Sox needed. In one of the strangest pitching lines you will see, Lopez walked six batters and only struck out one. The Flamingos only base knock came off the bat of Wilmer "Chappy" Chappell in the seventh frame. It was Lopez's fifteenth consecutive win, following fourteen that carried over from the regular season.[122]

The series switched to Miami Beach and peculiarly, it was the largest crowd of the series; 1,749. During the first two games held at Miami Stadium, the attendance had failed to surpass 1,500. It was by standards for the time a pitiful show of support for Miami's best season since the FIL's inception.[123] Anytime the Flamingos outdrew the Sun Sox was a rare event.

Martin, of course, was not thinking about how many people were in the seats. He was focused on wrapping up the series and moving on. His choice to start the third game was diminutive right-hander Seijas (14–8, 2.25) to square off against the towering 6'3" Bob Zachritz (15–7, 2.70) of Miami Beach.[124]

Always looking to keep his teammates loose, Dick McCoy good-naturedly teased his compadre Seijas. This strategy worked especially well on the night of September 7.

> Oh yeah, there was two Cubans; Lopez and Seijas. And Seijas I was always teasing him all the time. I'd say (in a Midwestern twang), "What's your name? Say Jes?" And he'd say, "No Mac; Say hoss." And I'd say, "Say Jess," again. I was the guy that would drive him nuts." [laughing heartily][125]

If Seijas had any case of nerves, the notion was quickly dispelled as he matched Zachritz inning for inning in zeroes through the first four innings. In the top of the fifth, and with two Sun Sox in scoring position, the next batter hit a ground ball that looked like a sure putout at the plate. Unfortunately, for the pink birds the toss-eluded catcher Reinaldo Corrales, who had replaced the always-reliable Emilio Cabrera earlier in the game, allowing both runners to score. It was all the runs that Seijas needed as he scattered seven hits dashing Miami Beach's hopes. There were plenty of handshakes and back slaps following the game during the celebration, but the Sun Sox knew the toughest test lay ahead as they waited to see how the outcome of the Havana-Tampa series played out.

A tropical cyclone the press labeled as a "baby hurricane," wreaked havoc with Havana and Tampa stretching out the games until September 10. Not as if the rain hadn't been troubling enough, but Tampa was playing the series under protest claiming that Havana was using an ineligible player, third baseman/pitcher Carlos "Patato" Pascual, brother of Camilo who was acquired by Havana. The complaint by Spicola was that Pascual had played with Big Spring of the Longhorn League on August 16 and 17 when he was supposed to be a member of the Cubans, a violation of league rules. Spicola, the Smokers' owner, was informed by O'Connell that he would toss out the first two games and agreed to let the teams replay both contests.[126]

Havana players and ownership were incensed. It set up a game three that proved to be a battle royale, with a home run by former major leaguer, Roberto Estalella proving to be the difference. The Cubans prevailed, 5 to 4 in what would have completed the sweep. But, in an odd twist to the protest verdict, Spicola conferred with O'Connell after his team lost to Havana for the third straight time, and despite winning the protest withdrew his complaint conceding the series to the Cubans. O'Connell praised Spicola saying, "one of the greatest shows of sportsmanship in the history of the league."[127] Spicola said, Havana beat us on the field and even though we won the protest it would have been useless to continue the playoff." It was another strange outcome in the ongoing saga of the always-bizarre FIL. With the decision reversed, the Cubans advanced to meet Miami for the league crown.[128]

In another odd arrangement to the curious FIL Shaughnessy playoffs, it was agreed that the championship games would all be played in Miami Stadium with a 2-3-2 format. Havana would be the home team for the first two games and last two games if the series were to go the full seven.

On September 11, the series for the whole bag of marbles kicked off in a peculiar fashion. It must have felt odd for the 4,453 fans in the stands to see Miami bat first and see Havana designated as the home team. Both managers chose their winningest pitchers to take to the bump. For Havana, Tony Lorenzo (17–10, 2.56) faced the Sun Sox's ace, Labe Dean.

Havana drew first blood tallying a single run in the bottom of the first inning. Miami answered in the second frame when after Rotzell and Siegert reached base on errors, and Ackeret drew a free pass putting "ducks on the pond." Ticco then singled sharply plating Rotzell and Siegert. Ticco then attempted to steal second, and upon see his teammate race for the steal, Ackeret broke for home stealing another run while his teammate was gunned out at second. The beat continued as the Sun Sox pounded Lorenzo for five runs and six hits in the first five innings. Rotzell's inside the park homer with a compadre aboard took the steam out of Havana in the fifth as the Dean spread out ten Cuban hits while allowing only two runs, in the opening night, 8 to 2 win.[129]

Lopez continued his dominance in game two, and once again silenced the Cubans bats. Miami scored six runs in the first four innings. In the opening frame, Montalbano and Rosa both hit singles. Rosa stole second and Montalbano scored when catcher Gilberto Valdivia's throw sailed into center field. Rosa tried to score but was nailed at the plate. Armstrong then hit a double and scored when Rotzell reached first base on an error. The inning proved to be all the offense that Miami needed as Lopez mowed through the Havana batting order.[130]

In the end, it was Lopez's fourth straight shutout and sixteenth consecutive win. He allowed only four hits during the whitewashing.[131] Although Lopez was regarded as a temperamental type, when focused, he had arguably the best stuff in the FIL. "There was something about a trait with some of these people," as Dick McCoy recalled. "If he didn't want to pitch, he'd have a headache or he'd be sick. Yeah, God, he was a good pitcher, but if he didn't want to pitch, or the moon phase wasn't right he'd get sick or something."[132] Fortunately, the moon over Miami was in the right phase.

Havana manager, Oscar Rodriguez made a surprising choice for the third game of the series. The Cubans' controversial late-season acquisition, Carlos Pascual, who American baseball fans also called "Patato" a derivation of his Cuban nickname, was chosen to face the Sox's Seijas. Although Pascual had been playing third base, he had begun to establish himself also as a decent pitcher with a 7–2 slate and 2.75 ERA in the notoriously hitter-friendly Class D Longhorn League. So impressed were the Washington Senators with his abilities that he was called up to the big club after the close of the FIL season for two late appearances.[133]

Pascual and Seijas matched scoreless stanzas through seven innings. In the eighth, Justo Azpiazu tripled and later scored on Estalella's long fly ball to break the deadlock. Miami failed to score in the bottom half of the same inning, and in the ninth a weary

Seijas allowed the bases to be loaded. This prompted Pep Martin to call on the lanky right-hander Darden, to extinguish the rally. The first batter he faced, Pascual, then helped his own cause with a no out, two-RBI single. Hiram Gonzalez followed with another singleton giving the Cubans a 4–0 lead. Miami scratched out a couple of runs in the bottom of the ninth, but it was too few, too late, as Havana prevailed, 4 to 2.[134]

A re-ignited Cuban squad was now looking to recapture the winning formula that drove them to the pennant. A confident Martin still had two aces up his sleeve for games four and five in Dean and Lopez scheduled to take their turns.

Dean, who had pitched 270 innings during the regular season, was approaching 300 for the year and concerns were beginning to surface whether or not he had the stamina for another quality start. Seemingly, up to the task, Dean relied on his defense for help as he gave up hits early, but was bailed out by fine defensive plays by Ackeret, Montalbano, and Rosa.

The Sun Sox put the first runs on the scoreboard in the bottom of the second inning. With two outs facing Lorenzo, Ackeret singled and stole second base. Ticco worked the count and was walked, followed by Patterson's base hit that scored Ackeret. With Dean, a .164 hitter during the regular season due up next, it looked as if Lorenzo would escape the inning with minor damage. Surprisingly, Dean slashed a single and Miami jumped to a 2 to 0 lead.[135]

Havana tied the score in the eighth, but in the bottom of the ninth, Ackeret doubled and reached third base on a sacrifice. Once again, Dean approached the plate, no doubt nervous, but came through in the clutch again with a single that garnered the Sun Sox the win and a commanding 3–1 edge in the series.[136]

Miami's confidence was spilling over the brim for the next day's game as the league's hottest pitcher Vicente Lopez took to the hill against Gil Torres (6–1, 1.27). Five thousand-seven hundred-seventy-seven fans filed into Miami Stadium, unbeknownst to them about to get more than their money's worth for the price of a ticket. The two Cuban hurlers battled for eight innings with neither yielding as much as a single run. Lopez put Havana down in the top of the ninth and at this point had given up only five hits. Torres confidently strolled to the mound for the bottom of the ninth poised to take his compadres into extra innings. However, the crack of the bat signaled trouble when Patterson hit one into the gap for a triple. George Tesnow followed and marched to the plate in an obvious high-pressure situation. Yet for the reserve infielder who had flown 65 combat missions over Germany during World War II as a U.S. Air Force bombardier, this was just a stroll in the park. What followed was pandemonium when he connected for a single, a walk-off winner. It set off a celebration that went on through the night. It was Miami's first championship since the Magicians took the FECL title in 1920.[137]

Elvie Darden, a newlywed in 1950 recanted in her quaint southern accent her memory of her husband and teammates' joyful celebration in the Miami Stadium clubhouse following the victory.

> They were all happy as they could be. And they, like I said, they had plenty to drink. And by the time the party was getting, they'd been there long enough they were beginning to feel their alcohol. Then they'd all start singing. Some would be singing and some would be talking, and some would be hugging . . . They had a good time and I enjoyed watching them because they was happy because they was getting a little extra money.[138]

For all intents and purposes, the Havana defeat spelled the end of their FIL dynasty. They would spend two more years battling it out in league play with less than positive results. However, better times lay ahead and by 1954 Havana secured a spot in the AAA International League just a step away from the major leagues.

Around the league, an alarm bell was sounding and reality was setting in that the FIL was facing financial difficulties. A sharp 22.7% drop in attendance tied to several factors including the boom of television watching that brought major league baseball into the comfort of peoples living rooms nationwide, and Havana's continued dominance that left fans in cities with much smaller populations such as Fort Lauderdale Lakeland and West Palm Beach with little hope of competing. Even Cuban fans seemed to have found winning monotonous, and they hungered for a higher level of play. Havana which had drawn over 200,000 fans every year since the FIL's inception, dropped to a low of 168,419.[139]

Lakeland, the smallest city in the circuit reported continuing financial losses. The Pilots were co-owned by forty members of the community and were ready to throw in the towel, but were saved by city leaders who agreed to $3,500 rebate on stadium rent that convinced the group of owners to hang on.[140]

The hardest hit of all of the cities was Miami Beach that experienced a 48% drop in their attendance from 90,682 in 1949 to 47,278.[141] Although GM Ryan had a done a yeoman's job of attracting talent on a shoestring budget, and putting a competitive team on the field, the community became indifferent to his club who played in an aging and rickety facility that paled in comparison to their neighbors across the causeway.

Finally conceding to mounting financial losses, a majority of the ownership group consisting of Sam Shapiro, Syd Gans, Maurice Gans, I.A Durbin, and four others agreed to sell their 33% interest in the Miami Beach club to a local automobile dealer, Leo Adeeb, and Joe Ryan.[142] Later, Carl Gardner would also sell his 33% share, while agreeing to stay on the club in a front office capacity.[143]

Adeeb and Ryan agreed to sell some of the team's stock to local citizens in an effort to build a strong connection with the civic-minded in the community. Later, the new ownership group made a concerted effort appearing before the city council asking for much-needed renovations to Flamingo Park, which was owned by the city of Miami Beach, as part of their agenda to revitalize baseball in the area.[144]

Baseball was saved for at least one more season in Miami Beach, but questions about the continued viability of the FIL would continue to play out. It was a topic of conversation for local hot stove fans, who anxiously anticipated seeing what the future held.

Final Standings

TEAM	W	L	GB
Havana	101	49	–
Miami	98	55	4.5
Tampa	85	60	13.5
Miami Beach	77	72	23.5
Fort Lauderdale	70	80	31
West Palm Beach	67	85	35
Lakeland	57	93	44
St. Petersburg	43	104	56.5

1951

Not since Miami Beach's Max Rosenfeld (1941, 1942, and 1946), had any manager held the reins of a club for three seasons in Miami. In an era when minor league managerial changes were as common as changing your socks; returning for his third campaign with the Sun Sox was the fun-loving but tough as nails, Pepper Martin.

H. B. Taber's offseason had been generally quiet. When asked about the status of Martin, Taber said, "I guess everything is going okay with Pepper." He added, "He never writes unless something goes wrong with his tractor." However, sure as the sun rises and sets, Martin reported to spring training camp in February ready to embark on another season.

Confidence was high in Sun Sox spring training camp and based on the previous season's happy ending, Miamians were predicting their hometown boys were set to end Havana's skein of five straight pennants. Most of the optimism centered on a crop of returnees from the 1950 squad including regulars; outfielder Paul Armstrong (.290, 38 RBIs), shortstop Gus Montalbano (.216, 57 runs), second sacker Knobby Rosa (.282, 68 runs), outfielder Rocky Rotzell (.307, 86 RBIs), pitcher Arturo Seijas (14–8, 2.25), and super utility man Barney Bridgers returning for his fourth season in Miami togs.[145]

Joining the veteran-laden club were the following: Dodger prospects Richard Lovell (10–3, 4.29) with Hazard, Kentucky of the Class D Mountain States League; Larry Ludtke (12–10, 3.93) from Sheboygan of the Class D Wisconsin State League; Dick Spady (6–6, 2.77) from Greenwood of the Class C Cotton States League; and first baseman Oscar Sierra who bashed 21 home runs at Hornell of the PONY League.[146]

The Sun Sox's brain trust of Taber and Gilliland remained active during the offseason securing talent. Key acquisitions were Ed Little that served at Syracuse of the International League as their third-string catcher, infielder Red Teague from the Cincinnati Reds organization who hit .327 with Wilmington of the Class D Tobacco State League, and 34-year-old Cuban star Gil Torres from Havana who could play either corner of the infield and pitch as well.[147]

Miami Beach was also blessed with their own group of return-ees counting; Ortelio Bosch (.194, 27 RBIs), the always depend-able backstop Emilio Cabrera (.243, 35 RBIs), Lou Colombo (.299, 11, 89) and hard luck hurlers Gaspar Del Monte (9–16, 3.09) and Bin Torres (6–10, 3.08).[148]

Conversely, the Flamingos were hit hard when three of their returnees who were expected to fill regular roles were called to serve in the armed forces. Infielders Don Server (50 games, .222), and Walter Halsall (74 games, .255) were called to active duty with the Marines at Camp Lejeune. Chucker Bill Buck (10–11, 3.57) received his call to service from the Army and reported to Camp Chaffee in Arkansas.[149] [150]

Although some news was bad, the Flamingos got a major positive shot in the arm from the Pensacola Fliers when the Southeastern League folded, and several of their players were transferred to Miami Beach including their player-manager George "Spec" Dozier. Like the Fliers, Miami Beach was a feeder team for the Atlanta Crackers, who in turn were affiliated with the National League's Boston Braves.[151]

Ryan had hired a proven winner in player-manager 29-year-young Spec Dozier from Pensacola during the offseason. It was a homecoming for Dozier who had started his professional baseball career with Miami Beach in 1941. Like many ballplayers, Dozier was drafted following the 1942 season. Spec proudly served his country as a member of the Army Air Corps in the Asiatic Theatre and Central Burma Campaign where he was highly decorated. Upon returning to the states he returned to the diamond and performed the dual role of skipper and receiver with Charleston of the Sally League, and Atlanta of the Southern Association.[152] Dozier, having gained valuable experience, then guided the Gainesville G-Men to the 1949 Florida State League pennant. He followed that up in 1950 by leading the Pensacola Fliers to the SEL championship.[153] When asked what his chances were for the upcoming season, Dozier was cautious in his assessment when he said, "No promises . . . I've heard about Havana winning five straight championships in this league."[154]

Dozier was very familiar with his incoming Fliers' players. The list included Charles "Chuck" Ehlman (.290, 4 HR), first baseman Forrest "Frosty" Kennedy who appeared in 10 games early in sea-son before a promotion, but batted .429, third baseman Robert

Lyons (125 games, .247), versatile Morton Smith (6 HR, .290 and 5–2, 4.14), and pitcher Richard "Dick" McMillin (13–10, 3.79).[155]

Many Flamingos fans were hopeful that the championship mentality brought by Dozier and his Pensacola teammates might bring them a league title. With the ownership group of Adeeb and Ryan in place and a new influx of cash flow, fans were expecting better results in the win column and on the field.

The biggest change for the faithful followers was not in the roster, but in their home field with the renovation of Flamingo Park. The dilapidated grandstands had been condemned and the city of Miami Beach put forth $18,000 towards a new roof, new seating, and other repairs that were long overdue to the facility. Although still not up to Miami Stadium standards, many of the issues that fans had complained about in the past had been addressed with the hopes that attendance would improve.[156]

Howard Kleinberg, who would later become editor of the *Miami News*, was a young reporter in 1951, and shared the following:

> I was a sports writer. My bylines appeared in the *Miami News* as a high school student in 1949. I was on staff in 1950 and I hadn't graduated high school yet. So, I was there and then stayed in sports from 1950 until 1963. I went over to the news desk at that point as an inside man. I got involved in things like the Kennedy assassination, Pope, somebody dying, and space explorations; an altogether different world.[157]

Kleinberg recalled the poor conditions at Flamingo Park, "What a rat house that was . . . I was in the press box that was ramshackle and was ready to fall down around me and at the game."[158] The ballpark seated just over 2,000, and the vast majority of games were filled with less than capacity crowds. Even after the upgrades to the ballpark, it was still considered rickety. Reporters like Kleinberg climbed up a metal staircase near the entrance of the ballpark that resembled a fire escape and trudged a few stories high climbing up to the austere press box that precariously overlooked the grandstands and the field. The scaffolding-like stairs are still in use today at the park.

With rosters decided, both Miami and Miami Beach opened their season on the circumspect date of Friday the 13th. As luck would hold, Miamians were greeted by overcast skies, which produced steady rains keeping many a paying customer at home. Although the field at Miami Stadium was ruled playable at 7 pm, Miami front office officials saw the lack of fan turnout as disappointing and used the weather as an excuse to postpone the lid-lifter with the motive of playing the next day with a better turnout at the gate. Privately, the same officials wanted to make a run at the annual Florida International League's attendance trophy that was awarded each year to the team with the highest home attendance for their opener, excluding Havana, and it was a guarantee that the paying crowd would be substantially better based on the forecast of bluer skies ahead.[159]

Meanwhile, the Flamingos traveled north to Fort Lauderdale, and in a sloppily played game which featured four errors by both sides, came out on top in a slugfest, 10 to 9. Uncharacteristically, Lions starter Chet Covington was roughed up and pulled in the eighth inning.[160] For Covington, it was his twenty-first different team in 13 years. Not surprisingly, Chesty Chet would not finish the season in Fort Lauderdale.

Miami Beach's offense took a major blow on April 19, when Colombo was lost for the season when he severely fractured his ankle while scrambling back to base during a loss to Havana.[161] So popular with the fans was the horn blower that he was awarded his own night on April 28 in which fans raised $455 for the jovial outfielder. Although Colombo was unable to attend the festivities, his teammate Mike Conroy acting as a stand-in was happy to accept the gift which also included a decorated cake that was presented by a pretty lass from Miami. Conroy delighted the crowd when he asked if a kiss went with cake.[162]

In Lou's absence his teammate, Bin Torres, pitched his best game of the season. Despite getting little support from the offense, which only mustered two hits, the resilient Puerto Rican native stood tall hurling ten shutout innings, as the Flamingos edged the Sun Sox, 1 to nothing in an extra frame.[163]

In addition, Conroy the 1949 FIL batting champ struggled early on with various nagging injuries including an early season slump garnering only three hits in 25 at-bats. "I think I'll start pitching." said a frustrated Conroy. He added, "I'm hitting like one."[164]

While the Flamingos struggled to remain at the .500 mark, Miami was slugging it out with Havana, St. Petersburg and Tampa for the top spot. On May 11, the Sun Sox had one of their most impressive wins of the season against St Petersburg. The Saints had slaughtered Fort Lauderdale the previous two nights by one-sided scores of 17 to 0, and 20 to 2, and looked to carry that momentum onward at Miami Stadium. However, the Sun Sox turned the tables on the surprised visitors and built an early 11 to 1 lead after six innings. Miami pasted 17 hits off four beleaguered Saints hurlers. Although starter Lovell faltered in the seventh inning, leading to a six-run Saints rally, his mates held on to win, 14 to 8. Miami (17–9) jumped into the league lead by percentage points ahead of St. Petersburg (19–11). By the close of the night, only 1½ games separated the Sun Sox from the fourth place Havana Cubans (16–11).[165]

Miami's lofty position at the top of the hill was short-lived as Tampa, after a sluggish 7–8 start, reeled off 39 wins in their next 50 games surging into first place. The Sun Sox (36–26) by then had fallen 8½ games off the pace into third place. The Saints (40–23) remained within striking distance five games to the arrears.

Miami's offense had been steady ranking third in the league in runs scored, but it was evident that the Sun Sox lacked stoppers at the top of the rotation like they had the year before with Dean and Lopez.

Both Dean and Lopez had earned their promotions during the spring and were pitching for the Dodgers affiliates at the AA level; Dean in Mobile, and Lopez in Fort Worth. Nevertheless, while Lopez was getting steady work with the Cats in Texas, his ex-teammate Dean had been used sparingly and mostly in mop-up duty. For Dean, who was used to being in the regular rotation, the lack of work showed poorly in his stat lines as he had appeared in only 13 games, having given up 43 hits in 34 innings, and earned only one win in four decisions.

In mid-June, Martin who had been asking for help received the good news that Dean was being re-assigned to Miami to get more work. Dean probably had mixed feelings when he was told by Bears manager Paul Chervinko of the demotion. Although the relegation came as a disappointing blow, the fact that he would receive regular work with the Sun Sox was a relief.

On June 16, Miami stood at 36–25 and in third place. Martin quickly inserted Dean into the starting rotation. His coming out was against Havana at Gran Stadium. Dean looked like his old self for the first four innings holding Havana scoreless. But, in the fifth inning, he began to unravel when Zardon led off the inning with a single, and Ramiro "Cuquíto" Vasquez drew a walk. Severino Mendez then tied the score with the second base hit of the inning. Dean followed by misplaying a ball allowing another run to score and by the end of the inning the Cubans had tacked on four runs, thus chasing Dean to the showers. Before the cigar smoke had cleared, a final tally showed Miami 2 to Havana's 5.[166]

Despite his initial rough outing, the acquisition of Dean came at an opportune time. Miami went reeling in the month of June losing 19 of 29 games and were in desperate need of mound support. Especially troublesome to skipper Martin were humiliating defeats to last place Fort Lauderdale, 11 to 1, and second division West Palm Beach 12 to 1, and Lakeland 10 to 1. During their June swoon, the Sun Sox were shutout six times and suffered through five other losses scratching out single runs.

A rusty Dean failed to notch a victory in his first two starts but finally earned a "W" on June 26, when he shut down Miami Beach, 8 to 2. After giving up a pair of tallies in the first inning, Labe settled into the form that made him the winningest pitcher in the FIL the year before, limiting the Flamingos to eight hits and doing his best impersonation of Harry Houdini, escaping several jams. A thankful Labe was indebted to several of his mates who touched Bin Torres, Billy Currie and Mort Smith for 13 base hits. Sierra was the chief contributor aiding the Sox's cause by driving in four runs.[167] From then on out Dean was nearly untouchable.

Indeed, the addition of Dean to Miami saw the beginning of a turnaround. The move solidified the staff that was in desperate need of an ace. The Sun Sox swept Tampa during a June 30–July 2 three-game series as Dean pitched ten quality innings during the first game. Seijas, who came on in relief in the tenth, garnered the win, an 11 inning affair; a 2 to 1 Miami victory. Always cool in the clutch Rotzell provided the walk-off single; a game-winner that thwarted Smokers' skipper Ben Chapman's unconventional strategy of repositioning his outfielders as a seven-man infield to cut down any chance of a ball escaping the infield.[168]

Whatever work that Dean had not received in Fort Worth, Martin was making up for in spades. The apex of the bald-headed veteran season came on August 16. A scant Thursday crowd of 1,072 filed through the turnstiles of Miami Stadium to see the hometown team take on lowly Fort Lauderdale in a doubleheader not knowing that they would witness a historic feat.[169]

The first game, which was by custom a seven-inning affair, had Dean scattering six Braves hits, as well as fanning two in the process. Rotzell and former Flamingo Ashton "Ash" Heckel, the latter recently acquired on option from St. Paul of the American Association, each drove in a run. The game was played in what today would be considered an unbelievable one hour and 18 minutes as the Sun Sox triumphed, 2 to 0.[170]

In the nightcap, a surprised crowd saw Dean take to the hill again to square off against former Beachite, Gaspar Del Monte. Martin had planned on using Seijas for the second game but continued with his veteran seeing how easy he had handled the Braves. Dean continued his mastery, as he once again shut out the free-swinging Fort Lauderdale batters; this time striking out seven and limiting the Lions to a trio of hits. Dean aided his own cause by driving in a run, as the Sun Sox completed the double-header sweep winning 4 to 0.[171] Interestingly both games combined were played in just under three hours.

The twin shutouts were a unique accomplishment. As a testament to Dean's feat, several other hurlers had pitched and won both games of a doubleheader, in major league history only one pitcher had ever matched Dean's performance of dual shutouts, that being Edward "Big Ed" Reulbach of the Chicago Cubs who blanked the Brooklyn Dodgers on both ends of a twin bill on September 26, 1908.[172] Thanks to Dean's performance the two wins vaulted Miami into second place, as St. Petersburg sat idle.

But, as Miami emerged out of their doldrums, reality in Miami Beach was setting in as hopes of a successful playoff run were diminishing. Ryan had already sold struggling frontline starter, Del Monte in mid-May[173] and then in another obvious cost-cutting move, the Flamingos agreed to sell 1949 batting champion Mike Conroy to Tampa. Conroy had struggled with various injuries all season long and had seen his batting average drop to an uncharacteristic .195.[174] The move would prove to be fortuitous for front-running Tampa as Conroy would bounce back and by the end of the season raised his average to .273.

The Flamingos had come to a crossroad. The hopes and dreams of revitalizing fan interest in Miami Beach with a winning club were waning. Team vice-president, Carl Gardner, who had spent 16 years early in his life on the stage as a song and dance man, had gone so far as to resort to doing commercials and telling stories and anecdotes about baseball and the players between innings over the public address system to heighten interest in the team. He always ended his shtick by telling everyone, "So bring your family and friends out to the ball game when we play . . ." followed by the upcoming team that was scheduled for the next game. The front office was counting on civic pride to kick in, their modest goal of averaging 1,000 per game versus the 650 they were drawing. "It's worth a try to get folks out to the ballpark," said Gardner. He added, "because unless you try a gag how do you know what laughs will be? I'll bring out some chorus girls to keep the fans interested. We need the business."[175]

The biggest event of the season was the brainchild of Joe Ryan. On August 17 and 18, Miami Stadium was scheduled to sit empty. What the enterprising Ryan suggested was pure Bill Veeck like in nature. He moved two scheduled game series (originally on the calendar for Lakeland at Miami Beach and Miami at Havana), and played all of the games at Miami Stadium under the banner of 'Fan Appreciation Night.' Each day fans would be treated to two games, and four teams, for the price of one and enjoy in scheduled festivities and giveaways.[176]

Not only did the games turn out to be thrillers; all four games were decided by single runs, but there was fun and entertainment for all. Part of the attraction was that orchids, and scatter-pins, were presented to the ladies who attended each night. Fans were also treated to fifty cent dinners, along with free ice cream cups that were handed out. In addition, ten turkeys, and five bicycles were awarded as prizes.[177]

What earned Ryan the most attention and found him earning the moniker of "Veeck of the Florida International League" was his idea of a milking contest that pitted Miami's Red Teague against Miami Beach's Mort "the Georgia Squire" Smith. The Sun Sox cause was aided by their skipper Martin who crooned to the cow while Teague manipulated the heifers utters to edge out Smith. Although the Flamingos protested the Sun Sox skipper's maneuver, in the end, it was seen as just clean fun for all that watched and participated.[178]

The umpires also joined in the bounty, receiving gifts by the Flamingos' Carl Gardner, as a token of appreciation for their services. In the end, it was estimated that gate receipts were 200 percent higher than was otherwise expected.[179]

Unfortunately, the aggressive efforts of Gardner and Ryan to drum up attendance went to no avail as local interest was indifferent at best except for the occasional meeting against the Sun Sox. Although overall league attendance had shown an increase by July of 12,000, attendance at Flamingo Park had dropped precipitously by 3,885.[180]

The Flamingos had not seen the plus side of .500 since mid-May yet there were some shining lights. George Greene and his battery mate Ehlman were both chosen as FIL all-stars and participated in the league all-star game that was played on July 19 at Miami Stadium. Greene would finish the season as Miami Beach's winningest pitcher posting a 17–14 mark and 3.21 ERA. Ehlman replaced Emilio "Cabby" Cabrera dealt to Class A, Wilkes-Barre. He batted a steady .254 in 117 games in Cabby's place.

The departure of Cabrera left the league minus one of its most colorful players. The fiery backstop, known for his intestinal fortitude and confrontational nature dealing with perceived injustices. Fans in Virginia were once so appreciative of his inspirational and spirited play that they presented him with $335 and carried him off the field in celebration.[181]

One of the most deserving pink birds not listed amongst the all-stars was a man who would become a minor league legend, Frosty Kennedy. The 5'10" solidly built 24-year-old Kennedy, frequently seen with a healthy chaw of tobacco in his mouth, was the only regular in Dozier's lineup to hit over .300 (.307) along with 7 home runs and 63 ribbies. Although those numbers were impressive in a league dominated by pitching, the cocky Frosty would go on to set a mark that put him amongst the elite in baseball history. Five years after moving on from Miami Beach, Kennedy would blast 60 homers for the Plainview Ponies of the Class B Southwestern League.[182] He would join an elite group of only eight minor league players to bash 60 or more circuit clouts in a season. (*note Joe Hauser was the only player to do it twice). During that magical year, he also batted .327 and collected 184 ribbies for good measure.

After the conclusion of the 1956 season, he was released as part of an organizational youth movement handed down by the Sacramento Solons of the Pacific Coast League who had a working agreement with the club. He would play one more season sharing time with the Boise Braves of the Class C Pioneer League and Savannah of the Class A Sally League. Ironically, he would close out his career with only seven more homers.[183]

Miami's roster was not without its own cast of characters. One of the most outgoing and memorable personalities was their all-star selection at shortstop, Gus Montalbano. Although a sure-handed flashy fielding shortstop, he was the exact opposite of Kennedy as a hitter. In his two years in Miami Montalbano flirted with the Mendoza line batting .217 in 1950 and .200 in 1951. Over his two seasons in the Magic City, the kid with the quick wit from the Bronx managed only four home runs.[184] Elvie Darden fondly remembered Montalbano's enthusiasm for the game; how he joked with his teammates to keep them loose. He recalled his excitement when he connected on a long ball, "He kissed the home run plate after he hit a home run . . . He was so proud he hit that home run that he kissed the plate when he bounced over it."[185]

Joining Montalbano on the all-star squad were Miami teammates Gil Torres, as a utility player, and outfielder Oscar Sierra. At 35 years old, Gilberto "Jibaríto" Torres was in the twilight of his baseball career that began during the 1934–35 season in the Cuban winter leagues with Havana. He was the son of Ricardo Torres, who played sparingly at first base and catcher for the Washington Senators from 1920–22, as well as 13 seasons in the Cuban winter leagues and no doubt learned the game well from his father.

Torres was truly a jack of all trades having played every position with the exception of catcher. Torres arrived at the major leagues in 1940 as part of scout Joe "Papa Joe" Cambria pipeline of signings that supplied the Washington Senators. Torres first appeared in two games in 1940 for the Nats without a plate appearance. With World War II raging over the next few years major league rosters were depleted as many ballplayers were called to serve overseas. This opened the door for Torres who was able to rejoin the Senators and earned a regular spot in 1944 and 1945. After the war, he did come back for one last season in 1946 and appeared in 63 games before finishing his career with 320 hits and a .252 lifetime batting average.[186]

Torres kept up his breakneck pace appearing in either the minor leagues or major leagues every year from 1935 through 1955 while correspondingly competing in the Cuban winter leagues until 1953. All in all, he would compete in 18 winter campaigns finishing 8th all-time in at-bats (2,561), and 9th in hits (694). He was twice named Most Valuable Player (1940–41, 1943–44) and 5 times hit over .300. In addition, he twice led the winter league in games pitched (13 in 1934–35, 27 in 1940–41), and led the league in win percentage in 1940–41 (.769). He also served four seasons as a manager with the 1946–47 Havana Reds, 1948–49 Marianao, and 1956–57 and 1957–58 Havana Lions.[187]

Although the Sun Sox (77–61) played valiantly the second half of the season winning three games more in the second half than the first half. Despite the team's efforts "The Wild Horse of the Osage" let his temper get away from him once more. Martin was being heckled by a fan during the August 11 game against Lakeland and he claimed he couldn't take it anymore and climbed over the fence then punched the man. After the game, police approached Martin, arrested him for assault, and held him on a $100 bond. Later he was docked $25 by the municipal court. League president, O'Connell took further action and Martin was fined $75. If it was not bad enough, Lakeland prevailed, 5 to 2.[188]

The Sun Sox were essentially outclassed by St. Petersburg (83–56) and regular season champs Tampa (90–50) whose pitching staffs proved to be deeper than Miami's. Miami Beach (68–74) finished a disappointing sixth place just ahead of West Palm Beach who had yet to enjoy a winning season since the league's inception.

The Shaughnessy playoffs once again featured the odd arrangement of the first place club, Tampa taking on the third-place finishers, Miami. While the second place team, St. Petersburg took on the fourth place, Lakeland who was making their second appearance ever in the playoffs.

Tampa opened up their series with Miami on September 4 with the home field advantage. Martin's chose to start his most experienced pitcher Dean, who had gone 11–7 since joining the team from Fort Worth against 7-year minor league veteran right-hander Arnie Atkins another mid-season acquisition who had also won 11 games with his new team.

Atkins proved to be more parsimonious when it came to giving up hits than walks. In seven innings of work, the Sun Sox managed only three hits off Atkins but took advantage of eight free passes and three errors to score seven runs against him. Miami tallied five runs in the third despite the only base hit being a double by Rosa that came between three Tampa miscues and three walks. The Sun Sox added two more runs in the fourth when Atkins walked three more batters and allowed an Armstrong single. Dean proved masterful by spreading out nine Smoker hits and striking out seven without allowing a run. Both Armstrong and Rotzell each accounted for three runs batted in helping the cause. Every Miami batter had at least one hit, the exception being catcher Ed Little. The final score was Miami 14 Tampa 0.[189]

Game two once again provided plenty of offensive fireworks. Tampa struck hard and fast posting nine runs on the scoreboard in the first three innings. Rene Solis was knocked out of the box in the first frame after walking Carlos Bernier and Conroy, giving up a single to Mike Hafenecker then a bases-clearing double to Earl Brucker. The Sun Sox scored four in the eighth on singles by Rosa, Armstrong, and Rotzell that were followed by Sierra's double and Teague's single. The Smokers winningest pitcher during the season Dale Matthewson earned the easy walk away win by 11 to 4.[190]

In a peculiar arrangement, Tampa moved on to play the final games in Miami, while St. Petersburg did the same against Lakeland. The Sun Sox looked poised and positioned to take the series as once again manhandled the Smokers by a score of 8 to 3. Rotzell again proved to be the offensive catalyst driving in three runs in the first inning with a bases-loaded triple; one of four hits on the day. Martin's decision to start a veteran Gil Torres proved to be fortuitous as the wily veteran was bent, but not broken by scattering nine hits while striking out six.[191]

After an off day, the series resumed. The day off proved a blessing as Martin was able to turn again to Dean with a much needed extra day of rest. Tensions had been running high during the whole series as Tampa's vaunted pitching staff had been anything but. Under fiery manager Chapman, frustrations reached the boiling point in the second inning when Torres sent a liner to the right-field fence. When he rounded second base Tampa's shortstop Lamar "Doc" Bowden was in his path and obstructed his progress. Butch Henline, the umpire at second base, mad the quick decision on the play by calling baserunner interference allowing Torres to advance to third. Smoker manager Chapman was incensed, felt that Torres had swung wide, and ran into Bowden either intentionally or unintentionally. Chapman continued in a rage and soon received the thumb that led to him being summarily tossed. Miami capitalized on their big break by scoring twice off of Tony Lorenzo in what would prove all the offense that the Sox needed. Dean posted his second straight playoff win allowing eight hits. Always tough in the clutch the crafty veteran was able to escape out of several jams thanks to some fine defensive plays by infielders Montalbano and Rosa and outfielders Armstrong and Sierra. An ecstatic hometown crowd celebrated as Miami earned the right by beating Tampa 4 to 1.[192]

The Sun Sox were set to face St. Petersburg, which had won a hard-fought series in five games against the Cinderella, Lakeland Pilots who had started the season by dropping their first eleven games. The Saints success was tied to their two-headed monster at the top of their pitching staff, one-time Boston Red Sox phenom righty Woody Rich (25–6, 2.34), and former St. Louis Browns southpaw Clarence "Hooks" Iott (22–12, 2.00). The two former major leaguers were joined by Elwood "Dinty" Moore (16–12, 2.44), and mid-season acquisition Charlie Cuellar (8–3, 2.69), a FIL fixture that rounded out the league's best mound corp.[193]

The best-of-seven series kicked off on a windy September 10 at Al Lang Field before 3,043 Saints rooters. Martin's choice was Rene Solis (4–3, 3.38), a late-season acquisition from Fort Worth, to go against slender right-sider, Dinty Moore.[194]

If one believes in omens, then they received no better evidence than what happened on the game's first play. The Saints first batter Angel Lopez hit a soft dribbler down the first base line in what looked like an easy out, but Teague ham-handed the ball as Lopez scampered safely across the bag. The next batter, Joe Clark reached base on fielder's choice as Lopez was forced at second. Tom Davis then singled Clark to third, and Billy Seal followed Davis with a pop fly to just over shortstop. However, the usually reliable Montalbano made the catch but had positioned himself so that he was unable to check the runner on third and Clark crossed the plate on the tag-up play putting St. Pete up, 1–0.[195]

The Saints tagged Solis for single runs in each of the first three innings. Miami's first and only score came in the top of the third frame when Solis led off with a single. Rosa then reached on a fielder's choice and advance on a rare Moore wild pitch. The Sox's third sacker, "Ash" Heckel then hit a long drive to Clark in left field, which he mishandled, and Rosa raced home from second to score.[196]

Moore, who only got stronger as the game rolled on, relied on his curveball to send Miami batters, one after another, back to the bench only giving up four singles while garnering 4 K's. Bob Hudson of the *St. Petersburg Times* called Moore's performance his best of the year. The Saints prevailed 4–0 to take the lid-lifter.[197]

The September 11 game was postponed because of heavy rains, but play resumed on the next day. In front of 3,512 rabidly cheering fans, Cuellar took the mound to face off against the Sun Sox's Torres.[198]

This time, St. Petersburg got off to an ominous start. Two errors, a single by Bridgers and a sacrifice fly gave Miami a 2–0 lead. Not to be discouraged the Saints offense reacted quickly to turn their bad fortune around. In the bottom of the first inning, the Saints battered Torres for three runs, a key blow delivered by Rudy Tanner's two-run double. Martin had seen enough and pulled Torres in favor of big 6'5" Larry Ludtke. Ludtke lasted until the eighth inning giving up only a run, but his teammates failed to string anything significant against Cuellar who held on for the complete game win, 4 to 3.[199]

The series shifted to Miami in a game that featured the two team's aces. Prognosticators were right on the mark when they predicted it would be a low scoring contest. Dean who characteristically started slow gave up a first-inning run when he walked Clark on four straight pitches. Clark later scored on a Seal single.[200]

The Saints added to their lead in the fifth inning when Clark tripled and scored on Davis's long fly ball to center fielder Sierra. Miami cut the lead in the seventh frame when leadoff batter Rotzell blasted a moon shot over the right-field fence. Rotzell hit the ball so hard that it ricocheted off the back of scoreboard behind the fence and back onto the playing field. Unfortunately, Miami did little against the veteran Rich who struck out three and allowed only six Sun Sox base hits. The final score showed St. Pete 2 Miami 1.[201]

With all the momentum on St. Petersburg side, Iott took the mound brimming with confidence. After all the imposing 6'2" lefty had just been signed by the Pittsburgh Pirates and wanted nothing better than to bring home a championship. Martin countered with Seijas, but for the third straight time, the Sun Sox allowed first-inning runs to put themselves in a hole. After allowing three singles and a double for two runs, Martin turned again to Ludtke to extinguish the rally.[202] [203]

In the bottom of first Miami cut the lead by one when Rosa reached base on shortstop Junior Dodgins' error, followed by Armstrong and Torres who both worked the count and drew walks. Sierra's long fly to center field scored Rosa as Miami cut the lead to 2 to 1.[204]

The Saints notched another run in the top of the fourth inning to increase their lead to 3–1. In the bottom half of the same frame, the Sun Sox answered for one tally when Rotzell doubled, Little clubbed a long fly that advanced the runner, and Montalbano singled with two outs driving in his teammate. Miami never threatened again as Iott slammed the door on them and the Saints completed the four-game sweep, winning the final, 3 to 2.[205]

As each of the players filed out of the dressing room anxious for the offseason to begin, there was one exception. Leaving Miami Stadium for the last time, Barney Bridgers was slower than the others departing. A fixture in the infield for three seasons in Miami, the kid from California who starred at North Hollywood High School in baseball, football and track went on to retire after ten seasons, leaving the long interminable bus rides and the occasional pleasant chartered flights to Havana behind. Although the diminutive Bridgers, who stood 5'6" and 145 pounds soaking wet, would never grace the field as a professional ballplayer again. He left the fans wherever he played knowing that he gave it everything he had. The curtain may have fallen, but he never left the game he loved. He went on to perform scouting duties for the St. Louis Cardinals and organized baseball camps for the youngsters of Etowah County, Alabama for several years.[206]

Although Bridgers was missed by many, the most shocking news came in November when H. B. Taber Jr. announced that Pepper Martin would not be returning as manager of the Sun Sox. He announced, "we don't want to get into a rut by having a manager too long." Speculations of past incidents involving the attacking of an umpire, getting into a physical altercation with a fan, and walking off the field in 1950 when booed by fans played a role in his dismissal. Despite two second-place finishes, a third-place finish and a league championship in 1951 the "Wild Horse of the Osage" left his position with a clear conscience knowing another job was well done. He would not be out of work long. Martin would soon find a new home just a stone's throw away.[207]

Final Standings

TEAM	W	L	GB
Tampa	90	50	–
St. Petersburg	83	56	6.5
Miami	77	61	12
Lakeland	71	68	18.5
Havana	68	71	21.5
Miami Beach	66	74	24
West Palm Beach	64	75	25.5
Fort Lauderdale	38	102	52

NOTES

1. Balfe, Bob. FIL Directors Seek President, *Palm Beach Post*, 1 November, 1948, p. 9.
2. Balfe, Bob. It's Post Time With Bob Balfe, *Palm Beach Post*, 14 November, 1948, p. 21.
3. Tripp, Robert. Phone interview with author, 20 October, 2014.
4. Wade, Gale. Phone interview with author, 25 July, 2014.
5. Baseball-reference.com.
6. Barthel, Thomas, *Pepper Martin: A Baseball Biography*, (Jefferson, North Carolina & London, McFarland & Company, Inc., 2003) p. 190.
7. Barthel, Thomas, *The Fierce Fun of Ducky Medwick*, (Lanham, Maryland, Scarecrow Press, 2003).
8. Spink, J.G. Taylor. Muscles Moves Into Master-Mind Role, *Sporting News*, 9 March, 1949, p. 8.
9. Ibid.
10. Burns, Jimmy. Giants 1-2-3 in N.L. Race—Old Stoney, *Sporting News*, 30 March, 1949, p. 10.
11. Spink, J.G. Taylor, Ernest J. Lanigan, Paul A. Rickart, and Cliff Kachline, *Sporting News Baseball Guide and Record Book 1949* (Charles C. Spink & Son: St. Louis, MO), p. 313.
12. Gonzalez, Gaspar. El Lanzador, *Miami New Times*, 18 April, 2002 retrieved from miaminewtimes.com/news.el-lanzador-6350991.
13. Figueredo, Jorge. *Cuban Baseball: A Statistical History 1878–1961*, (Jefferson, North Carolina & London, McFarland & Company, Inc., 2003), p. 314–315.
14. Figueredo, Jorge. *Béisbol Cubano: A un Paso de las Grandes Ligas: 1878–1961*, (Jefferson, North Carolina & London, McFarland & Company, Inc., 2005) p. 371.
15. Figueredo, Jorge. *Cuban Baseball: A Statistical History 1878–1961*, (Jefferson, North Carolina & London, McFarland & Company, Inc., 2003), p. 257.
16. Baseball-reference.com.
17. Spink, J.G. Taylor, Ernest J. Lanigan, Paul A. Rickart, and Cliff Kachline. *Sporting News Baseball Guide and Record Book 1949* (Charles C. Spink & Son: St. Louis, MO), 314. Baseball-reference.com listed Rotzell with 5 home runs for the season.
18. Baseball-reference.com.
19. Balfe, Bob. Tribe Out-Hits Sox, But Lose, *Palm Beach Post*, 5 April, 1949, p. 9.
20. Burns, Jimmy. Wild Horse Fined $25 for Cussin' Umpire; Player Fights Mark Game With Ducky's Club, *Sporting News*, 4 May, 1949, p. 37.

21. Burns, Jimmy. *Still Plenty of Power in Ducky's Bat*, Sporting News, April 20, 1949, p. 46.
22. Burns, Jimmy. Ducky, Pepper Meet—Result, Fireworks, *Sporting News*, 27 April, 1949, p. 37.
23. Ibid.
24. Ibid.
25. Ibid.
26. Burns, Jimmy. Wild Horse Fined $25 for Cussin' Umpire; Players Fights Mark Game With Ducky's Club, *Sporting News*, 4 May, 1949, p. 37.
27. Ibid.
28. *Sporting News*, 25 May, 1949, p. 37.
29. Wade, Gale. Phone interview with author, 25 July, 2014.
30. How They Stand, *Sporting News*, 8 June, 1949, p. 37.
31. *Palm Beach Post,* 5 June, 1949, p. 19.
32. Campos Still Tops League Hitting Race, *Palm Beach Post*, 5 June, 1949, p. 19.
33. Figueredo, Jorge. *Who's Who in Cuban Baseball, 1878–1961*, (McFarland & Co., Inc., Publishers: Jefferson, North Carolina and London, 2003), p. 152.
34. Burns, Jimmy. Spotlighting Sports, *Miami Herald*, 24 June, 1949, p. 12-A.
35. Minor League Class B Highlights, *Sporting News*, 29 June, 1949, p. 33.
36. *Miami Trips Marrero Third Straight Time*, Miami Herald, August 26, 1949, 4-D.
37. Martin Suspended, Fined $100 for Attacking Ump, *Sporting News*, 7 September, 1949, p. 41.
38. Martin Attacks Umpire, *Miami Herald*, 27 August, 1949.
39. Beahon, George, In This Corner, *Democrat and Chronicle* [Rochester, New York], 28 April, 1959, p. 32.
40. Tripp, Robert. Phone interview with author, 20 October, 2014.
41. Martin Gets Suspension For Balance Of Season, *Palm Beach Post*, September 2, 1949, 11.
42. Powell, Robert Andrew. Rough Diamond, *Miami New Times,* 15 August, 1996.
43. Butler, Guy. Chandler Will Head Opening Celebrities, *Miami News*, 31 August, 1949, p. 2-B.
44. Tripp, Robert. Phone interview with author, 20 October, 2014.
45. Butler, Guy. 13,007 View Opening: Colossal They Agree, *Miami News*, 1 September, 1949, p. 2-B.
46. McLemore, Morris. Morris McLemore Says, *Miami News*, 31 August, 1949, p. 3-B.
47. Burns, Jimmy. 13,007 See Sun Sox Open New Stadium With Victory, *Sporting News*, 7 September, 1949, p. 17.
48. Burns, Jimmy. Chandler Among Guests for Miami Park Opening, *Sporting News*, 31 August, 1949, p. 41.
49. Llanes, Rolando, *White Elephant: The Rise and Fall of Miami Baseball Stadium*, (Blurb Inc., 2010), p. 113.
50. Burns, Jimmy. 13,007 See Sun Sox Open New Stadium With Victory, *Sporting News*, 7 September, 1949, p. 17.
51. Baseball-reference.com.
52. Butler, Guy, Topic of the Tropics, *Miami News*, 2 September, 1949, p. 2-B.
53. McMullan, John. Martin Awaits Fate: Solis Hurls Windup Against Cubans, *Miami News*, 1 September, 1949, p. 4-B.
54. Ibid.
55. Ibid.
56. Ibid.
57. Wetstein, Mert. Like Public, Sox Get Thrills, *Miami News*, 1 September, 1949, p. 4-B.
58. Butler, Guy. 13,007 View Opening: Colossal They Agree, *Miami News*, 1 September, 1949.
59. Three Parking Lots Ready For Opening, *Miami News*, 31 August, 1949, p. 2-B.

60. Covington Ill, Advised to Quit, Palm *Beach Post (AP)*, 30 August, 1949, p. 8.
61. Spink, J.G. Taylor, Ernest J. Lanigan, Paul A. Rickart, and Cliff Kachline, *Sporting News Baseball Guide and Record Book 1950* (Charles C. Spink & Son: St. Louis, MO), 226.
62. FIL Playoffs, *Palm Beach Post*, 7 September, 1949, p. 12.
63. FIL Playoffs, *Palm Beach Post*, 8 September, 1949, p. 9.
64. FIL Playoffs, *Palm Beach Post*, 9 September, 1949, p. 12.
65. FIL Playoffs, *Palm Beach Post*, 10 September, 1949, p. 5.
66. Baseball-reference.com.
67. Spink, J.G. Taylor, Ernest J. Lanigan, Paul A. Rickart, and Cliff Kachline. *Sporting News Baseball Guide and Record Book 1950* (Charles C. Spink & Son: St. Louis, MO), p. 226.
68. Spink, J.G. Taylor, Ernest J. Lanigan, Paul A. Rickart, and Cliff Kachline, *Sporting News Baseball Guide and Record Book 1950* (Charles C. Spink & Son: St. Louis, MO), p. 226.
69. FIL Playoffs, *Palm Beach Post*, 7 September, 1949, p. 12.
70. Baseball-reference.com.Consuegra pitched for the Washington Senators (1950–53), Chicago White Sox (1953–56), Baltimore Orioles (1956–57), and New York Giants (1957).
71. FIL Playoffs, *Palm Beach Post*, 8 September, 1949, p. 9.
72. FIL Playoffs, *Palm Beach Post*, 10 September, 1949, p. 5.
73. FIL Playoffs, *Palm Beach Post*, 12 September, 1949, p. 5.
74. *Sporting News*, 21 September, 1949, p. 40.
75. *Sporting News*, 23 November, 1949, p. 19, credited Conroy with a .365 batting average versus baseball-reference.com, and the *Sporting News Baseball Guide and Record Book, 1950*, crediting him with a .359 batting average.
76. J.G. Taylor Spink, Ernest J. Lanigan, Paul A. Rickart, Cliff Kachline. *Sporting News Baseball Guide and Record Book 1950* (Charles C. Spink & Son: St. Louis, MO), p. 226. The league leader was Fred Bell of St. Petersburg with 24.
77. Alderton, George S. The Sports Grist, *Lansing State Journal*, 28 June, 1949, p. 16.
78. Haviland Wins Sun Sox Award, *Palm Beach Post*, 25 September, 1949, p. 15.
79. Burns, Jimmy. Pepper Can Stop Cubans-With Ted, Stan and DiMag, *Sporting News*, 28 December, 1949, p. 15.
80. Baseball-reference.com.
81. Medwick Loses Manager's Job, *St. Louis Post-Dispatch*, 16 September, 1949, p. 11-C.
82. Burns, Jimmy. Majors Strike Bonanza in New Miami Park, *Sporting News*, 29 March, 1950, p. 22.
83. Ibid.
84. Burns, Jimmy. Aleman, Cuban Millionaire Who Helped Build Swank Miami Stadium, Dies at 44, *Sporting News*, 5 April, 1950, p. 29.
85. *Sporting News*, 14 September, 1949, p. 39.
86. McCoy, Dick. Phone interview with author, 16 August, 2014.
87. Ibid.
88. Ackeret, Jim. Phone interview with the author, 25 July, 2015.
89. Wade, Gale. Phone interview with author, 25 July, 2014.
90. Baseball-reference.com.
91. Ibid.
92. Spink, J.G. Taylor, Ernest J. Lanigan, Paul A. Rickart, and Cliff Kachline, *Sporting News Baseball Guide and Record Book 1950* (Charles C. Spink & Son: St. Louis, MO), p. 228 (Ticco), p. 241 (Patterson).
93. Baseball-reference.com.
94. Ibid, p. 246–247.
95. *Sporting News*, Transactions, 8 February, 1950, p. 27.

96. O'Neill, Bill. The Jazz Trumpeter Lou Colombo Will Be Honored Sunday, *Cape Cod Times*, acquired 28 December, 2016 from www.capecodtimes.com/article/20120616/LIFE/206160303.

97. FIL Averages, *Palm Beach Post*, 30 April, 1950, p. 21. At the time Ray Sowins was listed at .346, Rocky Rotzell .333, Tommy Tabb .311, Ed Lewinksi .310, Mike Conroy .290, Jim Clark .288, and Lou Colombo .282.

98. *Palm Beach Post*, 23 April, 1950, p. 21.

99. *Palm Beach Post*, 24 April, 1950, p. 6.

100. Sun Sox Buy Memphis Fielder, *Palm Beach Post*, 26 May, 1950, p. 15.

101. *Sporting News*, 7 June, 1950, p. 37.

102. F-I Gate Down 76,116. *Sporting News*, 31 May, 1959, p. 38.

103. Baseball-reference.com. Florida International League.

104. Burns, Jimmy. Henline Likes Spirited Play of Cubans in F-I, *Sporting News*, 31 May, 1950, p. 38.

105. Baseball-reference.com. The 11 players included; Sandalio "Sandy" Consuegra, Bobby Estalella, Ramon Garcia, Julio Gonzalez, Rogelio Martinez, Rene Monteagudo, Julio Moreno, Tony "Mosquito" Ordeñana, Carlos Pascual, Gilberto Torres, and Santiago "Sandy" Ullrich.

106. Burns, Jimmy. Loop Delays Vote to Oust Havana Club, *Sporting News*, 21 June, 1950, p. 37.

107. Whoops! Shorts for Wild Horse in Miami Stint, *Sporting News*, 7 June, 1950, p. 37.

108. McCoy, Dick. Phone interview with author, 16 August, 2014.

109. Daniels, Stephen M. The Hollywood Stars, Retrieved 9 January, 2017 from research.sabr.org/journals/Hollywood-stars.

110. Ibid.

111. Burns, Jimmy. Rotzell Sale by Beach Due to Slim Gate, *Sporting News*, 9 August, 1950, p. 39.

112. Steelers Lose 9th Straight; Tourists Here, *Florence Morning News* [Florence, SC], 23 June, 1950, p. 10.

113. *Palm Beach Post*, 27 June, 1950, p. 8.

114. *Palm Beach Post*, 30 June, 1950, p. 15.

115. Hall, Dan. Sun Sox Edge Saints In 17-Inning Tussle, *St. Petersburg Times*, 8 August, 1950, p. 15.

116. Ibid.

117. Ibid.

118. Havana Nears Pennant In FIL Race, *Panama City News-Herald*, 31 August, 1950, p. 8.

119. Sox Dump Cubans, Braves Nip Tampa, *Palm Beach Post*, 1 September, 1950, p. 11.

120. *Palm Beach Post*, September 2, 1950, p. 10.

121. Sun Sox Win Playoff Debut, Tampa Shifts Play to Cuba, *Palm Beach Post*, September 6, 1950, p. 8.

122. Sox Blank Beach To Lead Playoffs, *Palm Beach Post*, 7 September, 1950, p. 9.

123. Attendance figures gathered from game results posted by Palm Beach Post, September 6–8.

124. Sox Win Playoff Series, *Palm Beach Post*, 8 September, 1950, p. 11.

125. McCoy, Dick. Phone interview with author, 16 August, 2014.

126. Protest Upheld, Smokers Concede Games to Havana, *Sporting News*, 20 September, 1950, p. 33.

127. Tampa Protest is Withdrawn, FIL Playoff Opens Tonight, *Palm Beach Post*, 11 September, 1950, p. 5.

128. Ibid.

129. Miami Grabs Playoff Opener, *Palm Beach Post*, 12 September, 1950, p. 9.

130. Sox Win Second Playoff Game, *Palm Beach Post*, 13 September, 1950, p. 12.

131. Ibid.
132. McCoy, Dick. Phone interview with author, 16 August, 2014.
133. Baseball-reference.com.
134. Potato Sacks Sox in Playoffs, 4–2, *Palm Beach Post*, 14 September, 1950, p. 9.
135. Sox Edge Cubans, 3–2, *St. Petersburg Times*, 15 September, 1950, p. 23.
136. Ibid.
137. Sun Sox Whip Cubans To Win FIL Playoffs, *St. Petersburg Times*, 17 September, 1950, p. 23.
138. Darden, Elvie. Phone interview with author, 23 January, 2017.
139. Baseball-reference.com. Year by year attendance figures of the Florida International League.
140. Burns, Jimmy. Florida Int. Host to Convention Has Troubles and Growing Pains, *Sporting News*, 6 December, 1950, p. 12.
141. Baseball-reference.com.
142. Miami Beach Team Is Sold, *Palm Beach Post*, 24 December, 1950, p. 15.
143. Jimmy Burns, Sporting News, *Miami Beach Flamingos in New Hands*, January 17, 1951, 12.
144. Ibid.
145. Baseball-reference.com FIL Hit Title Still Undecided, *Palm Beach Post*, 9 September, 1950, p. 18.
146. Ibid.
147. Ibid.
148. Baseball-reference.com.
149. *Sporting News*, Flamingos Hit Hard, 14 March, 1951, p. 31.
150. Baseball-reference.com.
151. Brown, Scott. *Baseball in Pensacola: America's Pastime and the City of Five* Flags (History Press, Charleston, SC, 2013).
152. www.legacy.com/obituaries/name/george-dozier-obituary?pid=1000000178976293.
153. Baseball-reference.com.
154. McMullan, John (Miami Daily News), New Blood, Cash Injected Into 1951 FIL Flamingos, *Palm Beach Post*, 5 April, 1951, p. 14.
155. Ibid.
156. Burns, Jimmy. Florida Int. Expects New Gate Record, *Sporting News*, 11 April, 1951, p. 18.
157. Kleinberg, Howard. Personal interview with the author, 9 July, 2013.
158. Kleinberg, Howard. Personal interview with the author, 9 July, 2013.
159. Balfe, Bob. Sox Postpone Lid-Lifter In Attempt To Win Trophy, *Palm Beach Post*, 14 April, 1951, p. 12.
160. Ibid.
161. *Sporting News*, 2 May, 1951, p. 31.
162. Burns, Jimmy. Miami Hill Star Gives Only 2 Hits, *Miami Herald*, April 29, 1951, 2-D.
163. Ibid.
164. Evans, Luther. Ludtke Halts Flamingo's On 6 Hits, *Miami Herald*, 21 April, 1951, p. 14-A.
165. Sox Regain Lead In FI-League, *Palm Beach Post*, 12 May, 1951, p. 6.
166. Hurler Hurts Own Cause With 2 Costly Misplays, *Miami Herald*, 17 June, 1951, p. 6-D.
167. Hall, Dan. Iott To Face Lakeland In Series Closer Tonight, *St. Petersburg Times*, 27 June, 1951, p. 11.
168. Kelley, Whitey. 2,569 See Miami Nab 2–1 Duel, *Miami Herald*, 1 July, 1951, p. 2-D.
169. Kraslow, Dave. Miami Right Hander Goes Route In Both Triumphs, *Miami Herald*, 17 August, 1951, p. 6-D.

170. Ibid.
171. Ibid.
172. Baseball-almanac.com/feats. Retrieved 1 March, 2017.
173. St. Pete 17-to-0 Winner, *Fort Lauderdale News*, 10 May, 1951, p. 2-B.
174. Conroy Bought By Miami Smokers, *Panama City News-Herald*, 8 July, 1958, p. 7. Headline misprinted as it was supposed to say Tampa Smokers.
175. Cuddy, Don. Player-Patter on Loud Speaker, *Sporting News*, 23 May, 1951, p. 1-2.
176. Cuddy, Don. Four Clubs Join 'Fan Appreciation Series', *Sporting News*, 29 August, 1951, p. 15.
177. Ibid.
178. Ibid.
179. Ibid.
180. FIL Attendance Up 12,000, *Tallahassee Democrat*, 8 July, 1951, p. 8.
181. Balfe, Bob. It's Post Time With, *Palm Beach Post*, 24 August, 1947, p. 13.
182. Luckyshow.org/baseball/49 HR, one season.html. Retrieved, 1 March, 2017.
183. Diamondsinthedusk.com, *Frosty Kennedy, "The Greatest Player Ever."* Retrieved, 1 March, 2017.
184. Baseball-reference.com.
185. Elvie Darden, phone interview with author, 23 January, 2017.
186. Baseball-reference.com.
187. Figueredo, Jorge. *Who's Who in Cuban Baseball, 1878–1961*, (McFarland & Co., Inc., Publishers: Jefferson, North Carolina and London, 2003), p. 81, 200, 201, 260, 261.
188. *Sporting News*, Costs Pepper $75 To Assault Fan, 5 September, 1951, p. 34.
189. Sun Sox Drub Smokers, 14–0, *St. Petersburg Times*, 5 September, 1951, p. 12.
190. FIL Foes Play Here Tonight, *Miami Herald*, 6 September, 1951, p. 6-D.
191. Burns, Jimmy. Miami Takes One-Game Lead In Playoff Set, *Miami Herald,* 7 September, 1951, p. 6-D.
192. Kelley, Whitey. Chapman Tossed Out In Rhubarb, *Miami Herald*, 9 September, 1951, p. 4-D.
193. Baseball-reference.com.
194. Ibid.
195. Hudson, Bob. Slim Right-Hander Stops Miami Nine On Four Hits, *St. Petersburg Times*, 11 September, 1951, p. 12.
196. Ibid.
197. Ibid.
198. Hudson, Bob. Saints Beat Sox, 4–3 To Stretch Series Lead, *St. Petersburg Times*, 13 September, 1951, p. 22.
199. Ibid.
200. Kelley, Whitey. Saints Post Third Win In Finals, *Miami Herald*, 14 September, 1951, p. 4-D.
201. Ibid.
202. Waters, Barney. 1,663 See Iott Serve 7-Hitter, *Miami Herald*, 15 September, 1951, p. 16-A.
203. Iott And Clark Shine As Locals Sweep Sun Sox, *St. Petersburg Times*, 15 September, 1951, p.10.
204. Ibid.
205. Ibid.
206. Goodson, Mike. Sports greats deserve recognition, *Gadsen Times,* 9 March, 2004, p. B-5.
207. Sun Sox Fire Pepper Martin, *Palm Beach Post*, 15 November, 1951, p. 11.

Royal Palm Grounds, circa 1910s (State Archives of Florida, Florida Memory)

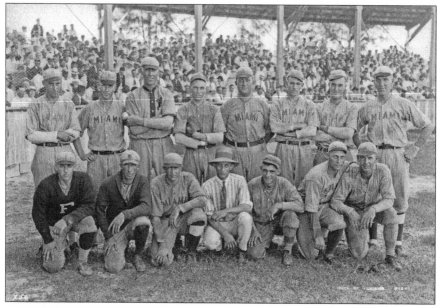

1921 Miami Magicians team photo (State Archives of Florida, Florida Memory)

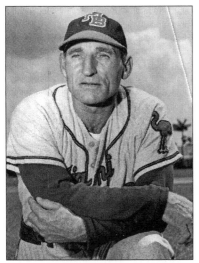

Manager Pepper Martin in his Flamingos regalia (Bob East, photographer, Miami News *Collection, HistoryMiami)*

Isey Bandrimer, 1920 Miami Magicians (Courtesy of the Bandrimer family)

1946 Miami Beach Flamingos at Miami airport (Stephen Smith photo collection)

MIAMI BEACH (130)

MAX ROSENFELD
Manager del Miami Beach

*Max Rosenfeld, 1946–47 Propagandas
Montiel, Cuban Baseball Card (Courtesy of
Cesar Lopez, baseball card collection)*

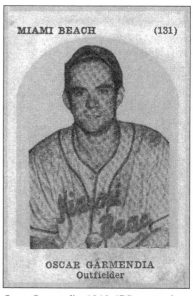

MIAMI BEACH (131)

OSCAR GARMENDIA
Outfielder

*Oscar Garmendia, 1946–47 Propagandas
Montiel, Cuban Baseball Card (Courtesy of
Cesar Lopez, baseball card collection)*

MIAMI SUN SOX (164)

HOWARD ERMISCH
Short Stop

*Howard Ermisch, 1946–47 Propagandas
Montiel, Cuban Baseball Card (Courtesy of
Cesar Lopez, baseball card collection)*

MIAMI SUN SOX (177)

PAUL WANER
Manager del Miami Sun Sox

*Paul Waner, 1946–47 Propagandas
Montiel, Cuban Baseball Card (Courtesy of
Cesar Lopez, baseball card collection)*

From left to right: Mel Nee, John Jakubov, and Walter Halsall, 1947 Miami Tourists (Miami News Collection, HistoryMiami)

The 1949 Reisler Bros. MVP trophy given to Miami Beach Flamingos Mike Conroy that is still in the family's possession to this day (Courtesy of Mike Conroy Jr.)

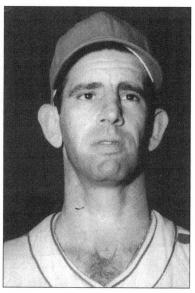

Roy Knepper (Courtesy of the Knepper family)

Emilio Cabrera, catcher for the 1949–51 Miami Beach Flamingos (Courtesy of Barbra Cabrera)

Pete Morant 1952 baseball card (Courtesy of Stephen Smith)

Knobby Rosa 1952 baseball card (Courtesy of Stephen Smith)

Bob Morem, 1948 Miami Tourists third baseman showing off his fielding skills (Courtesy of the Morem family)

From left to right: Chico Morilla, Nora Gonzalez, and her father on Chico and Nora's wedding day, 1949 (Miami News Collection, HistoryMiami)

1949 Miami Beach Flamingos team photo (Stephen Smith photo collection)

1950 Miami Sun Sox, Florida International League Championship team photo (Courtesy of the Darden family)

1952 Miami Sun Sox celebrating championship (Courtesy of Stephen Smith)

1956 Miami Marlins team photo (fan handout)

Satchel Paige on the mound at the Orange Bowl, August 7, 1956 (Lyn Pelham, photographer, Miami News Collection, HistoryMiami)

Satchel Paige and Woody Smith during a game sitting on the bench, 1956 (Lyn Pelham, photographer, Miami News Collection, HistoryMiami)

From left to right: Woody Smith, Bob Micelotta, and Ben Tompkins-anchored the Marlins infield 1956–1958 (Toby Massey, photographer, Miami News Collection, HistoryMiami)

Francisco "Pancho" Herrera, slugging first baseman for the 1957 and 1958 Miami Marlins (Miami News Collection, HistoryMiami)

Aerial view of Miami Stadium, circa 1960s (Walter Marks, photographer, Miami News Collection, HistoryMiami)

CHAPTER SEVEN

A GLORIOUS SEASON 1952

Many Miamians basked in the prosperity of the mid-1950s. Yet, not all that glitters is gold. The characterization as an idyllic time was not what it seemed as portrayed on television shows such as, *I Love Lucy* and *Ozzie and Harriet*. The reality of segregation was a fact of life throughout the U.S. In the Magic City, the Ku Klux Klan burned crosses on the lawn of the Miami Shores Community Church, just because of the perceived pro-black stance held by the congregation. These were disturbing actualities. On the baseball field, the first black players did not cross the color line of the Florida International League (FIL) until 1952, a full five years after Jackie Robinson's arrival in the major leagues.

An uneasy public also was digesting the so-called "Red Scare" brought on by the Cold War. Fears of communism created widespread paranoia. The black community, in particular, suffered as groups like the NAACP (National Association for the Advancement of Colored People) became labeled as incongruous and subversive by some in the community.

The Korean War began in June of 1950 and did not come to its conclusion until July of 1953. A notable loss came with the death of former 1948 Miami Tourists frontline catcher, Frederick Tschudin. An excellent handler of pitchers, Tschudin proved his mettle dealing with different personalities from the cocky Chet Covington to the kind-hearted Melvin Nee. Handy with the ash, he delivered a .273 batting average in 135 games behind the plate his lone season in Miami. Sadly, on March 14, 1952, Tschudin just shy of his 30th birthday conducted a flight-training mission aboard a North American T-6D Texan, and at some point during the assignment, the single-engine trainer suffered engine failure.

The plane crashed while attempting an emergency landing 12 miles northwest of Kingston, Georgia, killing Tschudin and his trainee Second Lieutenant Martin F. Gould.[1]

Miamians felt the effects of war and experienced great sadness with the death of 114, and 30 more listed as missing in action.[2] However, baseball continued to be a source of comfort and a buffer from the troubles and fears that surrounded everyone. The 1952 season was a welcome distraction in what proved to be the most exciting pennant race in FIL history.

1952

As the FIL approached its seventh campaign, its owners were concerned about shrinking attendance, and the survivability of the circuit. They were not alone; every level of minor league baseball nationwide experienced the same precipitous drop off in interest. Havana, once the stalwart of the league in fan support, had fallen from a high of 264,813 in 1947 to 83,051 in 1951. Overall FIL attendance, which peaked in 1949 at 899,171, dropped to 664,307 by 1951, a decrease of 26.1%.[3] Much of the woes were associated with the increased infringement of television viewing, which brought major league baseball, boxing, roller derby, wrestling, and Saturday college football into living rooms across America.[4] What many baseball historians considered the "Golden Age" of minor league baseball, which began in 1946, was at its end.

In 1951, only two FIL teams cleared the 100,000 mark in attendance, St. Petersburg at 139,464 and Miami 128,107.[5] Miami's numbers were especially disconcerting based upon their recent success on the diamond, and the fact that they played in a state-of-the-art stadium considered by many the best in minor league baseball. The situation had become so bad that the local press began to describe Miami Stadium as a "white elephant."

Miami Stadium finances were running in the red causing great concerns. Twenty-year-old Jose Aleman, Jr., reacted decisively by taking over control of operations and naming himself president of the organization. Looking to change the old guard, he ousted many of those associated with his father including the influential Harry B. Taber Sr., and Eddie Gilliland who had run the Sun Sox the previous three seasons. According to Jimmy Burns, "Disturbing to Aleman was the $29,000 annual charge for city and county taxes on a stadium which aside from baseball rentals has shown small return." He added, "The only revenue had come from charging the Sun Sox 25 cents of their gross receipts for rental and a similar sum from the Brooklyn Dodgers who used the park for exhibition games." Although a small income derived from the Kid Gavilan-Bobby Dykes boxing match, and rentals from the Roller Derby contests, these events did little to offset the mounting losses from the previous year.[6]

Assuming the role of Aleman, Jr.'s, most important advisor was George Salley, a local attorney. His task to assess the financial viability of Miami Stadium including whether or not to sell the property was unenviable.[7] From the fans perspective, the honeymoon with the ballpark had ended. As Rolando Llanes pointed out in his landmark book *White Elephant: The Rise and Fall of Miami Baseball Stadium*, "For the first time in Miami's young history a question arose that would haunt the city to this day: Was Miami a legitimate baseball town, or was it better suited for the once a year, name-brand appeal of spring training?"[8]

Not only were pecuniary concerns plaguing Sun Sox management, across the bay the Miami Beach franchise teetered on the verge of financial collapse. Only through the last minute actions of Paul D. Rust Jr., a minority stockholder-owner were the Flamingos rescued from going belly-up. On January 12, Rust purchased 100% of the team's stock and agreed to assume all other financial obligations tied to it. Rust, an avid yachtsman with a keen interest in tennis was a semi-retired owner with a controlling interest in a Kansas City lumber business at the time. He had only one previous connection to baseball, as president of the Optimists Club Miami Beach Little League.[9] Despite having relocated to Miami Beach four years earlier, Rust had become a strong advocate in the community. He affirmed that he purchased the stock, "to save baseball at the beach."[10]

Just like the Sun Sox front office, changes were also in store on the Beach. Carl Gardner, one of the three founders of Florida International League, active in club operations since 1946, and president of the Flamingos from 1946 to 1948 stepped aside. One of the most colorful executives in south Florida history said, "I've given a lot of effort and had a lot of pleasure from the Flamingos. Now it's time to retire and babysit for my grandson," said Gardner upon moving on to his next step in life.[11]

Nevertheless, some personnel remained. Returning were Leo Adeeb, who assumed the role of president, and Joe Ryan continuing in his dual role as vice president and general manager.[12] Most notably, Rust Jr., by keeping Ryan in his familiar job, proved to be a masterstroke. When Ryan put together his 1952 edition of the Flamingos, there were scant few predicting that this would be his winningest club in his long and storied career.

With new ownership in place, Ryan began his search for a new skipper. Candidates for the post boiled down to four well-respected former major leaguers including, Bobo Newsom, Pete Reiser, Roy Weatherly, and Whitlow Wyatt. One of the front-runners, Newsom dropped out of consideration as the *Sporting News* reported, ". . . because he did not relish the idea of flying to Havana."[13] However, Ryan's first choice boiled down to Wyatt. Surprisingly, after accepting the position, the former Brooklyn Dodger pitching star and Leo Durocher disciple, backed out of his contract choosing instead to go into the oil business.[14]

Ryan continued his search focusing on someone with excellent leadership on the field, as well as a potential draw at the gate. He soon made a surprising choice that set Miami abuzz and that no one saw coming. February 20, he announced Pepper Martin as the new manager. Flamingos management projected that the exceedingly popular "Wild Horse of the Osage" would pull in an additional 200 fans a game and over the course of the season 15,400 paying customers.[15] Martin's record of accomplishments in the FIL included a pair of second place finishes, one third place finish, and one league championship with the Sun Sox. Flamingos supporters felt optimistic about the upcoming season. The injection of energy that Martin brought gave them a reason to come out and support a team that could compete for the pennant.

Sun Sox fans were also optimistic. Brooklyn's Branch Rickey had confidence in Miami's prospects, and together with Aleman Jr., Sox management, and the Dodgers' brass, they were anxious to bring the pennant and championship to Miami again. Ever since the Dodgers had aligned themselves with Aleman Jr., they had lived up to their promise of supplying a steady stream of young talent and quality Cuban recruits. In addition, the Sun Sox had the blessing of abundant financial resources that Aleman Jr. brought to the table. It provided the Sun Sox with the ability to supplement his team with experienced players.

One of Miami's most important decisions came during the offseason with the announcement that 37-year-old Max Macon would take over as player-manager. "The Brooklyn organization is extremely happy with the appointment of Macon," said Harry Taber Jr. He added, "We feel his ability, sound judgment and colorful all-around play will satisfy the Miami fans."[16] Macon had ties to the Sunshine state, born on October 14, 1915, in Pensacola. At 18 years old, he signed his first contract with the St. Louis Cardinals and began his professional career with the Hutchinson Larks of the Class C Western Association. He showed an early propensity to be a two-way player putting up 15 wins against 11 losses on the mound, and occasionally taking the field while batting .216 which would serve him well later in his career. After a steady climb up the minor league ladder, he debuted with the Cardinals on April 21, 1938, pitching the last two-and-a-third innings against the Pittsburgh Pirates. He later pitched for the Dodgers (1940, 1942–43) but injured his arm. Max then re-invented himself as a first baseman during the war years with the Boston Braves where he spent the 1944 season, his last in the big leagues as a regular.[17]

Macon's last stop as a player came with Milwaukee of the American Association. While a member of the Brewers' he came to the realization that he had to make a career decision. Based upon his deep desire to continue in the game, he embarked on a new career as a minor league player-manager and in 1949 replaced William Jackson of the Modesto Reds of the Class C California League twenty-two games into the season. Despite his losing record, he proved himself adept as a leader, and an effective hitter, batting .383.[18]

Following the season, Macon applied for several coaching positions. Brooklyn management showed the most interest. Based upon his leadership abilities they offered him a position as a player-manager. His next assignment took him deep into Appalachian coal country with the Dodger's Class D affiliate in the Mountain States League at Hazard, Kentucky. His star student came along during his second season. His pupil, southpaw pitcher named Johnny Podres, went on to fame with the Dodgers, and later as a respected big league pitching coach. He absorbed much of his skipper's wisdom during his stay. In Macon's two seasons in Hazard, he guided the Bombers to a 169–82 record, as well as batted .392 in 1950 and .409 in 1951. During his second year, the Bombers finished in first place with a 93–33 slate and coasted to the league championship.[19]

Macon's success earned him a promotion. In 1952, the Sun Sox announced him as their new manager. When he arrived at spring training in Vero Beach, he found no shortage of capable youngsters and talented seasoned veterans. One player especially catching Macon's eye was a fleet-footed shortstop out of Cuba, Humberto "Chico" Fernandez. Fernandez would later go on to a successful eight-year big league career with the Dodgers, Detroit Tigers, New York Mets, and Philadelphia Phillies. He remembered his arrival in training camp that year, "They had those places where they used to keep the military people . . . And when I got there we had about 500 and some ballplayers."[20]

For Macon, cutting from the large herd of players the ones he most wanted, was like a cowboy trying to pick the best steer from a blue ribbon auction. Three of the most impressive young men he snatched were Fernandez, third baseman Dick Gray and a right-handed fire-baller from Canada, Billy Harris.

Joe Kwiatkowski, an outfielder assigned to Miami recalled, "I remember when they signed him [Fernandez]. They thought it was a big deal because he is going to help us win a pennant."[21] The slick-fielding Fernandez, spotted by Dodgers' scouts in the Cuban winter leagues, came to Miami as the most highly touted prospect having earned the honors the previous season with the Billings Mustangs as the Pioneer League's best shortstop. He proved a capable gloveman and handy with the war club having batted .284. Like Fernandez, Gray could also flash some leather, and held his own as a hitter stroking a solid .302 in 110 games for Valdosta of the Class D Georgia–Florida League. Gray's team-mate, twenty-year-old Harris (18–9, 2.10, 201 IP) joined him. The young pitcher's most impressive ability to paint the corners with his live fastball brought him much attention.[22 23]

Harris, a quiet good-natured sort, caught Macon's eye in spring training after he witnessed his devastating biting heater. Howard Kleinberg remembered that Harris' soon to be skipper baptized the young man with the nickname of a famous Dodgers pitcher that stuck with him during his entire stay in Miami. "The Dodgers had a pitcher named Kirby Higbe. And Billy's pitching style was a lot like Higbe's. And Max started calling him Higbe, and I started calling him Higbe."[24]

Along with Macon's stable of young bucks were returning veterans including, Paul Armstrong, catcher Ed Little, outfielder Rocky Rotzell, and hurlers Labe Dean, Arturo Seijas, Gilberto

Torres, and from the 1950 squad Billy Darden. Although *Miami News* sports writer, Morris McLemore predicted the Sun Sox to finish in second place behind St. Petersburg, the consensus by other league writers including Bob Balfe of the *Palm Beach Post*, forecasted the Sun Sox would take the flag. Miami Beach was pegged as a second division club.[25 26]

Macon quickly established a relationship with all of his players as being fair-minded, yet tough, as he expected a hundred percent effort. Although most of the Sun Sox respected their manager, his style did rub some of the Cuban veteran players the wrong way, most notably Seijas who would have several run-ins with Macon during the season.

Fernandez, coming in young and eager had a different perspective than his fellow compatriots. He instead benefitted from Macon's help and guidance. Macon saw firsthand the plight of what many Latin ballplayers were experiencing around the country and especially in the south. During the previous season in Hazard, a young Costa Rican pitcher, Danny Hayling felt the sting of racial threats, slurs, and intimidation and Macon had done his best to help the young man cope with the adversities. Like Hayling, Fernandez had experienced his own form of culture shock in Billings where almost no one spoke his native tongue. Macon wanted to ensure that Fernandez would not undergo the same abuse that Hayling had. When asked about how the FIL differed, Fernandez said, "I was lucky I went to the Sun Sox. That was my big break because all of those players that were there were Cubans from the Cuban teams."[27] Fernandez remembered how Macon went out of his way to help him adjust to Miami, although upon first arriving felt the cold shoulder of several of his teammates.

> Oh yes, to me he was the best manager for me because he used to be crazy about me . . . We came over here to Miami and nobody took me to eat or nothing. And I didn't know Miami, and he [Macon] showed me. He [Macon] was in a restaurant and he saw me walking around and he asked me what happened. He said, "Did you eat?" and I said, "No." He called for a meeting and told all the Cubans that if he ever asked me if I ate, and then if they didn't take care of me, that they had a fine. Max Macon was crazy about me.[28]

Life for the Cuban born players was difficult. Many of the players had racial slurs slung at them at times, and the language barrier always presented a problem. Aleman Jr. who was quite generous in his dealings with all of his players was even more sympathetic to his fellow countrymen. According to Kleinberg, "He was generous to his players, especially his Cuban players. Now, that's not a bias. The Cuban players were in a strange country and he was just trying to make them feel better. He didn't buy a can of beer for Max Macon (laughing), but Max was tough."[29]

Meanwhile, a busy Martin and Ryan continued to beat the bushes and worked the telephones looking for players while quietly building a team. Martin welcomed into the pink birds nest one of his favorite players from the Sun Sox, and a FIL fixture, Knobby Rosa. The spunky infielder had retired from baseball, but upon hearing about Martin's decision, he returned for one more season.[30] Rosa, a scrapper, wore his heart on his sleeve, exactly the type of player that Pepper loved because like himself, Rosa did not back down to anyone.

Kleinberg recalled confronting the fiery Rosa over an issue that offended the longtime FIL star and captured a bit of the nature of a fierce competitor.

> Knobby, he was really a cantankerous guy. One time, I don't remember whether it was with the Sun Sox in '51, or it was the Flamingos in '52, more likely it was with the Sun Sox. He chased me around the training table because of something I wrote. And he wanted to really lay me out. I had to run for my life. He was really a tough guy.[31]

However, Ryan's biggest coup involved the signing of two former major leaguers, Jesse Levan and Mizell "Whitey Platt, as well as one-time star of the Negro Leagues, Dave Barnhill.

At twenty years old, Jesse Levan earned a late September call-up with the Philadelphia Phillies after batting .309 and belting 19 home runs for Wilmington of the Class B Interstate League in 1947. After a "cup of coffee" in the city of Brotherly Love, he returned to the minor leagues for the next four seasons mostly in the lower classification with varying degrees of success. By 1951, a frustrated Levan had landed in the Class C Provincial League, a fast independent league that was a haven for black ballplayers, and major and minor league castoffs. While performing for

Saint-Hyacinthe, he batted a career-high .347 in 120 games.[32] Perhaps looking for a locale with warmer weather, and better pay, he showed up in the Flamingos' spring training camp looking for a job. Martin's initial assessment of the veteran was cool at best. According to teammate, Charles "Pete" Morant, his soon-to-be teammate, the wayward Levan changed his manager's mind later by making quite an impression on him.

> We were getting ready for the season. Jesse Levan, who wound up leading the league that year, I think there was a question mark in Pepper's mind as to whether he was going to make the ballclub or not. He [Martin] lined people up, and they had races, and Jesse just outran everybody. And he put him on the ballclub, and he won the batting title that year probably by, I'd have to look, by thirty points or so.[33]

Joining Levan as one of the Flamingos' most experienced hitters was Whitey Platt. His nickname was derived from his sandy-haired tuft. He was a local boy from West Palm Beach who attended Palm Beach High School and came to Miami Beach with the most major league experience. Platt previously appeared with the Chicago Cubs in both 1942 and 1943, was used almost exclusively as a pinch-hitter. He later caught on with the Chicago White Sox in 1946 and with the St. Louis Browns in 1948 and 1949. His best year being 1948 when he appeared in 123 games, connected for seven homers, and drove in 82 runs. Ironically, it was his second tour of duty with the Brownies having previously served as a batboy for them in his youth during spring training.[34]

And then there was the curious case of the well-traveled, Dave "Impo," or Skinny" Barnhill. Although he only stood at 5'7" and weighed 145 pounds, his contemporaries compared his fastball to the legendary Satchel Paige's own. Barnhill began his pro career in 1936 barnstorming with the Miami Giants, Zulu Giants (1937) and Ethiopian Clowns (1937–40).[35] He also spent time in the Negro Leagues with the New York Cubans (1941–49), the Cuban Winter League with Marianao (1947–48 through 1949–50),[36] and the Puerto Rican League with Humacao (1940–41).[37]

A 35-year-old Barnhill signed with the New York Giants in 1949 and reported to their top minor league affiliate the Minneapolis Millers of the AAA-American Association where he toiled for the next two seasons. Clearly, Barnhill's dreams of making it to the major leagues had long since faded, but he was still proving to be an effective starting pitcher. Later, the Oakland Oaks of the Pacific Coast League purchased his contract and that is where the story takes an interesting turn. Prior to the 1952 season he began to complain of arm pain and approached his manager Mel Ott telling him, "I might as well go home because I know I can't help you. Not this season at any rate." He stated that after pitching in an exhibition game a few days earlier that something snapped and his arm pained him so much that he could not sleep and left the team to retire to his home in Miami.[38] For whatever reasons that are lost to history, despite Barnhill's injured wing, Ryan took a flyer on the 38-year-old veteran and signed him. It proved a fortuitous move. Upon arriving in Miami Beach it was not long after that his aching right wing seemed to have healed.

Charlie Albury, an umpire over four seasons in the FIL remembered Barnhill and what an extraordinarily gifted pitcher he was. In particular, he recalled a special delivery that left one batter shaking his head at home plate. "He had a pitch he threw that twisted his wrist. And that ball . . . We were playing the Beach and he was up there and that guy [Barnhill] threw the first pitch. The guy [the batter] stepped back and said, 'What was the damn first pitch. And then he threw it again and that was Barnhill."[39]

Barnhill joined a staff that featured three veteran frontline pitchers, Dick McMillin, Chico Morilla, and Marshall O'Coine. Ryan further bolstered his starting rotation bringing in 20-year-old port-sider Pete Morant (15–7, 3.13) from Landis/Elkin of the Class D North Carolina State League.

Morant, who was signed right out of high school in 1951, joined shortstop Jack Caro in spring camp as one of the two youngest players on a squad of veteran players made up almost entirely of men in their mid-20s and early 30s. Morant had gone by his given name (Charles) his entire life, until he arrived in Landis. His manager then bestowed him with a nickname that he carried throughout his baseball career.

> I did not go by Charles at that time. The reason was when I went up to Landis, North Carolina I introduced myself to the skipper and he said, "Oh God, Charles. We got five Charles' and pick any other name." Well up in Pasco people started calling me Pete. Don't ask me why. So, I said, "Yeah, just call me Pete." Most of the time you look back at anything written you will see that my name is Pete Morant, not Charles.[40]

Nicknames aside, other additions to the roster were fan favorite and outfielder Lou Colombo who returned after missing almost the entire 1951 season with a severely injured ankle, outfielder-pitcher Mort Smith, and catcher Chuck Ehlman.

With rosters in place, both teams commenced the regular season on April 9. While Miami traveled north to Lakeland, history was made in Miami Beach's Flamingo Park. For the first time in the history of the FIL, black ballplayers took to the field. Jackie Robinson had broken major league baseball's color barrier on April 15, 1947, yet the FIL had been slow in making progress towards ending segregation in their "neck of the woods." Although several olive-skinned Cuban players like Carlos Bernier and Bobby Estalella had been stars in the league, team owners had been careful to stock their teams with men of lighter complexion in fear that fans would stay away from the ballparks.

When the Flamingos' George Handy took his position at second base, and Havana's Angel Scull stepped into the batter's box to lead off the game, the color line had finally been broken. Later in the bottom of the first inning Cubans' Silvio Garcia, who at one time was considered by Branch Rickey the choice to break major league baseball's color barrier, joined Handy and Scull when he trotted out to his position. Elsewhere around the league, other black ballplayers made their historic debuts including former New York Cubans Negro League star outfielder Claro Duany of Tampa,[41] and later shortstop and third baseman Woodrow "Woody" Means, formerly of the Negro League's Chattanooga Choo-Choos, with Fort Lauderdale on April 25.[42]

In general, most of the black ballplayers were well-received, at least while on the diamond, although occasional jeers and ugly remarks, especially in the northernmost FIL cities were still heard. At the same time, conditions outside of the baseball field remained difficult due to the ugly practice of Jim Crow laws. In most cities, black ballplayers were unable to stay in the same hotels with their club mates. Kleinberg witnessed firsthand how Miami star Chico Fernandez was able to get around the prejudicial attitudes of others and was able to share a room with his teammate.

> There were a couple of players in the league who were perceived as black and they had to stay at other hotels, not in Miami, but over the state. And Humberto Fernandez, who

later became known as Chico, he was an interesting guy in that he was black and yet he wasn't black. And I remember in Lakeland, which also had wedges of segregated areas. The Floridian Hotel, after a ball game, Humberto would put a little powder on his face so he could stay at the hotel.[43]

Others were less fortunate and felt the sting of racial prejudice. Morant remembered his two teammates Barnhill and Handy still faced obstacles in most of the cities they traveled to. Morant remembered, "And between he [Dave Barnhill] and George Handy . . . Before they could stay in hotels with us, they went someplace in the black community and left them off. And then we would go to the hotel in town someplace where we traveled."[44]

Surprisingly, the sportswriters made little mention of the historic appearances of Duany, Garcia, Handy and Scull on opening day from their respective cities. Nevertheless, the season kicked off with Miami coasting to an easy win over Lakeland on the road banging out 12 hits, including two singles and double by Macon, and Labe Dean throwing nine shutout innings for an easy 10 to 0 win.[45]

Miami Beach began their season in opposite fashion. Playing at home in front of 2,021, the combatants battled for 12 innings before a pair of errors; the first by Levan who dropped a fly ball, and then Caro who threw wild to second base on a force out attempt, led up to Morilla walking in the deciding run in the top of the final frame. Havana, stood tall behind former Washington Senator, Santiago "Sandy" Ullrich's fine pitching, and captured the 1 to 0 victory.[46]

The much anticipated first meeting between the Flamingos and Sun Sox finally occurred a week into the season with the clubs tangling on April 16 at Miami Stadium in front of 3,402. Kwiatkowski remembered how during the special pre-game ceremony to introduce the players from both teams that the always-colorful Martin had a unique spin when he announced his team.

If you knew Pepper Martin, or not he was a good old country boy. And he introduced his players, and he said to the fans, 'Now just because my boys are wearing the gray, just remember that they're still good clean cut American boys.' He was talking like they were rebels from the Civil War. I don't know why that stuck out, but it struck me funny at the time.[47]

With the festivities concluded it was time to play ball, and Miami scored first off Walt Nothe in the second frame after Armstrong singled, Gray drew a base on balls, and Macon singled driving in a run. Miami Beach knotted the score in the top of the eighth only to see the lead slip away when Armstrong, who had stroked a double earlier in the inning, scored on Cecil Dotson's sacrifice fly. The victory was the second of the season for Darden as he held the Flamingos to four hits. Final score Miami 2 Miami Beach 1.[48]

Although prognosticators said Miami would be atop the league race, it was Miami Beach that got off to a scorching start winning 21 of their first 30 games. On the morning of May 8, the Flamingos tied for first place with St. Petersburg, while Miami stood in fifth place at 15–15 having lost eight of their previous ten games.

That same evening the Sun Sox were on the verge of losing another game to Tampa while their nemesis Chet Covington stood on the mound taunting his opponents. Macon, who had committed an error earlier costing his team two runs, decided to take matters into his own hands. "We lost three in a row in Tampa and we had to win this one," said the vexed Macon. Although the Miami skipper had admitted to a dead arm, he took to the hill replacing Gil Torres, his starting pitcher. He then proceeded to retire five of the next six batters with ease striking out four.[49] With the score tied at two apiece in the bottom of the eighth inning, the fleet-footed Fernandez cleverly used some heads-up base running by first beating out a drag bunt, then tagging up all the way to third base on Armstrong's deep fly ball to right field. Fernandez then dashed home on Rotzell's sacrifice fly to center field that turned out to be the winning run as Miami prevailed, 3 to 2, Macon earning the win.[50]

The victory turned out to be a turning point in the Sun Sox season. From that point forward, Macon's charges played nearly flawless baseball until crossing the finish line. Miami launched the first of many winning streaks, which began when they won 27 of their next 30 games. During the run, Harris was a perfect 6–0, Torres was 4–1, and swingman Lowell Grosskopf was 4–0, which included a pair of his victories coming in relief.[51]

The Harris-Torres tandem was matchless when it came to their ability to win games all year long. Yet, the two were as opposite as night and day when it came to their background and personality.

Harris was born on December 3, 1931, in the Canadian town of Duguayville, New Brunswick. He was the prototypical hometown boy [who] made good. Like most Canadian youths, he grew up with a hockey stick in his hand, but unlike most, also played baseball when the weather permitted. In the end, the pull of the horsehide sphere was stronger than the lure of the slap shot. Harris's break came when Bill O'Connor, the Brooklyn Dodgers New England scout, spotted the burly 5'8" kid while pitching for the Maritime Champions Dieppe Junior Cardinals, and Moncton Legionnaires of the New Brunswick Senior League. Harris was offered a contract for $1,000, plus a $500 bonus if he stuck it out for longer than the first month.[52] During his 2008 Canadian Baseball Hall of Fame induction speech, Harris told the story of his train trip to Vero Beach for his first spring training with the Dodgers, and his chance encounter with a big husky, athlete heading to Dodgers spring training camp in Vero Beach who he struck up a conversation with.

> He looked at me and said, "You're not going to make it." And I said, "Why?" And he said, "You're way too small." Well, it just so happened we got on the same team in spring training, and after four months he got released and I was there (in professional baseball) for sixteen years.[53]

Harris earned his bonus by persevering his first season surviving the oppressive humidity, sweaty and bumpy bus rides, and poor playing fields at Valdosta. His talents on the hill produced 18 wins, which warranted a promotion the next season. Seeing how well Macon worked with pitchers, Harris's assignment to Miami was a natural fit. The young Canadian must have thought he had gone to baseball heaven. He had the opportunity to play in a major league level ballpark and travel to exotic spots like Havana by chartered plane and various sundry locales in Florida. Although never one to complain, Harris, known as being rather reserved, took exception when he took to the mound. "He was a very shy guy and one terrific pitcher," said Kleinberg.

Whereas Harris was more reserved and just beginning to build his professional resume, his counterpart Torres was brash and opinionated although generally likable. He had already earned star status in his native country of Cuba and was one of its most revered players. Born August 23, 1915, in Regla, Cuba he was the son of Ricardo, a star catcher and first baseman in the Cuban professional league during the middle-teens to the late 20s. The elder Torres appeared with the Washington Senators from 1920–22. Gilberto followed his father's footsteps and enjoyed an 18-year career in the Cuban winter leagues, as well as spending four seasons with the Senators in 1940, and 1944–1946.[54][55]

Nineteen-fifty-two would prove to be Torres' last great season in a stellar career that would stretch until 1955. Moreover, what a year it would be for him and the Sun Sox. He proved to be invaluable to Macon, for not only his pitching prowess but his versatility playing in the field and pinch-hitting. In a 2013 interview, Kleinberg recalled Torres.

> Torres was a revered man. This was way before Castro . . . He was terribly anti-American and was always complaining about America. And of course, as soon as Castro took over he became a darling of Castro. He took over the Cuban National team. I remember though. When he was in his prime with the Sun Sox he could be very nice . . . And after the game, we would all get on the ferry and go to Regla where he was a hero . . . The restaurant would stay open at night and they would put out a huge snapper with all kinds of onions and olive oil and olives.[56]

Torres' neighbor in Miami was the Darden family. Elvie and her husband Billy lived in one of the apartment buildings that Aleman Jr. made available to his players. One of her fondest memories was of Torres and the kindness he always showed towards their son, "In fifty-two, our son was maybe . . . , he was small. I guess he was about a year old. And we'd always have a chair down to block the door. And Torres would come by and talk to him. He would stick his hand in there holding onto that chair and would stop and talk with him . . . It was like we were just one big family."[57]

Harris and Torres started out the season well despite an overall poor start by Miami. On the other hand, Ryan, although pleased with his club's start, was concerned about his roster mix and began to tweak and strengthen his roster. Faced with reducing his roster to 17 players by May 9 he optioned Handy to Keokuk (Kernels) of the Class B Three-I League (he would return to Miami Beach later in the season), and Ken Munroe to Thibodaux (Giants) of the Class C Evangeline League. Ryan also dealt outfielder Clark

Henry and pitcher Harry Raulerson.[58] The transactions allowed more playing time for infielder George Wehmeyer who was more versatile than Handy and was a better gloveman, and outfielders Oscar Garmendia and Edmond Wilson.

By June 6, the Flamingos watched their league lead disappear to the hard-charging Sun Sox and instead were gazing up at Miami now 3½ games in front of the pack. A critical three-game set against the Sun Sox was on tap for the archrivals with pennant implications. Pitching the curtain raiser for Miami was Vicente Lopez. He returned to the Sun Sox earlier in the season from Fort Worth after receiving little work. Lopez was riding a remarkable 21-game win streak as a member of the Miami club dating back to 1950. Lopez won his last 16 decisions before a promotion to Fort Worth in 1950 and won his first five decisions to start the '52 season. The Flamingos' southpaw, Nothe, would oppose the fire-balling Lopez.[59]

Nothe was characteristic of many pitchers of his era. He lost his best years during service in World War II, in his case, serving with the Army Air Force.[60] After his honorable discharge from the service, he received an invitation to the 1946 Dodgers' spring training camp and inked a contract to play with their farm club in either Mobile or Fort Worth.[61] St. Paul of the American Association purchased him and he compiled a less than impressive 3–11 record and 4.44 ERA. Nothe returned the next year, assigned to Montreal of the International League where he toiled for two seasons before the Dodgers gave up on him and handed him his release. He then began his minor league sojourn with stops in Toledo, Hollywood, (California), Baltimore and Atlanta with poor to limited success.[62] By the spring of 1952, Nothe found himself vying for a roster spot with the Flamingos. Martin was impressed with what he saw and slotted him into the regular starting rotation.

Nothe was on his game that day putting down the Sun Sox with little complaint over the first three innings. The Flamingos put a pair of runs on the scoreboard in the third frame thanks to successive singles by Wehmeyer, Ray Williams, Levan, a pair of free passes and an error. Given the lead, Nothe confidently dominated Miami scattering six hits without giving up a run. One of the longest winning streaks in baseball screeched to a halt as the despondent Lopez moped off the mound. Miami Beach had pulled to within 2½ games of the league lead.[63]

The following day brought heavy rains and cancellation of the second game of the series necessitating a make-up doubleheader on June 8. Although the ballfield was damp, the spirits of Macon's club and Pepper's charges were anything but dank as both clubs warmed up prior to game time. Taking the mound in the seven-inning opening contest were two 20-year-old peach-faced kids, hard-throwing Harris for Miami and the crafty southpaw Morant for Miami Beach. Both pitchers were in the midst of their most sensational seasons.

In an odd twist, the Flamingos were the home team during the first game of the twin bill even though Miami Stadium played host. The home advantage switched back to the Sun Sox for the late match. The arrangement accommodated the 4,100 who turned out for what proved to be one of the highest attended contests of the year.[64]

Although Miami managed five hits and reached base on a couple of Flamingo errors, they failed to hit in the clutch and bring a runner across the plate. Rosa's leadoff triple in the first inning, followed later by a Levan single plated the only run of the game. It was a rare loss for Harris who would be on the losing end of only six games by the season's conclusion.[65]

In the nightcap, McMillin squared off against Grosskopf. Martin used a strategy more commonly used today and turned to three relief pitchers to bail out McMillin. Going into the eighth frame the Sun Sox held a 2 to 1 lead. In the ninth, the usually reliable Miami defense counted a couple of miscues, gave up a pair of singles, a safe bunt and a fielder's choice that led to a three-run outburst that proved to be the difference as Miami Beach came from behind to win 4 to 2. Newly signed Frank Smith, a former University of Miami football star (no relation to Mort Smith) sparked the rally with a single while serving as a pinch-hitter. Andy Elko, acquired early in the season from Atlanta of the Southern Association, would make 23 appearances including only 10 in relief, followed Smith to earn the save.[66][67] The Flamingos had closed the gap pulling within a half-game of the league-leading Sun Sox with the sweep.

Throughout the summer, both teams traded places in the standings with Miami usually on top. Much like 1968, the season of the pitcher in the major leagues, so it was the same with the FIL as several moundsmen around the league had record-breaking seasons. In Macon's case, he rode his best three starters, Harris, Torres and Dean while mixing and matching his fourth spot with Solis and Grosskopf; in particular, Harris and Torres who were on a record pace pitching several shutouts and maintaining microscopic ERAs below 1.00.

On the other hand, Martin skillfully mixed and matched ten different pitchers with unprecedented success. Five members of the Flamingos' staff would hurl over 100 innings and all with sub 2.00 ERAs. Nothe led all starters with 191 innings and tied Morant for the team lead in wins with 15. Barnhill, despite what was advertised as a bad arm, paced the club with a stingy 1.19 ERA while working 181 innings, a decent workload for a 38-year-old. Even super utility man Mort Smith figured in 82 innings with an impressive 2.09 ledger.[68]

The two clubs met again starting on June 30 for a three-game set at Miami Stadium. Nearly missing the series was Martin who once again came under the scrutiny of league officials for bad behavior. New FIL President Henry S. Baynard handed down a $75 fine and three-game suspension involving two prior incidences.[69] The first involved a dispute between Martin, and umpire Art Talley and his watch. The league's policy and local curfew laws stated that an inning was not to start after 11:50 pm. The issue of time came to a head during the second game of a doubleheader against West Palm Beach at Connie Mack Field (formerly Wright Park). The Indians won the opening game 4 to 0, a contest that featured a ninety-minute delay due to a heavy downpour of rain. The second contest did not begin until 11 pm, but according to league rules, the game must proceed even if the suspension was inevitable. According to Talley, his watch said 11:48 pm when the fourth inning ended. At the time, West Palm held a 1 to 0 lead. Martin went into a verbal tirade arguing that it was past the curfew and the game had to be suspended making it unofficial. Martin's contention was that Talley's watch was ten minutes slow, but Talley was having nothing of it. Neither team scored in the fifth frame, and in accordance with league rules was an official game. Although the Indians earned the 1 to 0 win, the game finished under protest by Martin.[70]

The second incident occurred on June 10 and concerned a heated exchange at home plate in Havana between Martin and umpire Archie Jones. The call in question came during a critical part of the contest in the sixth inning when the arbiter ruled a

Cubans' base-runner safe at home. Martin went into a diatribe, quarreling that the baserunner was out by a mile, but Jones stood firm despite the objections. Reportedly, Joe Ryan challenged the ruling by stating that a picture of the play showed the runner out by eight feet. The Cubans garnered the victory, 7 to 5, while Martin went to the showers.[71][72]

Despite the fine and suspension, Baynard delayed his sentence and allowed Martin to manage his team in the critical series against the Sun Sox.[73] In the lid-lifter, Macon sent Harris to the hill to face Barnhill. As was the case, in the majority of meetings between the two, it was a pitcher's duel. For five innings, neither team was able to put anything on the scoreboard but "goose eggs." In the bottom of the sixth, Barnhill ran into trouble when he loaded the bases. Having already developed a blister on his fingertip the veteran unleashed a wild pitch over the head of his backstop Ehlman allowing Harris to score from third base. Given all the support he needed, Harris bore down, and by the game's end, the burly Canuck scattered seven hits and allowed only one free pass, earning a 1 to 0, whitewashing win.[74]

The next evening, the second half of the Sun Sox's dynamic pitching duo took the hill against right-handed swingman Bob Palmer. With the score tied in the bottom of the eighth at one apiece, the Sun Sox exploded for four runs stringing together four hits, a balk, sacrifice fly, and a walk. Torres allowed eight hits, yet was touched for only a solitary tally as the Sun Sox prevailed, 5 to 1. The victory was his eleventh win and it stretched the Sun Sox's league lead to 3½ games.[75]

In the series finale, Darden's work completed the sweep of the series although not without a scare. Miami jumped to the lead scoring a pair in the first inning off Nothe on singles by Tom Murphy, Rotzell and Fernandez. Then added an additional score in the second when Dotson singled, Joe Kwiatkowski, Murphy and Armstrong coaxed a trio of "Annie Oakley's" forcing in Dotson. Darden cruised until the ninth inning when the Flamingos rallied. After Ray Williams drew a free pass, he advanced to third on Ehlman's, too hot to handle line drive off the glove of third baseman Gray. Edmond Wilson then smacked a double that plated a run, followed by Mort Smith grounding out which allowed Ehlman to race home for the second run. Nevertheless, Macon, with infinite patience, stuck with Darden who "dug down deep" slamming the door on Miami Beach and collecting his tenth win of the season.[76][77] Although naysayers were starting to write the Flamingos' epitaph because the Sun Sox built a 4½ game lead, their largest of the season, the pink birds were far from dead.

Both frontrunners remained hot through the month of July. They matched each other winning 19 of 28 games and separated themselves from their closest rival Tampa who had fallen 9½ games off the pace during a banner month full of highlights.

On July 10, Torres made history in Miami versus West Palm Beach. With two outs in the bottom of the ninth frame, the Indians' Gordon Bragg stepped up to the plate. The Sun Sox were clinging to a 1–0 lead. Torres had been relying on his trusty knuckleball all night and up to this point had yet to yield a base hit to the visitors. The only Indian to reach base was Butch Lawing on a walk in the fourth with two outs. The tension inside of Miami Stadium was at a fever pitch as the crowd stood on its feet. Bragg, looking for another butterfly to come in, instead was surprised when Torres fired an overhand curve, "I hadn't tried one all night," said Torres after the game. With a loud crack of the bat, Bragg connected, but the ball started drifting foul down the left field line. Armstrong, "on his horse" raced over, reached up, and caught the ball for the final out. Torres had completed the first no-hitter at Miami Stadium as his teammates mobbed him on the mound. It was Torres' ninth shutout and thirteenth victory against three losses.[78]

"The Miami press corps had touted Torres so much for using the knuckler that many thought that was his only pitch. "Gil was a character. He would throw that knuckleball," said teammate Kwiatkowski. "He would show them. You would see him knuckling that ball. The batters would see it and he was just phenomenal with that. You wonder how his arm lasted."[79]

However, Ed Little, Torres' catcher for the historic game, disputed that Torres was a one-dimensional pitcher who relied only on the knuckler. Little stated during a 2013 interview, "He was a regular pitcher with the ability to throw a knuckleball. He could throw a curve ball. He could throw any pitch you can think of, he could throw. His specialty was he could throw change-ups."[80]

Not only was the pennant race heating up, so was the Florida summer. Even though most games were at night, the incessant humidity and warm temperatures tested even the hardiest player's stamina. Many resorted to cooling off at the local cinema, which "featured" air conditioning. Kleinberg recalled that going to a movie theater was one way to beat the heat.

> That was the year, 1952. *Singing in the Rain* came out . . . Gene
> Kelly, Debbie Reynolds, and Donald O'Connor. In all of these
> towns, Lakeland and West Palm Beach they only had one movie
> there . . . And so if you wanted to cool off one day, I don't know
> how many times I saw *Singing in the Rain*, traveling around
> the Florida International League. And ballplayers would go too.
> Higbe, you know Dotson, and all of those guys would sit there
> in the cool air because there was always, *Singing in the Rain*.[81]

Martin, like everyone else, was looking for a way to avoid
the high temperatures. His well-founded ability to gain the edge
on his opponents came to fruition and on the night of July 14.
As fans filed into Flamingo Park, they were surprised to see the
hometown team donning shorts. Martin may have borrowed a
page from his own playbook as well as Hollywood Stars' manager
Fred Haney's, when both their clubs debuted in shorts in 1950.
Haney said, "It stands to reason that players should be faster
wearing them-and that half step going down to first alone wins or
loses many a game."[82] The knock-kneed Pepper must have been
quite the comical sight to the 1,841 fans that came out to view
the game.[83]

Once again, the youthful Harris found himself pitted against
veteran graybeard Barnhill. Miami broke the ice in the fourth
inning when Armstrong scored on Macon's single to right field.
The action picked up in the bottom of the same inning when
Colombo hit a slow-roller toward Jimmy Bragan at second. The
slow-moving Colombo chugged down the first base line. Umpire
Charlie Albury hesitated, and then animatedly ruled Lou out.
Martin had been in rare form all year in his battles with the umpires and as expected, he came charging onto the field with fire
in his eyes. While pleading his case, Martin out of frustration,
slammed his cap into the ground bringing on an automatic ejection from Albury. For Harris's part, he would escape the inning
unscathed and seemed in control and poised to win his second
consecutive 1–0 win against Barnhill. However, Platt had different plans. In the ninth frame, he led off with a ringing single to
left field. Johnny Podgajny, Martin's assistant coach, then called
on the speedy Wehmeyer to pinch run. Williams then sacrificed
Wehmeyer to second. Harris retired Eddie Wilson leaving only
weak hitting Ehlman between him and victory. After a pair of

wide tosses by Harris, Ehlman got the pitch he was looking for and drove the ball just over the head of Macon at first. Wehmeyer raced home from second with the tying run putting the game into extra innings. Ironically, in the ninth, Ehlman argued a ball and strike call and came close to receiving the thumb. Only the efforts of Podgajny to get between his catcher and the umpire prevented Ehlman from joining Martin for an early shower.[84] [85]

Harris and Barnhill continued toiling into the eleventh. In the bottom of the fateful inning, Levan started out by collecting his third single of the night. Wehmeyer looking to sacrifice the runner, overplaced a perfect roller towards Macon who picked up the ball, but threw it in the dirt towards second, allowing Levan to slide in safely; it was a costly error. Harris followed by getting Williams to fly out, but the speedy Levan tagged up to third. Wilson drew an intentional pass and once again, Ehlman stepped to the plate. Ehlman, a .220 hitter, who Martin hyperbolically described in a *Miami Herald* article as the smartest catcher who ever played for him, connected on Harris's first offering just far enough into right field for Rotzell to catch, but too far to nail Levan who raced home on the sacrifice to score the winning run. The final tally showed Flamingos 2 Sun Sox 1.[86] Miami Beach had closed the gap to ½ a game behind the Sun Sox.

The next day featured an action-packed doubleheader as 2,187 fans squeezed into Flamingo Park. The opener featured Torres against Morilla. Torres began the day battling a bad back but kept the Flamingos in check for the first five innings. In the sixth, with the Sun Sox enjoying a 1–0 lead, Torres got some help from fellow countryman Sierra who doubled off Morilla with the bases loaded extending Miami's lead to 4–0.[87]

In the bottom of the sixth, Miami Beach rallied when Levan tagged Torres and went deep with a three-run home run. Torres un-phased, settled down and the Flamingos were unable to touch him for the remainder of the game as he picked up his fourteenth win against three losses.[88]

In the nightcap, the tension between the two teams once again reached the boiling point. In the third inning, Kwiatkowski took a half-swing on a full count that umpire Butch Henline ruled a ball. As Kwiatkowski jogged down the line, Martin charged out of the dugout in a fury. He took a couple of handfuls of dirt and less than politely deposited it on Henline's shoes. His overt actions drew the umpire's thumb, and for the second night in a row, Martin was banished.[89]

With Kwiatkowski aggressively leading off first, Jimmy Bragan swung at a third strike as his teammate broke for second. Ehlman received the ball cleanly and threw a head-high rocket towards second that Wehmeyer caught and then aggressively put the tag into the face of Kwiatkowski while he slid into the bag. A few adult words exchanged between combatants followed with fisticuffs and soon thereafter both benches emptied. By the time the dust had cleared, both Kwiatkowski and Wehmeyer received ejections and warnings issued to both teams.[90]

Nevertheless, Miami Beach's starting pitcher Nothe, scattered seven hits. Bolstered by nine hits from his Flamingos teammates the pink birds went on to take the "curtain closer" by the final of 3–2.[91] It was the ninth time in sixteen meetings between the two teams that a one-run difference decided the winner.[92]

Miami and Miami Beach remained on torrid paces and tangled again on August 5. The Sun Sox held a two-game lead going into the three-game set and were confident going with Torres to start the series against Barnhill. Nonetheless, the Flamingos continued their mastery over the Sun Sox by taking the opening game of the series. Miami Beach got all the offense they needed in the first inning when Caro, Handy, Levan and Platt hit consecutive singles that staked them to a 1–0 lead. Miami Beach put up an insurance run in the next inning when Mort Smith scored on Wilson's single. Barnhill did the rest of the work, crafting the 2–0 shutout, and holding his opponents to six hits.[93]

The next evening proved to be one of the highlight games of the year with a most unusual outcome. The 3,000 plus that trooped into Miami Stadium got their money's worth for the price of their ducat. For the first seven innings, Harris and Nothe matched zeroes, the only difference being that Nothe had not allowed a single base runner. In the bottom of the seventh, with two outs, Kwiatkowski hit a hard grounder to Handy who booted the play resulting in an error. Nothe's "perfecto" ended, but by the end of regulation play, he had sustained the no-hitter. Unfortunately for him, his club mates had failed to score a run.[94]

All good things come to an end and in the bottom of the tenth, Bragan hit a "grass cutter" single past Handy that ended the no-no. Armstrong followed by sacrificing Bragan to second and Rotzell singled to right field plating Bragan It proved to be the only run, and two base hits, that blemished an otherwise near-perfect night. Although clearly disappointed, Nothe was the consummate team player when after the game he said, "Who cares whether I pitch a no-hitter or not. I got out there on the mound to win the baseball game; all other things are incidental." Harris, who had also pitched brilliantly, earned his nineteenth win and ninth shutout while stingily giving up only four hits a pair to Handy and Ray Williams.[95][96]

The Flamingos gained a measure of revenge in the rubber game against Macon's charges. McMillin struggled early, so Martin made an unconventional choice and turned to Smith. Smith, a jack-of-all-trades, not only played the infield and outfield but also pitched occasionally. Coming out of the bullpen in the second inning, he proceeded to hurl eight scoreless innings, baffling the Sun Sox with his change-up. Darden, like McMillin, was ineffective and pulled in the second. Unlike Smith, Grosskopf struggled, as the Flamingos prevailed 5 to 2. Martin exclaimed after the game that he had found a new secret weapon for the stretch run in Smith. Miami Beach was now within a game of Miami.[97]

In the continuing saga of the wild and wacky FIL, what happened next had immense repercussions on the pennant race. Up until now, the relationship between the Flamingos and Sun Sox management had been quite amicable. In fact, Sun Sox business manager Jerry Waring had turned to Ryan several times for help and advice on several matters. In spite of this, following the game on August 7, Waring filed charges with FIL president Baynard that during the Flamingos' win they had used an ineligible player. According to the *Sporting News*, "Waring contended that the protest was made (1) because he believed that he had finally caught Ryan off base disregarding various league rules, and (2) because the Flamingos have been carrying a roster of 19 players, instead of the legal 17 by misuse of league rules on suspension." Waring further stated in an unrelated matter, "One night the Beach changed players on the eligible list by suspending Bob Palmer for not reporting at the park. Actually, Palmer was sick in bed at his home."[98]

The protest spotlight shined brightly on Knobby Rosa, who had been on suspension for insubordination, then returned to action without the league offices not being properly informed. According to FIL rules, "that for a player to be eligible, the league must be informed before game time of a player's return to the active list." Ryan came to his own defense by advising Baynard that the wire was sent from the ballpark before the Sun Sox and Flamingos started their game at 8:15. Baynard later said that his secretary informed him that the message had not been received by the league's office until 9:45 that night. A furious Ryan shot back, "If the Sun Sox want a victory that badly, we'll give them one. I'd like to give them the one that hurt the worst."[99]

Baynard's final decision was official on August 18 and announced shortly before the Flamingos and Sun Sox squared off again. The ruling was upheld that the Sun Sox be awarded the win because of the use of an ineligible player, Rosa. Baynard asserted that the actual wire sent by Ryan was stamped in Miami at 9:02 pm a full 47 minutes after the game had started and that the letter notifying him on Rosa's return to the active list was postmarked at 10:00 pm. A furious Ryan offered, "The fact that we sent a wire showed we were acting in good faith." The decision was such an affront to Ryan that he tried to resign his position because he had hurt the Flamingos. "It was the lousiest decision I've ever heard of," said a steamed Ryan. Only upon the insistence of owner, Paul Rust Jr., and the Miami Beach players, did Ryan decide to stay.[100] [101]

Fodder from the fallout was all the motivation the Flamingos players needed that night as they readied to take out their frustrations on the Sun Sox. Martin commented, "What would you say that could be printed about such a thing if it happened to you. The boys were pretty mad about it, but we'll have to get back out here and try to win it on the field." In one of the highest attended games at Flamingo Park that year, 2,072 fans were evenly divided in their loyalties. Faithful Sun Sox followers made the short trip across town to see how each club would react.[102]

After Barnhill put Miami down in order in the top of the first inning, his teammates exploded for four runs in the bottom of the same frame off a stunned Torres. Miami's only score of the night came in the top of the second inning when Rotzell scored on Little's single to left field. Platt homered with two outs in the second inning to extend the lead to four runs again. Thereafter, both hurlers matched zeroes. Barnhill relied on his experience and cunning assortment of pitches limiting the Sox to eight hits; only one knock going for extra bases being a Little double. Rosa, Caro, Platt, and Colombo all stung Torres for a pair of hits as Miami Beach prevailed, 5 to 1. The Flamingos' victory would have been the twelfth consecutive if not for the Baynard decision.[103] Taking all into consideration, the Flamingos ended the evening a mere one-half game behind Miami. Following the game, Macon, commenting about the controversial decision by Baynard predicted, "I still don't think that game will decide the championship."[104]

The Flamingos departed for their next road trip. They followed their successful homestand dropping a doubleheader in Havana, a city notorious for its abundance of nightlife. Kwiatkowski recalled that one of the main sources of distractions were the casinos; not only for players, but also for their sometimes-traveling companions on chartered flights to Cuba.

> I remember they had casinos there, and we had a doctor friend traveling with us. And he thought he'd go to the casino and spend some money. I think this George Raft owned a, I think he owned the casino . . . .Yeah! I think he owned the place. And the doctor went in there. They gave us sport coats. You couldn't walk in unless you had a sport coat on . . . And we got in there and the doctor was there about five minutes and lost three hundred bucks . . . We didn't even button up our coats and we were on our way out.[105]

Gambling was not reserved for the luxury hotels and the gambling halls, Morant recalled how common wagering was always present and in the open in the grandstands of Gran Stadium.

> They had a nice ballpark there, but the thing that stuck in my memory was they had the fans fenced off from the field because they bet on everything. They bet on whether the next pitch was a strike, a ball, a home run, single, whatever it may be and they kept the fans away from the players.[106]

Not only were the Flamingos nearly unbeatable, so were the Sun Sox's duo of Harris and Torres. They continued to rack up wins both passing the twenty-win mark in August. Harris had already garnered his special victory on August 10 when Miami topped the former Fort Lauderdale club that had relocated to Key West during a 12 to 2 rout.[107] On August 28, Torres gained his twentieth in a hard-fought win against Tampa, 3 to 2. Dick Gray was the hero of the night driving in the game-winner that scored Macon from second base.[108] A testament to the dominance of the two Sox pitchers, by the end of the season, Harris and Torres would end up tied for the FIL record for most shutouts in a season with 12 each.[109]

By Labor Day, Miami Beach (96–48) found themselves trailing Miami (100–45) by 3½ games. Maybe Macon's prognostication concerning the Baynard decision was turning out to be true, but the Flamingos players had other ideas. Miami and Miami Beach were both scheduled key doubleheaders on the holiday as the Sun Sox took on the third place Tampa, while the pink birds faced woeful Lakeland.

The Flamingos needed some help and received it thanks to a pair of former major league hurlers. In the first game of the twin bill, 29-year-old Dale Matthewson, on his way to a 21-win season, held Miami to one hit earning the 1 to 0 complete game shutout win. In the nightcap, thirty-seven-year-old former major league veteran, Charles "Red" Barrett[110] followed, limiting the Sun Sox to four hits as the Smokers cruised to an easy 5 to 0 win.

While Miami dropped their two games, Miami Beach was taking advantage of a "sad sack" seventh place Lakeland club that finished the season with over 100 losses. In the opener, Morant uncharacteristically got into early trouble. Plagued by six Flamingos' errors, he thankfully received welcome aid from Morilla who provided excellent relief work along with a timely Levan home run, as the pink birds overcame an early deficit and prevailed, 8 to 7. In the late game, Nothe and reliever Morilla were both stellar. Together the pair held Lakeland to five hits, playing a key role in the twin bill sweep recording an 8 to 1 win. Overnight, Miami Beach had trimmed two games off the Sun Sox lead and narrowed the gap to one-and-a-half games.[111]

A Hollywood writer could not have scripted a better ending of the season scenario. On the final day of play, Miami held a 1½ game edge. If Miami Beach could take both ends of their doubleheader against Tampa at Plant Field, and if the Sun Sox were to lose to visiting St. Petersburg, it would set up a tie between the two teams and require a one-game playoff to settle the championship.

Adding even more theater to the down-to-the-wire pennant race was the never-ending drama that was so much a part of the FIL. It involved anger-fueled accusations by Joe Ryan that the Saints were not giving it their all, and they were handing the league flag to Miami. The latest controversy centered on St. Petersburg manager, Bill Herring's plan of using two pitchers per ballgame in order to rest his staff in preparation for the upcoming playoffs. Ryan perceived this as the Saints giving it less than their best effort. "We understand he will pull his starters at the end of five, even if he is pitching a no-hitter," explained Ryan and added, "At the other extreme, we are told he has said he will not pull that starter until five innings are played even if he is being clobbered."[112]

The specific games in question were the first two meetings between Miami and St. Petersburg during their season-ending series. In the opener, Herring left starter Joe Kirkland in the game despite giving up five runs in two innings of work during the Sox's win. In the second game Monte Lopez started and gave up three quick runs in the first inning on a pair of base on balls and a home run. Lopez then held Miami scoreless until the sixth when Herring himself came on to pitch. Ryan's contention expressively stated that "Lopez should not have been removed from the game as he was pitching effectively, and Herring should not have inserted himself as a reliever in Lopez's place since he had not pitched at all recently." Ryan had a valid complaint as other regular Saints pitchers were available, and Miami scored four runs off Herring due to a questionable hit and three Saints' errors. Two of the most egregious errors were by Max Gnagy. Ryan further grumbled that Gnagy was in the lineup because Herring had benched his regular shortstop Billy Spears in favor of a poor substitute. Although Spears was only hitting .218 at the time, his replacement would finish the season with a worse batting average of .145.[113]

Herring fired back, "When my pitchers aren't being hit hard, there is no reason to pull them. The balls hit off of Kirkland could have been fielded." In Lopez's case, Herring blamed poor defense and that Gnagy was in the lineup because Spears was suffering from food poisoning. Upon review by league president Baynard, his findings were that St. Petersburg had not thrown any of the games in question, but that Herring had virtually admitted that he placed the Shaughnessy playoffs, which the Saints can win, ahead of the pennant, which they can't, and that could be detrimental to baseball.[114]

Although Baynard overturned Ryan's protests, there was still a glimmer of hope for the Flamingos that still had a chance to tie for the regular season title. For a doubleheader with such high stakes, you would have never known by the size of the crowd in Tampa that pennant aspirations were on the line. The smallest crowd in the history of the FIL, 175 patrons, turned out to see if their fourth place Smokers could dash the Flamingos' hopes of a tie for the league lead.

For the few diehards in Plant Field, the lackluster effort by Tampa's offense turned out to be as anemic as their fan support. Miami Beach captured both ends of the double dip by scores of 4 to 0 and 4 to 1.[115] Elko was in command from the beginning twirling a shutout, and Morant was nearly as good earning his fifteenth win in the nightcap.[116]

Having completed the sweep of Tampa, the Flamingos retired to the tenth floor of the Thomas Jefferson Hotel to listen to the reconstructed broadcast of the St. Pete-Miami game on the radio. The announcers re-created the game account from information sent to them on a ticker tape. It was a very different environment at Miami Field as an energetic and emotional 2,824 Sun Sox rooters greeted the home team in anticipation of their club's first FIL pennant. Toeing the rubber for Miami was Torres, while Saints' manager Bill Herring sent his 19-year-old right-hander, Vicente Amor to the mound.

The Sun Sox did all their damage in the second inning. With one out, Sierra drilled a single, Kwiatkowski was retired, and Macon slapped a base hit. Amor intentionally walked Dotson to load the bases with an eye towards getting the next batter to hit into a double play. Gray spoiled those plans by singling in two runs before Fernandez drove in an additional score putting Miami in front, 3–0. Torres allowed a pair of runs, one in the sixth and one in the eighth, heading into the ninth with a one-run lead.[117]

After retiring Valdivia, Herring sent his best starting pitcher Iott to the batter's box and he promptly drilled a single to center field. The nervous crowd squirmed in their seats as Frank Gallardo stepped up to the plate. Gallardo then sent a sharp grounder to Fernandez at short who fielded the ball cleanly, stepped on second for the force, and fired to Macon at first to complete the double play. It set off the celebration with a scrum of players jumping for joy in the infield. Gray joyfully tackled Torres between home plate and the mound with Dotson and Macon piling on top. The fans hooted and hollered in their seats releasing their excitement like confetti in a New York City parade.[118] It was baseball cinema at its purest and best.

Meanwhile, at the Jefferson Hotel, a dejected bunch of Flamingos and front office staff hung their heads upon hearing the final. According to Frank Fox of *The Miami News*, "There was little comment on the 10th floor of the Thomas Jefferson Hotel where the Flamingos were quartered. A few doors slammed and there were a couple of mild expletives, but that was all."[119]

The opening round of the Shaughnessy playoffs squared-off Miami against Tampa and Miami Beach faced St. Petersburg. Much like the legendary 1951 National League championship game featuring Bobby Thomson's "Shot Heard 'Round the World," was the highlight of that season; the World Series that same year almost seemed anti-climactic. The less than enthusiastic writers from the *Miami Herald* felt the same when they summed up the upcoming FIL championship, "an effort to prove nothing." The Flamingos' players though, felt they *did* have something to prove.[120]

In the best-of-five series alignment, Miami and Miami Beach were given the choice of playing the first two games at home and the last three on the road or start with two on the road and the final three at home. The Sun Sox chose the former.

The Sun Sox entered the postseason without their regular backstop Ed Little, sidelined with an unspecified injury, leaving only Dotson to do catching chores. In Little's stead, Mike Napoli from Class B Newport News drew the assignment by the Dodgers to fill in, but with some objection and resistance from Miami Beach's front office. Ryan, still smarting from what he perceived as a pennant snatched away from his Flamingos, questioned whether the Sun Sox be allowed to use Napoli during the playoffs. "Waring's not going to beg 'im," said Ryan who eventually seceded, under the condition that Napoli only be used if Dotson came up injured so that the postseason could begin.[121]

Heavy rains and 20-game winner Rogelio Martinez greeted the host Miamians versus Martin's choice of young ace Billy Harris in front of a meager gathering of 1,024; the attendees no doubt discouraged by the previous downpour. Martinez had already beaten the Sun Sox four times during the regular season and loved nothing better than playing the role of the spoiler.[122]

Miami and Tampa matched single runs in the first inning. In the third, Miami briefly took the lead when the Mercury-heeled Fernandez singled, stole second, advanced to third on a Bragan sacrifice, then stole home staking the Sun Sox to a narrow 2–1 lead. In the fourth, Leonard Pecou's two-run single put the Smokers in front, 3–2. Harris nearly tied the game in seventh when he blasted a Martinez offering in what appeared to be a sure triple. However, Harris kept running in an attempt for an inside the park home run only to be gunned down at the plate on a perfect throw by Carlos "Yiqui" De Souza via an outfield relay.[123]

Buoyed by his teammate's excellent defense, Martinez received a boost while an exhausted Harris grabbed some pine in the top of the ninth inning. With two outs, Harris allowed Tampa to fill the bases. Macon took the stroll to the mound and called on Seijas who promptly slammed the door. However, Martinez shut down the Sun Sox in the bottom of the ninth earning himself a hard-fought fifth win against Miami, 3 to 2.[124]

Across town in St. Petersburg, in a rare offensive showcase, the Saints pounded out 11 hits to the Flamingos' 10. In what should have been a sign of things to come, before the game, Martin expressed that his staff was overworked having faced Tampa six times in the last four days. Miami Beach's pitchers showed signs of fatigue. Their sloppy defensive effort resulted in six errors, which cost them the game.[125]

In order to rest their staffs, both teams used five pitchers. The Saints tabbed their ace and 23 game winner, Iott to face the pink bird's Palmer. Contrary to predictions by the local sportswriters seeing a low scoring affair, instead both teams tied at the end of regulation at nine apiece. The deciding run came across in the tenth inning when Saints, Neb Wilson reached base after Eddie Wilson misplayed a wind-blown fly ball. Rogers McKee coaxed a free pass, followed by Spears who lifted a towering fly ball in the field and then was ruled out by the infield fly rule. Regrettably, the Flamingos' usually steady fielding Ray Williams let the ball bounce away from his grasp and Wilson raced to third. Williams then threw wide of third trying to get Wilson, allowing the enemy base runner to dash home and score the deciding run.[126]

Buoyed with confidence, St. Petersburg and Tampa put Miami Beach and Miami's backs to the wall. Despite their confidence the Flamingos and Sun Sox evened their series at one each, the former edging the Saints, 6 to 5 after coming back from a 4–0 deficit needed some nifty relief work by Podgajny to close the book.[127] While Miami turned to Torres who dominated tossing a five-hitter and extinguished the Smokers, 5 to 1.[128]

Game three had St. Petersburg bouncing back, and once again edging Miami Beach by one tally, 7 to 6, and Tampa handled Miami stopping them, 7 to 5. A 360-foot home run by Neb Wilson tied the score in the seventh inning, an eighth-inning tie-breaking single by Valdivia proved to be the difference-maker, and 5 1/3 innings of brilliant relief work by ex-Flamingos' O'Coine sent the Flamingos down to defeat. The Sun Sox were torpedoed by their poor defensive errors as they committed five errors during the losing effort. Despite garnering nine hits off the veteran Barrett, they were unable to overcome an early 6–0 deficit.

Game four in Miami Beach would be the only game during the series not decided by a single run. A sparse crowd of 600 met the Flamingos as they took the field, a sad commentary on how far local fan interest had sunk. Not to be dissuaded by the poor turnout, Andy Elko was up to the test allowing only two Saints hits although he was wild allowing nine free passes. The key blow of the day came off the bat of Levan who blasted a three-run home run in the first inning.[129]

Miami, in turn, evened their series at two apiece by edging Tampa, 3 to 2. Trailing 2–1 in the fourth inning, the Sun Sox knotted the score when Sierra and Dotson singled. Harris helped his own cause with the third "bingle" of the frame driving in a run. In the sixth inning, Sierra and Gabe Gabler each slapped singles, followed by Dotson who did the same, driving in Sierra with what turned out to be the game-winning RBI off Martinez. Harris finally put an end to Martinez the "Sun Sox Killer" and earned the complete game win allowing only six hits. The final showed Miami 3 Tampa 2.[130]

The fierce competition in the first four games of both series' promised to provide thrilling conclusions. For Miami Beach, there was extra motivation, to not only win but also strangely enough root for their rivals from across town. As *Miami Herald* beat writer, Whitey Kelley put it, "Almost to a man—from the front office to the bat boy—the Flamingos are hoping that it will be the Sun Sox. There's a little matter of the regular season pennant they lost by a single game that needs vindication."[131]

Martin's choice of pitchers was Nothe, the game starter in the earlier Flamingos 6–5 win. The 34-year-old port-sider was the second oldest member of the staff only outdone by Barnhill at 38. Elko's shutout on the previous night left Martin with several options if Nothe were to weaken, including a well-rested staff to come at the least sign of trouble. Toeing the rubber for St. Petersburg, right-hander Monte Lopez was hoping to pull off the upset.

Trailing 1–0 going into the fourth inning, Miami Beach exploded for five runs. Ray Williams primed the pump by slashing a single. Lou Colombo followed crushing his second double of the night tying the score at one. Lopez seemingly shaken by the blow issued free passes to Mort Smith and Ehlman, and then threw three straight balls to Nothe a .085 hitter during the regular season. Manager Herring had seen enough and strolled out to the hill pulling Lopez in favor of O'Coine. O'Coine who had been so effective in game three was not able to repeat his previous performance against his ex-teammates allowing Nothe to reach base and Rosa to single in the third run of the inning. By the end of the fourth Miami Beach held a 5–1 advantage.[132]

The Saints were not about to go down quietly. They rallied in the sixth inning recording three runs and knocking Nothe out of the box. With two outs, Martin called on Morilla who retired the only batter he faced in the inning. He continued to close out the game denying any further damage while earning the save. The celebration commenced with the Flamingos and their fans rushing onto the field creating a free for all of hugs, backslaps, and handshakes. The Beachites would have to wait for one more day to see the outcome of the Miami-Tampa series.[133]

Miami's hopes rested squarely on the shoulders of Torres and his fluttering knuckleball. Torres, as he had done so well all season long, continued to befuddle Tampa hitters by scattering five Tampa hits. Not surprisingly, a series rife with poor defensive play, a three-base error by the Saints Cecil Kaiser proved the difference. Kaiser misplayed a long fly ball off the bat of Gray, allowing Sierra and Gabler to score in the second inning. The Smokers netted three consecutive singles in the sixth, which essentially was their only threat as Tampa fell to Miami, 3 to 1. Although the Sun Sox celebration was more subdued since they were on enemy turf. There is no doubt the bus trip back to Miami was full of whoops and hollers.[134] The stage was set for the classic confrontation in what would prove to be the only inner-city championship in Miami history.

Going into the best-of-seven series final the local press affectionately dubbed the championship, the "Causeway Series." The players on both sides felt they had something to prove. The Flamingos came in with a "chip on their shoulders" feeling that they had earned the pennant only to have it snatched from them on a technicality and were seeking retribution. On the other hand, the Sun Sox felt they were the outright flag holders. The league ruled the contested game in their favor on August 7; they won the pennant "fair and square." The way they saw it, their rivals should quit "crying over spilled milk."

The much-anticipated curtain raiser at Miami Stadium featured the home team's Labe Dean facing Miami Beach's ageless wonder Dave Barnhill. Just over 3,300 fans pushed their way through the turnstiles expecting a pitcher's duel. After all, both hurlers had completed the season with ERA's south of 2.00. Although Dean started out, as the *Miami Herald's* Barney Waters described, "as a ball of fire" striking out a pair in the first inning, it was Barnhill's steady consistency in finding the edges of the strike zone that perplexed Sun Sox hitters.[135]

The Flamingos scored a pair of runs in the second inning thanks to a trio of singles and a pair of errors. Levan and Colombo's singles, followed by Gablers' throwing error, accounted for the first score. Ehlman also singled later in the inning extending the lead to 2–0. In the fifth frame, Handy propelled a double and scored adding another run. After Dean was relieved by Darden, the Flamingos tallied yet another score in the eighth, spotting them a 4–0 lead. Miami's only runs were accounted in the bottom of the ninth when Handy dropped a fly ball. Barnhill handcuffed the Sun Sox allowing only four hits and no earned runs, as the Flamingos took the first game, 4 to 2.[136]

Game two had Macon turning to his young ace Harris, squaring off against Morant who had recorded three of his fifteen wins against Miami. A crowd of 2,630 cheered loudly as their Sun Sox took the field. However, to their disapproval, Miami Beach struck first in the second stanza with a pair of runs. Miami had struggled offensively thus far in the finals. They finally exploded with four runs off Morant in the fourth stanza. The big knock came from Gray's triple that plated a pair of runs.[137]

The Flamingos, trailing 4–2, cut the lead by one in the top of the sixth when Caro drew the only walk of the evening off Harris and eventually advanced to third. Harris tried to pick Caro off base, but his errant throw was wide and Caro raced home. Miami then offset the run when they tagged Palmer, who had relieved Morant in the fourth, for another score giving them a 5–3 lead.[138]

The Flamingos threatened in the ninth when Handy reached base on a Fernandez error. Levan and Colombo stroked consecutive singles to right field, and Handy scored. Morilla came into the game to pinch-run for Colombo with no one out. Macon refused to go to his bullpen even though it was obvious that Harris was tired. "I intended to take Billy out after the next batter, but I figured (Ray) Williams would lay the ball down," said Macon in a postgame interview. He added, "I know Harris is a better fielder than either of my guys in the bullpen . . . (Lowell) Grosskopf or (Art) Seijas. So I left him in."[139]

Williams, the next batter known for his ability to place the ball where he wanted, fouled off the next two offerings. Williams now forced to swing away did just that and hit a scorcher towards Bragan who flipped to Fernandez who fired to first to complete the double play. Mort Smith followed tapping a slow roller to Bragan who tossed the horsehide to Gabler to end the game. The Sun Sox had evened the series at one apiece with a 5 to 4 victory.[140]

Game three shifted to Flamingo Park where inexplicably only 681 loyal Flamingos' rooters took their seats. At a time when fan interest should have been at its peak in Miami Beach, instead, the epigraph on the wall could not be more evident about the future of hardball on the beach.[141]

Nevertheless, the Flamingos came out playing with spirit. Andy Elko, who had previously shutout St. Petersburg in the playoffs, was again up to the task against Torres and the Sun Sox. Elko received a gift in the second inning when the usually re-liable Rotzell botched a Colombo fly ball allowing the slow-footed trumpet player to reach second. Williams then smacked a single advancing Colombo to third, followed by Platt's long fly ball to Armstrong in left field that was deep enough for Colombo to tag up from third with the pink birds first and only run.[142]

Miami's only threat came in the eighth inning when Gray started the inning with a single. Next came Dotson who hit a grounder wide of Handy at second base. It looked like Gray would reach scoring position. Instead of Handy taking a sure out at first, he wheeled around, threw to Caro, and covered second just in time to get Gray. Torres followed with an infield hit and Dotson dashed to third.[143]

The crowd, although small in numbers, was boisterous and on their feet as Fernandez stood at the plate. Elko was not too shaken, and once again found the strike zone to his liking catch-ing Fernandez looking on a third strike. Bragan followed with what looked like an inning-ending grounder to Caro, but the usually reliable Pensacolian ham-handed the play.[144]

With the bases loaded, Paul Armstrong, a dangerous contact hitter who batted .279 during the regular season, stepped up to the plate. Once again, Elko painted the corners on the strike zone and coaxed Armstrong into a ground ball that erased Bragan on a force play at second base. Elko went on to retire the sides in the ninth inning completing the whitewash.[145]

Elko, who was prone to wildness during the season, was on his game, not allowing a single free pass, and striking out three, while giving up only four Sox hits. He also was stellar on defense handling nine fielding chances without a blemish. It was a tough loss for Torres who pitched an excellent game, allowing only five hits, only to be undermined by an error.[146]

Miami had found themselves in the hole down two games to one. The main culprit had been their defense, the best in the league during the regular season that had committed seven errors versus Miami Beach's three. Game four would prove to be a turning point as the Sun Sox returned to their proficient selves on the field.

Macon's choice for game four was Darden, while Martin hoping to take a commanding three to one game lead in the series went with Nothe. It would be a short night for Nothe when tagged for a pair of runs in the first inning. Morilla relieved him in the second.[147]

Although Morilla proved effective, only allowing a run in the third on a Rotzell sacrifice fly, his mates failed to muster enough offense to overcome the early two-run deficit. The Flamingos biggest threat came in the fifth frame with one out when Darden got wild and walked Ehlman, Rosa, and Caro in succession. Macon had seen enough and turned to Dean out of the bullpen. The crafty "Old Labe" was able to escape the inning giving up only one run, an RBI single to Handy. For the first time in the series, the Sun Sox had played errorless ball and earned a hard-fought, 3 to 1 win.[148]

Torrential rains forced cancellation of the September 19 game in the second inning with the Flamingos holding a 1 to 0 lead. Hurricanes were frequent visitors to the area this time of the year. What concerned Macon more than anything was encountering a delay in the series due to the weather and possible blow of losing one of his regular players before its conclusion. Macon, in short order, got word that his regular third sacker, Dick Gray received his notice to report to Pittsburgh for his army draft physical.[149]

The day off did little for the Sun Sox. In game five, their recent bugaboo of shoddy defense, once again, came back to bite them. A five-run fourth inning proved the difference-maker as the Flamingos chased Sox starter Seijas. A trio of errors by Fernandez, Gray, and Seijas did the real damage as Miami Beach prevailed, 7 to 3. Barnhill and Palmer combined to hold the Sun Sox to eight hits and collect the win.[150]

Martin was looking to grab the championship in six games. He went with the hottest hand on the staff, Elko. It would not be an easy chore for the Flamingos as Macon's pick was Torres who had battled Elko in game three to a near standstill, only to be undone by an error.

Going into game six, Macon received good news twofold. First, Gray would be able to finish the series and secondly, Ed Little, who had been suffering from kidney problems, would be returning to action behind the plate.

A raucous crowd of 2,943 filled the stands at Miami Stadium. It was baseball drama at its best with the hometown in a do-or-die situation. Both Elko and Torres were in control from the beginning trading zeroes. In the sixth, Miami Beach appeared poised to take the lead. Handy singled past Bragan. Levan popped out, but Colombo advanced Handy on a ground ball. With two outs, Williams drilled a single to left. Armstrong fielded the ball cleanly as Handy rounded third heading for home. Armstrong came up throwing and on the bounce, Little received the heave in front of the plate just in time to lay the tag on Handy. Macon said after the game, "Armstrong doesn't have the strongest arm in the world. But he usually gets the ball in there when it's necessary. This was one of those times."[151]

The Sun Sox grabbed the lead in the seventh when Gray hit a searing ground ball down the third base line past Williams for a double. Little, seeking to move up the runner, bunted towards Elko who fielded the ball and alertly threw to Williams at third to get the racing Gray. Inexplicably, Williams failed to put the tag on Gray and instead threw to first in an attempt to get the plodding Little at first. The throw was late and runners were now on first and third. Fernandez received an intentional walk and Bragan smacked a long fly ball to center that allowed Gray to score with the first run of the game.[152]

Gray doubled again in the eighth inning plating Gabler for an insurance run putting Miami ahead, 2–0. All that was left for Torres to do was slam the door, which he did effectively. Although the Flamingos outhit the Sun Sox 8 to 4, Torres was able to minimize the damage thanks to his teammate's excellent defensive efforts, for the second time in series, playing errorless ball.[153]

The stage was set for a deciding game seven, and just like the previous games, it would prove to be a classic. Harris would take the hill for Miami, while Martin made the inexplicable choice of Mort Smith. This led many to second-guess his choice. Looking at the options at hand, Barnhill and Elko were out of the question since they had pitched recently and would be starting on short rest. Palmer was improbable having pitched in long relief only two days before. Since Morilla by this point was being used exclusively as a relief pitcher, Martin had the option of selecting McMillin, Morant, or Nothe as his starter. The most logical choice seemed to be Nothe, despite his poor performance in the fourth game. He had only pitched a little over an inning in his previous start and had been a stalwart of Martin all season long hurling in many key games. Martin seemed to be playing some kind of hunch, or was the Wild Horse of the Osage simply remembering Smith's August 7 performance of pitching eight scoreless innings of relief against Miami?

The atmosphere at Miami Stadium was electric as 4,097 fans filled the seats in anticipation of one of their local clubs taking home the whole bag of marbles and settling the question of who would wear the crown as the champions of the FIL. One can imagine that Miami fans must have felt the same excitement that the Brooklyn Dodgers, New York Giants, and New York Yankees experienced when World Series time rolled around for them, especially when it came to bragging rights in an inner-city series.

Just like Boston Red Sox manager Joe McCarthy's decision to choose Denny Galehouse in a one-game playoff against the Cleveland Indians to win the 1948 American League pennant backfired, so did Martin's choice have similar consequences.

This time Smith's changeup was not fooling any of the Sun Sox hitters as after Fernandez led off the first inning coaxing a base on balls, with one out, Armstrong stroked a double, driving in the game's first run. After retiring Rotzell, Smith got into trouble and Martin thought better of his decision calling on Morilla to get the last out and escape the inning with minimum damage.[154]

Miami tacked on a single run in the second inning when Gray doubled, and Harris helped his own cause duplicating Gray, putting Miami up 2–0. The impatient Martin then called on McMillin who fared little better when he also allowed a run in the third. After Armstrong reached base on a free pass, he followed by stealing second. After Rotzell was retired, Sierra punched a single to right field and Armstrong raced across home plate with Miami's third run.[155]

The Sun Sox added two more tallies, one in the fifth and one in the seventh innings. In the fifth stanza, Fernandez bashed a double, tagged up to third on Bragan's long fly ball, and scored on an Armstrong single. In the seventh, Elko, the fifth Flamingos' pitcher to appear, threw a tempting offering to Fernandez who connected and raced around the bags for a triple. Bragan followed with a single and the Sun Sox appeared as if they were in the driver's seat up 5–0.[156]

With Harris on the mound, and seemingly in control, fans began to head out the exits. It appeared for all intents and purposes the championship was in hand. But, just like their scrappy manager, there was still some fight left in the battered Beachites. In the eighth inning, Harris yielded a free pass and a couple of base hits, the biggest blow coming off the bat of Eddie Wilson, a two-run triple. Wilson later scored from third on Levan's sacrifice fly and suddenly as Florida afternoon rain showers, Miami Beach was back in the game cutting the lead to 5–3.[157]

Harris continued to struggle in the ninth. Ray Williams led off the inning with a ringing double towards Kwiatkowski in center field. Ehlman was retired on a pop fly and with Elko due up and Martin's bench already thinned out he called on Morant who hit only .212 during the season to pinch-hit. To everyone's surprise, Morant whacked a single putting the tying run on base.[158]

Macon, who probably should have relieved Harris in the eighth, was now in a pickle. Torres was already up in the bullpen and with two outs needed to squelch the rally and seal the deal, Macon turned to his veteran. The next batter up was the right-handed hitting Caro an excellent contact hitter. Caro was up to the task and hit a short single to right field bringing Williams across the plate and cutting the lead to 5–4. Rosa the next batsman saw nothing but the knuckleball from Torres and was unable to zero in on one of his offerings popping up gently behind home plate for Little to get under for the catch. A dejected Rosa slammed his bat in disgust and there were two outs.[159]

All of the Flamingos' hopes lay at the feet of Eddie Wilson, a .230 banjo hitter who appeared overmatched against the crafty Torres. The veteran hurler's confidence showed as he delivered the next pitch. Wilson connected on the offering, driving it to left field towards Armstrong. The ball hung in the air a precious few seconds before the swift outfielder raced over and gloved the long fly ball for the final out.[160]

It was pandemonium. Torres flung his cap in the air and his jubilant club mates swarmed him as the smiling Cuban sauntered off the mound. The dejected Flamingos sat stunned in the dugout; some just hung their heads, while others trudged to the locker room. The Sun Sox had proven they were the champions and no one could dispute that. "I'm delighted. That proves it wasn't a fluke," said Macon. He added, "They had a good ball club, but we had just a little bit better one. There was no bitterness. Both teams fought hard and fairly." In a gesture of good sportsmanship, Martin visited the Sun Sox locker room to commend all of the players and personnel. "I'm pleased that Pepper came in to congratulate us like the good guy that he is," said Macon. Martin added, "That Gil Torres is great. His knuckleball was too much for us."[161]

Elvie Darden and her late husband Billy were married for 61 years. She remained by his side all the years dating back to his playing days. Together they experienced with the entire Sun Sox team the joy of winning the championship for the second time. She also witnessed the heartwarming instance when the opposition's leader joined in on the festivities.

> So, it's just been one big family . . . I was not a drinker and they'd all be in the clubhouse having a good time. We'd be having a big party and they'd all be drinking . . . Pepper Martin come over after we won the game and he came and joined the party. And they all just had a ball with him being there . . . he was letting them all know that he was proud of them, and how well they had done.[162]

It was a crowning season in Miami baseball. It is hard to say whether winning breeds comradery, or vice versa, but for both teams, 1952 was special in many ways. Part of the special relationship nurtured by the two clubs was through the generous nature of their owners, Jose Aleman Jr., and Paul Rust Jr.

Aleman Jr. famously was very accommodating to players and their wives setting them up in nice apartments. "And they always fixed up the apartments . . . They would go ahead and put us in where we'd all kind of be in the same area together" said Elvie Darden.[163]

Aleman Jr. was also attentive when it came to his players and personnel by addressing their personal needs. One of the favorite activities the generous owner loved was taking his Sun Sox players out on his yacht for deep sea fishing excursions. Kwiatkowski, a New York guy, remembered one of these pleasure trips and a prank they pulled on their teammate Ed Little. Boys will be boys.

> He [Aleman Jr.] had a yacht and he asked some of the guys if they wanted to go deep sea fishing. We jumped at it. I know I was there. Ed Little was there. And I can't remember who the other guys were but, we went trolling for Marlin, you know where they have these lines off to the side of the boat. You hook something and it snaps the line. So anyway we were outside of Havana throwing in the ocean and Ed was sitting on one of the seats and then he wanted a beer, so he left his seat and went down in the galley there and was getting himself a beer. So while he was down there. Who was the coach? He was the assistant. He was everything. What the hell was his name?
>
> Bill Cates?
>
> Yeah, he decided when Ed was down there in the galley getting a beer, he towed his line in, got a bucket, a wooden bucket and he tied the bucket to the end of his line and they started hollerin' and when he got out there dragging a bucket they started hollering, "Ed, Ed, you got a bite, you got a bite." So, Ed comes running out. He gets in his chair. I can still picture it, he's sitting there, you know you pull and crank, pull and reel, pull and reel. He must have worked 45 minutes, and he pulled a bucket up. (laughing heartily). He [Little] laughed about it. He took it as a funny joke. I don't think he knew there was a bucket there. He thought there was a fish, you know because it never surfaced. But he kept working his butt off pulling that line in.[164]

Morant recalled not only the kindness of Rust Jr. but also that of Ryan.

> But, he was quite an owner. He cared for the ballpark. Joe Ryan did too. Joe did a lot of things that some people wouldn't . . . I remember one time we were playing over in the St. Pete and Lakeland area. And I was scheduled to pitch the opening game until we got back into town. He [Rust] actually flew me back to Miami to let me have a good night's rest for the next ball game.[165]

Yet, what should have been an offseason of good feelings and optimism quickly turned sour. Although basking in the glory of his second straight league championship, Macon announced that he would not be returning to guide the Sun Sox for the 1953 season. Rumors were that his replacement would be Torres. Macon cited troubles dealing with the temperamental Cuban players and a bizarre incident of spying by owner Aleman Jr. as his reasons to move on to greener pastures.

Although Aleman Jr. was altruistic to a fault, he had also become paranoid and so suspicious of Macon and what his players were saying that he had secretly installed microphones in the home dugout and wires that led to his private box of the stadium so that he could hear their conversations.[166] Kleinberg recalled how Macon had approached him upon discovering the wires.

> I was out in the field for batting practice, and Max asked me to come with him. And we went into the Sun Sox dugout, and he said, 'Look at this at the bench.' And he pulled out these wires; microphones. And he took me three times down the bench and they were tapping the bench to see what the players were saying about each other. It was just vicious. Max reported things to the Brooklyn Dodgers that Aleman was doing.[167]

Even more disturbing news came out of Miami Beach that came as no surprise to anyone. Rust Jr. announced that because of fan apathy that he was considering moving his franchise to Fort Lauderdale. Despite a winning club and an exciting down to the wire pennant race, the Flamingos had drawn a disappointing 52,000 fans for the year.[168] Even that may have been an exaggeration. Kleinberg remembered one incident in particular where Ryan may have exaggerated his customer count.

> Joe Ryan comes in the press box and says, "Tonight's atten-dance is seven-hundred-ninety-six." So Woodward puts down his pencil, and his scorebook and he says, "Howard, would you keep score for me for a minute." And off he goes. He leaves the press box. He comes back a half inning later and he says, "Mr. Joe Ryan, you are a liar. I counted only four hundred and some odd people except for the ones in the ladies room."[169]

As part of Minor League Baseball's 100th Anniversary celebra-tion in 2001, two veteran researchers presented their list of the 100 greatest minor league teams of the 20th century. Bill Weiss and Marshall Wright devised an evaluation system based upon league strength (as an example AAA level would score higher than D level), winning percentage, and total wins. The king of the hills was the 1934 Los Angeles Angels (137–50) of the Pacific Coast League. Coming in at the number forty spot was the Miami Sun Sox (104–48).[170] Led by the big three of Billy Harris (25–6, 0.83), Gil Torres (22–8, 0.86), and Billy Darden (16–9, 1.79) the Sox had the best top of the rotation in the FIL and were one of the greatest trios in the history of the minor leagues. Both Harris and Torres completed 12 shutouts, while Miami as a team blanked opponents 42 times.

The left side of the infield anchored by Fernandez and Gray, along with late-season transfer first baseman William "Gabe" Gabler all made it to the big leagues. Both player-manager Max Macon and Torres previously played in the majors. The rest of the roster was filled with several productive minor league vet-erans including, Paul Armstrong, Jimmy Bragan, Billy Darden, Labe Dean, Joe Kwiatkowski, Ed Little, Rocky Rotzell, and Oscar Sierra.

A testament to how good Miami was in the clutch, out of 57 games decided by a margin of one run they came out in front 35 times.[171] The Sox outscored opponents to the tune of 234 runs plating 549 against 315.[172]

Although Miami Beach lacked the marquee pitchers that their rivals boasted, Martin's staff had the most depth. Seven Flamingos' pitchers finished in double figures in victories led by Pete Morant (15–1, 1.84), Walt Nothe (15–8, 1.79), Dave Barnhill (13–8, 1.19),

Bob Palmer (13–9, 1.94), Dick McMillin (12–5, 2.27), and Andy Elko (11–2, 1.26).[173] So deep was the staff that Flamingos management was secure in selling the seventh not mentioned above, Marshall O'Coine in mid-August to St. Petersburg who ended up the season finishing 10–5 with a 1.45 ERA.[174]

The Flamingos also boasted the second best offense in the league scoring 603 runs just six behind the Saints. At the heart of their attack was Jesse Levan who not only snared the FIL batting title with a .334 batting average, but also led the league in hits (192), and RBIs (87).[175] Dave Exter, who pitched at Miami Beach High School and later appeared in two games for the Flamingos in 1954 remembered fondly what a great hitter Levan was, "He was a left-handed batter, stocky, he looked like Johnny Mize, and he could hit. He hit .330, .340 like nothing. And that league, the FIL, was a pitcher's league, nobody hit that high."[176]

Levan joined Whitey Platt as the only two former major leaguers on the roster. A talented supporting cast, many of whom enjoyed productive careers included, Jack Caro, Chuck Ehlman, Oscar Garmendia, Knobby Rosa, George Wehmeyer, and Ray "Razor" Williams.

Had the "fickle finger of fate" played a different hand, Miami Beach would have made the top 100 list instead of Miami. One is left to wonder "what if?" What if Baynard, had ruled in Ryan's favor regarding the Rosa incident? What if the suspended game against Palm Beach was later finished and the Flamingos won? What if Ryan's late-season protest surrounding the lack of effort displayed by St. Petersburg against Miami, received its proper consideration and changed the results?

The books closed on the 1952 season. At the October league meeting in Miami, all eight club owners insisted that "we will answer the bell for the upcoming season." In spite of the outward optimism, several problems plagued the FIL. For the first time, a team folded mid-season when Fort Lauderdale relocated to Key West. League-wide attendance fell from 664,307 to 494,062 a drop of 25.6%; Havana, once a mainstay in fan turnout, for the second straight year drew less than 100,000. Aleman Jr.'s absence from Miami for six weeks due to the Cuban government confiscating $300,000 worth of machinery from his farms, and the increasing losses mounting from Miami Stadium running in the red were causing increasing concern with the young owner, putting the future of the franchise in doubt. By the time opening day 1953 rolled around the FIL's look was quite different.

Final Standings

TEAM	W	L	GB
Miami	104	48	–
Miami Beach	103	49	1
Tampa	85	68	19.5
St. Petersburg	84	70	21
Havana	76	77	28.5
West Palm Beach	68	85	36.5
Lakeland	51	103	54
Fort Lauderdale / Key West	40	111	63.5

NOTES

1. Bedingfield Gary. *Baseball's Greatest Sacrifice*, Fred Tschudin, retrieved on 27 March, 2017 from www.baseballsgreatestsacrifice.com/biographies/tschudin_fred.html.
2. Parks, Arva Moore. *Miami The Magic City*, Miami, FL: Community Media, 2008, p. 208.
3. Baseball-reference.com.
4. Olson, James S. *Historical Dictionary of the 1950s*, (Greenwood Press, Westport, Connecticut, 2000), p. 286.
5. Baseball-reference.com.
6. Burns, Jimmy. Miami Club Nose-Dives at Gate as Rich Young Owner Moves In, *Sporting News*, 30 April, 1952, p. 36.
7. Ibid.
8. Llanes, Rolando. *White Elephant: The Rise and Fall of Miami Baseball Stadium*, (Blurb Inc., 2010), p. 144–145.
9. Cuddy, Don. Big Jump for Paul Rust—From Kid Loop to Pros, *Sporting News*, 23 January, 1952, p. 17.
10. Rust Acquires All Miami Beach Stock, *Panama City News-Herald*, 14 January, 1952, p. 5.
11. Ibid.
12. Ibid.
13. Flights To Cuba Eliminated Bobo as a Pilot Prospect, *Sporting News*, 5 March, 1952, p. 32.
14. *Sporting News*, 12 March, 1952, p. 22.
15. Burns, Jimmy. Wild Horse Leaps Over Miami Bay, *Sporting News*, 27 February, 1952, p. 18.
16. Max Macon, Former Major Leaguer Named Manager Of Sun Sox, *Miami Daily News*, 4 December, 1951, p. 13-A.
17. Baseball-reference.com.

18. Retrieved from http://californialeague.webs.com/seasons/1949.pdf, 28 March, 2017.
19. Ibid.
20. Fernandez, Humberto "Chico." Phone interview with author, 11 April, 2013.
21. Kwiatkowski, Joe. Phone interview with author, 13 September, 2013.
22. Ibid.
23. Milb.com.
24. Kleinberg, Howard. Personal interview with the author, 9 July, 2013.
25. McLemore, Morris. Now They're Off Here's The Finish, *Miami News*, 9 April, 1952, p. 3-B.
26. Balfe, Bob. It's Post Time, Time For The Annual Guessing Game, *Palm Beach Post*, 6 April, 1952, p. 21.
27. Fernandez, Humberto "Chico." Phone interview with author, 11 April, 2013.
28. Ibid.
29. Kleinberg, Howard. Personal interview with the author, 9 July, 2013.
30. *Sporting News*, 1 March, 1952, p. 32.
31. Kleinberg, Howard. Personal interview with the author, 9 July, 2013.
32. Baseball-reference.com.
33. Morant, Charles. Phone interview with author, 11 June, 2013.
34. Baseball-reference.com.
35. Negro Leagues Baseball Museum, Dave Barnhill, retrieved 28 March, 2017 from http://coe.k-state.edu/annex/nlbemuseum/history/players/barnhilld.html.
36. Figueredo, Jorge. *Who's Who in Cuban Baseball, 1878–1961*, (McFarland & Co., Inc., Publishers: Jefferson, North Carolina and London, 2003), p. 386–387.
37. Negro Leagues Baseball Museum, Dave Barnhill, retrieved 28 March, 2017 from http://coe.k-state.edu/annex/nlbemuseum/history/players/barnhilld.html.
38. Arm Ailing, Barnhill Quits Oaks, *Sporting News*, 9 April, 1952, p. 28.
39. Albury, Charlie. Personal interview with the author, 5 August, 2017.
40. Morant, Charles. Phone interview with author, 11 June, 2013.
41. Burns, Jimmy. Negro Players Well Received in the Fla-Int, *Sporting News*, 21 May, 1952, p. 34.
42. Meyer, Dick. Miami Sun Sox Win, 1–0, *Fort Lauderdale News*, 26 April, 1952, p. 2-B.
43. Kleinberg, Howard. Personal interview with the author, 9 July, 2013.
44. Morant, Charles. Phone interview with author, 11 June, 2013.
45. Havana Edges Beach; Miami, Tampa Win, *Palm Beach Post*, 10 April, 1952, p. 14.
46. Ibid.
47. Kwiatkowski, Joe. Phone interview with author, 13 September, 2013.
48. Kleinberg, Howard. Macon Pitches Dean After Beach Sweep, *Miami News*, 17 April, 1952, p. 17-A.
49. Woodward, Stanley. Miami Seeks Second Victory of Tampa, *Miami News*, 9 April, 1952, p. 4-B.
50. Ibid.
51. Statistics compiled from *Miami News*, 8 May through 6 June, 1952.
52. Schenley, Bill. Billy Harris, 80; Pitched for Brooklyn/LA Dodgers. Retrieved 5 May, 2017 from groups.google.com/forum/#!topic/alt.obituaries/rdEmkXgwKSw.
53. Retrieved from cooperstownersincanada.com, 10 May, 2017.
54. Baseball-reference.com. Ricardo Torres played parts of three seasons with the Washington Senators in 1920–22. He played in 22 games batting .297 and driving in three runs.
55. Figueredo, Jorge. *Who's Who in Cuban Baseball, 1878–1961*, (McFarland & Co., Inc., Publishers: Jefferson, North Carolina and London, 2003), p. 8, 200, 201.
56. Kleinberg, Howard. Personal interview with the author, 9 July, 2013.
57. Darden, Elvie. Phone interview with author, 23 January, 2017.

58. Fox, Frank. Beach Releases 5, On Road Trip, *Miami News*, 8 May, 1952, p. 27-A. Henry would land with Harrisburg of the Class B Interstate League where he batted .308, but retired following the season. Raulerson, was sent to Savannah of the South Atlantic League where he finished with an 0–7 record, in what would prove to be his last season of professional baseball.

59. *Sporting News*, Lopez' Streak Is Snapped After 21 Victories In Row, June 18, 1952, p. 35.

60. Bedingfield, Gary. *Baseball in Wartime, Walt Nothe*, retrieved on 10 April, 2016, from www.baseballinwartime.com/player_biographies/nothe_walt.htm.

61. Batting Title Again Pistol Pete's Target, *Sporting News*, 21 March, 1946, p. 10.

62. Baseball-reference.com.

63. FIL Roundup, *Palm Beach Post*, 7 June, 1952, p. 7.

64. Miami Beach Downs Miami In Twin Bill, *Fort Lauderdale News*, 9 June, 1952, p. 2-B.

65. Ibid.

66. Minor League Class B Highlights, *Sporting News*, 18 June, 1952, p. 35.

67. Miami Beach Downs Miami In Twin Bill, *Fort Lauderdale News*, 9 June, 1952, p. 2-B.

68. Baseball-reference.com.

69. Burns, Jimmy. Stormy Pepper Again Set Down, Draws $75 Fine, *Sporting News*, 9 July, 1952, p. 41.

70. Balfe, Bob. Indians Shut Out Flamingos Twice, 4–0, 1–0, *Palm Beach Post*, 27 May, 1952, p. 10.

71. Burns, Jimmy. Stormy Pepper Again Set Down, Draws $75 Fine, *Sporting News*, 9 July, 1952, p. 41.

72. FIL Roundup, *Palm Beach Post*, 11 June, 1952, p. 8.

73. Burns, Jimmy. Stormy Pepper Again Set Down, Draws $75 Fine, *Sporting News*, 9 July, 1952, p. 41.

74. Fox, Frank Wild Pitch Enables Miami To Hike Lead, *Miami News*, 1 July, 1952, p. 11-A.

75. Fox, Frank. Balk Call Is Key To Miami Score, *Miami News*, 2 July, 1952, p. 4-B.

76. Fox, Frank. Miami Hikes Lead, Battles Key West, *Miami News*, 3 July, 1952, p. 3-B.

77. FIL Roundup, *Palm Beach Post*, 3 July, 1952, p. 6.

78. Sun Sox Squeeze Past Locals 1–0, *Palm Beach Post*, 11 July, 1952, p. 11.

79. Kwiatkowski, Joe. Phone interview with author, 13 September, 2013.

80. Little, Ed. Phone interview with author, 28 May, 2012.

81. Kleinberg, Howard. Personal interview with the author, July 9, 2013.

82. Wolf, Al. Hollywood Stars Blossom Out In Shorts (for Speed*)*, *Los Angeles Times*, 2 April, 1950, p. 1.

83. Evans, Luther. Win Places Flamingos ½ Game Behind Leaders, *Miami Herald*, 15 July, 1952, p. 14-A.

84. Ibid.

85. Kleinberg, Howard. Flamingos Face Sun Sox Twice, *Miami News*, 15 July, 1952, p. 3-B.

86. Ibid.

87. Kleinberg, Howard. Miami Maintains F-I Lead, Plays Lakeland, *Miami News*, 16 July, 1952, p. 7-A.

88. Ibid.

89. Ibid.

90. Ibid.

91. Ibid.

92. Pilots Honor Service-Bound Pitcher Boyette, *Fort Lauderdale News*, 16 July, 1952, p. 2-B.

93. FIL Roundup, *Palm Beach Post*, 6 August, 1952, p. 6.

94. Kleinberg, Howard. Nothe's No-Hitter Spoiled As Sun Sox Win In Tenth, *Miami News,* 7 August, 1952, p. 3-C.
95. Ibid.
96. Walt Nothe Hurls 9 Hitless Innings, But Loses in Tenth, *Sporting News*, 20 August, 1952, p. 37.
97. Kleinberg, Howard. Secret Weapon Found By Flamingo Manager, *Miami News*, 8 August, 1952, p. 12-A.
98. Burns, Jimmy. Miami's Protest Ends Cross-Bay Beach Cordiality, *Sporting News*, 20 August, 1952, p. 37.
99. Ibid.
100. Burns, Jimmy. Beach Flaps Wings on Loss by a Forfeit, *Sporting News*, 27 August, 1952, p. 13.
101. Flamingos August 7 Win Reversed, *Miami Herald*, 19 August, 1952, p. 13-A.
102. Ibid.
103. Burns, Jimmy. Beach Flaps Wings on Loss by a Forfeit, *Sporting News*, 27 August, 1952, p. 13.
104. Flamingos August 7 Win Reversed, *Miami Herald*, 19 August, 1952, p. 13-A.
105. Kwiatkowski, Joe. Phone interview with author, 13 September, 2013.
106. Morant, Charles. Phone interview with author, 11 June, 2013.
107. Burns, Jimmy. Sox Score Seven Runs In Sixth, *Miami Herald*, 10 August, 1952, p. 8-D.
108. Sun Sox Take Ninth Win In Row, In Drive For F-I League Flag, *Fort Lauderdale News*, 29 August, 1952, p. 10-A.
109. Baseball-reference.com.
110. Baseball-reference.com. Barrett pitched 11 seasons in major leagues, all in the National League, with Cincinnati (1937–40), Boston (1943–45, 1947–49), and St. Louis (1945–46). He finished his career with a 69–69 won-loss record including a 23–9 season in 1945 pitching most of the season with the St. Louis Cardinals.
111. Tampa Melts Sox' Lead Over Beach, *Fort Lauderdale News,* 2 September, 1952, p. 11-A.
112. Beck, Bill. Miami Beach Charges Saints Played Dead In Sun Sox Series, *St. Petersburg Times,* 7 September, 1952, p. 1-C & 4-C.
113. Ibid.
114. Ibid.
115. Miami Nips Saints, Clinches Flag, *St. Petersburg Times*, 7 September, 1952, p. 1-C.
116. Frank Fox, Two Wins Fail To Save Beach, *Miami News*, September 7, 1952, p. 1-C & 3-C.
117. Kleinberg, Howard. Sun Sox Beat St. Pete To Clinch F-I Pennant, *Miami News*, 7 September, 1952, p. 1-C & 3-C.
118. Ibid.
119. Fox, Frank. Two Wins Fail To Save Beach, *Miami News*, 7 September, p. 1952, p. 1-C & 3-C.
120. Miami, Tampa Clash In 1st Playoff Tonight, *Miami Herald*, 8 September, 1952, p. 2-B.
121. Ibid.
122. *Sporting News*, 17 September, 1952, p. 35.
123. Kelley, Whitey. Martinez Outduels Billy Harris, *Miami Herald*, 9 September, 1952, p. 2-B.
124. Ibid.
125. Saints, Flamingos To Open Playoffs, *St. Petersburg Times*, 8 September, 1952, p 13.
126. Flamingos Guilty Of Six Errors, *Miami Herald*, 9 September, 1952, p. 2-B.
127. 2,497 See Flamingos Connect For 12 Hits, *Miami Herald*, 10 September, 1952, p. 4-D.

128. *Sporting News*, 17 September, 1952, p. 35.
129. Kelley, Whitey. Levan's 3-Run Homer Helps Elko's 2-Hitter, *Miami Herald*, 12 September, 1952, p. 2-C.
130. Series Tied By Miami As Harris Wins, 3–2, *Miami Herald*, 13 September, 1952, p. 16-A.
131. Kelley, Whitey. Beach Uses Big Fourth To Oust St. Pete, 5–4, *Miami Herald*, 13 September, p. 16-A.
132. Ibid.
133. Ibid.
134. Sporting News, September 24, 1952, 32.
135. Waters, Barney. Dave Loses Shutout on Error, *Miami Herald*, 15 September, 1952, p. 4-B.
136. Ibid.
137. Evans, Luther. Sun Sox Halt Late Rally To Even Series, 1–1, *Miami Herald*, 17 September, 1952, p. 2-B.
138. Ibid.
139. Ibid.
140. Ibid.
141. Burns, Jimmy. Elko Shuts Out Sun Sox, 1–0, *Miami Herald*, 18 September, 1952, p. 2-B & 3-B.
142. Ibid.
143. Ibid.
144. Ibid.
145. Ibid.
146. Ibid.
147. Kelley, Whitey. Early Lead Pays Miami Dividends, *Miami Herald*, 19 September, 1952, p. 1-D & 4-D.
148. Ibid.
149. Sox, Beach Rained Out; Play Tonight, *Miami Herald*, 20 September, 1952, p. 14-A.
150. Sporting News, October 1, 1952, 55.
151. Burns, Jimmy. Series Ends Tonight At Stadium, *Miami Herald*, 22 September, 1952, p. 16-A & 18-A.
152. Ibid.
153. Ibid.
154. Burns, Jimmy. Torres' Sparkling Relief Stint Saves Sox' Victory, *Miami Herald*, 23 September, p. 1952, 15-A & 16-A.
155. Ibid.
156. Ibid.
157. Ibid.
158. Ibid.
159. Ibid.
160. Ibid.
161. Max Macon 'Delighted' Over Sun Sox Triumph, *Miami Herald*, 23 September, 1952, p. 16-A.
162. Darden, Elvie. Phone interview with author, 23 January, 2017.
163. Darden, Elvie. Phone interview with author, 23 January, 2017.
164. Kwiatkowski, Joe. Phone interview with author, 13 September, 2013.
165. Morant, Charles. Phone interview with author, 11 June, 2013.
166. Burns, Jimmy. Macon Makin' Tracks Away From Miami, *Sporting News*, 1 October, 1952, p. 55.
167. Kleinberg, Howard. Personal interview with the author, 9 July, 2013.
168. Burns, Jimmy. Macon Makin' Tracks Away From Miami, *Sporting News*, 1 October, 1952, p. 55.
169. Kleinberg, Howard. Personal interview with the author, 9 July, 2013.

170. Milb.com.
171. Sox Host Tampa, Beach Plays Saints, *Fort Lauderdale News*, 8 September, 1952, p. 3-B.
172. Baseball-reference.com.
173. Ibid.
174. Souped-Up Saints Regain 4th Place, *Palm Beach Post*, 19 August, 1952, p. 6.
175. Ibid.
176. Exter, Dave. Personal interview with author, 21 June, 2017.

CHAPTER EIGHT

THE F.I.NAL EPITAPH

On January 20, 1953, retired five-star General Dwight D. Eisenhower was inaugurated president of the United States. A sense of optimism swept the country with hopes of the new administration ending the Korean War. By July 27 that same year, hostilities ceased with a compromise agreed upon creating the Demilitarized Zone along the 39th Parallel.

War veterans returned to find new jobs and opportunities for those with the desire to succeed. With employment on the rise, the age of "buy now and pay later" begins to take shape. Reflected in this era is the ease of acquiring credit on a new vehicle and a boom in the auto industry.

In Miami and across the country people flock to the movie theatres to view such classic flicks as *From Here to Eternity, Gentlemen Prefer Blondes* starring the platinum bombshell, Marilyn Monroe, and *The Robe* for those of a more religious and historic persuasion. Frankie Laine's, *I Believe* and Perry Como's *Don't Let the Stars Get in Your Eyes*, could be heard on WIOD originating its signal from the 79th Street Causeway tower to the suburbs, to downtown, and to the beaches. Miami like the rest of America is changing, yet with it, a certain age of innocence is coming to its end.

1953

The Florida International League exhibited a very different look to fans in 1953. Returning to his post as league president, Phil O'Connell took on the unenviable task of trying to save the floundering league. The ongoing financial troubles that many of the franchises were experiencing came home to roost in an ominous way. Havana, Lakeland, Miami, Miami Beach, and Tampa were all in trouble. Lakeland was the first casualty. Perennial bottom feeders, and already in the league's smallest market, they were doomed by lack of fan support. Tampa was nearly the second club to throw in the towel after Tom Spicola announced his intention to sell his franchise to a group of local citizens. He later changed his mind and decided to give it a go for one more season.[1] Key West followed Lakeland as the second franchise to fold although not by their ownership's choice. Despite surprisingly good fan support for a last place club adopted from Fort Lauderdale, FIL officials decided to drop the Conchs in order to accommodate a balanced six-team format.[2]

The other geographical areas of concern for O'Connell were the Miami and Miami Beach situations. Whispers and hearsay had been swirling since August 1952 of the possible sale of Miami Stadium. Rumors ran rampant due to the conspicuous absence of Jose Aleman Jr. at late-season home games. Jimmy Burns, reported in *The Sporting News*, that the Sun Sox owner was having financial difficulties and conjectured, "One theory was that Aleman feared to leave Cuba where the government had taken over some of his farm machinery." Adding on to the young owner's problems were reported losses of $59,436.84 from his stadium. Aleman's attorney, George Salley commented on his client's situation saying, "Anything a man owns can be bought. I imagine Aleman would sell the stadium, but it would cost the buyer more than $1,500,000." Salley confirmed the cost of the stadium to be $2,000,000 and, like many others, referred to the stadium as a "white elephant."[3]

Aleman Jr. was not alone in experiencing financial woes. Paul Rust Jr. had also taken a beating monetarily. Despite the success of the Flamingos on the field, he announced that he would pull up stakes after having drawn a paltry 52,000 in 1952.

Three cities pursued Rust Jr. with enticements to move his team. The contenders included Fort Lauderdale, Hollywood, and Key West.[4] Hollywood was the first to drop out of the bidding unable to garner adequate financial support. The Conch city was more persistent and made a strong play offering free rent concessions, and guaranteed strong fan support in a last ditch effort to gain entry into the league that ultimately failed.[5] FIL officials most likely felt that the city would be unable to support a team over the long haul. Key West did receive one consolation prize, agreeing to a one-year part-time arrangement with the troubled Havana club on a deal that allowed the Cubans to play an unspecified number of their home games, including opening day, at Wickers Field. By the conclusion of the season, it would take another sixteen years before fans in the Keys would see a minor league franchise come to fruition.[6]

Fort Lauderdale ultimately won the rights to host the Flamingos. The city closed the deal by presenting the team with the best perquisites including, free rent, renovations to the ballpark, and free light bills courtesy of Florida Power and Light.[7]

With the departure of Miami Beach to Fort Lauderdale, the Sun Sox had the total Miami geographic area to themselves. Baseball would have a much different feel in the Magic City minus the natural rivalry that had been so much part of its scene dating back to 1940. Most of the familiar cities were still in the league, Fort Lauderdale, Havana, Miami, St. Petersburg, Tampa, and West Palm Beach. The FIL trimmed down a 140-game schedule for the first time since the league's inaugural season and reverted to a split season arrangement to determine playoff positions. In addition, clubs could only sign eight veteran players versus twelve allowed the previous season.[8]

With the new alignment in place, Sun Sox management addressed their most pressing need for a new pilot, following the exodus of Max Macon to Double A Fort Worth. On January 19, they announced that 30-year-old Andrew "Doc" Alexson would take over as their new player-manager.[9] Although still youthful by managerial standards, first impressions were sometimes deceiving. Alexson spent the previous four years in the Brooklyn system starting with Valdosta of the Class D Georgia-Florida League in 1949. He guided the team to an 86–54 record and second place finish. Doc was then assigned to the Hornell Dodgers of the Class D Pennsylvania-Ohio-New York League where he settled from 1950 to 1952 and enjoyed three winning seasons while making playoff appearances every year including a league championship in 1951, compiling a cumulative .596 winning percentage (307–208).[10]

Alexson's managerial successes aside, the left-handed batting first baseman had also proven adept with the stick, batting .300 six of his seven seasons in the minors since originally signed by the Detroit Tigers in 1947. Sun Sox secretary-treasurer, Jose

M. Garcia glowingly reported in the *Miami Herald*, "He seemed to suit our needs and qualifications best." Wasting no time, upon arriving in Miami, Alexson immediately hooked up with Bill Cates his assistant coach who filled his new boss in on what to expect. Alexson jokingly expressed his own thoughts on assessing the FIL, "When Pepper was in the Brooklyn organization he gave everyone up in Vero the impression that the FI was a third major league."[11]

Alexson was joined by Cates as they made the annual trek to Vero Beach for the "rites of spring" to prepare for the season. The Sun Sox's roster once again featured a mix of veterans and up and coming prospects from the Dodgers' farm system. Four notable returnees with prior seasons with the club were, Paul Armstrong (4th season), Ed Little (3rd season), Arturo Seijas (5th season), and Oscar Sierra (3rd season). Also coming back for his second season was right-hander Richard Lovell a 13 game-winner for the 1951 Sox.

Three prize prospects graduating from Class C Santa Barbara of the California League were shortstop Willie Davis, second baseman Gerald "Hoot" Didier, and outfielder Asdrubal Baro all that participated in the crowded Dodgers spring training camp. Didier shared his experience of what it was like upon his arrival at Vero Beach.

> When I went to my first minor league camp they had about 500 players there. Unbelievable, and when you signed with them if you signed a Double-A, or Triple-A contract when you went to spring training you were, you know you were known and were given a uniform of that team . . . As I remember people who had contracts from A down to D wore colored numbers. And that's how many guys they had in spring training. It was unbelievable. I think there were a couple of other teams that had those many players.[12]

Coming into the season, the most conspicuous weakness for the Sun Sox were their lack of strong pitching prospects that the Dodgers had so generously supplied them in the past. In particular were the assignments of Joe Bernier with a less than impressive 3–13 record between Class A Elmira (Eastern League), and Class B Lancaster (Interstate League), Joe Gushanas (3–9, 5.76) from Class B Asheville (Tri-State League), and Art Raynor a rookie who last made headlines chucking for Bucknell University in 1950. However, one of the most intriguing prospects was 24-year-old righty McKinley "Mac" Mosley who compiled a 25–6 record in two seasons at Class D Hazard, Kentucky, including a perfect 10–0 slate in 1952.[13]

Miami opened the season in rousing fashion taking a pair of victories at the expense of West Palm Beach before returning home for their opening game. Only 2,371 paid customers attended the festivities at Miami Stadium for raising of the championship flag; less than half the expected crowd.[14]

The honorable mayor of Miami, Chelsie J. Senerchia threw out the first pitch that sailed well over the head of the commissioner, Ian MacVicar.[15] The pitch was an ominous foretelling of things to come. By the end of the season, six members of the Sun Sox pitching staff suffered through cases of wildness and averaged in excess of four walks per game, Eleuterio "Tellito" Lopez and Mac Mosley being the worst offenders at 7.3 and 7.2 respectively.[16]

League president O'Connell presented and raised the championship banner to a broadly smiling Aleman Jr., in front of the wildly cheering home crowd. It must have been especially gratifying to the returning Sun Sox who had rejoiced in the bowels of Miami Stadium just seven months before.[17]

The hometown team did little to disappoint their fans as they extended their winning streak to three games. The big blow of the night came off the bat of Baro who smashed a 345-foot two-run tater over the left center field wall, part of a five-run third inning. On the mound, Mosley did his part restricting the visiting West Palm Beach Indians to five hits and nearly threw a shutout. Only his own error on an attempted pickoff at first base and an error by Alexson availed the visitors of their only tally on the evening as the Sun Sox prevailed, 7 to 1.[18]

Miami continued their winning ways surging into May. They started out the month thrashing Fort Lauderdale, 17 to 3 on a night that proceeds went to the Northside Kiwanis Club to aid needy children. The youngsters were not the only ones in need of assistance as Sun Sox hitters pummeled six Lions' hurlers for 15 hits in front of their largest crowd of the season; 5,363 at Miami Stadium. Pepper Martin was so desperate he even used left fielder Jim Davis in a relief role in order to try to stop the onslaught.[19]

The most notable difference to fans and players in the early going of the season was the introduction of a livelier baseball that resulted in higher scoring contests. The reason for this, in a league notoriously known as a pitcher's league, was the decision by owners as a solution to spark lagging attendance. One of the clearest examples was the Fort Lauderdale versus Miami series on May 1–3. The three-game set, found Pepper Martin using 13 different pitchers yielding 37 hits and 31 runs during the three-game set. On the other side of the diamond, Alexson employed ten hurlers who surrendered 35 hits and 25 tallies. In the final game of the series, five home runs were jacked out of long ball unfriendly Miami Stadium. It was almost half the total hit during the entirety of 1952.[20]

In spite of the injection of added offense league-wide, attendance continued its precipitous decline, with the exception of Fort Lauderdale that averaged better than 2,000 for their first five home games. According to the *Sporting News*, some owners were going as far as to blame the influx of "Negroes" into the league. They also reported that, "Tampa officials have admitted that they have had some objections to the use of Negro players and said around 15 regular-season ticket purchasers did not re-new their orders on that grounds." Nevertheless, Jerry Waring, Miami's business manager stated, "We have had some letters-all-anonymous-objecting to the Negroes," He added, "But there has been no concerted objection, and we do not consider that one of the main reasons for our decline in attendance."[21]

Every team, with the exception of West Palm Beach, carried at least two black ballplayers on their roster. Baro and Clyde Parris were arguably two of Miami's best players. Later, on his way to join the Sun Sox, Maury Wills from Pueblo became the third. The best argument against the influx of "players of color," hurting gate numbers was exemplified by Fort Lauderdale who had four blacks including; Dave Barnhill, Johnny Davis, George Handy, and future major leaguer Ed Charles. The *Sporting News* reported, "Miami also has accepted calmly the appearance of Negroes in the lineups of the University of Miami's football opponents . . . Neither did the attendance at these or later games show a decline."[22]

Although some owners around the FIL subversively voiced their concerns about black ballplayers negatively affecting attendance, in fact, there were other more tangible factors resulting in the precipitous drop of fan support. The most obvious reason stemmed from the introduction of television that allowed greater access to major league baseball games thus keeping fans at home. In addition, Miamians were increasingly attending Jai Alai matches, and betting on local horse and dog races as an alternative distraction. Contrary to what some espoused, there was no evidence proving that the introduction of players of color had a negative impact on gate receipts.

In an effort to increase fan support, FIL club owners copied what other leagues were doing nationwide to bring paying customers back into the seats. Increasingly team owners were aggressive in promoting their teams using gimmicks and creative ideas to lure fans including using stunts like alligator wrestling, men's and women's wrestling, beauty contests, and family nights with cut-rate ticket prices. "I'm tired of hearing the magnates cry about poor attendance and doing anything to help improve the situation," exclaimed Joe Ryan.[23] Increasingly apparent, the game on the field was no longer enough to hold the average Joe's interest.

One factor rarely mentioned as having a negative impact on the popularity of the game was the practice of segregation at ballparks. All African-Americans, forced to sit in their own separate sections because of Jim Crow mores, a potential fan base was neglected by the prejudices of the day. Essentially, they were discouraged to attend ballgames thus reducing potential gate receipts.

When Wills reached Miami in late May, he experienced the prejudicial harsh realities that existed outside of the white lines and they hit him harder than a Barnhill fastball. Fortunately, for Wills, Clyde Parris, an ex-Negro Leaguer, assigned as his roomie proved to be a godsend. A native of Panama, Parris gained notoriety playing for the 1946 and 1947 New York Black Yankees and was well acquainted with the narrow-minded views held by a predominately-white society and was adept at avoiding its many pitfalls. He served as a mentor to Wills, helping him negotiate through some of the obstacles that he confronted, including dealing with not being able to stay in the same hotels or eat at certain restaurants with teammates. The pair gained an instant friendship that Wills shared with me.

> He was an outstanding player and could hit too. But, in those days, this is 1953, and I mean you almost got to be super before they would call you up . . . Jackie Robinson had just broken the color line in 1947. You see there was a lot more proving to be done. Yeah, he used to laugh at me because I would sit on that porch and eat something. And that was my lunch . . . He [Parris] was from Panama and he was freer to do things than I was. But, he was a good player. I really admired him.[24]

Wills, who grew up in Washington D.C., was a son of a Baptist minister. The Brooklyn Dodgers signed him at 17-years-old out of high school. One of thirteen children he grew up attending church and taught to be well mannered by his father. By the time, he arrived in the Magic City he was only 20 years old. He recalled what it was like for him during his stay in Miami.

> Another experience I had in Miami was that I couldn't stay with my teammates. When we went on road trips, I couldn't eat where they ate. That's the first time I had run into that in my lifetime . . . Just to think that I could go to another country, a third world country at that, and eat where everybody else ate. I couldn't in Miami, my own country. Anyway, I didn't complain. I went through it, but it helped me to grow.[25]

The versatile Wills who played several different positions so impressed Alexson that he replaced the struggling .200 hitting shortstop Jasper Spears with the new arrival. Batting leadoff, playing shortstop and outfield the young speedster's presence improved the club both defensively and offensively as they precariously held onto first place just ahead of Fort Lauderdale.[26] Wills made his first appearance on May 24, against Tampa substituting for Sierra late in the game in center field during a 10 to 0 loss to Tampa on the road. Although not getting an official at-bat in that game, Wills would find increased playing time as the season progressed mostly at his familiar position at short.[27]

Having played for authoritarian, George Pfister in Pueblo, Wills found his new skipper more to his liking having also played for Alexson at Hornell in 1951. He shared how and why he came to the Sun Sox.

> He [Pfister] was gruff and scraping . . . So, one of my teammates, a buddy, a black guy who was a veteran said to me, and this was a life lesson, "I don't know why he singled you out and embarrassed you in front of everybody." I said, "What am I supposed to do?" He said, "Well, if he does it to you, just tell him to take his club and shove it." Would you believe that ten days later, maybe two weeks, this man had another meeting and he singled me out? And he ragged on me, and I said, "Hey, don't get on me. If you don't like the way I'm playing I'll go somewhere else and play." And the next day I was on

a train going to Miami. That's how I got there. That was a life lesson, not to listen to other people . . . Speak first, and think for yourself.[28]

With Wills now batting at the top of the order, the previous leadoff man Didier dropped to a lower slot in the lineup. Wills speed brought a dimension to the Sun Sox that they had not had since Chico Fernandez. Didier recanted, "He [Wills] had a hell of an arm and ran like a deer."[29] Going into the month of June, the hard-charging Fort Lauderdale Lions had much improved since their loss to Miami, 17 to 3 at the beginning of May. As of June 7, the Lions had won 21 of their last 30 games and overtaken the Sun Sox as league leaders.

Although half of the inner city rivalry had moved north, the bad blood between the two foes still percolated. Verbal run-ins, hard slides to break up double plays and high spikes were the norm between the two. The Fort Lauderdale roster included eight members from the 1952 Flamingos including, Ehlman, Elko, Handy, Levan, Morilla, Nothe, Wehmeyer and Williams. As a group, they all felt they still had a score to settle with the Sun Sox and justifiably motivated to grab the ultimate FIL prize.

Levan was arguably the best hitter in the brief history of the Flamingos and the FIL. During his three seasons, he won two batting titles (1952, 1954). Dave Exter was a Miami Beach High School graduate, who had a brief fling pitching with the Flamingos in 1954. He also enjoyed a five-year minor league career. Exter reminisced with me about one of the greatest batters he ever saw.

> He was a left-handed batter, stocky, he looked like Johnny Mize, and he could hit. He hit .330, .340 like nothing. And that league, the FIL, was a pitcher's league. Nobody hit that high. What a hitter.[30]

Miami temporarily got the upper hand and tied for the top spot taking the opener of the June 7 double dip, by the score of 9 to 3. Despite Alexson and Little being tossed for arguing an umpire's decision, their teammates stepped up and took three Lions hurlers to task banging out nine hits in the seven-inning affair. Lovell pitched $5\frac{1}{3}$ innings before being relieved by Joe Bernier. The pair combined to limit Ft. Lauderdale to five hits. Willie Davis had the big blow of the night homering in the second inning.

In the second game, Miami let a 3–1 lead escape them in the sixth inning allowing four runs, two that were walked home by Raynor in relief, handing the Lions a 5–3 lead which stood up as the final. Pepper Martin spewed his customary venom at the conclusion of the contest when he officially lodged a protest accusing Alexson of giving signals outside of the game.[31] An infuriated Alexson (ejected earlier for arguing calls) retorted by lodging a counter-protest and said, "What did they want me to do-go home." Alexson admitted that he had retreated behind a fence between the press box and the grandstand, but did not say if he flashed signals from afar. League president, O'Connell later ruled against the protests and the results of the twin bill stood.[32]

The month of June separated the pretenders from the contenders. By the time, the Sun Sox traveled to Fort Lauderdale on July 1, their slim half-game lead in mid-June had vanished, the product of the Lions reeling off 16 wins in 18 games to finish the month. They stretched their league lead to a season-high six games.

The animosity between the two rivals reached a farcical level. Miami's front office knowing that ballplayers have a propensity for being superstitious instigated a cleverly constructed ruse to put a hex on the visiting Lions. They organized a "Beat Fort Lauderdale Night," painted black cats, and the number 13 on the walls of the visitor's dugout of Miami Stadium at the June 24 contest.[33] At least for one night, the spell worked its supernatural force as Miami prevailed, 3 to 2 before 1,632. The big blast of the night came off the bat of shortstop Willie Davis, a three-run dinger off Winston Brown in the second.[34]

Behind the scenes of the continuing hostilities between the Sox and the Lions was the ongoing feud between Joe Ryan and the Sox's business manager Jerry Waring. The bad blood dated back to the previous year's incident involving Knobby Rosa that reversed a Flamingos win costing Miami Beach the pennant. The strife between the two reared its ugly head when the Lions and Sun Sox clashed at the beginning of July.

With what the *Miami News* termed, "the newest in a long series of taffy-pulls," Ryan yanked the plug on WINZ's Denny Kirwan and Johnny Schulte who were broadcasting the opening game of the series between the Lions and Sox at West Side Park. The announcers called the first two innings without incident before Ryan confronted them. He promptly advised both broadcasters while they were working the mics that his club's policy stated, "the radio station did not have permission to broadcast the game until 9:15." This, of course, is well after the game had begun. Waring angrily confronted Ryan and let him know, not so diplomatically, that before the season Ryan himself had sent a letter to the Miami club authorizing unrestricted broadcasting rights. In an otherwise calm press box, the two nearly came to blows. Waring's last words were letting it be known that the next time Ryan and his club visited Miami Stadium that they could expect a very cool reception.[35]

While Ryan and Waring were going at it off the field, Fort Lauderdale handed it to Miami on the field. The Lions pounded out 12 hits off Bernier and Gushanas, including a trio of home runs, thumping the Sox 10 to 1. Iott earned the "W" striking out eight and limiting Sox hitters to six singles.[36]

That same night fans attending the game in Fort Lauderdale received word by loudspeaker that Tampa owner Tom Spicola sold his fifth place Smokers to a group of local businesspersons for $17,500 including team uniforms.[37] It was a devastating blow to the league, losing one of its staunchest supporters, as the FIL continued to unravel.

First Half Standings

TEAM	W	L	GB
Fort Lauderdale	53	27	–
Miami	44	32	7
St. Petersburg	40	37	11.5
Havana	33	41	17
West Palm Beach	31	47	21.
Tampa	32	49	21.5

By mid-season's Fourth of July weekend, Miami had dropped to seven games off the pace, still resting in second place. Even Waring confessed that the Sun Sox were a cut below Fort Lauderdale and called upon the parent Dodgers for help. Especially troubling was the work of the Sox's bullpen. Alexson had become so frustrated with their efforts, that he inserted himself in relief during a 7 to 2 loss to the Lions before the break.[38]

Brooklyn's brass answered Waring's plea sending pitcher, Danny Hayling from Class A Pueblo, and catcher, Ronnie Dacko from Class B Asheville. Listed at 6'4" Hayling, the more intriguing of the two new arrivals, came only two years removed from a 21-win season as a member of the Hazard Bombers of the Class D Mountain States League. Alexson assessed his new pitcher by saying, "He is supposed to have a real live fastball and good stuff to go with it." He added, "His big trouble is control, and not having pitched in quite a while he may have a tough time in his first start."[39]

Whatever concerns Alexson might have had were laid to rest when Hayling took the mound for the first time. The visiting West Palm Beach Indians mustered only five hits and a single tally. The big Costa Rican struck out six, as the Sun Sox coasted to a 7 to 1 win. It was Miami's seventeenth win in nineteen tries against the Tribe. Outspoken Ed Little, when asked to evaluate the pitcher's performance, was uncharacteristically short in his assessment saying, "Good." On the other hand, when the light-hitting catcher was asked to share his thoughts on his two-hit performance he said, "They loved me."[40]

By the July 15 All-Star game, the Sun Sox had kept pace with the Lions, with identical 8–3 records. Fort Lauderdale hosted the FIL version of the mid-summer classic at West Side Park. Miami fielded seven players including, Armstrong (LF), Baro (RF), Bernier (P), Little (C), Montalbano (SS), Parris (3B), and Sierra (CF). Joining the Miami bunch was a cast of the best of the other FIL teams that battled Fort Lauderdale into extra innings. In the top of the twelfth and Morilla working on the mound, with a runner on first, Baro stepped to the plate. Looking for the right pitch, Baro cocked his bat and drove an offering 345 feet over the left-centerfield fence giving the All-Stars, an 8 to 6 lead. Denis Jent representing St. Petersburg pitched the bottom of the frame and shut down the Lions securing the win. Hall of Famer Al Simmons, one of almost 3,000 in attendance, praised both teams for their strong effort. He appraised the Fort Lauderdale club by remarking, "They are a great Class B team. I don't see how they can miss winning the second half too."[41]

As Simmons had predicted, the Lions outdistanced the rest of the FIL in the second half. Fort Lauderdale's eight-game lead over second place Miami with 14 games to go looked insurmountable. Manager Martin admitted it was just about impossible for his club to blow it. The consensus, the Sox only chance of catching the front-runners was sweeping the Lions in the upcoming five-game homestand.[42]

On August 21, a sizable crowd of 2,317 turned out for the opening twin bill to kick off the final series between the two rivals. Right-hander Seijas took to the hill to challenge Lions ace, Iott. The diminutive Cuban got off to a shaky start allowing a pair of runs in the first inning. He hit hard all night. By the end of the fifth, he had given up four runs leaving Miami trailing 4 to 3.[43]

After Miami tied the score in the bottom of the sixth, Seijas, who finished the season with a minuscule .119 batting average, approached the plate with the bases loaded and two outs. It was a decision that left many in the crowd scratching their heads. Elko who had entered the game in relief promptly struck the opposing hurler out to end the inning. Seijas pitched to one batter in the seventh, but after giving up a bunt base hit, Bernier came in for relief and silenced the Lions from there on out. After Wills and Baro each hit singles in the bottom of the seventh, Armstrong followed with the third base hit of the inning supplying the Sun Sox with a 5 to 4 victory.[44]

In the nightcap, the two rivals went at it again. The Sun Sox built an early 6–1 lead going into the seventh inning. Raynor was cruising along smoother than a Hudson Hornet when suddenly the wheels came off, and the Lions pushed across four unanswered runs. With base runners on the corners, Handy followed smacking a double into left field plating one run to knot the score. Following close behind with the go-ahead score was Mario Marsalisi. The catcher Dako was blocking the plate and as the throw came in from left field, Marsalisi appeared to have beaten the heave based on the catcher applying a late tag. To the surprise of most in the stands, home plate umpire Albury saw it differently and thumbed the runner out ending the inning. Martin was beside himself and exploded as he bolted from the first base coach's box in a rage.

Albury and Martin already had a history of several confrontations and this one proved to be another doozy. They did not call him the "Wild Horse of the Osage" for nothing; Martin grabbed Albury by the shoulder and began arguing his case. Levan who was in the on-deck circle also joined the melee and in "short order" ejections followed for both. Later, Martin claimed that Albury originally called the runner safe and then changed his decision. "As God looks down in judgment, by the court of appeals, that man was safe." Albury later defended his action and said, "Sure the runner beat the throw and I started to signal he was safe. But then I see that the catcher has him blocked off. No question about it." Regardless of the decision, Sierra hit a solo walk-off jack in the tenth inning off Bill Currie, delivering another win, 5 to 4 for Miami.[45]

The Sun Sox, hoping to build on their momentum by taking the doubleheader, faced their old nemesis in the third game of the set, Chet Covington. Ryan, not wanting to take any chances on a monumental collapse enticed the 42-year out of retirement and signed him hoping to squeeze one more bit of magic out of his weary arm.[46]

Chesty had a long history serving as Miami's antagonist having defeated them on a regular basis in previous years. In the past, disconcerted fans formed the "Beat Lefty Covington Club" in an effort to rile their longtime nemesis. Yet, despite their catcalls and pointed gibes, their jeers only strengthened his resolve to win. Alexson's hopes of discouraging the old warhorse rested on the shoulders of young Hayling.[47]

"Lefty" came out a little shaky in the first inning giving up a run, but soon shook off the cobwebs and regained his past form. Thanks to some welcome offensive support, going into the eighth inning Covington enjoyed a 5–1 lead. In the bottom half of the same frame, the cantankerous veteran retired the first two batters. Baro followed with a single and Parris smacked a double into the gap plating his teammate. Martin, seeing that his starter weakened, sauntered to the hill to make the pitching change. The rubber-armed competitor, known to refuse to leave the mound, uncharacteristically said, "Glad to see you" and handed "Old Pep" the ball. Iott took over and finished the job closing out the game, delivering the Lions a 5 to 2 win.[48]

Fort Lauderdale shutout the Sun Sox, 2 to 0, dowsing any hopes Miami held of making a run at the top spot. The big left-hander, Iott returned to the bump and out-dueled Bernier while striking out ten, and stingily allowing only four singles. The Lions stretched their lead to eight games, and Alexson's charges essentially ran up the white flag.[49]

Miami played poorly down the stretch dropping six of their last nine games, while St. Petersburg took advantage of the Sun Sox's poor play winning seven of their last eight games, thereby leap-frogging over Miami into second place in the second half.

Second Half Standings

TEAM	W	L	GB
Fort Lauderdale	39	19	–
St. Petersburg	32	25	6.5
Miami	32	26	7
Havana	30	28	9
West Palm Beach	26	33	13.5
Tampa	14	42	24

The stage was set for the postseason. Miami limped into the playoffs matched up against St. Petersburg in a best-of-five draw, while Fort Lauderdale drew fourth place Havana in the opposite semi-final series.

The Sun Sox loaded up in their traveling bus and headed northwest along Alligator Alley (present day Interstate 75) to Al Lang Field. A crowd of 1,484 greeted the visitors, a large crowd considering that only 382 came out in Fort Lauderdale. Both teams matched zeroes until the bottom of the ninth inning. Bernier allowed Pete Stroud, Stan Milankovich and Gene Hassell to reach base in quick succession. Don Richards was retired on a grounder to third baseman Parris. The ex-Negro Leaguer fired the ball home to Little for the force out. Seemingly having dodged a bullet, Bernier could not find the strike zone facing the next batter, Robert Stowe, and walked him with "ducks on the pond." St. Pete gladly accepted the gift and a 1 to 0 victory.[50]

Miami was unable to catch many breaks in the series. The Sun Sox lost game two, 5 to 4, and game three, 6 to 5, both heartbreakers. Bernier was the culprit in the finale, after coming into the game in the seventh in relief of Seijas, he tired in the twelfth inning. A double by German Pizarro, allowed Stowe to race in and score with the walk-off winner ending Miami's season.[51]

Much to the chagrin of Miami Beach citizens, the Fort Lauderdale Lions under the guidance of Martin, with a host of former Flamingos, went on to dump Havana three games to one, and then captured the Shaughnessy playoffs downing St. Petersburg in six games.

There were concerns surrounding the survival of the FIL at season's end. In order to maintain the six-team format, Roberto "Bobby" Maduro who took over the Havana franchise at mid-season received authorization from President O'Connell to explore the viability of adding a second team from the Cuban island.[52] This was in response to fears that league stalwarts, St. Petersburg and Tampa would fold due to their financial troubles. St. Pete officials petitioned the city to free them from their debts tied to the use of Al Lang Field, as well as unpaid electrical bills. Saints owner, Vernon Eckert went as far as offering to sell 80 percent of his stock for one dollar if the bidder was willing to assume all of the clubs obligations.[53] In addition, Tampa announced their intent to file an application for membership in the Class A South Atlantic League thus, making their exit.

In a further twist, Paul Rust and Joe Ryan presented a plan to Jose Aleman Jr., and Jerry Waring to put together a partnership to bring Triple-A baseball to Miami. The management of the Sun Sox response was a firm, "not interested."[54] However, the seed of the idea planted would later sprout and bring forth a whole crop of far-reaching repercussions that influenced Miami baseball to this day.

Final Standings

TEAM	W	L	GB
Fort Lauderdale	92	46	–
Miami	76	58	14
St. Petersburg	72	62	18
Havana	63	69	26
West Palm Beach	57	80	34.5
Tampa	46	91	45.5

1954

To surmise that the Florida International League was in trouble would be an understatement. Despite the outward appearance portrayed by the owners who maintained that the league was strong, the evidence was contrary to their outlook.

The biggest blow to the league's sustainability came on January 12, when Bobby Maduro, the owner of the Cubans franchise, announced that Havana was leaving the FIL to join the Triple-A International League (IL). He had been aggressively courting IL president, Frank Shaughnessy with promises including, guarantees of round-trip airfares for the other seven clubs in the league, and assurances of attendance clearing the 300,000 mark at the 30,000 seat Gran Stadium.[55] Any hope of establishing another franchise on the island of Cuba as a member of the FIL was no longer practicable.

Seeing, "the handwriting on the wall," and the likelihood of the FIL folding, Paul Rust Jr., owner of the Fort Lauderdale club began to explore his options including selling the team. He was relieved to discover that a letter written to league president O'Connell from Robert J. Reidy, a Chicago industrialist, expressed an interest and intention to purchase the Lions franchise. Reidy, who lived part of the year in Coral Gables, purportedly made an offer of over $20,000 to buy the club. The two men reached an agreement and closed the deal transferring ownership in quick fashion. As part of the arrangement, Reidy arranged the transfer of his team to Miami Beach when the city council agreed to $14,000 in requested improvements to Flamingo Park.[56]

The new owner retained Joe Ryan to run the club. One of his first decisions was purchasing Ed Little, voted the Sun Sox's most popular player in 1953. The straight-talking receiver, purchased for $300, accepted the duties of not only serving as the team's starting catcher but also agreed to act as its promotional director.[57]

At least temporarily, the Reidy purchase brought hope that the FIL would survive. Although the goal was to put together an eight-team league, with Maduro's departure and his promise of two Cubans teams joining the circuit being out of the question, all eyes turned towards Key West or Tallahassee to round out a six-team format. Despite a strong effort by a Lou Carbonell headed group representing the Keys, league officials awarded Tallahassee the sixth spot seeing the city as a more viable location for stability and increased attendance.[58]

Outwardly, the league's situation seemingly improved, still there were concerns about the stability of Miami. Aleman Jr.'s financial problems tied to Miami Stadium were draining his monetary resources. In order to recoup some of his losses, he resorted to renting the stadium out for a horse show and rodeo. This attracted some scorn from the parent Brooklyn Dodgers who were concerned about the condition of the playing surface come spring training. In addition, there was a great deal of trepidation surrounding the Sun Sox's situation because of the absence of their owner and the inability of the club to hire a business manager for months. To the Dodgers, it seemed as if the situation in Miami was in complete disarray.[59]

Nevertheless, Dodgers prospects and returning veterans received their assignment to Miami and ventured south in anticipation of the season. Twenty-three-year-old shortstop Carlyle Staab and his younger colleagues were thrilled upon arriving in Miami. They even got a break on their daily meals at a popular local establishment, where they partook of their famous apple pie a la mode. Staab shared his memories:

> When we walked into that stadium [Miami Stadium], you know all of the guys thought they had died and gone to heaven because that was a beautiful stadium then, and like you say it was state-of-the-art compared to the other minor league stadiums around the country. There was no question about that.
>
> I remember there were three or four of us that bought these food tickets from the Howard Johnson's restaurant. And they would give you twenty dollars-worth of meals for I think, sixteen dollars . . . You'd get in and have a meal and they would punch your ticket for what you bought, which for us at the time was a good deal because, you know, everyone was trying to save money on food.[60]

The season opened with heavy rains and several cancellations. It was a portentous sign of things to come. Miami's curtain-raiser was disheartening as a small gathering of 1,504 attended only to have the contest postponed because of heavy showers. Meanwhile, at Tampa, only 1,400 passed through the turnstiles to witness the Flamingos rip the Smokers, 5 to 1. Adding insult to injury, Miami's entire three-game opening homestand suffered through a daily deluge of rain forcing cancellation of every game. By the time, they were finally able to play on April 9, only 826 paying customers turned out.[61]

Miami Beach's home opener on April 12 did little to encourage their new owner. A sparse congregation of 1,312 passed through the turnstiles. Mayor Harold Shapiro threw out the first ball and shortly thereafter, he was joined by Reidy and new league president, Dale Miller (replaced O'Connell who stepped aside due to increased responsibilities related to his law firm) as the group addressed the crowd with encouraging words. Twenty-two-year-old right-hander, Bob Hines went the route holding the Smokers to six hits, doing his part in helping to earn the Flamingos the, 7 to 3 win.[62]

The ongoing problems plaguing the FIL came to a head on May 5 when both Miami and Tampa withdrew from the league after playing their last game. In front of a scant crowd of 633 at West Palm Beach, the Sun Sox fell to the Indians, 6 to 5. George Wasconis, a local boy that graduated from Edison High School took the loss.[63]

Earlier that same day, the Sun Sox, represented by Al Rubio and Joe Paul met with league directors and president, Miller in a last ditch effort to save the team. During a five and a half hour nerve-wracking meeting inside Miami Stadium's cocktail bar with league directors, Rubio informed attendees that during his prior visit with Aleman Jr. in Cuba, he was instructed that not a penny more would be invested into the Sun Sox. Rubio, given full authority to make any decisions concerning the Sun Sox by his boss, then made it official that Miami was dropping out of the league. In the end, the specter of pecuniary losses was too difficult to overcome. The Miami club reported losses of $10,000, attributed to five of their first twelve games postponed because of bad weather and poor attendance. The Tampa ownership group, seeing this as an opportune time to cut their own losses followed suit. The remaining four club owners promised to finish the season expressing their regrets over the losses.[64][65]

The Sun Sox's success on the field certainly had not been a deterrent to fan support, but future generations of owners learned, the many distractions that come with the territory in south Florida are hard to overcome. During the 1940s and 50s, the horse and dog races held in Hialeah, Jai Alai, and the lure of surf and sand all played a role in diverting the attention of paying public from the baseball diamond. Another factor to be considered is the transient nature of the population lacking deep roots and loyalties to the local team, not to mention the constant rain that comes each summer.

Amongst the swirl of continued dire news, the two most positive voices emerging from the chaos were those of Reidy and Ryan. Both men had their sights set on a higher goal, that of preserving baseball in Miami. Together they boldly predicted that the city would move up to a higher classification as a member of the AAA International League, following in the footsteps of Havana.

As part of the league re-organization, many of the Dodgers prospects were re-assigned, and a few members of the Sun Sox not privileged with a major league affiliation joined Miami Beach to form a new team under the banner of the Greater Miami Flamingos. The eternally optimistic Reidy acquired full territorial rights and negotiated a beneficial deal for the use of Miami Field rent free courtesy of the Miami City Commission along with pledges from civic clubs to sponsor ticket sales. Reidy and Ryan agreed that the favorable arrangement for the use of Miami Field as a more central location was conducive to better attendance than remaining in Miami Beach where fan apathy had reached a new low. Reidy enthusiastically predicted a bright future and an even better and faster league in 1955. It was clear that Reidy had his sights set on moving up in classification to a higher level in the near future with a clear understanding that the end of the FIL was inevitable. "We must explore every possibility to make a success in the Miami area now that we are the only team here," said Ryan. He added, "We are going forward to get the best ball we can at all times."[66 67]

On May 18, the Flamingos played their last game at Flamingo Park. Only 350 patrons (165 actual tickets sold) showed an interest in paying their respects to the death of professional baseball on the beach. The ballpark was empty as a church on a Monday morning. "After the crowds we've had here, there is only one way to go. That's up.," said a candid Little whose comments reflected all the players' feelings. He added, "I think everybody on the club is glad. We have missed the crowds." For the record Hines, who relieved starter Herve Cos in the eighth inning, earned the win. The big southpaw helped his own cause by laying down a well-placed bunt that forced an errant throw by St. Petersburg's hurler, Jeff Davis over the first baseman's head allowing the winning run to cross the plate.[68]

On May 22, the former Beachites debuted at Miami Field. For Pepper Martin, it was a homecoming, having previously managed the Sun Sox there. He and all the players made it a point to reach out to the 839 fans, shake hands, and share kind words of appreciation for showing their support. During the three-game homestand against West Palm Beach, 1,829 welcomed Martin's charges with open arms and encouragement.

In his regular *Miami News* sports column, Morris McLemore speculated why baseball had failed at Miami Beach. He blamed the hotels with nightclub licenses for making a strong effort to keep their patrons on the premises to spend money and the absence of bookies and bettors who used to frequent Flamingo Park.

"The absence of free-flowing 10-dollar bills between fans also figures. A former part owner of the club estimated 400 gamblers
a night infested the Beach ballyard at one time, living off each
other in the summer and trying to survive until the next crop of
plump turkeys showed up in the autumn, ready for plucking at
horses, roulette or whatever." The unnamed former stakeholder
quoted in the article said, "When the gamblers disappeared after
the Kefauvers came through, there went baseball."[69]

Despite Reidy and Ryan's sanguinity, and the revamped
Greater Miami club running neck and neck with St. Petersburg
in a taut second half pennant race, interest in the club continued
to wane. In order to stimulate attendance Reidy and Ryan put together a plan that offering fans free admission for a pair of home
games scheduled for Tuesday, July 13 and Wednesday, July 14
games. Reidy had tried this is a publicity stunt earlier in May, but
as luck would have it the game was rained out. St. Petersburg
used a version of this same gimmick by offering local business to
buy out the ballpark for the night for $700 and then offering free
tickets to anyone attending. The promotion worked so well that
the Saints drew over 22,000 for a five-game homestand in June.[70]

The July 13 game met with less than expected success. Reidy's
"free admission night" drew 2,044, about eleven times more than
attracted the previous night when only 189 paid customers, but
far less than the 4,000+ crowd expected. Although the final count
seen by the press as disappointing, to be fair, the offer of free ducats advertised to the public on short notice probably depressed
the final numbers. However, the terminally half-full versus half-
empty outlook owner was cheered by the turnout and went so far
as announcing over the intercom that if more than 4,000 fans
came out for the next night's contest he would give away a vehicle. Following the game, he boldly predicted he would do better
on Wednesday and declared, "I think we'll have plenty of people.
I believe we'll go over 4,000. I am still happy over that Tuesday
crowd." Almost lost in all the excitement, the Flamingos upended
Palm Beach, 12 to 5 as Labe Dean in his fourth go around in
Miami earned the win.[71] [72]

If there was ever anyone that believed in omens, their greatest
suspicions received convincing substantiation by what transpired
on that Wednesday night. Heavy rains pelted Miami Field, and
with that, it seemed as if hope and whatever momentum built the
previous night to lure fans went down the drain.

The all-star break provided a temporary respite from an otherwise disheartening season. Many players were concerned about their future, if the league folded.

Regardless of the ominous cloud hanging over the league, the front-running St. Petersburg Saints moved forward hosting the midsummer classic at Lang Field against the best players from the remaining three clubs. The Flamingos filled out most of the roster that included; Martin (manager), Little (C), Levan (1B), Dan Morejon (3B), Armstrong (LF), Wehmeyer (utility infielder), Frank Smith (utility outfielder), Winston Brown (P), Dean (P), Hines, (P), and Solis (P).[73]

The July 19 all-star game proved to be the last gasp of in the life remaining in the FIL. The Miami led contingent proved instrumental in the blasting of the Saints in front of 2,296 by the one-sided score of, 7 to 1. Morejon went 3-for-4, and Levan drove in a couple of runs providing more than enough offense. Veteran Labe Dean held the opposition to one run and four hits in three innings of work, garnering the victory.[74]

By July 26, the ailing FIL pulled the plug and officially disbanded when West Palm Beach announced their intention to step down to Class D in 1955, and Tallahassee withdrew from the league when their directors were unable to raise a required $5,000 fee. Reidy made a last-ditch effort offering to buy the Jacksonville Beach Class D Florida State League team and relocate it to Miami. Sea Birds co-owner Julian Jackson rebuffed the offer ending Miami's last hope. A determined Reidy contacted minor league commissioner, George Trautman asking for permission to continue to operate as a two-team league. The recommendation was rejected. Clearly, Reidy's motive to save the failing league involved protecting his territorial rights in hopes of joining either the Southern Association or International League in 1955. By not finishing the season, any claim that the Chicago industrialist had on the Miami territory became void even though Ryan maintained that was not the case.[75][76] Soon after, a disenchanted Reidy faded from the scene in Miami no doubt discouraged by the chain of events that undermined his last ditch to save baseball in Miami under his ownership.

Many reasons factored into the ultimate collapse of the FIL. Jimmy Burns, a sports columnist for the *Miami Herald*, blamed the four-club competition as failing to grab the interest of the fans. He also pointed out that travel expenses incurred by the other teams when making the trek to Tallahassee amounted to an extra $400 in expenditures putting an additional strain on the budgets of teams that were already struggling financially.[77]

Further, the encroachment of television was changing American culture and their choice of entertainment. Whereas a family once jumped into their car and drove to the ballpark to see their local team, more and more they stayed home to watch their favorite program on the screen. Major league baseball and other sports like boxing, and college football were simply more accessible to the masses.

The FIL, which started out with so much bluster and promise, after nine seasons faded out with little more than a whimper. For all the league's faults, an inordinate amount of great moments, and eccentric personalities more than offset the negative. The FIL was ahead of its time when it ushered in international play in the Caribbean and was the first minor league operation to organize chartered flights. Two cities, Miami and Tampa became major league cities, including St. Petersburg serving as the home of the Rays at Tropicana Field. It will always be up for debate if the political situation in Havana had not shifted towards communism, would the Cuban capital have also joined the majors in time. The slogan that accompanied the Sugar Kings logo, "Un paso mas y llegamos" ("One More Step and We Arrived"), stated Maduro's goal for his club that never came to realization.

In the summer of 1955, Miami Stadium remained silent. With its reappearance in the spring of 1956, the most colorful characters to ever cross baseball's landscape emerged. Along with it, the Magic City enjoyed the highest class of baseball yet.

Final Standings

TEAM	W	L	GB
St. Petersburg	64	37	–
Miami Beach / Miami**	63	39	1.5
West Palm Beach	47	51	14.5
Tallahassee	22	76	40.5
Miami*	13	12	
Tampa*	17	11	

* Miami and Tampa disbanded on May 5
** Miami Beach relocated to Miami on May 22
The FIL disbanded on July 26 and St. Petersburg was ruled league champion

NOTES

1.   Burns, Jimmy. Miami Beach, Fla. Int Club, Shifted to Fort Lauderdale, *Sporting News*, 25 February, 1953, p. 33.
2.   Warner, Ralph. Havana Dispute Puts FIL On Spot, *Miami News*, 11 April, 1953, p. 1-B.
3.   Burns, Jimmy. Miami Stadium for Sale? A Bid May Tell Story, *Sporting News*, 21 January, 1953, p. 20.
4.   Reaction Favorable To Baseball Revival In Broward County, *Fort Lauderdale News*, 28 October, 1952, p. 2-B.
5.   Dick Meyer. Time Out for Sports, *Fort Lauderdale News*, January 23, 1953, p. 14.
6.   Baseball-reference.com. Key West was an affiliate of the San Diego Padres in 1969 as a member of the Florida State League finishing 67–63. They existed as a co-op minor league team from 1972 through 1973, before their affiliation with the Chicago Cubs in 1974 as a member of the FSL. Over those three years, they accumulated a 156–248 record.
7.   Burns, Jimmy. Miami Beach, Fla. Int Club, Shifted to Fort Lauderdale, *Sporting News*, 25 February, 1953, p. 33.
8.   Warner, Ralph. F-I League Starts Tonight, Sun Sox Meet West Palm, *Miami News*, 15 April, 1953, p. 3-B.
9.   Whitey Kelley. Pony Pilot 4-Year Vet But Only 30, *Miami Herald*, 19 January, 1953, p. 3-D.
10. Baseball-reference.com. His record was 81–43 in 1950, 71–55 in 1951, and 69–56 in 1952.
11. Kelley, Whitey. Pony Pilot 4-Year Vet But Only 30, *Miami Herald*, 19 January, 1953, p. 3-D.
12. Didier, Gerald. Phone interview with author, 6 August, 2014.
13. Baseball-reference.com.
14. Kelley, Whitey. 2,371 Watch Mac Mosley's Five-Hitter, *Miami Herald*, 18 April, 1953, p. 14-A.
15. Burns, Jimmy. Mayor Uncorks a Wild Pitch, *Miami Herald*, 18 April, 1953, p. 14-A.
16. Baseball-reference.com.
17. Kelley, Whitey. 2,371 Watch Mac Mosley's Five-Hitter, *Miami Herald*, 18 April, 1953, p. 14-A.
18. Ibid.
19. Warner, Ralph. Very Tamed Lions Face Miami Again, *Miami News*, 2 May, 1953, p. 10-B.
20. Homer, Hurlers Parade In F-I, *Sporting News*, 13 May, 1953, p. 34.
21. Burns, Jimmy. Negroes' Gate Effect Debated in Fla. Int, *Sporting News*, 6 May, 1953, p. 1 & 4.
22. Ibid.
23. Burns, Jimmy. 'Gator Wrestling Among Gate Baits Tried by Fla. Int, *Sporting News*, 10 June, 1953, p. 14.
24. Wills, Maury. Phone interview with author, 3 August, 2014.
25. Ibid.
26. Kelley, Whitey. 2,116 See Cubans Waste 10 Blows In First Game, *Miami Herald*, 23 May, 1953, p. 17-A.
27. 6-Run 2nd Destroys Sox Hopes, *Miami Herald*, 25 May, 1953, p. 5-D.
28. Wills, Maury. Phone interview with author, 3 August, 2014.
29. Didier, Gerald. Phone interview with author, 6 August, 2014.
30. Exter, Dave. Personal interview with author, 21 June, 2017.

31. Miami Pitchers Walk 2 Runs Across in Finale, *Miami Herald*, 8 June, 1953, p. 3-D.
32. Burns, Jimmy. Game Played Under Double Protest, *Miami Herald*, 9 June, 1953, p. 1-D.
33. *Miami Herald*, Staff Photo, 25 June, 1953, p. 4-B.
34. Pettijohn, Fred. Top F-I Clubs Vie In Miami, *Fort Lauderdale News*, June 25, 1953, p. 2-B.
35. Warner, Ralph. Lions Pulling Away From Miami's Sox, *Miami News*, 2 July, 1953, p. 12-A.
36. Ibid.
37. Ibid.
38. Meyer, Dick. Brown Due To Pitch Sox Finale, *Fort Lauderdale News*, 3 July, 1953, p. 8-A.
39. Grace, Art. Big Negro, Hayling, Will Begin Work Now, *Miami News*, 6 July, 1953, p. 13-A.
40. Warner, Ralph. New Pitcher Keeps Sun Sox Jinx Alive, *Miami News*, 7 July, 1953, p. 9-A.
41. Warner, Ralph. Lions Still Rated Invincible Despite Loss To All-Stars, *Miami News*, 16 July, 1953, p. 2-B.
42. Grace, Art. Lions Play Single Game Hear Today, *Miami News*, 22 August, 1953, p. 7-A.
43. Ibid.
44. Martin Grabs Ump In Wild 7th, *Fort Lauderdale News*, 22 August, 1953, p. 2-B.
45. Grace, Art. Last-Innings Sox Scores Beat Lauderdale Twice, *Miami News*, 22 August, 1953, p. 7-A.
46. Add Covington, *Fort Lauderdale News*, 22 August, 1953, p. 7-A.
47. Old Lefty Needs Aid From Iott, *Fort Lauderdale News*, 23 August, 1953, p. 1-B.
48. Ibid.
49. Grace, Art. Split Extinguishes Sun Sox Hope For Second-Half Flag, *Miami News*, 24 August, 1953, p. 11-A.
50. Burt, Lonnie. Saints Win Playoff Opener From Sun Sox, *St. Petersburg Times*, 1 to 0, 4 September, 1953, p. 11.
51. Burt, Lonnie. Saints Sweep Sox Playoff In 12-Inning Drama, 6–5, *St. Petersburg Times*, 6 September, 1953, p. 1-C & 3-C.
52. Burns, Jimmy. FI League Seeks Second Club to Play in Havana, *Sporting News*, 28 October, 1953, p. 22.
53. St. Pete Club Priced at $1-If Bidder Assumes Debt, *Sporting News*, 28 October, 1953, p. 22.
54. Warner, Ralph. Sun Sox May Present 'Triple A' Entry Here, *Miami News*, 20 November, 1953, p. 14-A.
55. Daniel, Dan. It's Official Now—Richmond and Havana Enter Int, *Sporting News*, 20 January, 1954, p. 15.
56. Burns, Jimmy. Chicagoan Buys Fort Lauderdale Florida Int Club, *Sporting News*, 10 February, 1954, p. 35.
57. Jimmy Burns. Jimmy. Promotion Chief Little May Catch for Flamingos, *Sporting News*, 17 March, 1954, p. 26.
58. Burns, Jimmy. Dale Miller Named Prexy of Florida Int, *Sporting News*, 24 February, 1954, p. 29.
59. Warner, Ralph. No 'Smugitis" For Dodgers, *Miami News*, 1 March, 1954, p. 10-A.
60. Staab, Carlyle. Phone interview with author, June 10, 2014.
61. Burns, Jimmy. St. Pete Pulls 3,589 to Top F-I Openers, *Sporting News*, 21 April, 1954, p. 24.
62. Ralph Warner, Ed Little's Hitting Boosts Flamingos Baseball Hopes, *Miami News*, April 13, 1954, p. 12-A.
63. Flamingos Add Game To Lead By FIL Action, *Miami News*, 6 May, 1954, p. B-1.

64. McLemore, Morris. Stadium Story Needs Telling, *Miami News*, 6 May, 1954, p. B-1.

65. Warner, Ralph. Beach Seeks Miami Site, Sox Quit FIL, *Miami News*, 6 May, 1954, p. B-1.

66. Burns, Jimmy. Bob Reidy Sets Sights on Higher Loop for Miami, *Sporting News*, 2 June, 1954, p. 37.

67. Warner, Ralph. Beach Seeks Miami Site, Sox Quit FIL, *Miami News*, 6 May, 1954, p. B-1.

68. Warner, Ralph. 'Greater Miami Flamingos' Jubilant Over Park Switch', *Miami News*, 19 May, 1954, p. B-1.

69. McLemore, Morris. Flamingos Take To Air Again, *Miami News*, 19 May, 1954, p. B-1.

70. Warner, Ralph. Enterprise Sells Out Ballpark, *Miami News*, 28 June, 1954, p. 10-A.

71. Burns, Jimmy. Reidy's Free Gate at Miami Draws 2,044, *Sporting News*, 21 July, 1954, p. 39.

72. Warner, Ralph. Next Two Nights Determine Future Of Miami Baseball, *Miami* News, July 14, 1954, p. 11-A.

73. United Press, "Flamingo Players Dominate FIL's All-Star Game Roster," *Miami News*, July 15, 1954, 16-A.

74. "Miami Stars Lead Victory Over Saints," *Miami News*, July 20, 1954, p. 11-A.

75. Jimmy Burns. "Fla.-Int Tosses in Sponge When Cut to Two Clubs," *Sporting News*, August 4, 1954, 13.

76. "FSL Transfer Decision Due By Thursday," *Miami Daily News (AP)*, 28 July, 1954, p. 13-A.

77. Burns, Jimmy. "Fla.-Int Tosses in Sponge When Cut to Two Clubs," *Sporting News*, August 4, 1954, p. 13.

CHAPTER NINE

THE ORIGINAL MIAMI MARLINS 1955–1958

A new form of music coined "rock 'n roll" was sweeping the nation, and the youth of America was "rocking around the clock" to Bill Haley and the Comets. A swivel-hipped young man from Memphis named Elvis Presley had female fans swooning, and men dancing in their blue suede shoes.

In the south, the Civil Rights movement was gaining momentum. On December 1, 1955, Rosa Parks refused to give up her seat on a bus to a white passenger in Montgomery, Alabama setting the stage for the end of segregation. The incident became a centerpiece for the growing movement of equal rights for all.

Miamians intently followed events in Cuba, where Fidel Castro, the leader of a revolutionary movement fought to take control of the country. Hundreds of thousands of Cuban refugees fled the communist oppressed country; most never to return. The migration changed the face of the Magic City forever.

Baseball in Miami continued to evolve. Miami Stadium's history of separate seating for black patrons was about to end. Jim Crow laws were dying a slow death. A baseball icon would win Miamians over with his free-spirited approach to the game and a rubber arm that despite his advanced age continued to make even the best hitters look foolish. Entering from stage right, legendary baseball icon, Leroy "Satchel" Paige.

1955

The January 14 headline across the *Miami Daily News* announced, "Miami's Chance For Baseball Declared 50–50." Joe Ryan remained tenacious in his efforts to bring baseball to Miami in 1955. Always the optimist, the bespectacled dynamo was holding out hopes of fielding a team in a proposed new league consisting of Fort Lauderdale, Fort Pierce, Hollywood, Key West, and West Palm Beach with the possibility of Fort Myers, St. Petersburg and Tampa joining. "A Class C league would keep interest alive until we get another chance for higher classification franchise," Ryan declared.[1]

While he scrambled to arrange for baseball alignment in Miami, Robert Reidy the co-owner of Continental Trailer Co. was in Chicago with eyes fixed on the goal of acquiring a franchise at the Triple-A level. He missed the best chance at bringing the International League (IL) to Miami in December of 1954 when a local group hatched a plan to bring summer jai alai to the area and quickly signed an option to purchase Miami Stadium essentially blocking their concerted efforts.[2]

By February, Reidy resigned himself to the fact that at least for one more season he had to find an affiliation in the lower minors. He was hopeful that one of a pair of well-established leagues, the Class B Tri-State League or the Class D Florida State League (FSL), would court Miami with enticements to join their leagues, and reach an agreement to begin play in the spring. In the interim, Reidy remained committed to seeing Miami acquire baseball for the 1955 season when he said, "Miami is my home and it is where I want a baseball team."[3]

Then again, the best-laid plans of mice and men sometimes go awry. The first bad news came when Tri-State League officials expressed concerns that travel expenses made it unrealistic for Miami's admittance.[4] On the eve of April Fools' Day (April 1), a surprising decision was handed down. FSL President John Krider announced they were taking a pass on Miami. This was perhaps as a result of Miami Stadium's uncertain status, and projected short stay in the league. Despite Reidy's financial commitment of the required $2,500 entrance fee, and his rock-solid financial stability, West Palm Beach, a competitor in the bidding for the one opening in the league won out earning the spot. The decision was perplexing since West Palm Beach ownership was short on funds and its playing facilities fell short of what Miami had to offer. The disappointing blow to Reidy was understated when he sorrowfully expressed, "This is our last chance for baseball in Miami for 1955."[5]

The crack of the bat, the pop of horsehide against leather gloves, and the chatter of the ballpark was noticeably absent by the time the regular season started. The *Miami Herald* and *Miami Daily News* sports sections filled their pages with major league scuttlebutt and box scores, but local fandom missed the live action on the field. Nonetheless, there was a sense of optimism that baseball would return next year. The continued rumors that the IL was serious about Miami as part of their league continued to fuel hopes.

Reidy and Ryan worked frantically to bring hardball back to the Magic City by 1956. Meanwhile, the ongoing saga that surrounded the back and forth negotiations involving the sale of Miami Stadium continued. Like the albatross hanging from the neck of the Ancient Mariner, so the once widely hailed ballpark continued to weigh mightily on Jose Aleman Jr. To offset his continuing losses he resorted to scheduling roller derby and boxing matches to fill the bill until the better moneymaking proposition of eight Brooklyn Dodgers spring training exhibition games rolled around in March.

As far back as February, George Salley, the attorney representing Aleman Jr., dangled an enticing proposal to the city of Miami asking $950,000 to purchase Miami Stadium. However, city commissioners were less than enthused with the proposition, and instead were seeking alternative financing options including a lease, and/or a price tag of $750,000.[6]

Negotiations involving the possible sale carried on throughout the spring and into the summer. More than once, a deal appeared imminent only to have one disagreement or another hold matters up. As early as March 16, it looked as if an agreement was finalized for $850,000, however, city commissioners developed "cold feet" and backed out.[7] Through all the tumult, the young owner remained confident he could make a deal and at least rent the stadium out during the summer.

Although unable to secure the sale of Miami Stadium, on September 2, he reached an agreement with the city for a two-year lease amounting to $60,000.[8] After a few kinks were "ironed out," the final signatures were put on paper on October 26.[9] The agreement opened the door for some level of organized baseball's return. Local fans were hungry for a higher caliber of play and most of the talk by local rags remained focused on Triple-A baseball as the best option for Miami, in either the American Association (AA), or International League.

The Milwaukee Braves, looking for a change of venue, were the strongest suitors and familiar with the facilities having played several exhibition games in spring training against the Dodgers at Miami Stadium. The Wisconsin group represented the first major league club making overtures towards relocating their flagship Triple A affiliate to Miami. The Braves association with Toledo, a member of the AA, experienced financial problems due to poor attendance. Braves officials stated that pressure from major league baseball, plus television exposure from nearby Detroit and Cleveland hurt attendance and thus posed a problem for the continuing viability of the Toledo franchise.[10]

Meanwhile, Frank "Shag" Shaughnessy, president of the IL remained the strongest proponent towards bringing baseball back to Miami by 1956 as part the league he oversaw. "Well, if Miami can make an offer, you can bet Shaughnessy would be on his way down there to sew it up for the Syracuse berth," stated IL officials. They added, "It's just a mater [sic] of fixing financial responsibility to get something concrete rolling."[11]

The proverbial clock was ticking, and the once biggest supporter of bringing baseball back to Miami, Reidy, had since re-focused his efforts with an eye towards developing a new four-team winter league called the Sunshine League with games scheduled during January and February of 1956. Essentially, he had taken himself out of the running as an owner of an IL team. According to Norris Anderson of the *Miami Daily News*, "Both Shaughnessy and Reidy have emphasized that it would be necessary to move a franchise to Miami, "sometime in October" if the necessary preparations for baseball in 1956 could be completed." He added, "Even a man of Reidy's vast energies could not be expected to promote two teams in two leagues in a city where organized baseball has died." He joined forces with another well-to-do business owner and sportsman, William B. MacDonald to start their new league. Ultimately, it would fail to come to fruition.[12]

Still, locals held out hope that the IL would make a move on short notice and bring Miami into the league. The main candidate, the financially strapped Syracuse Chiefs owner, Martin Haske, continued to look favorably on Miami as the best relocation option. Moreover, there were rumors of the IL's Richmond, having its own financial problems tied to a tax issue, as having interest in relocating further south.

Closely following all the developments were the recently appointed Miami Stadium committee and its manager, Knox Eldredge. In his opinion, "There are not enough year-around events to support the Stadium without a higher classification of baseball. He added, "I think the people of Miami will support baseball if it is in a higher league such as the International League."[13]

On December 1, Milwaukee management announced that Miami was the first choice for relocation of the Toledo affiliate, but instead they opted to move the club to Wichita, Kansas; remaining a member of the AA. Braves GM, John Quinn stated, "Miami was our original choice, but a thorough check of a trial schedule including that city proved to us that such a move would be unfeasible because of the transportation problems and expenses involved."[14]

As one door closed, another one opened. In an unexpected twist, St. Louis businessperson, Sidney "Sid" Salomon Jr. stepped into the void left by Reidy and the Milwaukee contingent. Salomon Jr., an avid sports enthusiast who earned his fortune in the insurance business, had previously been one of a consortium of owners with the American League's St. Louis Browns before their sale and move to Baltimore to become the Orioles.[15] His intentions to buy the Syracuse Chiefs and relocate them to Miami came into play due to an interesting set of circumstances.

At the same time, the AA was holding their winter meetings in Columbus, Ohio, Salomon Jr. and his business partner Elliot Stein were in town closing a deal on a restaurant. According to Bill Veeck in his legendary biography, *Veeck as in Wreck*, while sitting down at a table enjoying his meal, Salomon Jr. commented on some of the dealings during the minor league meetings. He opined what a mistake it was for the AA to pass up an opportunity to place the Toledo club in Miami, and proclaimed, "If I could buy a club I wouldn't hesitate to move it to Miami." Unbeknownst to him, Syracuse Chiefs owner, Haske was sitting at the next table. Upon overhearing the conversation, Haske reached over, tapped Salomon's shoulder, and said, "OK, you've bought yourself a club."[16] With that, a deal was finalized for the purchase price of $100,000.

Unfortunately, and much to the dismay of Salomon Jr., the purchase and transfer of the Syracuse club to Miami proved to be problematic. On December 8, the local citizenry organized a rally at the War Memorial Building in order to raise $50,000 to buy Haske's stock and prevent the club from moving. More than 400 fans turned out on a miserable night when the weather was so dreary it should have turned most people away. Surprisingly, the baseball supporters raised $54,840. A perplexed Haske seemed shocked by the show of support since the Chiefs had only drawn 109,173 the previous season.[17]

Salomon Jr., although initially disappointed when he said, "It looks like we have wasted a lot of effort," later expressed to Jimmy Burns of the *Miami Herald*, that he firmly believed Miami would support Triple-A ball, despite the failure of the Class B brand.[18]

Salomon's and Stein's next move was securing help from Bill Veeck, a close friend and former business partner of theirs while associated with the St. Louis Browns. At the time, Veeck was living on his sprawling ranch in southwest New Mexico in semi-retirement and immediately accepted an offer to serve as Executive Vice-President to promote the team. "I think everyone realizes that Veeck is one of the greatest promoters in baseball and the type who would build the sport here," exclaimed Salomon.[19] *The Sporting News* reported that Veeck said, he would "help out in any way I can," in getting his former associates . . . off on the right foot in Miami's entry in Triple-A ball."[20]

Veeck, or "Sports Shirt Bill" as the press liked to call him, known as a maverick and master showman was a baseball pioneer in the art of promoting his teams. His outrageous stunts were legendary, including having 3'7" Eddie Gaedel pinch hit in a game; as well as "Grandstands Manager Day" (where fans voted on strategy). There were also fireworks, musicians ambling through the stands, and entertainers like Max Patkin and Jackie Price performing their classic baseball "shtick." Veeck made his first splash initially as an owner setting attendance records with Milwaukee of the American Association before moving on to the Cleveland Indians where he did the same, followed by the Browns. He had been "chomping at the bit" to get back in the game ever since fellow stodgy, and conservative fellow American League owners had forced him out of major league baseball prior to the relocation of the financially troubled Browns to Baltimore in 1954. Veeck's promotions and stunts ran against the grain of baseball establishment that held the belief that the game on the field was enough to bring fans into the stands. Bill saw the "Miami opportunity" as a way to get back into baseball with an eye towards the city becoming part of the major leagues in four to five years. Shirley Povich of the *Washington Post-Times* noted, "Bill Veeck. The Big Operator is coming back into baseball at the same level from which he leaped to notoriety-the minor leagues . . . Veeck is giving it another whirl, with everybody aware he won't be content to stay in the minors."[21]

On December 20, the second effort by Salomon Jr. and Stein to purchase the Syracuse Chiefs for $100,000 received approval.[22] Despite efforts by Pat Miller, president of the Syracuse fan organization, and a proposed lawsuit to retain the franchise, Salomon Jr., and Veeck moved forward to prepare for their arrival to Miami.[23] President Shaughnessy glowingly predicted, "Our league is now secure from change for the next ten years."[24]

On December 26, Veeck arrived in Miami, after a 13-hour flight from New Mexico. With his signature wide-open white sports shirt, wooden leg, (his limb amputated during WWII; he was struck by the recoil of an anti-aircraft gun), and thirteen pages of questions in hand, he shared his intentions with local reporters. First on his agenda, securing a lease at Miami Stadium. Some other nuggets he shared; that he considered Miami a major league city, that he intended to sprinkle the team's roster with veterans to complement the players provided by the Philadelphia Phillies per their working agreement, to continue his policy of providing outside entertainment at games, and allowing the fans to vote for the team nickname. He wasted no time visiting Salomon Jr.'s home in Miami Beach to plan the future.[25]

From his suite at the top of the McAllister Hotel, Bill began negotiating a lease with city and stadium officials. It was a tall task since there was no guarantee of reaching a deal. Through it all, the perpetually optimistic "Sport Shirt Bill" was confident he would secure an agreement. It turned out to be a challenging process with time becoming a major factor and spring training only a couple of months away. Veeck was seeking a 10-year lease to give permanence to the franchise. To his dismay, he discovered that the city had only a two-year lease with Aleman Jr., which also included an $850,000 option to buy. "We're running out of time," asserted Veeck. He added, "it would have been best if all of these things had been tied together three months ago but that was impossible. Now, however, we've got to move and move quickly."[26]

Despite difficult negotiations, fans remained optimistic that hardball would return. Based upon the strong financial backing by Salomon Jr., and baseball's most forward-thinking publicity man Veeck, the future of Miami baseball looked rosy. However, as previous owners had discovered, every rose had its thorns.

1956

Finding success in the Miami baseball market had always proven to be a hard coconut to crack. Miami proper, at the time, counted a population of approximately 375,000, with many of its residents transplanted from other areas of the country. A significant percentage of them hailed from cities where major league baseball was well established. The consensus was that they were more interested in the sun, surf, and sand than action on the diamond. Not to mention the pull of Jai Alai and the horse and dog tracks that served as an added distraction.

Veeck, not deterred by naysayers, moved quickly to promote the team while continuing tough negotiations with the city of Miami on a stadium lease. He left no rock or speaking engagement unturned while he was in town. Besides keeping his face in the forefront of the sports page, he also arranged with the *Miami Herald* to promote a contest for its readers to name the team, with the winner awarded box seat season tickets. Five hundred fans, before the "Name the Team" promotion began, had already offered suggestions for the team moniker.[27] Some of the more creative entries included; The Alligators, Palms, Pelicans, Sabre Jets, Sailfish, Sea Gulls, Sols (short for Solars) Sun Rays, Sunshines, and Tarpons.[28] [29] The eventual winning entry sent in by Earl E. Purpus suggesting "Marlins" earned him the prized ducats.[30]

In addition, a 25-word essay promotion to grant the honor of being the team's first batboy drew a huge response from the local youth. Veeck was keenly aware of the importance of involving kids and the influence they had on their parents directly related to ticket sales. Tim Anagnost, then 13-years old, recalled his first encounter with "Sport Shirt Bill" and how he became the Marlins first home team batboy.

I remember when we got to the top ten. I had it made. I said to myself, "This is wonderful." I got season tickets now for this baseball season and that was it. I had no aspirations, you know, of actually winning the contest . . . So we got to the interview, and I remember this vividly and I don't know why it happened because I was really not a wise guy, it just blurted out . . . I walked into this room for the final interview thing and there were these men sitting around this long table, like a conference table . . . And I thought it was Bill Veeck who said, "Come on in and sit down and relax." And I looked at him and I said, "That's easy for you to say." And I don't know why I said that but they all started laughing, and I started laughing, and I think that's what won me the contest.[31]

Veeck brought into his fold some of his most trusted cohorts. With Elliot Stein already in position as the team treasurer, he named long-time baseball man, Eddie Stumpf as General Manager (GM). Stumpf started his professional career in 1915 as a catcher with the Aurora Foxes of the Bi-State League. He began his relationship with Veeck during the time Bill owned the Milwaukee Brewers of the AA and served as overseer of the club's minor league system. He later worked for Veeck with the Cleveland Indians, as business director. In addition, he served as GM of the Indianapolis Indians of the AA. Besides, a relatively unsuccessful playing career in the minors, Stumpf also served as a manager in the All-American Girls Professional Baseball League (Rockford Peaches in 1943 and Kenosha Comets in 1945), a scout, and held down various front office jobs.[32] [33]

Veeck, on Stumpf's recommendation, further bolstered his front office brain trust by naming Joe Ryan as the Marlins business manager. They both recognized that there was no one more in tune with the local baseball scene than Ryan who had worked tirelessly to bring baseball back to Miami.[34] Morris McLemore of the *Miami Herald* noted in his column of January 6, "Since baseball died here, Ryan had done nothing but try to revive it and his interest kept the pot aboil long after others had turned down their wicks.[35]

Despite the delays on a finalized stadium lease, enthusiasm for the arrival of the Marlins reached a fevered pitch. Veeck's early prediction of attendance reaching 500,000 did not seem out of the realm of possibility. By the middle of January, the club had received 2,000 ticket requests for opening day, and orders for about 300 box seats. Those numbers might have been better were it not for the fact that the front office was limited to using a solitary phone by stadium officials for sales. "There's no telling how many more ticket orders we could be taking if the fans could get their calls in. But with only one telephone, it's awfully tough," said Stumpf.[36]

After much anticipation, on January 29, Stumpf announced that the club filled the position of manager by naming Don Osborn to the helm. "Osborn is a solid baseball man, a great fundamentalist and a real student of pitching. He is even-tempered and he works well with his men. I would compare him to the Al Lopez type of manager," said the new GM. The selection surprised many Miamians, although rumors had pegged him as the favorite, they were expecting Veeck to follow his usual pattern of making a splash and selecting a high profile name to the post. In this case, Phillies management that retained their association since the transfer of the club from Syracuse, insisted on selecting someone already proven from their own system.[37]

Although Osborn's name was new to Miami fans, the highly respected skipper had already established a successful record of accomplishments. The former PCL star pitcher, and Idaho native, received his first assignment as a player-manager in 1941 for Vancouver of the Class B Western International League (WIL). There, he led the Capilanos to two winning campaigns, and a pennant in 1942. He followed by managing a pair of seasons at Macon of the Class A Sally League (1948–49), Nashville of the Double-A Southern Association (1950–51), back to Spokane Class A WIL (1952–54), and Schenectady of the Class A Eastern League compiling a .560 win percentage. He had yet to experience a losing season, finished out of first division only once, and produced four championships in ten years.[38] [39]

Osborn would later go on to become a highly successful pitching coach with the Pittsburgh Pirates. Although never known to possess an overpowering fastball or great movement on his pitches, during his playing career he used control and changed speeds to get batters out. His teammates on the 1943 Los Angeles Angels gave him the nickname, "Wizard of Oz," a reference to his ability to get hitters out with less than impressive stuff. This would serve him well in his post-baseball career.[40]

Still, Veeck was Veeck, and although Osborn was lacking big-name appeal, it did not stop the tireless promoter from bringing a marquee name. As part of the coaching staff, he hired Hall-of-Famer Jimmie Foxx to act as a first base coach during home games and batting instructor. Foxx, who held a coaching position at the University of Miami, welcomed the chance to assist by passing on his vast knowledge of hitting.[41] Later, he received kudos for his work with Bob Bowman and Ed Bouchee helping them with their batting stroke.[42]

Veeck continued hard-fought discussions to close a lease deal on Miami Stadium. At one point, out of frustration with city officials, Veeck rolled up his trousers exposing his artificial leg. He bluntly said, "Here, you might as well have this too!"[43] The obvious humor of the moment relieved tensions between the parties and finally, after numerous hard days of negotiations of hammering out all the fine details, a two-year lease to rent Miami Stadium reached completion. On hand to sign the final agreement were Ryan, Stumpf, and local attorney, John G. Thompson, acting team secretary who witnessed the signing of the documents. Triple-A baseball was official.[44]

Veeck turned his focus to Plant City, Florida where the Chiefs had trained the season before. While Stumpf looked on, Mayor Otis Andrews, City Manager T. J. McCall, and Commissioner Henry S. Moody signed the necessary documents procuring Adelson Field as the Marlins spring training home.[45] Excitement surrounding the Marlins was so high that city leaders guaranteed 1,000 paid admissions for each home game. In conjunction with the city's gesture, the visitors agreed to direct 25% of gate receipts towards boys' little league programs in Plant City. Marlins' pitchers and catchers reported to spring training March 10th.

Much of the attention in the preseason surrounded the young stable of pitching prospects making positive impressions at the big club's training site in Clearwater. "I never saw so many good pitchers in a baseball camp. It's the best crop I ever worked with," said Phillies pitching coach Whitlow Wyatt. Minor league director Gene Martin chimed in, "You can say we've got a youth movement going. We want to grow out talent out there on the farms. Miami will get the cream of our minor league players."[46] Out of the crop of hurlers assigned to Plant City, 20-year-old 6'4", 208 lb., right-hander, Don Cardwell (10–9, 3.77) from Schenectady of the Class A Eastern League, 22-year-old Jim "Bear" Owens (15–11,

3.11) a carryover from Syracuse, and southpaw, Gene Snyder (from 1950 to 1952 won 41 games between Class D and Class A), all made their presence known. Joining them were the less heralded 6'4" husky righty, Richard "Turk" Farrell, relief specialist, Angelo LiPetri, one-time Phillies bonus baby Tommy "Money Bags" Qualters and quirky port-sider, Seth Morehead, all made their mark.

Early season prognostications saw Miami as a "dark horse" in the IL race. The returning league champion Montreal Royals and the veteran-ladened Toronto Maple Leafs received the nods to snatch the IL flag. As the season approached, Veeck stressed, "To get that winner, we're going to supplement our working agreement with the Phillies by buying the players we need." It was the age-old conundrum of the constant give and take, between the parent club wanting prospects to play on a daily basis, versus ownership's focus on signing talent to help them win. Veeck had already inked four former major leaguers among them, ex-St. Louis Browns Willard Brown and Dick Kokos; 38-year old former big league third baseman, slugger Sid Gordon; ex-Cincinnati Reds and Detroit Tigers fly-chaser, George Lerchen.[47] Gordon would also serve as a coach.

Osborn continued to pare down his roster with the approaching close of spring training. Many of his concerns centered on the veterans brought into camp that had not proven to be in playing shape. The first to receive his walking papers, former Negro League star, Willard Brown, sold outright to Austin of the Big State League. On the other side of the coin and staying on, first baseman, Ed Bouchee, and second baseman Ben Tompkins, a fixture in Miami for the next three seasons. Both received rave reviews for their hustle and quality of play.[48]

By the end of spring training, the Phillies sent reinforcements with major league experience. Newcomers included outfielder, Mel Clark (Philadelphia 1951–55), backstop, Jim Command (Philadelphia 1954–55), shortstop, Robert "Mickey Micelotta (Philadelphia 1954–55), outfielder, Ed Mierkowicz (Detroit 1945, 47, 48 and St. Louis NL 1950), and catcher, Gus Niarhos (New York AL 1946, 48, 49, 50, Chicago AL 1950, 51, Boston AL 1952, 53, and Philadelphia 1954).

Never in Miami's history had so much excitement been generated around an opening day. Much of the anticipation centered on Veeck's gift for unique promotions, and fans did not know what to expect when the Marlins kicked off the season at Miami Stadium on April 18 against the Buffalo Bisons.

Stadium workers hurriedly rushed to put the final touches on the ballpark repairing neglected box seats, applying fresh coats of paint, and hanging patriotic red, white and blue banners on the upper portion of the façade. This was the big coming out party and Veeck, like a skillful magician, was pulling out all of the rabbits from his bag of tricks to ensure the shindig was a success.

Fans began arriving early, greeted by the imposing twenty-foot high blazing reddish-orange neon letters above the front entrance spelling out M-I-A-M-I S-T-A-D-I-U-M, streamed by the anxious ticket-takers accepting their ducats. Upon entry, a carnival-like atmosphere pulsed through the stadium with electric vivacity. Frank Shaughnessy, IL President, and Florida senator George Smathers, were present overseeing the action.[49] Also in attendance were Chet Covington, Phil O'Connell, Tiny Parker, and Tom Spicola, familiar names from the FIL of the past.[50]

Veeck, as usual, did not disappoint. Max Patkin, baseball's most renowned clown, performed his funny contortions and mocking behavior on the field, and Barnum and Bailey's Josephine Berosini walked across a 150-foot high tightrope strung between two of the outfield light towers. If that was not enough, recently signed former Browns, Tigers, and White Sox hurler, Bob "Sugar" Cain arrived on the field delivered by a city cab, and minstrels strolled through the stands crooning to the crowd. As part of the pregame extravaganza, each Marlins starter received an introduction by the public address announcer, accompanied by a spotlight aimed in their direction. During the presentations, a green, red, and white pyrotechnics display that spelled out "Hi Fans" welcomed all in attendance.[51 52 53]

There was more to come, the scheduled contest on the field, and something unexpected that would turn Miami on its ear. Taking the mound for the home team was 6'3" right-hander, Thornton Kipper squaring off against the Bisons' southpaw, Bill Froats. Neither team tallied a run in the initial frame, but the fans' eyes quickly turned to the skies spying a helicopter circling the stadium. Soon, the bubble-headed whirlybird began its descent towards the diamond. Kipper and the rest of the Marlins' infielders began to scatter as the craft touched down directly behind the pitcher's mound, near the infield to the rear of second base.

Witnesses to the landing have varying accounts, but Anagnost said he could remember what happened like it was yesterday.

> I am sure the helicopter landed in either short right or center-field. I am positive it did not land on the pitcher's mound as some people described. Regardless, the blades kicked up quite a dust storm. As for the helicopter incident, I vividly remember that the wind carried all this dust towards the box seats behind third base. The men and women were all dressed up because it was opening night and as the dust carried over the dugout, I could hear a lot of profanity! That was one promotion by Bill Veeck that didn't quite go as planned.[54]

Wilbur Johnson watching from the dugout recalled that the women in the box seats got the worst of it. He laughed heartily while reminiscing about that opening night.

> It was a beautiful night. They have white dresses on and they were dressed to kill. It was a warm night and they had a little sweat on them, and dust blew all over their outfits. That was not one of their better nights.[55]

Out of the swirling cloud of dust came a tall and thin black man, glove in hand, wearing his home off-white uniform, trimmed in medium blue and orange with a satin blue Marlins warm-up jacket. The entrance was a great surprise to the fans and the mystery man's soon-to-be teammates. Over the loudspeaker, Satchel Paige's introduction drew wild applause.[56][57] "We had heard some rumors about something that was going on, but even the players didn't know officially," said pitcher Jack Spring.[58] Many in attendance recognized Leroy "Satchel" Paige as he emerged from the blowing dirt and headed toward Don Osborn in the dugout. Outfielder, Mel Clark reminisced about the incident.

> I'll tell you, in the first game he arrived in a helicopter. Yes, I was in right field when the helicopter came and started coming down. It just kept coming down, and our pitcher [Thornton Kipper] was looking around for cover, you know. He got out of the way or it would have landed on the mound. Satchel walked over to the dugout and told the manager [Don Osborn], he said, "My name is Satchel Paige and I'm here ready to pitch."[59]

The helicopter's landing was scheduled earlier in the evening. However, the stadium lights went dark during the introduction of the players and a loss of communication between staff and the pilot forced the whirly bird to circle high above until the second inning. At the same time, Joe Ryan was worried that the stunt would backfire because the helicopter was running low on fuel. Fortunately, everything went off without a hitch, and after Paige's "how-do-you-do's" with Osborn, he then made a beeline to the bullpen and took up residence in what would become his rocking chair.[60] Spring recalled that he appeared a little shaken by the whole ordeal.

> At the time I was a relief pitcher. I was out in the bullpen along the left field line as I recall, and here he came out, out there and he said, "Holy man." It was one of those bubble fronts, you know where they open. His eyes were as big as saucers.[61]

Satchel assured the press that he had everything under control. He stated, "There weren't no chance at all that I'd fall outta that thing. It don't have a door to keep you in, but I was holding on tight."[62] His teammates met him with smiles and handshakes as he got comfortable for the evening. Qualters, although happy to see him, admitted having concerns at the time.

> Finally it comes opening day. I'm still there and I'm absolutely amazed I made the ball club. All of the sudden here comes a helicopter in and it lands beside the mound and who comes out but Satchel Paige. And I thought, "You old son-of-a-gun, you just took my job," you know [laughing]. And it had turned out that they had cut another guy; it wasn't me.[63]

Buffalo scored first plating a pair of runs in the third before Miami answered with a five-run salvo in the bottom of the same frame. In the sixth inning, the entertainment continued unexpectedly. Leadoff hitter David Mann found himself in a rundown between first and second base. Pitcher Fred Hahn planted a hard tag on Mann landing the runner on his back. Mann argued that he was safe, and would not relent with the umpiring crew as he headed toward the dugout. Left fielder Johnny Blatnik crossed paths with Mann and less than politely told him to get off the field. Mann retorted with a few adult adjectives before feeling a hard blow to his back. Mann retaliated and punched Blatnik; with both benches running onto the field. By the time order was restored both men had been ejected.[64] [65]

The festivities were successful; the Marlins prevailed over Buffalo, 10 to 3. Most everyone went home delighted. Veeck even offered to pay for the dry cleaning bills of the few fans who left the stadium in soiled clothing. Four Buffalo hurlers combined to do their part in helping Miami to win by allowing 13 walks. Gordon reached base all five of his at-bats including a single and a double. Larry Novak, who hit the first Marlins home run while pinch-hitting for Mierkowicz in the third frame, and Micelotta both drove in a trio of runs. Bob Greenwood corralled the win coming in relief for Kipper in the fourth inning getting the new franchise off on the right foot.

The only disappointment, described as "mild" by Norris Anderson, was the below-expected attendance. The anticipated sellout drew only 8,816; less than the predicted 13,000 spectators. Stumpf commented after the game, "Some of the general admission customers were probably scared out of the opening night because they figured seats would not be available."[66]

With opening night now in the books, the question in everyone's mind was, "What is going on with Satchel Paige?" As early as January 24, Veeck allegedly had planted rumors with the press that he might sign the ageless Paige, "You can't tell about Leroy. He's just likely to pop up," confessed "Sport Shirt Bill." Few took the rumors seriously. Behind the scenes, Veeck approached Paige, who was contemplating retirement in early April, and convinced him to sign a $15,000 contract that included a percentage of the gate receipts.[67] Osborn had his own ideas about using Paige. Although the new Marlins' field general went along with Veeck on Paige's grand entrance, he was not interested in the 49-year-old hurler taking up a roster spot. Veeck made it clear, "He came down to pitch for us." So, he had a proposition, the same that he presented to then skeptical Indians player/manager Lou Boudreau in 1948 after signing Paige, "You line up your nine best hitters, and you tell them you're going to give them ten dollars for every base hit they get off him . . . I'm paying." Veeck specified, if anyone got a hit, Osborn was not obligated to keep the ageless wonder. He agreed. When Satch struck out all nine hitters, the thoroughly impressed manager changed his mind, and endorsed retaining the star pitcher.[68]

The future Hall of Famer's first outing came four days into the season on April 22 against the Rochester Red Wings. The Marlins dropped the first game of the doubleheader 10 to 6 during an 18-inning marathon. The second game, a seven-inning affair, the league's custom, saw Cardwell pitch into the last inning holding on to a 3 to 2 lead. After getting into trouble putting runners on first and second with two outs, Osborn relieved his starter of his duties and signaled for Paige. The veteran laboriously strolled to the mound, as was his style. The only blemish on the closer's performance was when Niarhos let one offering get past him for a passed ball, but the "cool as a cucumber" veteran coaxed the next batter, Mel Nelson, to hit a grounder to the mound ending the game.[69] Jack Spring remembered the unique way that Paige closed out the game that left more than a few jaws dropping.

> I think it was maybe his first appearance and he came in relief in the ninth inning, and there must have been two outs . . . But anyway, he came in and the hitter hit a one-hopper right back at him. You know, not real hard, or just a nice and easy one or two bouncer. He caught the ball, and our dugout was on the third base side, but he turned and started walking off the field like he was leaving. Like he caught it in the air or something. He lifted his left arm and whipped the ball underneath his left arm with his right and threw a perfect strike to first base and just nipped the runner at the end of the game. And Don Osborn was almost passed out in the dugout. He was having a heart attack. [Laughing heartily][70]

Following a couple more short relief appearances, Paige made his debut as a starter during the second game of a double dip against Montreal on April 29. What would become a familiar role throughout the season, he would pitch the short end of the seven-inning doubleheaders and in between return to his relief specialist duties.

Returning to Miami for the first time since the memorable 1952 season were former Sun Sox greats, Chico Fernandez and Billy Harris. This time they were representing the opposition. Harris drew the unenviable task of starting and facing Paige. Armed with his famous array of colorfully named tosses like the Bee-Ball, Four-Day Creeper, Jump Ball, and Trouble Ball, the 49-year-young veteran confounded the Royals' hitters allowing a paltry four singles and striking out the same count in the 3-to-0 shutout. Bowman who hit a home run to aid in the winning cause recalled, "Yeah, he had the old hesitation blooper that he used every once in a while. He'd step out and then he'd release the ball kind of belatedly in a blooper style trajectory," relayed Bowman.[71] Paige assessed his performance afterward by declaring, "After 29 years in this racket, my arm felt pretty good out there today. He added, "They say I can't go seven innings; well I showed them. Now I guess I gotta show 'em I can go nine." One of the first out of the dugout with a congratulatory handshake was Osborn.[72]

His performances aside, the Marlins struggling offense, and shabby defensive play, were the main culprits. Beginning on April 30, after a disheartening 10-inning, 6 to 5 loss at the hands of the Royals at Miami Stadium, the club went on a ten-game tailspin. It was evident that the struggling Marlins offense and shabby defensive play were the main culprits. It was apparent that Gordon was no longer able to handle the everyday duties at the hot corner. Although still effective with the stick, his range and skills in the field had deteriorated to the point that Osborn resorted to using 35-year-old Don Richmond and utility-man Wilbur "Moose" Johnson instead. The club was counting on Clark, one of its mainstays, who had a batting average hovering around the "Mendoza Line" (a demarcation for poor hitters).

Witnessing how the team was struggling, Salomon Jr. and Veeck began delivering on their commitment of bringing a winning club to Miami by signing new players. On May 10, 32-year-old Cal Abrams was purchased from the Chicago White Sox. The one-time Dodgers prize prospect, addressed the Marlins most pressing need, offense.[73] In the days before SABRmetrics and measures like OPS+ and WAR assessed a player's value, ballplayers were judged more rigorously on their batting average. Coming off the 1955 season with the Orioles, after hitting only .243, his numbers to the novice fan were not impressive. Upon closer review, Abrams, an on-base "machine," reached the bag at a nifty .413. His best season came in 1953 with the Pittsburgh Pirates (119 games, .286, 15 HR, 66 runs, .368 OBP).[74] He also held his own in the outfield playing all three spots well, and was the perfect table-setter to bat in front of sluggers like Bouchee and Bowman.

Abram's presence at the top of the order brought new life to the Marlins offense. When they defeated Buffalo, 10 to 3 on

June 9, they reached the .500 mark for the first time since May 3 and climbed into the first division. Niarhos' three ribbies and a Bowman homer sparked the win, bailing out shaky starter Morehead, yanked for Greenwood in the fifth inning. The opportunistic Greenwood went on to earn his third win of the season.[75]

Adding depth to the club, Turk Farrell returned on June 10 after a 10-week hiatus due to a broken ankle suffered in spring training. In his first appearance, he pitched a scoreless inning in relief duty and followed that up two nights later hurling five frames out of the bullpen against Rochester earning his first victory.[76] He then joined ace Cardwell as two main cogs in the rotation. Meanwhile the last of the ex-Browns, excluding Paige, Duane Pillette originally signed by Veeck, received a promotion to the Phillies.[77][78]

Bolstered by the return of Farrell, the Marlins stable of young pitchers were performing well, yet it was the oldest of the corps that grabbed the headlines. On the night of July 11, at Havana's Gran Stadium, two of baseball's most senior members met in a game for the ages or aged (depending on your point of view). Promotionally motivated, the Sugar Kings brought back hurler Conrado "Connie" Marrero to make a starting appearance against the Marlins slotted starter, Paige. Although reported as 41, Marrero, the former Washington Senator and a long-time Cuban Winter League star was actually 45. The wily veterans took the mound against each other that evening with a combined age of 95 years, 111 days. In a classic duel under the stars, Paige and Marrero each toiled six innings in the stifling heat and humidity before retiring for the evening. Mel Clark shared his thoughts on the game.

> I enjoyed playing with Satchel Paige. He was quite a guy you know. I enjoyed him very much. But, I remember one day we were playing in Cuba. He, Satchel was pitching and starting. And there was a pitcher, Connie Marrero who had pitched for the Washington Senators. He was starting for Havana and Satchel had him one to nothing. And the bases were loaded in the fifth [actually the sixth inning], and I can remember this very well. And he worked the count three and two and struck the guy out. We won the game one to nothing and he walked off the mound told the manager [Osborn] to take him out and said, "That's all I had left."[79]

Both of the graybeards allowed five hits, but Satch was more dominant striking out eight to Connie's four. The only run of the game came on Ray Holton's single that plated Novak. Paige's sixth win of the season received some needed help from LiPetri who worked the last three innings to earn a save.[80][81] Fittingly, as Satch was so famously quoted for saying, "Age is a question of mind over matter. If you don't mind it doesn't matter."[82]

More changes came to the roster by the outset of July. "I said at the start of the season that if we were in first division on July 4th, we would gun for the pennant this year," said Salomon Jr. The owner lived up to his word. Catcher Ray Holton was acquired from Louisville, and Toby Atwell, another backstop from Omaha of the American Association to help spell Niarhos behind the plate.[83] Then on July 7, a blockbuster trade was completed that sent Clark, Wilbur Johnson and Kipper to Louisville for infielder Pompeyo "YoYo" Davalillo, first baseman-outfielder Roy Hawes, pitcher Tony Ponce, and Dario Rubinstein.[84] Ultimately, only Davalillo and Holton made substantial contributions.

The parent Phillies also sent reinforcements reassigning Jim Owens after a disappointing 0–4 record. The "Bear" won 15 games for Syracuse the previous season and led the IL in strikeouts with 161, but failed to live up to his promise in Philadelphia.[85] Upon arrival at Miami, many of his former teammates from the parent club greeted him, including outfielder, Glen Gorbous optioned to Miami two months earlier at the end of May.[86]

The biggest deal was yet to come. A sore spot for the Marlins existed at the hot corner. A revolving door of players tried to fill the void, including newly acquired Davalillo (more suited to play second base), with little success. For some time, Salomon Jr. and Stumpf had been pursuing Forest "Woody" Smith of the Havana Sugar Kings, but failed in their efforts to secure his services. Finally, on July 25, the two teams were able to reach an amicable agreement for a purchase price of $15,000.[87] He was held in such high regard by his peers, that when the deal was consummated it sent a shockwave throughout the IL. So much so that Greg Mulleavy, manager of the Montreal Royals, predicted that with him on third base, Miami would win the pennant.[88] Salomon Jr. was all in with a goal to capture the pennant.

Smith, one of the most popular players in the IL was thrilled to leave Havana and play in Miami. "He didn't like Havana and told me at the all-star [sic] game in Toronto that he wasn't going back the next year," added Mulleavy.[89] In his first game in Miami Stadium, a raucous crowd of 5,658 greeted the handsome blonde-tufted third sacker with wild applause when announced in the starting lineup. There were many in the stands that remembered him from his FIL days playing for West Palm Beach in 1951. His debut was magical. He smacked four singles in four at-bats and played flawless defense leading the Marlins to a 4 to 3 win over league-leading Toronto. After the game, an enthusiastic and re-lieved Smith said, "Whew! What a game to win! This ball club is going all the way."[90] It was a grand start for a man that would one day become a Miami baseball icon.

The rejuvenated Marlins reached the top of the standings on July 30 when they edged Buffalo at Offerman Stadium, 6 to 5. Woody Smith led the way with a single, triple and home run while driving in four runs. Farrell earned his seventh win against a trio of defeats, and despite the temperatures in the low 60s, Paige, who always found the chilling weather disagreeable, came on in the bottom of the ninth and retired Norm Sherry on three straight side-arm curveballs.[91] Jack Spring recalled how Satchel and frosty weather were disagreeable partners.

> Another thing he did when it was real cold and he wasn't pitch-ing, or he wasn't starting, he would just stay in the clubhouse where it was warm. He wouldn't sit out on the bench. Yeah, he didn't like cold weather.[92]

While the team was enjoying their success on the diamond, Veeck was planning what would go down in minor league baseball history as one of its most famous games. It was billed as, "The Baseball Party to end all Baseball Parties" with old "Satch" taking center stage as the main attraction to pitch against the visiting Columbus Jets.[93] Although Paige agreed to take on the starting as-signment, he had reservations. His reluctance stemmed from the possibility of another helicopter entrance. "There ain't gonna be any parachutin' or anything like that for me," he said. Veeck as-sured him that he would not be repeating that stunt, which eased his mind.[94] It was pure Veeck working his promotional magic and the city of Miami was under his spell.

In order to accommodate an anticipated crowd of over 50,000, the only venue in town large enough to host such an enormous event, was the Orange Bowl. After much negotiating, Veeck arranged to use the famous football venue on August 7. His intention was breaking the major league attendance record of 72,562 set on August 3, 1948 (when he owned the Indians); and the minor league record of 56,391 set on April 17, 1941 in Jersey City.[95]

Veeck assembled a cavalcade of entertainment stars mostly from the music industry to perform, compliments of Coy Poe Productions. Performances began an hour-and-a-half before the 7:30 game's slated start time. Ticket prices were a reasonable fifty-five cents with a hefty percentage of the proceeds going towards the kids at the Columbus Club. Local labor organizations had already sold 21,000 ducats, exceeding their quota. Greeting the fans at the entrances were four Dixieland bands. Once inside, the Russ Morgan Band, Cab Calloway, Merv Griffin, Patricia Manville, Helen O'Connell, Ginny Simms, Margaret Whiting, and the dance team of Bud and Cece Robinson performed. Moreover, populating the stands were several baseball dignitaries including Hall of Famers Jimmie Foxx and Dazzy Vance, IL president Shaughnessy, minor league czar George Trautman, and Max Patkin performing his madcap sideline routine.[96]

The packed house viewed a most unusual sight on the former gridiron. In order to accommodate a baseball field, a unique layout and ground rules were set up. The field dimensions were a cozy 216 feet down the right field line, and 250 feet down the left field line. A temporary outfield fence was constructed, which included a twelve-foot high screen built foul line to foul line; keeping balls in the park. Any ball hit over the improvised enclosure was considered a two-bagger, unless hit above the second ramp of the north side stands, or the first ramp in left field, resulting in a home run. In addition, any ball hit between the west end zone and bleachers were ground rule doubles.[97] Players must have been drooling over the prospect of hitting in this bandbox.

It was a prototypical Miami night in August. Game-time temperature felt like the 90s, with 85% humidity. When the festivities ended, the umpire called out the familiar, "Play Ball!" To the delight of the hometown contingent, Tompkins got the party started hitting a 365-foot solo shot off a Bob Kuzava offering out of the park in the first inning. "He threw me a fastball and I tagged it," said the bespectacled second sacker.

In the second inning, the Marlins put two runners aboard with two out. Instead of pitching to Micelotta, Kuzava opted to intentionally walk the shortstop and face Paige for an easy out.

Going into the night, Satch had only driven in one run all season long, but the slight by the opposition seemed to have put a burr under his saddle. At this stage of his career, he no longer was the hitter he once was. Anagnost recalled how the pitching icon was in earnest when it came to batting.

> He took his hitting very seriously, but he never got any hits . . . He took it so seriously that he would put "SP" on the hand end of his bat . . . All the position players had their names inscribed on their bats just like the big leaguers . . . pitchers did not have that. But Satchel Paige had found a bat apparently that he liked . . . so anytime that he got into a game, starting or as a reliever, I had to make sure and get that bat.[98]

While the crowd anticipated the end of the inning, Paige had other ideas. After the first strike delivery, with the next offering, the fans heard the crack of the bat and rose to their feet. Anagnost witnessed in disbelief, from the sidelines, the dramatic moment that could have come right out of the book of a Hollywood scriptwriter. Later one of his teammates exclaimed, "Yeh, he got sore at (Bob) Kuzava because he walked (Bob) Micelotta to get to him."[99] Anagnost remembered the moment.

> I think it probably went in the gap in left field. And the ball just kept rolling and rolling because left field [actually center field] had to be four hundred feet [estimated distance 330 feet] or more instead of the normal dimensions. So, the ball just kept rolling. It got past the outfield and he [outfielder] had to go chase it down.
>
> The bases were loaded and all three runs score . . . I can't believe it, Satchel Paige has just hit an inside the park home run . . . And I look back and Satchel Paige is walking into second base. Anyone would have been rounding third.[100]

No one was more surprised than Kuzava. The veteran who had pitched in two World Series with the Yankees and had nine seasons under his belt in the big leagues, found humor in the most improbable event. "I'm laughing because Satchel Paige hit a double off of me. Leroy hit a double. And he stood at second base, and he was laughing at me, and I laughed back at him. He was a great guy."[101]

Paige's pitching was nearly flawless for six innings confounding the opposing hitters with his double and triple windup, a variety of arm angle pitches, and the hesitation; all the while regaling the captive audience. However, the excitement of the evening took its toll and Satch began tiring in the seventh after giving up a run. By the eighth, with two outs, he had run out of gas having given up another run. Getting the call from the bullpen was Jack Spring who retired the last four batters in a row to end the game. The Marlins had come out the winners by a 6 to 2 tally.[102]

The game was widely hailed a success. *The Sporting News* headline declared, "Marlins Set 57,713 Gate High at Orange Bowl Show." "I am grateful to the Miami fans for this turnout," said Salomon Jr. Shaughnessy heaped even more praise when he said, "It was a great thing for baseball. There aren't many guys who would have given the receipts to charity like Salomon did." Veeck gleefully reported, "This proves Miami likes baseball, the Marlins, and first-class entertainment."[103] Although the final attendance figure was reduced to 51,713 and ultimately failed to surpass the previous minor league record set in 1941, there were actually more people in the seats than there were in Jersey City's Roosevelt Stadium fifteen years earlier. Since fans purchased extra ducats in support of the World War II effort, the estimated number of actual people in the seats was closer to 34,000; far below Miami's true number.[104]

For Paige, the game represented yet another milestone in his heap of accomplishments amassed in a career that felt like it was never going to end. Turning 50 years old, he proved he was still a force and arguably the biggest drawing card in baseball.

Satch's entertainment value was unquestionable, but what fans did not see was the relationship he had with his teammates and the positive effect he had on and off the field. Qualters, recounted how encouragement from Paige saved his career.

> We're in a game, and it's very early in the season . . . This was my first shot, here I am in Triple-A baseball. It felt like to me, I had made it to the majors. From the time I was a little kid, I was never afraid of anything, or anybody, as long as I had a couple of rocks in my pocket which I carried all the time or a baseball in my hand . . . And I come in a game and I get out there on the mound . . . I'm taking my warmup tosses and I get the shakes. I mean I became petrified. I know I haven't felt

anything like that in my life. And you can't bullshit another ballplayer, you know. Ballplayers can sense that. They can see it where nobody else can.

Somehow or another I got them out. I threw the ball up there and they hit it at somebody, or whatever, and I got out of the inning. And I went home that night and I'm trying to figure how I can, how I can quit and go home. Not because of the fans or anything like that, just that I couldn't stand the thought of players on the team thinking that I was a coward. I mean that was something that I had never gone through before.

So, we were in the bullpen the next night . . . I'm sitting beside Satch and finally a couple of innings go along. Finally, he coms and hits me on the leg and he said, 'What's the matter, son?' I didn't know what to do, so I just told him the truth and I told him what happened. And he started laughing. He said, 'I'm going to tell you, son. Those sons-of-a-bitches can beat ya, but they can't eat ya.' So, I get back up there and I take my warmup tosses . . . I'm standing there and I start getting the shakes again, you know. I just thought, *That's it, the sons-of-a-bitches beat me, but you can't eat me.* From that day on I could hardly wait to get out there. But Satch, without question saved my career.[105]

Besides being the resident sage on the team, Paige also bonded with his teammates by participating in never-ending locker room hijinks. The chief instigators were a group of three hell-raisers, Farrell, Morehead, and Owens that became infamous in baseball history for their barroom brawls, carousing, drinking, and non-stop mischief. Although some of the cast of characters changed in subsequent years and included Jack Meyer, essentially Farrell and Owens remained the ringleaders. Around baseball circles, the sobriquet, "The Dalton Gang," was given to the madcap trio, a reference to the infamous outlaws from the old west that robbed banks and trains.

The gang's antics came to light for the first time in Syracuse on June 25, 1955 when they were performing for the Chiefs. Reporter Normile A. Hannon, from the local *Post-Standard*, allegedly provoked Farrell and Morehead. They severely beat him inside of Pierre's Restaurant, a local establishment. While the two attackers pummeled Hannon, Owens with arms raised advised onlookers in the bar to stay out of the situation. They faced

assault charges, but both were acquitted by the judge because of
contradicting testimonies from the witnesses. However, the incident, and others involving team members, cast a negative shadow
over the Chiefs. Jack Spring recalled his experience while a member of the Syracuse team.

> They got into a little hot water up in Syracuse and almost got
> us run out of town. But, Farrell got in a fight in a bar and beat
> some guy up pretty good. It turns out the guy was some kind of
> sportswriter. I was married, and my wife was there and other
> married guys wives were afraid to go out in public because
> they might get recognized . . . The baseball players didn't have
> a very good reputation in Syracuse after that incident.[106]

Wilbur Johnson, although only with the Marlins for half the
season, remembered some of the carrying-on involving the Dalton
Gang. They especially enjoyed antagonizing Paige.

> Oh yeah, he was a character [Satchel Paige] . . . He loved play-
> ing with that Jim Owens and Seth Morehead. They would
> throw buckets of water at each other. Then sometimes they
> would miss and they would get another bunch of guys in the
> locker room next to them. But the players just loved him. He
> had magnetism, that's all he gave them.[107]

Qualters remembers how Paige especially drew the attention
of Farrell, Morehead, and Owens and was always on the alert
himself.

> Farrell, Seth Morehead, Jim Owens. They were, oh jeez, I can't
> think of the guy's name. He was an outfield. But they called
> them the "Dalton Gang." They, I mean they just, I don't care
> if it was on the field or off the field they were constantly doing
> something. I mean they were absolutely nuts. They were good
> guys, but oh man you had to cover your back all the time
> because you didn't know what was happening. They picked
> on Satch a lot, but Satch loved it because they gave him all
> of their attention. They nailed his shoes to the floor and all
> kinds of crap. He'd come in and get dressed an he'd be sitting
> around there and the first thing he'd do was shake out his uni-
> form to make sure there was no bugs or beetles in his sanitary
> socks. And they'd nail his hat to the locker . . . He used to spin

around on his stool, slide his feet into his shoes, tighten them up and then he'd get up and to go and have his shoes nailed to the ground. He'd almost kill himself coming out of his shoes.[108]

Anagnost recalls how Paige took it all in stride.

> The things that Satchel Paige, that they did to him. For some reason, they must have liked him a lot because you don't do this to people that you don't like. It was just pranks they were pulling . . . They had these stand-up lockers and they nailed his uniform to the wall of the locker. There never was any animosity . . . I never saw Satchel Paige with any animosity, or anger, or anything like that. So, I don't think he got upset about it.
>
> Another night we had laundry hampers after the game you would take the uniforms and everything and throw them into these laundry hampers to be laundered for the next day. or whatever. Instead of throwing everything into the laundry hamper, they threw as much as they could, whatever they had in his standup locker. So, it was completely filled up with stuff.[109]

The tomfoolery of the Gang had no boundaries. It even extended outside of the locker room and with their teammates. In a 1963 interview in the *Miami News*, Farrell shared a story involving some gun-play that scared some prison inmates at Miami Stadium.

> One morning we went into the dugout to try out some guns we had, he recalled. Some prisoners from the stockade were cleaning up the field, but we didn't know who they were. We began shooting at the bat-rack in one corner of the dugout from the opposite corner. Well, all hell broke loose.
>
> The prisoners acted like they thought they were being executed by the guards and the armed guards in the stands came rushing down on the field apparently thinking it was a prison break or something.

Farrell recounted that he, Morehead and Owens, seeing what happened, hid in the locker room while the guards searched everywhere for the culprits. Farrell took refuge in a toilet stall standing on the lid, Owens squeezed himself into a locker, and Morehead leaped into a hamper covering himself with dirty laundry. "The guards came searching, but couldn't find us," said Farrell. General Manager, Stumpf heard what happened, and forthwith confiscated the guns and locked them away until the season's end.[110]

Although most of the Dalton Gang's pranks were innocent play amongst teammates, there was the more rowdy side of one of the groups that reared its ugly head. The day after the Orange Bowl game, Owens sauntered into the clubhouse two hours before and as the *Miami News* reported, "showed up more than slightly tipsy." He was in no condition to pitch that night resulting in a scuffle, knocking the 22-year old pitcher unconscious. The club remained silent about the identity of the other person involved in the physical altercation.[111] [112] When an ambulance arrived on the scene, a police officer reported that a kid fell from the bleachers, but *Miami News* photographer Tobey Massey snapped a picture that appeared in the next day's edition of the newspaper showing the hurler lying on a stretcher and being whisked away from the ballpark.[113] The attempt to cover up Owens' discretion soon became public.

Under the threat of suspension, he thought better of his misdeeds and later apologized, but not before being handed a $250 fine. In a printed statement to the press, he said, "I am certainly sorry that the whole thing happened. It was a terribly sad thing for me to do and any punishment given to me is deserved." He also apologized to Marlins management, teammates, fans and kids for his behavior.[114]

Qualters recalled a story that captured the personality and spirit of the "Bear" and his constant struggle with the bottle and self-control.

> Roy Hamey is the general manager, Mayo Smith, the manager, and the coaching staff; I guess everyone was in there. And Roy Hamey says to Owens, "We've about had it with you. You're going to have to make up your mind what you're going to be. You can either be an alcoholic or a ballplayer. You can't be both, Now, we want an answer and we want it right now. What's it going to be?" And he [Owens] looked around at everybody and said, "Can I have a couple of days to think it over?" [laughing]

> I mean here's a guy, if there ever was a major league pitcher, this guy is it . . . Yeah, that's the story. I wasn't in the room but that's the story.[115]

The Bears' transgression seemed like a foreshadowing of things to come. Only two games behind Toronto for the league lead following the gala Orange Bowl game, Miami settled into mediocrity winning only 16 of their last 36 games. They settled into third place 5½ games off the pace, barely ahead of Montreal. The main reason for the Marlins' woes proved to be their inability to score runs to support the second-best staff in the league. They finished fifth in the IL in scoring. Foxx, one of the greatest hitters of all time lamented, "I wish some one [sic] would open up that bank vault that is holding all our base hits."[116]

In the opening round of the playoffs Miami suffered the unfortunate fate of playing Rochester. The Red Wings dominated the Marlins during the regular season taking 16 of 21 games. Rochester continued their standout play against Miami in the playoffs taking the best-of-seven series in five games. It was small consolation that under skipper Dixie Walker's leadership, the Red Wings upset Toronto in the finals to take home the Governor's Cup as champions of the IL.[117]

In spite of their postseason failures, Salomon Jr. was satisfied with the club's initial season despite the late start in putting the team together, and a reported loss of $50,000 on the books at year's end. "Next year we hope to have our club set during spring training instead of being forced to build during the season," said the optimistic owner. Counting two home playoff games, the Marlins finished the season drawing 295,496 just short of the projected 300,000 the owner predicted at the beginning of the season.[118]

Several players moved on to Philadelphia the next season. Bouchee made the biggest splash leading all National League rookies in games played (154), at-bats (574), hits (168), doubles (35), and triples (8) while batting .293, bashing 17 round-trippers, and driving in 76.[119]

Two of the three Dalton Gang members moved onto the Phillies roster in 1957. Only Owens, called into military service, was missing. Nevertheless, they would be reunited later, and draw national attention for their disorderly conduct. The trio's exploits away from the field became legendary in June of 1960, when *Sports*

Illustrated writer Walter Bingham's controversial article exposed the rowdy group's wild ways.[120] Despite his raucous behavior, Farrell was a significant contributor to the City of Brotherly Love going 10–2 with a 2.38 ERA while saving 10 games. Fellow hurler Don Cardwell made good and finished with a 4–8 mark and 4.91 ERA in 128.1 innings. Cardwell, Farrell, and Owens would go on to have substantial major league careers while Morehead would fade from the scene in 1961 after winning only five games and losing nineteen.

No one was expecting any changes during the offseason, yet behind the scenes Salomon Jr., increasingly busy with other interests, made it known he wanted to sell the club. Perhaps harkening back to Veeck's suggestions when he purchased the team from Haske, he remembered:

> I am about to give you some very good advice. Go back to the restaurant, tap the shoulder of the guy at the table on the other side of you and ask him if he wants to buy a ball club. If that doesn't work, go out into the street and try to spot some lamb walking by. If you don't have a buyer by nightfall, see if you can't give it to somebody. Believe me, it will be cheaper.[121]

During the annual December 3 Orange Bowl luncheon, Oscar Dooly, a Miami broker in charge of selling Miami Stadium, approached multi-millionaire communications magnate George B. Storer and in casual conversation asked, "How'd you like to buy the Marlins?" Storer had actively pursued buying into a baseball franchise as recently as 1955 when he made an unsuccessful bid to buy the Detroit Tigers from the Briggs family. In 1956, he failed again when throwing his hat into the ring to purchase the Miami club. Two days later, Storer, Dooly and Van C. Kussrow met, and over lunch, agreed with Salomon Jr., Stein, John Thompson, and Veeck to purchase the Marlins for $250,000. By December 7, all the details hammered out, the team changed hands to the sole owner, Salomon Jr.[122]

In the aftermath, Salomon Jr. announced that he made a small profit on the deal and was leaving baseball behind. Foxx and Gordon parted ways with Osborn. Veeck resigned from his position and returned to his ranch in New Mexico where he began actively trying to purchase the Ringling Brothers Circus. With "Sport Shirt Bill's" departure, some of the magic that so captivated baseball fans was gone. The only consolation that Miamians had was that at least Satch was returning for another season.

Final Standings

TEAM	W	L	GB
Toronto	86	66	–
Rochester	83	67	2
Miami	80	71	5.5
Montreal	80	72	6
Richmond	74	79	12.5
Havana	72	82	15
Columbus	69	84	17.5
Buffalo	64	87	21.5

1957

What possessed an otherwise successful businessman like George B. Storer to purchase a minor league baseball team? Especially an individual with the foresight and business acumen to build a successful company that was a leader in its field. In the 50s, being a team owner was a money-losing proposition; a road paved with disappointment; sprinkled with moments of adulation, if the club did well. Does an otherwise prudent and shrewd-minded person such as Storer throw caution to the wind to realize a personal dream? On the other side of the coin, was it a competent business decision ensuring additional income for the flagship WGBS? After all, having the broadcast rights to a sports team that is popular has always been a financial generator for TV and radio outlets over the years.

Storer, the product of a well-to-do family, originally from Toledo, Ohio was educated in Florida and Wyoming before attending Cornell University. Although he did not graduate from college, it was evident at an early age he had strong business instincts. At the age of 25, he formed a partnership with his brother-in-law J. Harold Ryan and obtained a franchise from Speedene gas products. In order to advertise the business venture, they sought local radio as a means of promotion and were so impressed with the medium's power that they eventually bought WTAL radio, which

later became WSPD. Storer soon became enthralled with the airwaves and thereafter acquired other broadcasting stations before
expanding into television and building a communications empire.[123] With local WGBS in Miami already under his company's
umbrella, Storer planned to use this outlet to stimulate baseball
in the area while increasing his overall listenership.

One of Storer's first acts, most likely on the recommendation
of Sid Salomon Jr., was hiring Bill "Big Bill" Durney to replace
Ed Edwards as the play-by-play man. In addition, Jerry "Sonny"
Hirsch would serve as his sidekick. Big Bill had previously served
as a jack-of-all-trades working with Veeck when he owned the
St. Louis Browns. Durney, a robust fellow with boundless energy and an appetite to match, did everything from acting as the
teams' traveling secretary, promotions and publicity director, as
well as handling the mic in the broadcast booth. His work with
the legendary Buddy Blattner and Dizzy Dean with the Browns,
drew praise from his audience and peers.[124] Together Durney and
Hirsch quickly developed a positive rapport and created a loyal
following throughout the south Florida area. Hirsch, who once
served as a batboy for the Miami Beach Flamingos, would later go
on to a celebrated career as the longtime voice of the University of
Miami football for over 30 years.

Turnover in the front office is as inevitable as death and taxes
when new ownership takes over. After spending a busy offseason
lining up contracts and getting the roster ready for spring training, Eddie Stumpf was relieved from his position as GM. Taking
his place was the industrious, Joe Ryan. Before leaving, Stumpf
complimented his successor saying, "I always called him the
Ironheaded [sic] Dutchman and liked the guy. You might fault
him sometimes on little things but never about energy or sincerity
of purpose." He added, "I'm all for him-I was playing for his dad
when Joe was born and we've been friends all his life."[125]

Players and coaches began to arrive in early March at the new
spring training site at Stuart, Florida's Sailfish Park. The biggest surprise of camp was the early appearance of Satchel Paige.
Osborn opined, "I'll be satisfied if he shows up by the time spring
training is half over." Osborn was pleased when Paige arrived early toting his vast array of baggage. The former Negro League star
lifted the spirits of everyone including his skipper who credited
him with saving 15 games over and above the 11 that he won.[126]

One of the many curiosities surrounding Satch was his ability to keep his right wing in shape. One of two methods he used over the years was rubbing a mysterious oily elixir that he claimed to have discovered in 1935 when pitching for a semi-pro team in Bismarck, North Dakota. When questioned about his secrets he proclaimed, "I've already contacted my Indian friend who makes my special snake oil." In his autobiography, *Maybe I'll Pitch Forever*, Paige recounts how he came across the magic concoction.

"The summer of 1935 I was around Bismarck so much that I got to know a bunch of Indians up there real well. I think they were Sioux or something.

> They took a real liking to me, too, and those Indians watched me good. They even gave me some snake oil. Seems there were all these poisonous snakes around there like they had in Venezuela, and those Indians were afraid one of them might nip me, maybe one of them rattlesnakes.
>
> When they gave me the oil, they said, "That's hot stuff. Don't use it on anything but snake bites."
>
> "You sure it's hot?" I asked.
>
> "Yes. Too hot for anything but snake bites."
>
> Now that put me to thinking. Up in the north like where I was, it was just too cold for my liking. If that stuff was hot, it might be just what I needed to keep my arm loose.
>
> So I tried it on my arm, even though those Indians said it would burn me up. It didn't. It was just fine and I started using it after every game.[127]

Tom Qualters was in awe seeing his teammate use another method to keep his arm loose.

> Satch would unscrew the nozzle on the shower head so that there was one heavy strong bead that would come down and he would turn that thing on and gradually make it hotter, and hotter. He did that all his life and go back out there. I sometimes wonder about this icing thing? You couldn't stick your hand under there, it was burning. . . . I'm telling you the steam would come out of there.[128]

With the conclusion of spring training, the Marlins broke camp with high hopes of garnering their first International League crown. Norris Anderson of the *Miami News* predicted, "Miami is improved over last year at this previous stage."[129] Jimmy Burns in his assessment for *The Sporting News* went even further, predicting the Marlins to finish in second place.[130] Baseball prognosticators felt that Miami should do better in 1957. They believed the team's slow start was because of the previous year's hastily-built roster. In addition, Satchel, arguably their best pitcher, did not arrive until opening day.

A crop of familiar faces populated the squad, including pitchers, Qualters, Snyder, infielders Tompkins (2B), Micelotta (SS), Woody Smith (3B), outfielders Abrams (CF), and Novak (LF).[131] Joining the veterans were three highly regarded prospects that included former Stanford football star Chuck Essegian (28 HR, .366) out of Salem, Class B Northwest League, and burly Cuban slugger Francisco "Pancho" Herrera (.286 14, 88) taking over first base for Bouchee, and fleet-footed pasture worker, Don Landrum (.282, 98 Runs, 18 SB) both from Schenectady Class A Eastern League.[132]

Arriving at camp were several new prospects. Making the leap from Wilson of the Class B Carolina League, Earl Hunsinger (187 IP, 14–9, 3.08), and Roman "Ray" Semproch (210 IP, 13–13, 2.91), joined a foursome of other impressive newcomers including John Anderson (154 IP, 8–5, 2.10), Richard "Dick" Bunker (202 IP, 17–8, 2.09), Bob Conley (160 IP, 16–5, 2.31), and Henry "Hank" Mason (205 IP, 15–11, 2.28) from Schenectady. Anderson, Conley, and Hunsinger made brief appearances with the Marlins in 1956.[133]

Brought on board to guide the young hurlers, the Marlins signed two experienced catchers, 32-year-old Johnny Bucha and 40-year-old Clyde McCullough. Both backstops were old school hard-nosed competitors known for having no qualms at blocking the plate and being firm with their batterymates. Bucha was up and down between the bush leagues and and majors, appearing briefly in 1948 and 1950 with the St. Louis Cardinals. He also served as the main backstop with the Detroit Tigers in 1953. Earl Hunsinger recalled that the stocky catcher served a dual role with the team; several players would go to Bucha for a trim. "Johnny was getting up in age and Johnny was the clubhouse barber," said Hunsinger.[134] By his final year as a professional, McCullough had worn the "tools of ignorance" for 16 seasons; Chicago Cubs (12) and Pittsburgh Pirates (4).[135] He gained a semblance of fame on

May 12, 1955, catching Sam "Toothpick" Jones' no-hitter, the first by a black pitcher in major league history.[136]

With their roster in place, the Marlins headed south to Miami Stadium to kick off the season on April 17. Osborn announced the surprising choice of 26-year-old Semproch as his opening day starter to face Toronto's Don Johnson, a veteran of six big league seasons.

Storer wanted to make a splash for the opener, and spared no expense by employing the services of Ernie Seiler, famous for organizing the annual New Year's Day Orange Bowl football extravaganzas. The gala featured a float complete with beauty queens entering the stadium to the Dixieland sound of "*When the Saints Go Marching In.*" One hundred members of the Miami High School Marching band complete with baton twirling majorettes entertained the crowd of 6,688 that passed through the turn-stiles.[137] Players were ushered onto the field on a float, pulled by a tractor, with Osborn at the head. During team introductions, each member burst through a breakaway banner, with Landrum leading the way. Miami's number one fan, Joe Yates, a blind con-cessionaire from the county courthouse threw out the first ball. A dramatic rendition of the "Star Spangled Banner" followed ac-companied by fireworks.[138] Veeck would have been proud.

The fans got their monies worth as both teams battled to a 3 to 3 sixteen-inning tie. Both Storer and Maple Leafs' owner Jack Kent Cooke watched the proceedings, enduring to the valiant end. The game was called at 12:55 A.M., due to a 16-inning curfew set by the IL. By then, about 1,500 of the 6,688 fans stayed to cheer the hometown boys. Semproch proved up to the task mixing his slider and sinker to perfection permitting only four hits and two runs over nine innings of work. Landrum was the hitting star go-ing 4 for 8 and scoring two of the Marlins' runs.[139]

The good feelings lasted for the first few weeks of the season. Miami, in sole possession of first place with a 14–6 slate on May 9, soon thereafter began a slide and dropped to seventh place with a 25–30 record. Storer promised during the preseason that he would provide a winning club and spend what was necessary to ensure that. He was proving to be a man of his word and ap-proved moves to bolster the fortunes of his sagging franchise.

Ryan began working his magic on the phones looking for avail-able talent and making deals. It was the beginning of a series of moves to put the team in contention for a playoff spot. On May 8, the Marlins purchased Bobby Young, a former infielder with the Browns, Indians, and Orioles.[140]

June brought a frenzy of activity. On May 12, former 1950 Phillies pennant-winning "Whiz Kids" hurler Bubba Church was optioned to Miami by the Chicago Cubs affiliate Portland of the PCL. The veteran had not pitched professionally since 1955 and was working in his insurance business having voluntarily retired. He decided to give it one more shot and agreed not only to pitch, but to assist Osborn as a coach.[141] The next day the club procured outfielder Whitey Herzog from Washington (AL),[142] and right-handed pitcher Howie Judson from Seattle of the PCL.[143] Herzog hit .245 and drove in 35 runs in 117 games the previous season with the Senators, but had fallen in disfavor having batted only .167 in 78 at-bats. Judson came with a less than impressive 4–6, 4.86 in 46.1, but possessed a resume of seven big league seasons (17–37, 4.29) with Chicago (AL), and Cincinnati.[144] Ryan, following a familiar pattern of his preference of signing veterans, was hoping that the newest acquisitions would catch lightning in a bottle and the change of scenery would spark increased production.

Slowly but surely the Marlins, with their injection of new talent, began to climb up the standings. As the members became accustomed to their new teammates, Herzog, in particular, witnessed the legendary persona that was Satchel Paige and saw firsthand his legendary control that left Whitey speechless.

> So one night I said to Satchel, I said, "Satch, you're always talking about your control." And I said, "There is a hole in the right field wall, if a batter hits it through, they get $100,000. "If I walked off sixty feet six inches do you think you could throw a ball through that hole on three tries?" And he called everybody "Wild Child." He said to me, "Wild Child, does the ball fit in the hole?" I'll never forget what he said. Oh yeah, it fits and it barely fits don't get me wrong. It was just about the size of a baseball where the ball did fit in the hole. He said, "I'll be out here tomorrow evening at 5 o'clock." And he said, "I'll bet ya a fifth of Old Forester." That's what he drank, Old Forester Bourbon, "that I can do that." So anyway, I marked it off the next night while we were taking batting practice and here comes Satch. And I marked off the sixty feet six inches. And he took not one warmup at all. He took the first ball and

he put it up by his eyes and threw the ball at that hole from the pitcher's length sixty feet six inches and the first one hit in the hole and went "Berrrr" and came back out. It chattered in the hole. And I'll be damned if he didn't throw the next one right through that hole. So I owed him a fifth of Old Forester.[145]

Whether it was Old Forester or Canadian Club, it was the same result; recalled differently by Dick Bunker. The feat occurred in Montreal's Delorimier Stadium.

We were in right field playing Skidoodle. They had a big sign there and it said, "$10,000 if you ever hit a ball in a regulation game." The odds are probably fifty million to one. Whitey said to Satch, "I'll bet you can't throw a ball through that hole." And Satch says, "Well, what do you want to bet? How about a case of Canadian Club?" That's what he drank. He loved Canadian Club. So, he stood about forty feet away and threw the first ball; it was pretty close. The second ball went right through the hole.[146]

Ryan continued to be active in July putting together deals. On July 1, he obtained outright from the Phillies, Saul Rogovin (48–48, 4.06), who brought his eight years of major league experience to the table.[147] Still looking to add some punch to the listless Marlins' offense, outfielder Stu Locklin (44 games, .310, 3, 24) was purchased from San Diego of the PCL.[148]

Ryan kept wheeling and dealing adding veteran mound help. Before the end of the month, he also procured John "Windy" McCall from the Boston Red Sox [149] and Charles "Red" Adams (2–4, 4.19) from Los Angeles of the PCL.[150]

Although Storer lived up to his promise of delivering a winning club even at further expense, the first signs of financial trouble became evident after the sale of Abrams. Ryan disclosed the attendance numbers. The reported first 51 home dates reflected they were down 57,000, (the previous year's figures complimented by the inclusion of the famous Orange Bowl game that brought in 51,713).

Adding insult to injury, the assemblage of new acquisitions the Marlins had allocated for, failed to deliver wins. By August 3, the team reached the .500 mark for the first time since June 8 thanks to an impressive 12 to 9 victory, which landed them in fifth place, half-a-game behind the Rochester Red Wings. Aided by an uncharacteristically strong wind blowing towards the outfield, three of Miami's best, Locklin, McCullough and Young all homered helping Qualters, in relief, earn his ninth "W" of the season.[151]

Miami followed their climb in the standing by dropping seven of ten games prior to their northern swing to Canada. The Marlins began their Montreal series traveling to play the Royals in Quebec City at Stade Canac (locals called it "Parc Victoria"). Strategically, the change of venue attracted more fans. Noticeably, absent from the 75-mile side road trip was Paige. Although Miami dispatched the Royals on a chilly 50-degree night in easy fashion, 10 to 3, the absence of his Sunday relief ace drew the ire of Osborn who was well aware of the wayward pitcher's propensity to avoid chilly conditions.[152]

Tompkins remembered how Satch shunned old "Jack Frost," and lived by his own set of rules when it came to making an appearance.

> Amazing character could throw as hard as anyone in the league if the weather was warm. If the weather was cold he might not even show up . . . We were in Buffalo, and he warmed up in the clubhouse with his jacket on. He didn't do well. But the thing with Miami, he might not even be around and be out somewhere listening to the game. He'd say, "I just got to go, they need me." And he'd show up in his uniform ready to pitch.[153]

The tolerant Osborn realized that you could not control Paige like his other players, but repeatedly showing up late for games and bending of the rules had tested his patience once too often. Rumors had it that Paige missed the bus while searching for his suitcase full of clothes at the airport, while another theory had Paige fearful of taking the bus to Quebec City. What turned out to be a harrowing bus ride, McCall said, "If I live through this. I'll live to see Satch get somewhere on time."[154] It was likely a combination of all the aforementioned including the frigid conditions that explained his nonappearance.

Regardless, Osborn doled out his punishment by scheduling Paige to pitch the next evening at Delorimier Stadium. "I'll teach Satch that he's gotta make it on time for those buses," said the annoyed skipper. Satch's reply as reported by the *Miami Daily*

News revealed, "Ah have the wrong danged clothes for this h'yar dogsled weather."[155]

The next night, his performance was less than spectacular. He allowed three runs in six innings of work including giving up a home run to Jim Gentile and a pair of triples, one to Bobby Del Greco and another to pitcher, Rene Valdes. The 7 to 0 defeat saw his record drop to 7 wins and 6 losses. Miami (60–65) stood in fifth place, 10 games behind first-place Buffalo, but only 2½ games to the rear of fourth place Rochester.[156]

When the August 19 IL All-Star game arrived, Miami (62–67) was still resting in fifth place. Fans in each IL city chose their team's starting lineup, however, the absence of a Marlins player was noteworthy; they did not receive adequate support. Toronto manager, Dixie Walker, named Landrum and Woody Smith to represent Miami against the Brooklyn Dodgers. Smith drew the starting assignment when Rochester's Frank Verdi missed the game due to a sprained thumb. Smith performed well going 2 for 5 with a single, double, and run batted in. However, the IL stars only managed four hits total and the Dodgers prevailed 2 to 1.[157]

An obvious omission for the second straight season was that of Paige. "This stuck in old Satch's craw," stated Osborn. He had pitched his heart out the two previous nights against the Maple Leafs and as his manager said, "He wanted to show Dixie." At this point in the season, Satchel had appeared in 33 games and was flashing a sparkling 2.66 ERA.[158] Two of the four pitchers named by Walker as all-stars had higher ERAs compared to Paige.[159] Documentation of Walker and his racist attitude dated back to the spring of 1947. As a player with the Dodgers, he started a petition amongst his teammates stating that if Jackie Robinson was a member of the team, they would not play. His decision raised eyebrows with fans and the press, by his exclusion of the baseball icon from the all-star roster.

While Buffalo and Toronto were fighting for the top spot, and Richmond ensconced in third place, Miami was in a three-way race "drag 'em out" battle for the final playoff position with Havana and Rochester. On September 2, the Marlins began an eight-game home and away set against rival Havana to finish out the season. Rochester closed out the season on a northern swing opening against Toronto before finishing with Montreal, both series' on the road.

It was the ideal ending to a less than perfect season for both clubs. The Marlins (70–75) and Rochester (71–76), tied for fourth place, were keenly aware of Havana (69–77) in the rearview mirror. The rivalry with the Cuban city only 228 miles as the crow flies, dates back to 1946 and the clubs inclusion to the Florida International League. Osborn knew the importance of the series not only from the standpoint of earning a playoff spot but because of the bitter rivalry that existed between the two combatants. He warned the media about the Sugar Kings when he said, "That's the club I've said all along we've got to beat face to face to get in the playoffs." The cautious skipper picked Paige to square off against 23-year-old righty, Orlando Peña, and left-hander Bunker to face Havana's Jose Santiago.[160]

In the opening game, in front of 2,090, Paige tamed the visitors shutting them out 3 to 0. He retired the first twenty-three batters he faced before giving up a base hit. In the process, he earned his ninth win of the season and struck out eight. Landrum, McCullough, and Micelotta each drove in a run. "I only tossed eight or 10 curves. My fastball was workin' for me today," said a satisfied Paige.[161]

In the nightcap, Osborn's hunch proved fortuitous when he chose Bunker. One of only two lefties on the staff, Bunker's last win had come on June 26 and was a surprise choice since having seen most of his recent action as a reliever.[162]

After the regulation nine stanzas, both teams were tied at one apiece on the scoreboard. In stifling heat and humidity, Bunker persisted into extra innings. By the top of the sixteenth frame, with two outs, the port-sider from Norwood, Massachusetts had spent his last ounce of energy. Only one strike away from ending the inning he conferred with his catcher and related his story of how he cleverly used an illegal pitch to escape the inning unscathed.

> You know why I remember it? Because it was ninety degrees out and the flag was blowing straight down. I'm serious it was so hot. I know I pitched a long time and I was about ready to drop. And the guy came up. I never threw a spitter. I taught Satchel, this is the truth, I taught Satchel Paige how to throw a spitter. He used to show me. I said, "Satch, the idea of a spitter is you can't touch a seam. When you wet your hand and to put it on the ball, it can't be on the seam, it's got to be below the seam, you know off seam."

So I remember I never threw a spitter in my life, but I called timeout and I don't remember who was catching that game, it could've been Johnny Bucha, but anyway he came out. They had their best hitter up, a third baseman I can't think, they called him the "White Rat" or something like that, he was a great hitter. And I said to Johnny, "Man, I mean I am tired," and he keeps fouling off pitches and I'm tired, and I said, "I'm going to load one up. I'm going to throw a spitter at him and see what happens and if it doesn't do anything I don't care." So he said, "OK." He went back and I loaded this up and I threw a spitter and the ball broke about a foot, you know, and it struck him out and I think that ended the game. I don't remember the score, it was two to one. I pitched the whole sixteen innings? Oh my god, well that's a true story. I remember throwing that pitch and the guy turned around and looked at Bucha or who-ever was catching and said that was a spitter. You know he says, "He doesn't throw a spitter." And I think he wiped the ball on the ground.[163]

In the bottom of the same frame, with one out, Tompkins stepped to the plate with Bucha hugging second base and stroked a single to right-center field off reliever Mike Cuellar. Bucha chugged home for the winning tally, ending the marathon, and earning the Marlins a 2 to 1 win.[164]

Although the Sugar Kings came back the next night by roughing up Tom Qualters to defeat Miami 6 to 1,[165] the Marlins bounced back in fine form in their final home game of the season by shutting out Havana, 5 to 0. In the pre-game ceremonies, Woody Smith was honored as the team's most valuable player, Don Landrum as the most popular player, Frank Herrera as the best rookie, and Ray Semproch as the most valuable pitcher. After the game, club officials announced attendance for the year came in at 185,794. It was a bitter disappointment for Storer and Ryan. Even with Miami and Rochester tied and holding on to hopes of a playoff berth, fans were not taking notice. It was a drop of almost 50,000 from the year before, or over 100,000 when accounting for the Orange Bowl extravaganza.[166]

Still, ownership was hopeful of success if the Marlins qualified for the Shaughnessy playoffs and a shot at the Governor's Cup. Going into the final series in Havana, Miami remained tied with Rochester for the final postseason position. Havana's hopes were on life support. In order for the Sugar Kings to qualify for the playoffs, they needed to sweep the Marlins and for Rochester to lose all of their remaining games.

In the lid-lifter at Gran Stadium, Miami experienced their all too common bugaboo that plagued them all season long, the inability to put runs on the board. Facing 39-year-old southpaw Panamanian Pat Scantlebury, the Marlins offense managed only four singles. The former Negro League star known for his pinpoint control had a reputation for doctoring the ball and used every means at his disposal to fool hitters. Teammate Sparky Anderson, who went on to a successful career as one of baseball's all-time greatest managers remembered, "When I was with Toronto we had a pitcher named Pat Scantlebury who lined his wristband with tacks and he'd glue a whole piece of sandpaper in the webbing of his glove."[167] The 8–0 loss dropped them one-half-game behind the idle Red Wings. After the game, a frustrated Osborn said, "There's no way in the world to win a ballgame," he allowed, without runs . . ."[168]

The team's hopes once again fell on the doorstep of Paige. Ol' Satch had dominated the Sugar Kings just four days earlier, and Osborn was counting on a repeat performance. However, concerns arose when the veteran remained in his room all day. The *Miami Daily News* reported he was suffering from small miseries that had him uncomfortable. He was also worried, since his teammates had produced only five runs for him in his last four starts.[169] Nevertheless, in classic Paige style, he stepped up and performed as only he could.

Trailing one to nothing in the sixth, Miami's bats came to life. Thanks to a two-RBI triple by Micelotta, who later scored on second baseman Jesus Mora's error, the Marlins staked themselves to a 3 to 1 lead. Satchel continued to baffle the home team hitters allowing a single base hit between the third and ninth innings. With one out in the ninth, the Sugar Kings cut the lead by a run after Daniel Morejon smashed a home run over the left field wall. When Osborn approached the mound, and without protesting, the former Negro League star handed him the ball; a surrender to heat and humidity that had taken its toll. Semproch got the call from the bullpen and promptly recorded the last two outs to earn the save. The final tally showed Miami 3 Havana 2. Teamed with Rochester's 3 to 2 loss at Toronto, the Marlins regained fourth place.[170]

Havana, eliminated from the playoff picture, was eager to play the role of the spoiler in the third game of the set. Manager Nap Reyes' choice to start was rookie Cuellar, facing 32-year-old Church. The Sugar Kings jumped out to a 2 to 1 lead by the end of three innings. Bubba looked out of sorts on many hard hit smashes that fortunately for him found their way to well-placed defenders. "For the first three innings I didn't have a thing," said Church, but added, "and then Osborn told me I was standing up too straight when I was throwing."[171] The advice worked wonders and Church silenced Havana the rest of the way. The score was tied in the fourth. The Marlins plated a trio of runs in the fifth that started with a line drive off the bat of Tompkins. Peña, who relieved Cuellar, was struck in the head. He was removed from the field on a stretcher. At that point, the Sugar Kings came unraveled. Locklin followed with a double and Herrera drove both runners in with a single. At the end of the sixth inning, the Marlins led 5 to 2.[172]

News had reached the bench that Toronto had just shutout Rochester, 2 to 0. With victory a few outs away, Church breezed through the Havana hitters the rest of the way garnering the 7 to 2 win. During the process, he allowed only five hits while striking out five and giving up a solitary base on balls. Herrera and Marv Blaylock were the offensive stars of the night driving in three and two runs respectively.[173] The Marlins celebration on the field was no doubt disconcerting to the few Cubans in the stands.

With their playoff spot secured the Marlins drew the unenviable task of playing against first-place Toronto in the opening round for the chance at the Governor's Cup. The Fish were heavy underdogs considering their below .500 record. Key performer Herzog was finished for the season (bum shoulder), and Qualters received his call up to the Phillies, prior to the end of the season.[174]

The 2-3–2 format featured the first two games at Maple Leaf Stadium, then to Miami, and if necessary, the last two games back to Toronto. The Leafs edged out Buffalo in a taut pennant race by one-half-game earning them their third pennant in four years. Yet despite their regular season success, they had not experienced a league championship since 1934. The Toronto line-up featured a collection of dangerous hitters including, Mike Goliat (28, 83, .296), Sam Jethroe (15, 83 runs, .274), Lew Morton (25, 60, .270), and IL legend Rocky Nelson (28, 102, .294). They were no slouches pitching either with Don Johnson (17–7, 2.96), Jim

Pearce (15–8, 3.65), Humberto Robinson (18–7, 2.95), and reliever extraordinaire Bobby Tiefenauer (68 games, 118 IP, 6–6, 2.14).

An interesting twist occurred prior to the opening game of the series. The Marlins filed an official protest with IL officials against Toronto requesting that Leafs' management abstain from setting off rockets every time their club scored. The origin of the complaint dated back to August 17 when Don Osborn protested a game in Toronto. The Leafs were ahead by two runs when both Locklin and Landrum got on their horses and chased a low-liner into left-center field that skipped its way to the outfield wall. The scoreboard attendant saw that a run was about to score, as was the teams' custom, he prematurely set off the fireworks that startled both Landrum and Locklin. By the time the two recovered from the blast, Hector Rodriguez had coasted into third tying the game. Osborn strongly argued his case that the blast interfered with the play and the run not be allowed, but the umpiring crew would not be swayed. Despite the explosive event, Miami went on to win the game 6 to 5, and the protest dismissed.[175]

A raucous crowd of 7,649 turned out on a cool September 11 night, thinking that beating the Marlins was like "shooting fish in a barrel." They were soon disappointed as Semproch, using his sinkerball to perfection, shut down the hometown batters by scattering nine singles and allowing two walks in a 6 to 0 white-washing. The big blow of the night came off the bat of Woody Smith, a two-run shot off Pearce in the second.[176] This time Miami had silenced the rockets in their own way.

Toronto got retribution in game two pounding Judson for five runs forcing him out of the game in the second frame with no outs. Adams, Bunker, and Rogovin fared little better in relief as Walker's charges thumped Miami, 10 to 4, to even the series. Don Johnson, the one-time major leaguer earned the win.[177]

Game three of the series shifted to Miami Stadium. Paige was sterling for the first six innings tossing shutout ball before giving up four unearned runs and the lead in the seventh. Miami tied the score in the bottom of the same frame on a Tompkins pinch-hit single scoring Woody Smith. The Marlins jumped on the usually "lights out" Tiefenauer in the bottom of the eighth. The clutch hit of the inning was a double by McCullough that plated Blaylock and Smith.[178]

Miami's hopes of wrapping up the series at home by taking the next two games were dashed when Toronto bounced back taking game four behind Eddie Blake's fine performance holding the fish to only three hits. Rocky Nelson had the big blows of the night bashing two home runs, leading the Leafs to a 6 to 1 victory.[179]

The baseball God's blessed Miami with a break the following day when heavy rains forced a postponement of play. It was a blessing, as Osborn's pitching staff was showing signs of fatigue. The extra day also allowed the thankful manager to turn to his ace Semproch. The crafty right-hander proved to be the Marlins best starter after getting off to an early season slow start. Miami hitters teed off on Pearce and Ross Grimsley (the latter, father of his namesake that also pitched big league ball) for six runs in the fourth, salting away the 8 to 4 win. Semproch, who relied on his sinkerball for most of the evening, earned the complete game "W" despite allowing ten base hits.[180]

Toronto was confident they would take the series by returning to their home field. Following the game five loss, Leafs pasture grazer Lew Morton chimed, "That humidity in Miami fogged us out." He added, "Up here we'll start feeling our oats." Don Johnson returned to the hill to oppose Bunker (6–10).[181]

The Norwood native looked like the same pitcher that was so masterful in Havana silencing the Sugar Kings' bats for sixteen innings, repeated his domination by holding the hometown team to four hits. Trailing the Leafs one to nothing going into the eighth inning, Osborn used a pinch hitter for Bunker in the eighth and then turned to Hank Mason to try to hold Toronto. Landrum homered in the eighth to knot the score, followed by his teammates scoring a pair more in the top of the ninth to take a 3–1 lead. A Locklin double followed by a Herrera triple proved to be the difference maker. Mason put the Leafs down in order to end the game and earn the win. The silent disappointment of fans in Toronto could be heard all the way to Miami. Local fandom tuned in to Durney and Hirsch masterfully recreating the game from a ticker tape feed at WGBS studios, calling the finale. The victory was indeed a stroke of magic for the aptly named city. Their next opponent Buffalo eliminated Richmond in five games.[182]

Paige drew the starting assignment to face the Bisons and their hitting star and longtime nemesis, Luke Easter. Both had a friendship dating back to Paige's barnstorming and Negro League days. Semproch recalled how the two of them used to jaw at each other, what we call trash-talking today.

I'll tell you one thing, he [Paige] and Luke Easter used to go at it. I'll tell you that was funny. The people used to love it because he would holler to Luke, "Here comes the curveball. Hit it, Luke . . ." We had a lot of fun. Oh yeah, those two I'll tell ya it was like Laurel and Hardy. I didn't have no problem with him. I used to throw outside anyway. He tried to hit the ball out of the ballpark, you know.[183]

Off the field, Easter and Paige were best of friends, but on the diamond, they were competitors. The pair would even trade vehicles during the season to travel. Anagnost remembered one particular meeting between them that summed up their competitiveness and mutual respect.

There was a great confrontation that I saw between Satchel Paige and Luke Easter. Luke Easter played for Buffalo, and he was a left-handed hitter. And of all the time I was the batboy, I saw very, very few home runs go out of right field. Somebody told me much later that because of the wind currents, or something, the wind would hold up the ball in right field. I remember Luke Easter getting up against Satchel Paige. And they would talk to each other. You know you could see them. I couldn't actually hear everything they were saying, but I know they were talking to each other. Satchel Paige apparent liked to talk to people and Luke Easter was talking back. And I'm watching this and then I see the longest home run I've ever seen in right field hit by Luke Easter off of Satchel Paige.[184]

Jack Spring added a postscript concerning the monster blast.

Anyway, he hit a home run off of Satch in the first inning and Satch kind of walked around the infield shook his finger at him, and yelled at him as he went around the bases, "That's all you're getting big boy. That's it. That's all you're getting." And by God, he struck him out, as I recall, the next two times, or three, whatever and he didn't get another smell out of it. We were dying in the dugout laughing. He kind of walked around the edge of the grass and followed him around and said, "You ain't getting no more."[185]

In an ill-omened start to the series at Offerman Stadium, Paige was not his usual self, allowing ten hits over the first seven innings, and the Miami bats once again went silent. Glenn Cox pitched his second shutout of the playoffs while surrendering only three singles. The final score showed Buffalo 2 Miami 0.[186]

The Marlins did little to distinguish themselves in the finals eventually dropping the series in five games. Of all the indignities, Paige was the losing pitcher in the fifth game when the Marlins fell, 7 to 1. Yet, even in defeat, the third game of the series would go down as one of the greatest performances by a Miami pitcher. Down two games to none, Osborn got the bad news that Semproch was suffering from a bad case of the flu. While mulling over who would start in place of his ace, Semproch convinced his skipper that he was ready to go. Begrudgingly, Osborn agreed and then proceeded to watch as both teams battled for sixteen innings tied at one apiece. Finally, seeing his starter spent, and adding on the indignities of suffering a painful blister, Osborn sent McCullough in to pinch-hit for Semproch, but the Marlins were unable to score. In the top of the seventeenth, the Bisons took the lead, but Miami tied the score again in the bottom of the same frame when with two outs, Herrera smacked a two-bagger and Smith followed, driving his teammate in. McCall silenced Buffalo in the top of the eighteenth. Micelotta led off the inning with a single, followed by Cox uncharacteristically walking McCall, then intentionally walked Landrum. Tompkins proceeded to hit into what looked like a rally-killing double play. With two out, Cox intentionally walked Locklin, to face Herrera. But his control escaped him, and he walked Pancho, forcing in the winning run.[187] Semproch recalled, "I went sixteen innings in that game, and I was going to be sent home from Buffalo because I started to get the flu," said Semproch. He added, "And, oh well, there was doctoring. They weren't going to pitch me, but I insisted . . . I went sixteen innings. We won the game."[188]

Considering the season-long inconsistent play and fourth place finish, the team went further than anyone had expected. While the Bisons' players packed up and headed to Denver for the Little World Series, the Marlins dispersed to various locales to work in offseason jobs, play winter league ball, or just enjoy a well-deserved rest. Both Blaylock and Landrum received news to report to Philadelphia as late-season call-ups.

Surprisingly, Satchel Paige (10-8, 2.42, 119 IP) and Woody Smith (.273, 14, 73) were overlooked by Phillies management for promotion. Smith, in particular, played gold glove caliber defense.

In Paige's case, it was most likely two-fold. One, the Phillies were slow signing and promoting black ballplayers. It was not until April 22, 1957, that John Kennedy made his debut in a Philadelphia uniform, a full ten years after Jackie Robinson broke the color barrier. Kennedy's stay was brief, appearing in five games and only making two plate appearances before being re-assigned to Class B High Point-Thomasville of the Carolina League.[189] Secondly, Hamey and team brass simply considered Paige too old based upon his 51 years.

The Smith oversight was also hard to understand based on the poor play of the Phillies' third sacker, Willie "Puddin' Head" Jones. His .218 batting average and nine homers were career lows since becoming a regular in 1949. Moreover, one-time rookie sensation Ted Kazanski, Jones backup, showed little power hitting only three home runs in part-time duty.[190]

The likely reason Smith did not receive a promotion to the big club, was due to a personal difference between he and Phillies GM Haney. Tom Qualters shared a story that brought this to light.

> Yeah, Woody Smith, I'll tell you a little story about him . . . He was probably the best defensive third baseman you could ever see. He was unbelievable, but he had a weak bat . . . He had come to spring training, while down there, and it was in Florida. We just needed a body and there was no chance he was going to make the team. And it was just obvious. I don't know what the hell they were thinking, they just didn't treat him right. They just didn't show any interest in him at all and he just packed his stuff and went home. Well, Roy Hamey was the general manager and he blackballed Woody.[191]

Although other clubs around major league baseball showed interest in Smith, the Phillies had no plans to deal him. He returned for another season to Miami in 1958. Storer and Ryan were more than happy to see the fan favorite return for another campaign.

While Ryan remained active building his next season's roster, Storer had much bigger concerns. Aleman Jr. announced he was returning to manage Miami Stadium, and the yearly battle to acquire a beneficial lease raised financial concerns, and whether or not the Marlins would stay in Miami.[192] Their sagging attendance dipped to just over 185,000; ranking sixth in the IL, less than half of what the biggest draw (Buffalo) attracted. The league reported an overall gain of 121,000.[193] The offseason would prove to be busy and stressful.

Final Standings

TEAM	W	L	GB
Toronto	88	65	–
Buffalo	88	66	.5
Richmond	81	73	7.5
Miami	75	78	13
Rochester	74	80	14.5
Havana	72	82	16.5
Columbus	69	85	19.5
Montreal	68	86	20.5

1958

For the third straight year, the future of minor league baseball in Miami was uncertain. The recurring battle to negotiate a stadium lease grew more complicated with the presence of its owner and his insistence on selling what had become known as "the white elephant", Miami Stadium. Meanwhile, he worried about political unrest in his native country. In a *Miami News* series, Aleman reportedly stated his preference that Fulgencio Batista relinquish control of the country, rather than have a revolution. He said, "I'm not in this for politics, all I want is for Cuba to return to a democracy.[194] Aleman Jr. was proving to be a burr in the saddle of Storer, who made every effort to keep the team in Miami. Adding further to the already difficult situation was IL president Shaughnessy's demand that the Marlins finalize an arrangement for a home ballpark by January 22.[195]

After the young tycoon's rejection of a $40,000 lease, Storer began exploring other options. His eyes turned towards the Orange Bowl as a possible venue and went a step further conferring with

Sam Wolfson, owner of the Class A Jacksonville Braves about the possibility of moving the team there.[196]

On January 18, Storer announced, "We've done everything we can to keep the team here, but the chips are down and we've got to move." The possible relocation sites were Jacksonville and Tampa.[197]

That next day, the city commission convened an emergency meeting to make their decision. Otis Shiver, who had fought for the city to surrender its option to buy Miami Stadium for $850,000, changed his mind and said, "I just decided we couldn't afford to lose baseball."[198] By a unanimous vote, the city agreed to purchase the stadium, thus allowing the Marlins to stay. An overjoyed Storer proclaimed, "All I can say is that I'm tickled pink."[199] With the announcement, Ryan jumped into action announcing that tickets would go on sale.[200] Due to a two-month delay in signing a lease, there was a significant loss of ticket sales, and the continued instability of the future of the club's viability in Miami was discouraging fan loyalty.

Preparations for spring training in Melbourne began immediately as players began trickling into camp. One of the first to announce that he was reporting early was Paige. Having spent the preseason in Kansas City tinkering around his house, he was anxious to return to Florida and declared that he planned to do some fishing and catch the Ringling Bros. and Barnum & Bailey Circus scheduled to appear in Miami.[201]

The biggest change during the offseason was a turn in managers. The Marlins front office revealed on October 20, 1957, that Osborn and coach Eddie Miller would not be retained.[202] After considering several options for the post, Ryan and Storer's choice to take his place was recently fired Cleveland Indians skipper, Major "Kerby" Farrell. Coming off a frustrating season in which he had finished in sixth place (76–77), the Tennessee native son, had been successfully piloting clubs in the minors since 1941 beginning with Erie of the Class C Middle Atlantic League. A first baseman by trade, Farrell began his playing career in 1932 with Vicksburg of the Class C Cotton States League and worked his way up through the various levels of the bush leagues, before logging two years in the big leagues during the war years with the Boston Braves (1943), and the Chicago White Sox (1945). His greatest successes as a field general came in 1954 and 1956 with the American Association's Indianapolis Indians when he led his club to pennants both years, and a league championship and Junior World Series title in the latter campaign. He copped two minor league manager of the year awards in Indianapolis and later won another in 1962 with the Jacksonville Suns, the only person ever to win three such awards.[203]

A great deal of optimism surrounded the Marlins as they prepared for the season and wrapped up their 21-games exhibition schedule. A slew of familiar faces returned including, Bucha, Essegian, Landrum, Micelotta, Woody Smith, Tompkins, and Bobby Young. Also back were pitchers, Bunker, Cardwell from the 1956 club, Conley, Mason, Windy McCall and of course Paige.

The most impressive of the fresh new faces were pitcher Dallas Green (12–9, 4.02) from Class B High Point-Thomasville, first base phenomenon Fred Hopke (10, 90, .337) out of Class C Salt Lake City, and Freddie Van Dusen, Green's teammate from the year before who thumped 25 home runs while batting a cool .310. The most intriguing prospect was 6'3", 215 lb. Hopke. Although considered a less capable fielder than the departed Herrera, during the spring he was arguably the Marlins best hitter bashing eight dingers, collecting 21 RBI's, and batting .306 during 21 exhibition games.[204]

Hopke had not only made an impression with the Phillies and Marlins brass, but with his new teammates. Several of whom offered him some financial advice. He exclaimed, "I went to Melbourne and I had that kind of spring . . . I had old-timers coming up to me telling me, 'you better ask for $20,000.' You know you are so in awe of everything you know. And they ripped up my contract and they gave me $100 more and I thought I was doing great."[205]

Hopke's spring experience had many rewarding moments, and humorous ones as well, but his most vivid memories were the ones that involved crossing paths with a baseball immortal.

> I was very, very fortunate. In Melbourne, I was walking to go to batting practice, right? And a Cadillac comes riding right across the field. And I looked at the groundskeeper and said what's this? He said, "That's Satchel." That's how I met Satchel Paige he drove a Cadillac right on the field.
>
> This is a funny story. He took me fishing. He says, "Do you fish?" I said, "I love fishing." I'd never fished in my life. [laughing] So he took, we went out to the causeway, and he gave me

a fishing pole and I threw it under the pier. You know my first cast. He said, "Oh, let me outta here." What a man he was. Everything they said about that guy was true.[206]

Following a productive exhibition season in which the Marlins compiled a 14–7 slate, expectations were running high coming into opening night at Miami Stadium. Morris McLemore's assessment of the club for 1958, "The Marlins are in a better position psychologically, financially, and team-wise than they were for either of their previous openings." He also pointed out the more heavily weighted veteran club and a well-knit group of pitchers should ensure the team's success.[207]

Early season results would not bear out McLemore's optimism. Opening day against Rochester proved to be an ominous start to the season. Although the Marlins outhit the Red Wings, 12 hits against 8, they dropped the contest 2 to 1 in front of 5,191 at Miami Stadium. The only run tallied by the hometown clan occurred in the first inning thanks to Hopke's single to center field. Everything taken into account, the Marlins stranded eleven runners and Conley absorbed the loss.

Miami started out slowly and found themselves residing in the second division. Their struggles were not limited to the diamond. On April 23, Paige found himself on the wrong side of the law, arrested by the police for speeding and driving without a license. The next day, brought before Metropolitan Judge Charles H. Snowden, the good magistrate, ardent Marlins fan, and University of Miami graduate, sentenced Paige to 20 days in jail. In an unusual decision, the judge deferred adjudication until October 1 and agreed to reduce the punishment by one day for each time Paige recorded a win, every run he scored, and for every time he struck out Luke Easter. "He'll have to do a little better than he did last year though," said Snowden.[208]

Satchel's off the field exploits such as showing up late for games at his convenience, and general disregard for rules, tolerated by Osborn the previous two seasons, began grating on the strict disciplinarian Farrell and Ryan as well.

Notwithstanding the team's poor showing, Storer again stepped up to the plate to right the ship and live up to his further promise of providing Miami a winning club. Prior to the early May road trip to Havana, the Marlins acquired the services of pitcher Mickey McDermott from the Detroit Tigers. The one time Boston

Red Sox, "can't miss prospect," was the quintessential pitcher, "with a million dollar arm and a ten cent head." Known to be as wild off the field as on the mound, he wasted no time making an impression on Miami fans. McDermott's pitching struggles at this point of his eleventh season in the big leagues were well known, and he announced that he was trying to resurrect his career as an everyday player at first base or in the outfield. On May 11, Farrell put him in the lineup to play first base, and to everyone's surprise, he went two for two, with a home run and two RBIs. Paige did his part pitching a seven-inning three-hitter and garnering his third win of the season, a Miami, 2 to 1 victory over the Sugar Kings.[209]

McDermott was one of many zany characters that passed through Miami. His reputation as a philanderer, drinker, and nightclub singer preceded him. His most egregious offenses included punching *Boston Globe* reporter, Bob Holbrook in 1953, altercations with Jimmy Piersall during the time his teammate was suffering from well-publicized mental breakdown issues, and 1956 when the Miami Beach Police Department arrested the madcap hurler for making out with his wife while parked in a vehicle. During the latter, he resisted arrest and later jumped bail. As recently as 1958 in spring training, he was involved in a late hours scuffle with the notoriously short-tempered Billy Martin.[210] McDermott admitted in his book, *A Funny Thing Happened on the Way to Cooperstown.*

> I lost my identity and took on a new one. I became a character actor-the dumb left-handed drunk. I was on a train going the wrong way, and I didn't know how to get off. That was serious, but being serious hurt too much, so I did funny. Turned everything into a joke on me. The clown laughing on the outside and hating what's happening to him on the inside.[211]

The final game against the Sugar Kings concluded a long trip that had already found the team traveling from Montreal to Toronto to Columbus. Boys will be boys and a group of players decided to let their hair down and partake of more than a few adult beverages while enjoying the nightlife in the clubs of Havana. The main culprits were Church, Green, McCall, and of course McDermott.

I remember stories about one trip over to Cuba, over to Havana, where they were ready to get on a plane and they can't find them [teammates]. And I think it might have been the group, or was it a group of four pitchers they couldn't find when they board the plane and come back. And they are looking all over the airport, and they found them sitting around a pillar on the floor with sombreros over their heads looking Mexican and just sitting on the floor of the airport. I think they finally got them rounded up and got them on the plane.[212]

The effects of the previous night were evident on "Fireworks Night." The Virginians hammered the Marlins, 13 to 2. Two of the sombrero perpetrators, McCall who came in to relieve Robert Frederick, surrendered six runs in two innings of work. McDermott, in right field, went 0 for 5. The loss dropped Miami's record to 9–18.

The next day, GM Ryan, no doubt disappointed by the previous days' results opened his door and found that Church had left his sombrero in his office. That night the Marlins in a rare offensive outburst outslugged Richmond, 10 to 7. Although Church claimed not to be superstitious, he left the hat in place as a sign of good luck. That night, Farrell borrowed a pen from Sonny Hirsch. Following the victory, he refused to return the ballpoint, claiming superstition. He continued to use it until the club lost.[213] Whether or not it was an irrational belief, there was some type of magic in the air because the Marlins rattled off seven straight wins, one short of the club record set in 1956, climbing from seventh to fourth place.

Ryan, inspired by the club's recent improved play, made his second major acquisition, a move to shore up the defense and offense by acquiring infielder,[214] Jerry Snyder from the Washington Senators. The 28-year-old Oklahoma native arrived in the nation's capital in 1952 serving as primarily a backup second baseman and shortstop. Although his .230 career batting average was not turning any heads, Snyder was a capable glove man who had a lifetime fielding average of .971.[215]

Pitching continued to be the Marlins strength. Cardwell, in particular, drew the attention of Phillies brass for his fine work as the ace of the Marlins' mound corp. On May 24, the imposing 6'4" left-hander gave up a first-inning grand slam to Jack Phillips and then proceeded to pitch shutout ball the rest of way. In the process, he mowed down 14 Bisons to earn his third win of the season and broke the previous Marlins strikeout record of 13, set by Earl Hunsinger on April 29, 1956, ironically against Buffalo.[216] By July, Cardwell received the call-up from Philadelphia he had been waiting for and departed Miami posting a 12–5 ledger, and 2.34 ERA in 150 innings of work.[217]

On July 13, the Marlins (49–48) elevated themselves over the .500 mark sweeping a pair from Columbus. Warren Hacker, sent down by Philadelphia to replace Cardwell, eased the pain of losing their ace shutting out the Jets in the lid-lifter, 6 to 0. Paige started and finished the 7-inning second game. Although he took pride in his hitting, during this juncture of his career his skill with the lumber had greatly eroded (his lifetime average as a Marlin, .090 in 100 at-bats). Still, he was capable of surprising his opponents (remember the Orange Bowl game) and helped his own cause by laying down a successful bunt on a squeeze play scoring Bert Hamric from third during the 3 to 1 win, his eighth "W" of the season.[218]

Although the Marlins play had improved markedly coming off a slow start, attendance continued to lag. Team officials were blaming the 10–20 start for the declivitous attendance numbers. By the middle of July, team officials reported a marked drop of over 25,000. Despite promotions like "Camera Night," "Family Night," and "Fireworks Night,"[219] several games had drawn crowds of less than 2,000. Ryan had instigated a plan at the beginning of the season to move Saturday home games to afternoons instead of evenings, and allowing 17-year olds (or younger), free admittance. Yet, despite his efforts, it failed to bring in the amount of paying customers he anticipated. Ryan admitted, "Aside from a few hundred paid admissions, we have not gained anything other than the intangible value of giving kids a chance to see baseball without paying admission."[220] Behind the scenes, Storer's enthusiasm about the future of Miami baseball and the establishment of a major league franchise in the future was beginning to wane.

Miami continued to battle in a close race for the final two playoff berths. It boiled down to a three-team race between Columbus, Rochester, and the Marlins. Woody Smith continued to be the peerless team leader on and off the field and was in the midst of his best season with the Fish. On the night of July 17, a researcher with the IL who had taken notice of Smith's play

verified that he had surpassed the record for most consecutive errorless games at the hot corner with 84, breaking the old one held
by Irving Jeffries of Montreal with 56. During the skein, Woody
handled 276 chances.[221] Two nights later, he would extend the
record 85 games before dropping a pop fly that opened the door
to a Havana win at Gran Stadium, 3 to 2. In total, he was flawless
in 283 chances.[222]

The continued hallmark of the Marlins play was the defense
and pitching. By the season's end, they finished tops in the IL in
both categories. On the other side of the coin, the offense continued to be a sore spot and ranking seventh in the league just a
smidgeon ahead of Havana. Miami also had a propensity to lose
one-run games; 30 of their first 68 losses were by a single tally.[223]
By season's end, league-leading Montreal scored 137 more runs
than Miami.[224]

Serving as a further distraction was the ongoing friction between Farrell and Ryan concerning Paige's continuing disregard
for team rules. Satch's repeated failure to show up at the ballpark,
the persistent missing of flights, and his coming and going on
a whim, finally reached its climax. Snyder imparted, "We would
take a plane to various cities. Maybe a couple days later Satch
would show up. I don't know how he'd get there, but he didn't go
with the team. He added, "I don't think he liked airplanes."[225]

The discord between Paige and management reached its apex
on August 2, when Satch charged that the club owed him back
salary and meal money that in turn caused him to miss the outgoing flight to Rochester. Ryan countered by stating that they had
accommodated his star attraction by paying salary advances and
that he did not pay out Paige's meal money because he was not
on the plane.[226]

Paige was on hand to make his start the next night in
Rochester, but was shelled and lasted only six innings in a 5 to 1
loss. On August 5, Ryan announced that he was handing down a
suspension for disregard of team rules and placed the pitcher on
the inactive list.[227] In response, he retorted, "All I want them to do
is pay me what they think they owes me and let me go free." He
followed by requesting his unconditional release so that he could
take his talents elsewhere.[228]

The suspension would have far-reaching consequences.
Although Paige returned to the Marlins, he had made up his mind
that he would not return for another season. Satchel slated to
make an important start against Toronto on the road on August

8, found his replacement, Johnny Gray taking the hill. The former Athletics, Indians, and Phillies hurler exited after five innings of work after giving up five runs, a loss to the Maple Leafs, 5 to 1.[229] During this critical juncture of the season, when every game counts, the loss of the veteran had a significant impact on the final standings.

Ryan later lifted the suspension and stated, "Paige wants to pitch and we think everything will be okay."[230] On August 17, Satch pitched his customary second game of a doubleheader and stifled the visiting Bisons, 6 to 1. He helped his cause by smacking a pair of singles and driving in a run. He had been after Marlins management to provide him with a lighter bat. Afterward, he handed out credit to Bob Usher for his newfound success at the plate. After seeing his teammate crush a homer in the opener of the double dip, the ageless hurler, asked to use his bat for the nightcap. 'I sees him hit that three-run home run in the first game and I sees he has a light bat you can swish around some. I tells him I wants the loan of it when I'm up there battin.'" It was Satchel's only two base hits that year, and victory number ten. It proved to be his last of the season.[231]

Jerry Snyder, who faced some of the best pitchers in the history of the game, including Paige, during his time in the American League, remembered that at this stage, the future Hall-of-Famer had lost some zip on his fastball, but he knew how to pitch and had pinpoint control.

> He usually pitched the second game of a doubleheader. And we'd only play seven-inning games . . . And he'd always give us a good outing. We usually won those games too. I don't know what his record was, but he spotted the ball. He didn't have great stuff, you know like a blazing fastball, but he knew where he was going to throw it. He'd throw a little sinker in on you tight. Then he'd throw a little slider on the outside corner. And a pitch like that I never could hit. But, I never could guess what he was going to throw.[232]

Going into September, the Marlins continued to jockey for the final playoff spot, while Rochester had already secured the third spot. Columbus was coming off a four-game sweep of Havana, while Miami took two of three games on the road from Richmond. The temperamental Farrell, nicknamed "Shaky" by his players because of his nervous mannerisms, blew up in a fit of frustration after hearing of the Sugar Kings poor play. He expressed his aggravation to a Columbus writer saying, "That Havana club blew four straight to Columbus. They handed you four games," said Farrell. His accusation was that essentially Havana laid down for the Jets. The Sugar Kings outscored 34 to 10, raised the suspicions of some baseball people who shared their opinions with the Marlins skipper.[233]

In order for Miami to slip in the back door and grab fourth place they needed to take at least three out of four from Columbus on the road, and hope for the best against Havana to close the season, if they had any hopes of catching the Jets.

In a series-opening doubleheader, Paige was sharp, but his teammates failed to offer any support as the Jets prevailed, 2 to 0. Green pitched the nightcap and kept Miami hopes alive for at least a tie, striking out eleven and earning the complete game win, 8 to 1. Tompkins and Landrum each contributed three hits, and Smith drove in a pair of runs.[234] Miami achieved their goal by taking the final two games of the set by scores of 4 to 3, and 11 to 2. Hacker was sterling in the finale winning his fifth of the year and holding the Jets to five hits while striking out nine.[235]

Miami's precarious situation found them 2½ games behind Columbus. The Jets had four games against Richmond still to play, while Miami came home to face archrival Havana in a three-game stanza. Even if the Marlins swept the series with the Cubans, they needed the Virginians to take three of four to snatch fourth place.

Columbus opened up their series splitting their doubleheader in Richmond dropping the first game, 10 to 6, but squeezing out a win the second game scoring five runs in the ninth and holding on to win, 7 to 6. At the same time, Miami, thanks to a six-run outburst in the third inning, prevailed 7 to 2, getting excellent work out of Bunker who went the distance limiting the Sugar Kings to a pair of runs on two hits.[236]

The next evening saw another fine pitching performance, this time from Dallas Green. The big Delawarean went into the sixth inning stingily giving up one hit before a fit of wildness found him pulled in favor of McCall. With the bases loaded, Windy retired the next two batters and proceeded to close out the 2 to 0 victory.[237] Meanwhile, Columbus came back from an early 4–2 deficit to defeat Richmond, 7 to 4.[238]

A Marlins' win combined with a Jets loss would put Miami into the playoffs. Farrell called on Hacker to bring the prize home. The tall sidearm slinger was no longer the fastball pitcher he once was and now relied more on his slow curve, changeup, and knuckleball to fool opponents. Sometimes the ball boys, or batboys, donned the tools of ignorance and warmed up the pitchers. Young Bill Durney Jr., a chip off the old block, was one of the lucky few who took on the envious duties of trying to catch Hacker and his elusive deliveries.

> I can remember he used to just wear out my left shoulder because his ball moved so much. I thought I was all set to catch the ball and that thing would miss, it would move so much, it would miss my glove and wear out my left shoulder. I had a chest protector on and some shoulder protection. As a four-teen, or fifteen-year-old kid, I wasn't used to seeing that kind of movement on a pitch. This was just during batting practice. He used to wear me out. I remember that.[239]

All the marbles were riding on this last game. In pre-game ceremonies, Woody Smith received two awards, one as the team's most valuable and the other as the most popular player. It was the second consecutive season that the St. Louis native accepted the hardware as voted by the local press.[240]

Hacker ran into trouble early and pulled by Farrell in favor of Mason with the Cubans ahead, 3 to 1. Every inning, announcers Durney and Hirsch kept anxious fans abreast of the status of the Columbus-Richmond game. The Marlins tacked on a run in the seventh but were unable to muster any more support falling short, 3 to 2. Columbus squelched the Fish's last hope when the score came across the loudspeaker that the Vees had coasted to an early 9 to 4 victory sewing up fourth place. A deflated Miami club fought hard until the end and had nothing to hang their heads over. Storer met with the club in the locker room after the loss and congratulated them for their efforts.

The three main contributing factors to the Marlins failures were their inability to win on the road, a poor 32–44 slate, and a 20–33 record in games decided by one-run. Several distractions on the field were harder to measure, but Paige's absence during a critical stretch of the season, and McDermott's antics off the field may have cost a win or two changing the complexion of the playoff race.

Equally disappointing was the Marlins performance at the box office. Final attendance numbers showed 183,681, down 22,075 from the year before.[241] Unfortunately, the final count did not include the nearly 100,000 youths admitted free. Storer reported his losses were between $125,000 and $135,000, a figure that no good businessman would tolerate. Although he held firm to his belief that Miami would respond to a winning club, he later stated in December, "The only way I would think of continuing, would be for the club to break even this next season."[242]

Changes were in order for the offseason. Behind the scenes, Storer was looking for a change of major league affiliation with the hopes that a new influx of talent would change the fortunes of his franchise. "Out with the old, in with the new" triggered the club's biggest change before year's end. Paige's exit from the Magic City was inevitable due to the continuing tension between himself and skipper Farrell and Ryan. Old Satch was not a man to be controlled, and as his history had shown, time and time again when his situation was not to his liking he found another venue that was more hospitable. Surprisingly, the next stop for Paige was not with another club but instead accepting an offer from Hollywood to become an actor. He proclaimed, "it looks like me and baseball is through." The communications magnet announced that he would not be returning to Miami for another season, but instead accepted an offer to play a role in a movie with Robert Mitchum and Julie London filming in Durango, Mexico called *The Wonderful Country*.[243] Paige was optimistic and stepped briskly into a new career that he hoped would bring him success and continued attention. Miami had lost its brightest star, and the baseball scene was never the same again. Yet, another colorful character from the not-so-distant past was about to enter the Magic City stage.

Final Standings

TEAM	W	L	GB
Montreal	90	63	–
Toronto	87	65	2.5
Rochester	77	75	12.5
Columbus	77	77	13.5
Miami	75	78	15
Richmond	71	82	19
Buffalo	69	83	21
Havana	65	88	25

NOTES

1. Miami's Final Chance For Baseball Declared 50–50, *Miami Daily News*, 14 January, 1955, evening ed.: p. 16-A.
2. Harris, Steve. Miami Stadium Offered To City For $950,000, *Miami Daily News*, 16 February, 1955, evening ed.: p. 14-A.
3. Anderson, Norris. Tri-State League Seeks Miami Entry, *Miami Daily News*, 8 February, 1955, evening ed.: p. 13-A.
4. Reidy Rebuffed Again But Will Keep Trying, *Miami Daily News*, 14 February, 1955, p. 10-A.
5. Anderson, Norris. FSL Passes Up Solvent Miami, *Miami Daily News*, 1 April, 1955, p. 13-A.
6. Harris, Steve. Miami Stadium Offered To City For $950,000, *Miami Daily News*, 16 February, 1955, evening ed.: p. 14-A.
7. Anderson, Norris. High Classification Baseball In Miami?, *Miami Daily News*, 16 March, 1955, evening ed.: p. 19-A.
8. Jose Aleman Signs Lease for Stadium, *Miami Daily News*, 2 September, 1955, home ed.: p. 11-A.
9. City Signs Miami Stadium Lease, *Miami Daily News*, 27 October, 1955, final home ed.: p. 3-D.
10. Miami May Get Toledo Berth, *Miami Daily News*, 11 September, 1955, final home ed.: p. 8-C.
11. Anderson, Norris. AAA League Awaits Deal From Miami, *Miami Daily News*, 12 October, 1955, final home ed.: p. 1-D.
12. Anderson, Norris. Winter Loop Seen Killing Summer Ball, *Miami Daily News*, 15 October, 1955, final home ed.: p. 3-B.
13. Anderson, Norris. 'Must Have AAA Baseball', *Miami Daily News*, 3 November, 1955, final home ed.: p. 4-D.
14. Associated Press, Miami Now Makes Bid For IL Club, *Miami Daily News*, 1 December, 1955, home ed.: p. 1-D.
15. Stlouisco.com. Suson Park, retrieved, 5 December, 2017. *https://www.stlouisco.com/Portals/8/docs/Document%20Library/.../SusonHistory.pdf.*
16. Veeck, Bill with Linn, Ed. *Veeck as in Wreck*, Chicago (University of Chicago Press, 1962), p. 311–312.

17. Durkin, Jack. Syracuse Drive to Say in Int Goes 'Over Top', *Sporting News*, 14 December, 1955, p. 14.

18. Burns, Jimmy. Miami Again Disappointed; 'Effort Wasted'-Salomon, *Sporting News*, 14 December 28, 1955, p. 14.

19. Anderson, Norris. Veeck Promises To Run Miami Club For Salomon, *Miami Daily News*, 7 December, 1955, final home ed.: 3-D.

20. Kailer, J.D. Veeck Hails Miami's Entry Into Int as Common-Sense Realignment Move, *Sporting News*, 28 December, 1955, p. 5.

21. Miami Only a Stop on Veeck's Return to Big Time, *Sporting News*, 4 January, 1956, p. 13.

22. Burns, Jimmy. Owners Salomon and Stein Get Veeck as Drum-Beater, *Sporting News*, 28 December, 1955, p. 5.

23. Durkin, Jack. Syracuse Group Files Suit to Restrain Move to Miami, *Sporting News*, 28 December, 1955, final home edition.: p.5.

24. Kritzer, Cy. Int's Now Tabbed 'Millionaire Loop', *Sporting News*, 28 December, 1955, p. 5.

25. Anderson, Norris. Bill Veeck Hits Town, 'Starts Taking Over', *Miami Daily News*, 26 December, 1955, final home ed.: p. 14-A.

26. McLemore, Morris. Stadium Lease May Botch Miami's Baseball Situation, *Miami Daily News*, 29 December, 1955, final home edition.: p. 2-D.

27. Team Name Contest Rules Announced, *Miami Daily News*, 16 January, 1956, home edition.: p. 14-A.

28. Anderson, Norris. Sports Today, *Miami Daily News*, 11 January, 1956, home edition.: p. 3-D.

29. Anderson, Norris. Sports Today, *Miami Daily News*, 15 January, 1956, home edition.: p. 6-D.

30. Anderson, Norris. Club Picks 'Marlins' As Team Nickname, *Miami Daily News*, 22 January, 1956, home edition.: p. 1-B.

31. Anagnost, Tim. Personal interview with author, 9 May, 2010.

32. Nordquist, Helen. Stumpf, Edward "Eddie" retrieved 14 January, 2018 from aagpbl.org/index.cfm by wikipedia.com.

33. Baseball-reference.com. Stumpf managed the 1939 Tarboro Serpents, 1941–42 Janesville Cubs was well as worked in the aforementioned front offices.

34. Anderson, Norris. Phils' Hamey Meets Veeck, *Miami Daily News*, 6 January, 1956, home edition.: p. 13-A.

35. McLemore, Morris. Plans Booming For Ball Club, *Miami Daily News*, 6 January, 1956, home edition.: p. 13-A

36. Anderson, Norris. Will City, Team Agree?, *Miami Daily News*, 17 January, 1956, final edition.: p. 14-A.

37. Burns, Jimmy. Osborn, Phillies' Choice, Named Miami Manager, *Sporting News*, 8 February, 1956, p.32.

38. Ibid.

39. Baseball-reference.com. Osborn's championships came with Vancouver (1942), Macon (1949), Nashville (1950), and Spokane (1953).

40. Golenbock, Peter. *Wrigleyville: A Magical History Tour of the Chicago Cubs* (St. Martins Griffin: New York, 2007) p. 326.

41. Anderson, Norris. Marlins Add Jimmy Fox As Coach, Aid To Kids, *Miami News*, 26 February, 1956, home edition.: p. 2-B.

42. *Sporting News*, 27 June, 1956, p. 34.

43. Anderson, Norris. The Duke's Mixture, *Miami Daily News*, 28 January, 1956, final edition.: 1-B.

44. Stadium Lease Finally Signed, *Miami Daily News*, 14 February, 1956, blue streak edition.: p. 5-A.

45. Plant City Chosen As Camp Site, *Miami Daily News*, 29 January, 1956, home edition.: p. 2-B.

46. Anderson, Norris. Phillies And Marlins 'Happy' With Young Pitching Talent, *Miami Daily News*, 24 February, 1956, final edition.: p. 2-B.
47. Anderson, Norris. Marlins Ready For AAA Ball; Advance Good, *Miami Daily News*, 8 March, 1956, final edition.: 4-D.
48. Anderson, Norris. Spring Of Marlins Impresses Phillies, *Miami Daily News*, 30 March, 1956, home edition.: p. 12-A.
49. McLemore, Morris. Nothing Lacking But Fans, *Miami Daily News*, 18 April, 1956, home edition.: p. D-1.
50. Four Prominent in Old Days of FIL, See Miami's Opener, *Sporting News*, 27 April, 1956, p. 27.
51. Anderson, Norris. Marlins And Veeck Off To Great Start, *Miami Daily News*, 18 April, 1956, home edition.: p. D-1.
52. McLemore, Morris. Nothing Lacking But Fans, *Miami Daily News*, 18 April, 1956, home edition.: p. D-1.
53. Burns, Jimmy. 8,806 at Marlins' Game See Fireworks and Delivery of Satchmo by Helicopter, *Sporting News*, 25 April, 1956, p. 27.
54. Anagnost, Tim. Email correspondence with author, 21 and 22 January, 2018.
55. Johnson, Wilbur. Phone interview with author, 11 March, 2010.
56. Spivey, Donald. *If You Were Only White: The Life of Leroy "Satchel" Paige.* Columbia, MO: University of Missouri Press, 2012, p. 260–261.
57. Veeck, Bill & Linn, Ed. *Veeck As In Wreck: The Autobiography of Bill* Veeck (University of Chicago Press, 2001), p. 188–189.
58. Spring, Jack. Phone interview with author, 16 March, 2010.
59. Clark, Mel. Phone interview with author, 15 March, 2010.
60. Tye, Larry. *Satchel: The Life and Times of an American Legend.* New York: Random House, 2007, p.234.
61. Spring, Jack. Phone interview with author, 16 March, 2010.
62. McLemore, Morris. Nothing Lacking But Fans, *Miami Daily News*, 18 April, 1956, home edition.: p. D-1.
63. Qualters, Tom. Phone interview with author, 5 March, 2010.
64. McLemore, Morris. Nothing Lacking But Fans, *Miami Daily News*, 18 April, 1956, home edition.: p. D-1.
65. Burns, Jimmy. Veeck Proves He's Still Master At Entertaining Baseball Fans, 18 April, 1956, *Miami Herald*, p. 1-D.
66. Anderson, Norris. Marlins And Veeck Off To Great Start, *Miami Daily News*, 18 April, 1956, home edition.: p. D-1.
67. Ribowsky, Mark. *Don't Look Back: Satchel Paige in the Shadows of Baseball*, (Simon & Schuster: New York), p. 309–310. Some reports stated $10,000 plus a percentage of gate receipts.
68. Veeck, Bill & Linn, Ed. *Veeck As In Wreck: The Autobiography of Bill Veeck* (University of Chicago Press, 2001), p. 188–189.
69. Kleinberg, Howard. Marlins Play 7½ Hours Without Finding Hitter, *Miami Daily News*, 23 April, 1956, final edition.: p. 10-A.
70. Spring, Jack. Phone interview with author, 16 March, 2010.
71. Bowman, Bob. Phone interview with author, 22 February, 2010.
72. Anderson, Norris. Marlins Close Home Stand, Go After Seventh Straight, *Miami Daily News*, 30 April, 1956, home edition.: p. 18-A.
73. Anderson, Norris. Marlins Lose Seventh, May Get Phils Owens, *Miami Daily News*, 11 May, 1956, final edition.: p. 13-A.
74. Baseball-reference.com. Abrams played with Brooklyn (1949–52), Cincinnati (1952), Pittsburgh (1953–54), Baltimore (1954–55), and Chicago AL (1956).
75. Anderson, Norris. Marlins Overpower Buffalo, Move Into Tie For Fourth, *Miami Daily News*, 10 June, 1956, final edition.: p. 1-B.
76. *Sporting News*, 20 June, 1956, p. 28.

77. Anderson, Norris. Marlins Hope To End 'Great Northern Jinx', *Miami Daily News*, 11 June, 1956, final edition.: p. 15-A.
78. McLemore, Morris. Owens IL Strikeout King Of 1955 Sent To Marlins, *Miami Daily News*, 6 July, 1956, final edition.: p. 14-A.
79. Clark, Mel. Phone interview with author, 15 March, 2010.
80. Anderson, Norris. Scantlebury Faces Farrell, Miami-Havana Series Ends, *Miami Daily News*, 12 July, 1956, home edition.: p. 2-D.
81. Paige, 48, Beats Marrero 41, Pitching Duel, 1 to 0. *Sporting News*, 18 July, 1956, p. 34.
82. Satchelpaige.com, retrieved 2 March, 2018.
83. McLemore, Morris. Worst Over For Marlins, Play At Columbus Tonight, *Miami Daily News*, 6 July, 1956, home edition.: p. 14-A.
84. Anderson, Norris. Miami, Senators Trade 7 Players, *Miami Daily News*, 8 July, 1956, final edition.: p. 1-B.
85. McLemore, Morris. Owens IL Strikeout King Of 1955 Sent To Marlins, *Miami Daily News*, 6 July, 1956, final edition.: p. 14-A.
86. Sporting News, 30 May, 1956, p. 38.
87. Sporting News, 8 August, 1956, p. 28.
88. Ibid.
89. Ibid.
90. Anderson, Norris. Marlins Dunk Leaders, Tackle Royals Tonight, *Miami Daily News*, 27 July, 1956, home edition.: p. 9-A.
91. Anderson, Norris. Marlins Play Doubleheader With Buffalo, *Miami News*, 31 July, 1956, home edition." p. 8-A.
92. Spring, Jack. Phone interview with author, 16 March, 2010.
93. Anderson, Norris. Extravaganza (And Baseball) May Draw Record Attendance, *Miami Daily News,* 7 August, 1956, home edition.: p. 11-A.
94. Paige, Leroy Satchel (as told to David Lipman), *Maybe I'll Pitch Forever*, (Lincoln: University of Nebraska Press, 1993) p. 271–272.
95. Baseball-reference.com
96. Anderson, Norris. Extravaganza (And Baseball) May Draw Record Attendance, *Miami Daily News,* 7 August, 1956, home edition.: p. 11-A.
97. Ibid.
98. Anagnost, Tim. Personal interview with author, 9 May, 2010.
99. Anderson, Norris. Extravaganza (And Baseball) May Draw Record Attendance, *Miami Daily News*, 7 August, 1956, home edition.: p. 13-A.
100. Ibid.
101. Kuzava, Bob. Phone interview with author, 15 May, 2010.
102. Anderson, Norris. Extravaganza (And Baseball) May Draw Record Attendance, *Miami Daily News*, 7 August, 1956, home edition.: p. 13-A.
103. Burns, Jimmy. Marlins Set 57,713 Gate High at Orange Bowl Show, *Sporting News*, 15 August, 1956, p.17.
104. *Associated Press*, Jersey City Sells 61,640 Tickets For Loop Opener, *Courier-News*, 18 April, 1941, p.15.
105. Qualters, Tom. Phone interview with author, 5 March, 2010.
106. Spring, Jack. Phone interview with author, 16 March, 2010.
107. Johnson, Wilbur. Phone interview with author, 11 March, 2010.
108. Qualters, Tom. Phone interview with author, 5 March, 2010.
109. Anagnost, Tim. Personal interview with author, 9 May, 2010.
110. Fitzgerald, Tommy. Cutup Farrell Slices Baseball's Baloney, *Miami Daily News*, 6 June, 1963, metropolitan edition.: p. 4-D.
111. Bonafede, Dom. Was Jim Owens Hurt In Fight?, *Miami Daily News*, 9 August, 1956, final edition.: p. 1-A.
112. McLemore, Morris. Owens Hospitalized Following 'Argument', *Miami Daily News*, 9 August, 1956, final edition.: p. 2-D.

113. Ibid.
114. Jim Owens To Pitch For Miami Saturday, *Miami Daily News*, 10 August, 1956, final edition.: p. 12-A.
115. Qualters, Tom. Phone interview with author, 5 March, 2010.
116. Anderson, Norris. Marlins Sink Again, 2–1, Held To Just Three Hits, *Miami Daily News*, 12 August, 1956, final edition.: p. 1-B.
117. Baseball-reference.com
118. Anderson, Norris. Marlin Officials Mapping Plans For 1957 Season, *Miami Daily News*, 17 September, 1956, home edition.: p. 10-A.
119. Baseball-reference.com.
120. Bingham, Walter. The Dalton Gang Rides Again, *Sports Illustrated*, 13 June, 1960.
121. Veeck, Bill & Linn, Ed. *Veeck As In Wreck: The Autobiography of Bill* Veeck (University of Chicago Press, 2001), p. 311–312.
122. Burns, Jimmy. Marlins Sold to Storer in Speedy Deal, *Sporting News*, 19 December, 1956, p. 28.
123. Stirling, Christopher H, O'Dell, Cary & Keith, Michael. *Biographical Dictionary of American Radio* (New York: Routledge-Taylor & Francis Group, 2011), p. 366–367.
124. Anderson, Norris. Marlins Sign Bill Durney; Title Unsure, *Miami Daily News*, 9 January, 1957, final edition.: p. 2-D.
125. McLemore, Morris. A New Complexion, *Miami Daily News*, 15 March, 1957, final edition.: p. 8-A.
126. Burns, Jimmy. Satchel Checks on Snake Oil; He's All Set for Spring Drills, *Sporting News*, 13 March, 1957, p. 36.
127. Paige, Leroy Satchel (as told to David Lipman. *Maybe I'll Pitch Forever*, (Lincoln: University of Nebraska Press, 1993) p. 97.
128. Qualters, Tom. Phone interview with author, 5 March, 2010.
129. Anderson, Norris. Marlins Much Improved, *Miami Sunday News*, 14 April, 1957, home edition.: p. 6-B.
130. Burns, Jimmy. Leafs, Champions of '56, Again Int Team to Beat, *Sporting News*, 13 February, 1957, p. 28.
131. Ibid.
132. Sporting News Official Baseball Guide, 1957, (Spink, C. & Taylor J.G.: St.Louis, MO). Eastern League statistics.
133. Baseball-reference.com.
134. Hunsinger, Earl. Phone interview with author 15 March, 2010.
135. Ibid.
136. Hernon, Jack. Cubs Pitcher Trims Bucs on No-Hitter, *Pittsburgh Post-Gazette*, 13 May, 1955, p.22.
137. Burns, Jimmy. Sieler Whips Up Spectacular' At Marlin Opener, *Sporting News*, 24 April, 1957 p. 27.
138. Anderson, Norris. Marlins, Leafs Try Again Tonight After 5-Hour Try, *Miami Daily News*, 18 April, 1957, home edition.: p. 18-A & p. 19-A.
139. Ibid.
140. Bobby Young To Join Club On Road Trip, *Miami Daily News*, 9 May, 1957, final edition.: p. 5-D.
141. Miami Gets Church On Club Option, *Miami Daily News*, 12 June, 1957, final edition.: p. 15-A.
142. McLemore, Morris. Miami Closes Toronto Series, *Miami Daily News*, 13 June, 1957, final edition.: p. 4-D.
143. Marlins Buy Another Former Big-Leaguer, *Miami Daily News*, 13 June, 1957, final edition.: p. 4-D.
144. Baseball-reference.com.
145. Herzog, Whitey. Phone interview with author, 18 August, 2014.

146. Bunker, Richard. Personal interview with author, 15 January, 2011.
147. Marlins Get Rogovin From Phils, *Miami Daily News*, 1 July, 1957, blue streak edition.: p. 1-A.
148. Miami Buys Stu Locklin .310 Hitter, *Miami Daily News*, 3 July, 1957, home edition.: p. 10-A.
149. Marlins Buy Star Lefty, *Miami Daily News*, 19 July, 1957, final edition.: 1-B.
150. Miami Drills Today, Seek More Base Hits, *Miami Daily News*, home edition.: p. 8-A.
151. Anderson, Norris. 3rd Marlin Rally Nips Red Wings 12–9, *Miami Daily News*, 4 August, 1957, final edition.: p. 1-B.
152. Anderson, Norris. Osborn To Start Satchel Against Montreal Tonight, *Miami Daily News*, 14 August, 1957, home edition.: p. 3-D.
153. Tompkins, Ben. Phone interview with author, 2 March, 2010.
154. Anderson, Norris. Osborn To Start Satchel Against Montreal Tonight, *Miami Daily News*, 14 August, 1957, home edition.: p. 3-D.
155. Ibid.
156. Anderson, Norris. Marlins Miss Another Chance, *Miami Daily News*, 15 August, 1957, home edition.: p. 3-D.
157. Anderson, Norris. Marlins Lose In 14, League Play Stops For All-Star Game, *Miami Daily News,* 19 August, 1957, final edition.: p. 11-A.
158. Ibid.
159. Baseball-reference.com. Pitchers who appeared in the All-star game were Jim Coates (Richmond), Jackie Collum (Montreal), Miguel "Mike" Cuellar (Havana), and Lynn Lovenguth (Rochester).
160. Anderson, Norris. Marlins Facing Havana In Season's Final Set, *Miami Daily News*, 2 September, 1957, final edition.: p. 19-A.
161. Anderson, Norris. Osborn Names Pitchers For Remainder Of Year, *Miami Daily News*, 3 September, 1957, final edition.: p. 13-A.
162. Ibid.
163. Bunker, Richard. Personal interview with author, 15 January, 2011.
164. Anderson, Norris. Osborn Names Pitchers For Remainder Of Year, *Miami Daily News*, 3 September, 1957, final edition.: p. 13-A.
165. Anderson, Norris. Ray Semproch To Pitch Home Finale For Miami, *Miami Daily News*, 4 September, 1957, final edition.: 2-D.
166. Anderson, Norris. Marlins Head For Havana And Final Set Of Season, *Miami Daily News*, 5 September, 1957, home edition.: p. 20-A.
167. Womach, Graham. Pat Scantlebury, The Ancient Rookie, Retrieved 1 March, 2018 from nationalpastimemuseum.com/article/pat-scantlebury-ancient-rookie.
168. McLemore, Morris. Ol' Satch Elected To Pull Marlins Back To Fourth Place, *Miami Daily News,* 6 September, 1957, home edition.: p. 9-A.
169. McLemore, Morris. Marlins Cling To Fourth, Seeking Clincher Tonight, *Miami Daily News*, 7 September, 1957, final edition.: p. 1-B.
170. Ibid.
171. McLemore, Morris. Great Finish Put Marlins Fourth, *Miami Daily News*, 8 September, 1957, final edition.: p. 4-B.
172. McLemore, Morris. Marlins Clinch Fourth Place With Victory Over *Cubans*, *Miami Daily News*, final edition.: p. 1-B.
173. Ibid.
174. *Sporting News*, 18 September, 1957, p. 35.
175. Osborn 'Blows Up,' Game Over Firing of Rocket, *Sporting News*, 28 August, 1957, p. 38.
176. *Sporting News*, 18 September, 1957, p. 44.
177. *Sporting News*, 25 September, 1957, p. 36.
178. Anderson, Norris. Marlins Cop 2–1 Lead In IL Playoffs, *Miami Daily News*, 14 September, 1957, home edition.: p. 1-B.

179. *Sporting News*, 25 September, 1957, p. 36.
180. Anderson, Norris. Bunker Tries For Clincher Tonight, *Miami Daily News*, 17 September, 1957, home edition.: p. 14-A.
181. Ibid.
182. Anderson, Norris. Paige Pitches As Marlins Begin Series With Buffalo, *Miami Daily News*, 18 September, 1957, final edition.: p. 2-D.
183. Semproch, Ray. Phone interview with author, 11 April, 2010.
184. Anagnost, Tim. Personal interview with author, 9 May, 2010.
185. Spring, Jack. Phone interview with author, 16 March, 2010.
186. *Sporting News*, 25 September, 1957, p. 36.
187. *Sporting News*, 2 October, 1957, p. 54.
188. Semproch, Ray. Phone interview with author, 11 April, 2010.
189. Baseball-reference.com.
190. Baseball-reference.com.
191. Qualters, Tom. Phone interview with author, 5 March, 2010.
192. Anderson, Norris. *Stadium Gets New Boss Friday*, *Miami Daily News*, 3 September, 1957, home edition.: p. 1-D.
193. Bisons, 385,620 Draw Tops Minors, Int Gate Up 121,000, *Sporting News*, 25 September, 1957, p. 36.
194. Roberts, Jack W. Aleman Calls Batista Crux Of Difficulty, *Miami Sunday News*, 9 June, 1957, final edition.: 1-A.
195. Shag Gives Marlins Until Jan. 22 to Find Ball Park, *Sporting News*, 8 January, 1958, p. 16.
196. Storer's $40,000 Lease Bid For Miami Stadium Refused, *Sporting News*, 15 January, 1958, p.24.
197. Anderson, Norris. Marlins To Leave Miami As County Turns Down Plan To Lease Stadium, *Miami News*, 19 January, 1958, final home edition.: p. 1-C.
198. Burns, Jimmy. City Official's Pride In Miami Saves Marlins, *Sporting News*, 29 January, 1958, p. 9.
199. Anderson, Norris. Storer 'Tickled Pink' Over Deal, *Miami News*, 20 January, 1958, metropolitan edition.: 1-C.
200. Burns, Jimmy. City Official's Pride In Miami Saves Marlins, *Sporting News*, 29 January, 1958, p. 9.
201. Burns, Jimmy. Satch to Report to Marlins Early-Wants to See Circus, *Sporting News*, 12 February, 1958, p. 28.
202. Don Osborn Ousted As Marlins Manager, *Miami Sunday News*, 20 October, 1957,home edition.: p. 1-B.
203. Baseball-reference.com. Farrell is also listed as playing for Jackson in 1932, but according to an interview conducted by Morris McLemore of the Miami News, 10 December, 1957, p. 2-C Farrell stated, "The book says I played at Jackson, Mississippi, in the Cotton States League that year. Never did. I was at Vicksburg and the team busted up and some of the players went to Jackson but not me."
204. Marlins Set For Opener, *Miami News*, 15 April, 1958, metropolitan edition.: p. 1-C
205. Hopke, Fred. Phone interview with author, 20 February, 2011.
206. Ibid.
207. McLemore, Morris. Strength Where It's Needed, *Miami News*, 16 April, 1958, metropolitan edition.: p. 1-D.
208. Kelly, Bella. Satch Sentenced To Win, *Miami News*, 24 April, 1958, metropolitan edition.: p. 1-A.
209. Burns, Jimmy, McDermott Hope to Bat Way Back to Majors With Miami, *Sporting News*, 31 May, 1958, p. 32.
210. Mickey McDermott And Mr. Hyde, *Miami News*, 22 August, 1958, metropolitan edition.: p. 1-C.

211. McDermott, Mickey with Eisenberg, Howard. *A Funny Thing Happened on the Way to Cooperstown* (Chicago: Triumph Books: 2003), p.236.

212. Durney Jr., Bill. Phone interview with author, 21 December, 2010.

213. Marlins Win Seven In Row, One Short of Club Record, *Sporting News*, 28 May, 1958, p. 31.

214. Kritzer, Cy. Help From Majors Scrambles Picture, *Sporting News*, 21 May, 1958, p. 31.

215. Baseball-reference.com

216. Anderson, Norris. Miami Bats Ring Out 8–4 Win, *Miami News*, 25 May, 1958, final edition.: 1-C.

217. Two Straight Shutouts Speed Cardwell's Recall by Phils, *Sporting News*, 16 July, 1958, p. 33.

218. Anderson, Norris. Miami After 3rd Place, Faces Vees, *Miami News*, 14 July, 1958, metropolitan edition.: p. 1-C.

219. *Sporting News*, p. 36.

220. Burns, Jimmy. Saturday Sun Tilts at Miami Drawing Kids, *Sporting News*, p. 16.

221. Anderson, Norris. *Smith's I.L. Fielding Record Verified*, *Miami News*, 18 July, 1958, metropolitan edition.: p. 1-C.

222. Boots Snaps Smith's Record Fielding Skein, Beats Miami, *Sporting News*, p. 30.

223. *Sporting News*, p. 38.

224. Baseball-reference.com.

225. Snyder, Jerry. Phone interview with author, 23 August, 2014.

226. Burns, Jimmy. Paige Suspended by Miami to Climax a Hectic Interlude, *Sporting News*, p. 36.

227. Ibid.

228. Fitzgerald, Tommy. Paige Asks Release, *Miami News*, 5 August, 1958, metropolitan edition.: p. 1-C.

229. *Sporting News*, p. 30.

230. Burns, Jimmy. Paige's Suspension Lifted, Old Satch Rejoins Marlins, *Sporting News*, p. 36.

231. Anderson, Norris. Paige, Usher Parlay 1 Bat, Whip Bisons, *Miami News*, 18 August, 1958, metropolitan edition.: p. 1-C.

232. Snyder, Jerry. Phone interview with author, 23 August, 2014.

233. Flora, Earl. Farrell Fined $300 by Trautman for Saying Kings 'Tossed Series', *Sporting News*, 10 September, 1958, p. 29.

234. Marlins Split, End In Sight?, *Miami News*, 2, September, 1959, metropolitan edition.: p. 4-C.

235. Marlins Still Alive, *Miami News*, 4 September, 1958, metropolitan edition.: p. 1-C.

236. Anderson, Norris. Marlins In 'Must' Game, *Miami News*, 6 September, 1958, metropolitan edition.: p. 1-B.

237. Anderson, Norris. Who Said Marlins Are Dead? Pressure's On Columbus Now!, *Miami News*, 7 September, 1958, late sports edition.: p. 1-C.

238. *Sporting News*, 17 September, 1958, p. 38.

239. Durney Jr., Bill. Phone interview with author, 21 December, 2010.

240. *Sporting News*, 17 September, 1958, p. 38

241. Burns, Jimmy. *Storer*, Marlins' Boss, Wants Club in Third Major, *Sporting News*, 17 September, 1958, p.40.

242. Burns, Jimmy. Miami's Storer Seeking Exit in Red Ink Deluge, *Sporting News*, 17 December, 1958, p. 21.

243. Is Satch Through? *Special to the Miami News*, 16 December, 1958, racing edition.: p. 3-C.

CHAPTER TEN

A NEW BIRD IN TOWN

The citizens of the United States, and those especially in Miami, turned their eyes south with nervous curiosity as a new leader emerged on the world stage. The charismatic (as the press described him), bearded Fidel Castro and his revolutionaries wrestled power from Cuban President Fulgencio Batista. The country's former leader fled Havana as armed olive drabbed clad rebels and pro-Castro supporters flooded the streets in celebration. Miamians were unsure of what their future held as the threat of a missile strike from the south came to the forefront, and a host of Cuban refugees' streamed into the city escaping a country soon mired in political oppression.

On the baseball diamond, another leader is dethroned. Perennial pennant winners New York Yankees watch as the "Go-Go Sox" from Chicago steal the bases and hearts of Americans. Overseen by the creative mind of owner Bill Veeck, his club snatches the American League pennant, only later defeated by the Los Angeles Dodgers in the World Series. The following year order is restored in the baseball universe and the Yankees return to prominence winning the AL pennant, only to find the upstart Pittsburgh Pirates upsetting them in the 1960 World Series.

Bobby Darin's, *Mack the Knife*, and *Dream Lover* filled the airwaves, and westerns like *Bonanza*, *The Rifleman,* and *Wagon Train* entertain audiences on the television. A new decade is around the corner and as Americans warm up to the good times, meanwhile, the heightened threat of an escalating "Cold War," conveys a chilling message.

The landscape of Miami is changing in step with the country, not only physically, but also culturally. Baseball is taking a back seat to political conflicts to the south and the distractions that only this beautiful city can offer.

1959

Imperturbable owner George Storer made it clear that 1959 was the "make it or break it" year with the Marlins as their franchise owner. If the team could not show financial viability, then the communications magnate would put the club up for sale. Over the past three seasons, he had been more than patient while experiencing losses amounting to $282,500 over that period.[1]

Part of Storer's perseverance was his staunch belief in Miami as a feasible baseball market capable of supporting a major league team. In 1956, Storer, who held the broadcasting rights to Detroit Tigers baseball games, was one of several individuals and groups that made bids or showed interest in purchasing the Briggs family-owned franchise. Among others, interested bidders were: a consortium of Bill Veeck-organized investors; actor Clark Gable; and IL Toronto Maple Leafs owner Jack Kent Cooke. The latter went on to acquire the National Hockey League's Los Angeles Kings; National Basketball Association's Los Angeles Lakers, and the National Football League's Washington Redskins. All failed in their bids.[2]

A new year brought significant changes to the Marlins on and off the field, the first being the change of their major league affiliation. Miami and the Philadelphia Phillies mutually agreed to break their ties, and the Phillies management established a new working agreement with Buffalo of the International League. Originally, Storer and GM Joe Ryan planned to act as an independent team within the same league, but soon reconsidered that decision and arranged a new working relationship with the Baltimore Orioles. Ryan also established loose ties with the Detroit Tigers and Washington Senators in order to acquire additional talent. The Marlins were one of two Triple-A affiliates of the parent club, the other being the Vancouver Mounties of the Pacific Coast League. It was the beginning of an "on and off" relationship between Miami and Baltimore that would span the next 32 years including the Birds' calling Miami their spring training home.[3 4]

Ryan, with Storer's blessing, named a new manager to replace Kerby Farrell. Hoping to revive diminishing fan support the club announced the return of the passionate and flamboyant, John Leonard "Pepper" Martin. The highly popular skipper that captured the hearts of Miami fans while managing the Sun Sox and Flamingos of the Florida International League was elated over the opportunity to return to the Magic City. "I'm happy to be back in my old haunts," exclaimed Martin. The "Wild Horse of the Osage" made it known he hoped that his managerial experience would lead him to a big league coaching position.[5]

Prior to spring training, Ryan worked hard always looking for ways to stimulate fan interest in the Marlins. In addition, he organized the Gold Coast Grapefruit League featuring four other upper-level minor league teams in the area competing against each other. The circuit included the Dallas Rangers (Pompano Beach) and Indianapolis Indians (Hollywood) of the American Association, as well as the Memphis Chicks (Fort Lauderdale) from the Southern Association.

Martin and his assistant coach Bill Cates greeted several returning players reporting to camp, and due to the change of organization, there were also a host of new faces. Cates, a Key West Conch, previously served as Pepper's right-hand man during their FIL years together. To serve as pitching coach, Martin added Lloyd "Gimpy" Brown. A veteran of 12 major league seasons, long-time Miami resident, and a member of the 1946 Sun Sox.[6] Heading up the list of familiar mugs was John "The Quiet Man" Anderson (P), Johnny Bucha (C), Bert Hamric (OF), Windy McCall (P), Mickey McDermott (P), Jerry Snyder (IF), and fan-favorite, Woody Smith (3B). Among the list of newcomers were highly-touted prospects such as pitcher Artie Kay (18–12, 3.75, 180 IP), and outfielder, Chuck "Snuffy" Oertel (.313, 5, 51) from Louisville of the American Association, Jim Archer (14–18, 3.54, 244 IP), from San Antonio of the Double-A Texas League, outfielder/third baseman, Leo Burke (.307, 17, 71), Knoxville Class A Sally League who also batted .455 in 11 at-bats in a brief trial with the Orioles, and making the biggest jump was fleet-footed pasture-worker Fred "Squeaky" Valentine (.319, 16, 55, 27 SB), Wilson Class B Carolina League.[7]

Archer, in particular, was an intriguing addition. Known for his control, he was your typical pitch-to-contact hurler who handed out free passes like Jack Benny handed out dollar bills. He learned his craft at an early age growing up in Max Meadows, Virginia. A childhood game led to achieving a major league dream.

Well, I started out, I guess, when I started walking. It seemed like I always had a baseball in my hand . . . I was born and raised in a little country town in a four-room house . . . We had a well, and we drew our water from the well. That well was on a concrete slab, and the concrete slab it was 8 x 10 square. It was about 8–10 inches on one end and I used to throw the baseball up in there and pretend that I was pitching. I could throw where I could get a groundball back, and I could throw it where I could get a fly ball. That's the way I played back and forth until I wore the cover off the baseball, then I would tape it with black tape.[8]

On April 13, the Marlins formally announced the release of 52-year-old Satchel Paige. In a typical Ryan move, he then signed another veteran hurler, Virgil "Fire" Trucks who was just shy of his 42nd birthday. Trucks made a name for himself as a frontline starter with the Tigers from the mid-1940s until 1952, later toiling for the St. Louis Browns, Chicago White Sox, Kansas City Athletics, and New York Yankees compiling a 177–135 lifetime mark.[9] Despite the high hopes Ryan had for Trucks, this old-timer would not work out nearly as well. His season, and professional career ended by June due to disciplinary problems and a 10-day suspension related to missing a team flight.[10] He appeared in four games and worked only seven innings.[11][12]

Martin announced 34-year old veteran right-hander Harry Byrd, as his opening night starter at Miami Stadium. He would go up against the defending IL champions, Montreal Royals. The former American League rookie-of-the-year winner who had struggled mightily since going 15–15 with the Philadelphia Athletics in 1952 was hoping to regain some of his past form and earn a ticket back to the big leagues. He had last pitched in the majors for the Detroit Tigers in 1957 going 4–3 with 3.36 ERA posting 51 innings.[13]

On an unusually chilly night in Miami, a disappointing crowd of 3,504 turned out to greet the Marlins new addition. Fans were met with unusually cold weather, but warm feelings abounded when the club honored Woody Smith in pre-game festivities. With teammates and ownership at his side, Smith received his second consecutive "Rawlings Silver Glove Award"; the trophy bestowed for the best at his position in the minor leagues. In attendance was

Storer, although happy for Smith, he was less than pleased by the show of fan support for opening day. Around the IL, Columbus (14,138), Havana (14,106), and Buffalo (7,116) all drew more than double what Miami attracted. The excuse that cold weather kept fans away could not be justified as Columbus reported game temperatures at 56 degrees, two degrees below Miami, yet still nearly sold out their home opener. Nevertheless, in a 14-inning marathon, the Marlins persevered, 7 to 6, thanks to Billy Davidson's sacrifice fly that scored pinch runner Rolf Scheel and excellent relief work from Mickey McDermott who collected the "W".[14]

Early season results had the Marlins charging quickly out of the gate and by May 14, they stood at 19–11 in first place. However, the injury list was becoming a cause for concern. Veterans Loren Babe (torn Achilles tendon and removal of calcium from his heel), McDermott (pulled muscle), McCall (sore arm), Trucks (back trouble), and Snyder (torn ligament) missed significant playing time.[15] Furthermore, shortstop Castleman was playing on bad knees, and Johnny Bucha, suffering from various nagging injuries, began sharing time with Steve Korcheck on loan from the Washington Senators.

Jerry Snyder remembered the sad case of long-time minor league star Loren Babe, who appeared briefly with the Yankees in 1952 and 1953 before landing a regular spot with the Athletics that same season. He lasted only two seasons in the big leagues but had a productive 15-year career mostly in the high minors. Like many of his fellow ballplayers, his body was subjected to much abuse over the course of years. Players in the bush leagues faced many behind-the-scenes difficulties that fans did not see. Nevertheless, it was very much a reality for them.

> One sad story . . . He tore his Achilles tendon and he was flat broke. I think I loaned him twenty dollars or something. But hell, I was flat broke too. You know in spring training you never would hardly have enough money to make it through until your first check . . . Anyway, I talked to Storer and said, "Look, you got a lot of money. Help this guy." I didn't say it like that, but he should help him because he had been with us earlier, and I think he did finally. At least he could get home because he had to retire. It was that bad. And you tear your Achilles then, and you were through usually. That's one of the sad times. That's how tough it was if you really wanted to play

ball, and you had to make as much money working in a packing house.[16]

Forced to fill the gaps left by injuries, Ryan purchased the contracts of first sacker, Norm Zauchin and 30-year-old right-sider,
Vito Valentinetti from the Washington Senators. It was a part of
the continued commitment by Storer to field a competitive club.[17]

Miami's hopes were that Zauchin, a Michigan native who
made a splash in his second year in the big leagues in 1955 with
the Boston Red Sox when he slugged 27 home runs and drove
in 93 runs, would do the same in Marlins' togs. Since his breakout year, Norm found himself relegated to bench duty after the
Sox acquired Mickey Vernon. Traded to the Senators in 1958, he
failed to produce to the Nats' expectations in his two seasons and
was unable to earn a regular spot in their lineup.[18]

In Valentinetti's case, he brought with him five years of major
league experience used mostly as a relief pitcher. He appeared in
one game with the White Sox in 1954 and returned to the majors
in 1956 with the Chicago Cubs for a pair of campaigns. He also
toiled in Cleveland, Detroit and Washington putting together a
13–14 ledger and 4.73 ERA.[19]

Fueling the success of the Marlins was the top-flight pitching
of John Anderson and Jack "Fat Jack" Fisher. Anderson (4–1,
1.55), and Fisher (6–0, 1.83) combined for over half the club's
wins. Byrd was proving to be a consistent innings eater, and
Archer was emerging as an effective starter. Although most of
the players on offense were struggling, Castleman was proving a
stalwart in the order, placing third in the league in batting average at .336, and Smith was close behind with a .326 average, 8
round-trippers, and a league-leading 36 RBIs.[20]

Fisher was catching the collective eyes of the Orioles brass,
and it was not for his trumpet playing that he sometimes pulled
out to entertain his teammates, but his dominant chucking of
the horsehide sphere. Coming off a season in Class B Wilson of
the Carolina League in which he fashioned a 14–11 record, in his
first seven appearances with the "Fish" he posted a perfect 6–0
record, hurling 61 innings, and stingily allowing 15 earned runs.
Bill Durney remarked on the ability of the 20-year-old phenomenon, "Fisher has all the tools."[21] Indeed, by June 22, the Orioles
recalled the fast-baller after he compiled an 8–4 record. What
may have been his most impressive accomplishment though was

marrying his sweetheart Judy Mack only eight days before receiving the good news delivered by Orioles skipper, Paul Richards. Earning the promotion to Baltimore was the icing on the cake.[22]

The promotion of Fisher, along with injuries that sidelined regular contributors, Burke (spike wound), Castleman (knee), and Snyder (hip), profoundly affected the Marlins as they dropped to fourth place. The list of walking wounded became so severe that upon Burke's return, the projected starting outfielder converted to second base under the watchful eye of Martin. Even Woody Smith, who was dealing with his own hand injury, filled in at shortstop briefly for the first time in his career.

In return for Fisher, the Orioles optioned 32-year-old reliever George Zuverink (0–1. 4.15, 13 IP) to Miami. In addition, the team acquired 30-year-old Herb Moford (2–2, 3.38, 32 IP) from Minneapolis of the American Association, a farm club of the Red Sox.[23][24] Oddly, the Marlins did not make a significant move to bolster the offense, nor did the Orioles offer any relief.

Picking up the mantle as the team's ace was John Anderson. The reserved right-hander had a reputation of staying to himself thus earning his nickname, coined by his teammates as, "The Quiet Man." The Phillies had given up on him following the 1958 season, and Miami was quick to sign him outright. Given a chance to pitch regularly, Anderson found the key to his newfound success was his ability to disguise his knuckler using the same motion that he threw his fastball. His skipper Martin was so high on him he pronounced, "After this season it will be acknowledged that the Phillies made their greatest mistake in letting Anderson get away."[25]

Although the Marlins' struggles continued, Pepper stayed as popular as ever with the Miami Stadium faithful. Still a fiery competitor, the passing years had somewhat mellowed the "Wild Horse of the Osage." Those FIL days of attacking umpires and fans were behind him. Bobby Willis, an infielder who came over from the Washington Senators organization remembered his colorful manager and the joy of playing for a baseball icon.

> Well, you know Pepper was a clown . . . You know back in those days we enjoyed playing baseball . . . I think he was somewhere in his mid-60s then. I'm not sure, but he could still, you know, reach his foot up and touch his toes over his head. His steal sign was a wink. He looked at you and winked

and that was his steal signal. He was a, you know, none of the
fancy one-two-three-four-five, whatever signs. He just cupped
his eyes and winked at you. So, you know he was just an en-
joyable person to play around and to play ball with.[26]

At this point in his career, Martin had become more of a "plug
the players into the slots in the lineup" type of manager, versus
a teacher. Zuverink recalled, after hitting the only circuit clout
of his professional career, that Pepper did not miss a photo opportunity if it presented itself.

> He messed around and sat down most of the time. I mean he
> didn't show anybody anything, but he just had the name . . . I
> got a picture when I hit that home run and him congratulating
> me with a big smile. I keep it because he's Pepper Martin.[27]

Valentinetti fondly described Martin entertaining his teammates with many of his crazy antics that he acquired dating back
to his "Gas House Gang Days" in St. Louis.

He was a jolly guy, you know. He rarely got mad and I didn't
see him get angry at anybody. He would go along, kind of a funny
guy, and always playing those tricks with the ball. He used to flip
'em around his back and under his legs and over his head.[28]

It was not that the usually sunny Martin never lost his temper. He did have his moments. Regardless, he always had the
respect of his players. Burke shared a special memory of a time
when his manager exhibited some of his fury in the dugout.

> He always smoked this pipe and I remember we had a big burly
> pitcher who pitched. I think he was with the White Sox, and
> his name was Harry Byrd. Or, was it the Athletics? Well any-
> how, he came to us to pitch, and he pitching a game, and
> he wasn't doing too well . . . Pepper came out and Harry didn't
> want to come out. And he [Byrd] really raised cane . . . He
> [the reliever] came in and while Pepper was greeting the relief
> pitcher Harry went over, and hit that pipe and broke it. After
> the game proceeded, Pepper went to get his pipe and saw that
> it was broken and he became furious. He just, he challenged
> the whole team, if any of you guys are man enough to stand
> up and admit who did it he said, "I'll fight you right here." And
> nobody did, not even Harry."[29]

Martin's celebrity was evident wherever he went, and his popularity had diminished little over the years. Revered not only in the U.S. but also in Cuba, Havana fans flocked to games just to get a glimpse of him. Korcheck recalled how he met a certain dictator through Pepper and they had a memorable evening of baseball talk.

> Of course, fifty-nine, Castro took over, and we went to play Havana that year. I'm going to guess, in about April, maybe even into May. And we stayed at the Havana Hilton which was Fidel Castro's headquarters. And we were checking into the hotel. They had two .50 caliber machine guns at each side of the entryway. And you know, didn't give you a hell of a lot of joy.
>
> But anyhow, after we played the night game, of course, you always played the night game, we got back to the hotel. And Pepper Martin and I just happened to be standing together and he looked over and said, "I believe that is Fidel Castro." And you know he had an entourage with him and he said go talk with him. And at the time I had four years of Spanish and was fairly fluent in Spanish. I graduated in college in fifty-four, so a couple of years went by, but I was still fairly fluent.
>
> Pepper said, "So go over there and see if we can talk to him." I said, "Hell, I don't want to go over there we'll get shot." And anyhow, I finally did and found out immediately that Castro was an absolute baseball fanatic. And so Pepper and I went over there and we talked with him until about 5 o'clock in the morning . . . He just wanted to talk baseball, didn't say anything about the revolution or anything.[30]

Meeting dictators aside, Martin had his hands full with other issues. His main protagonist was the irrepressible, Mickey McDermott that trouble followed wherever he went. On July 17, the Miami Beach police officers pulled him over, this time for running a stop light at a high rate of speed while driving intoxicated. It was the third time they had dealt with McDermott in the past two and a half years. His most recent offenses were refusing to produce identification, and causing a disorderly ruckus at a local bar on the 79th Street Causeway. This incident found him thrown in the "hoosegow" for four hours while he sobered up. Fines for his misdeed totaled $150 for drunk driving, $50 for speeding, and $15 for running the stop light.[31]

Archer related his favorite story about his madcap teammate they sometimes called "Maury" that enjoyed living life on the edge. Despite seen by fans and media as a hard case that experienced a wide range of mood swings, he did show a softer side to his personality.

> Mickey McDermott. I'll never forget this guy. Yeah, he pitched for the Red Sox. And his mother-in-law was related to Bart Riley, a criminal attorney. As a matter-of-fact, Mickey said that he [Riley] was Al Capone's attorney. And I had been in front of his house in Miami Beach but I never, of course, went in . . . This guy [McDermott] was amazing to watch for his age he could throw a baseball. It felt like a brick when you caught it. He just had a very strong arm. He was a character. He was drinking later on in his life and he showed up late for a ball-game in Havana one night and Pepper brought him in and talked to him and Mickey come out and he said, "That's the only person in this world that brought tears to my eyes" He said, "He must be something else, cause I've been a hard-ass all my life and he actually made me cry." He was a character.

McDermott fancied himself a first-rate entertainer. Indeed, blessed with a singing voice that rivaled professional crooners he was not shy about showing off his vocal skills any time or any place. While a member of the Red Sox, he sang in clubs around the league, and during the offseason performed in the Catskills at the peak of his career.[32] One of his favorite spots was Havana where his roommate usually found the room to himself because Mickey sang and partied into all hours of the night at the hotel lounge. Leo Burke witnessed firsthand, more than once, his care-free teammate perform.

> He sang with a group and we were down in Miami, I'm sorry in Havana. And after the team went up to the rooms and then came back down to eat there in the lobby . . . Actually, what had happened is Mickey had been relieved early in the game so he got dressed and went back to the hotel. And when we came back, we were going down there, and as we went down Pepper was getting on the elevator to go up, and he asked us if any of us had seen Mickey. And we said, "No we hadn't." And with that he got off the elevator, I guess, and we continued to

go down, and on the mezzanine floor on the elevator stop, and they had a band playing there, and we heard this guy singing a tune. And that was a song that Mickey used to sing in his group so we knew where Mickey was then.[33]

McDermott's troubles were not isolated to his off the field antics, on the field he continued to struggle. The Marlins plan was to develop the troubled pitcher into a hitter as a first baseman-outfielder while occasionally using him as a spot starter or reliever. As it turned out, the experiment had mixed results. By season's end, his 120 at-bats amounted to a .250 batting average, five home runs, and eight runs batted in. Unfortunately, his pitching worsened and he compiled a sorry record of three wins, 7 losses, and 5.66 ERA while working 71 innings.[34]

The Marlins continued as strong contenders for the pennant through July 14 following Anderson pitching a gem allowing only two hits to the visiting Vees, a complete game whitewashing, 2 to 0. The Miami victory improved their record to 49–43 and teamed with first place Buffalo's, 2 to 1 loss to Montreal left them one game out of the league lead.[35]

What followed next was a disastrous run as Pepper's charges dropped 31 of their next 48 games. By August 27, the team plummeted to seventh place, putting any thought of making the playoffs in serious doubt. Despite the emergence of starting pitchers Anderson (12–8, 2.69), Archer (13–7, 2.94), and relief specialist Artie Kay (6–6, 2.19), the Marlins were unable to overcome their weak offensive attack that produced an average of 3.5 runs per game, and a porous defense that ranked fifth in the IL.[36]

Storer announced the team was swimming in red ink and rumors were flying that the Marlins were considering offers to sell Anderson for $50,000 and possibly the team as a whole. Other speculation held that Storer would hold out one more season and try to sell off the contracts of their assemblage of veteran players including, Bucha, Byrd, Hamric, Smith, Snyder, Bunky Stewart, Jose Valdivieso, Willis, and Zauchin. What was fueling talk was the possible development of a second major league called the Continental League that would directly compete with the AL and NL.[37] Naturally, the new circuit would be looking for players to stock its rosters. Storer had already shown a strong interest in bringing major league baseball to Miami going back to when he purchased the Marlins in 1957.[38]

By the time the annual IL All-Star game rolled around the Marlins were battling to stay out of the league basement. Two Miami representatives, Anderson and Smith, participated in the annual classic against the Pittsburgh Pirates. Both fared well, Smith going one for two driving in a run, while Anderson pitched a scoreless inning. Surprisingly, the IL All-stars dispatched the visiting Pirates in Columbus, 14 to 6.[39]

Showing little chance of making a run at the Shaughnessy playoffs, attendance at Miami Stadium reached a new low. By the end of the season, 173,900 had passed through the turnstiles, a drop of 9,781 from the year before. It was the fourth consecutive year of decreasing gate. The only factor that kept the books from closing in the black was a fund developed by the major leagues for player development that distributed $22,500 to each club and the sale of some of the Marlins players to other clubs. Miami (71–83) finished the season in seventh place only two games in front of Toronto.[40]

Despite the many lowlights of the losing campaign, there were some high points of note. Sportswriters and sportscasters voted Woody Smith (.274, 16, 78), the team's most valuable player; John Anderson (12–9, 2.74), most valuable pitcher; and Fred Valentine (.257, 11, 39, 28 SB), most popular player. Other notable achievements were garnered by Jim Archer who led the club in victories with 13, Artie Kay (7–6, 2.01) third in the IL in ERA, and Foster Castleman (.313 6, 36) who finished third in the batting race.[41]

Disappointed Marlins' fans watched from a distance as Buffalo grabbed the pennant with a roster of players, many who had been with Miami the year before. However, the Bisons fared poorly in the postseason, dropping their opening round series to Richmond four games to one. Third-place Havana, that finished the season with an 80–73 record, handled Richmond in the next round taking the best-of-seven series in six games, then shocked the baseball world stunning the Minneapolis Millers (95–67) of the American Association in the Little World Series in seven games. The finale was settled at Gran Stadium in the Cuban capital.[42]

At the close of the season, Jimmy Burns of the *Miami Herald* predicted that Storer was prepared to give Miami one more chance. Pepper Martin expressed that he would like to return and guide the team again.[43] With the Orioles announcing a full working agreement for the 1960 season, and the use of Miami Stadium for spring training, all indications were that there would be little changing. On the other hand, negotiations carried on behind the scenes, soon brought changes. Al Vincent (a Paul Richards protégé), was named Marlins manager, taking Martin's place for the 1960 season.[44]

Vincent, a disciplinarian and highly regarded teacher, brought with him 15-years of managing experience at the A1 level and above. He enjoyed his greatest successes in the Texas League winning three league championships and one pennant in 12 seasons between Beaumont, Dallas, and Tulsa.[45]

Many a sad face accompanied the departure of the lovable, but fiery Pepper Martin. He was famous for quoting Biblical scripture and showed a paternal love for his players to a fault. Everyone spoke highly of him. To the men in blue, he was a fly in the ointment, yet his down-home nature, love of the game, and willingness to utilize any resource to win, earned him the love and respect of countless fans. Even those who had felt his fiery brimstone wrath, admired him. The Wild Horse of the Osage rode off into the sunset with no regrets and the memories of his exploits still recounted to this day.

Final Standings

TEAM	W	L	GB
Buffalo	89	64	–
Columbus	84	70	5.5
Havana	80	73	9
Richmond	76	78	13.5
Rochester	74	80	15.5
Montreal	72	82	17.5
Miami	71	83	18.5
Toronto	69	85	20.5

1960

From all appearances, George Storer was willing to give the Marlins another year to pan out. Yet subtle clues were emerging behind the scenes that the communication tycoon's commitment of developing Miami into a viable minor league franchise, and ultimately using it as a stepping-stone to bring either major league baseball or a franchise in the proposed Continental Baseball League to the Magic City, was unlikely.

In mid-December of 1959, Storer announced that he submitted a formal application to the National Football League with the intention of bringing professional football to Miami by 1962. Rumors soon followed that his focus had shifted from baseball to the gridiron.[46] Ultimately, just as his bid for ownership of the Detroit Tigers failed, so did his NFL aspirations.

On the evening of January 2, an official statement disclosed that Storer had sold the Miami franchise to retired sportsman and millionaire William "Bill" MacDonald for what was rumored to be between $225,000 and $250,000. The new owner, as generous as he was rotund, made his money in the trucking and mobile home manufacturing business. He then sold off his commercial interests, concentrating on sports-related dalliances. Bill had high hopes for the Marlins.[47 48]

The idea and decision to make a bid for the Marlins was a spontaneous one. During a peaceful evening with his wife, who he nicknamed "Snoozie," and his two daughters (9 and 11 years old), MacDonald thought out loud, "I think I'll buy the Marlins." Snoozie commented, "That's nice." At the same time, his oldest daughter Vickie reacted excitedly saying, "Please, please daddy-please buy the Marlins." MacDonald curiously asked why she was interested and she responded, "Because if you do, we'll be able to sit in the press box. And I can have all the popcorn I want." With that, the next day, MacDonald put the gears in motion, and in short order, found himself the owner of an International League club.[49]

Unlike Storer, MacDonald brought with him experience as an owner of a baseball team. Just three years earlier, he purchased the financially troubled Tampa Tarpons of the Class D Florida State League. Against long odds, he turned the fortunes of the club around through promotions and gimmicks attracting an impressive 85,031 fans through the turnstiles, an almost unheard of number at the time for the lowest level of organized baseball.[50]

Interestingly, the Marlins newest owner held little aspirations of a financial windfall when he said, "I don't think we will make money with the Miami club but I do think we may be able to break even."[51] However, he optimistically added, "An interesting, exciting ball club is the main thing for drawing people and I think we'll have it with our full working agreement with Baltimore which has the best young players in baseball."

For the first time since the establishment of Miami in the International League, the emphasis on a veteran-laden club would take the backseat instead to a youth-oriented roster. Under the watchful eye of field boss Al Vincent, there were three prospects out of Amarillo of the Class AA Texas League (TL), shortstop, Jerry Adair (6, 73, .309), outfielder Angelo Dagres (10, 64, .336), and TL batting champion, Al Nagel (27, 123 .344). Added into the mix, for good measure, was "bonus baby" outfielder Dave Nicholson, signed for $100,000 by the Orioles in 1958, he earned the promotion after bashing 35 home runs and driving in 115 runs at Class C Aberdeen, and right-hander, Wes Stock (6–6, 3.40), along with his teammate fleet-footed Barry Shetrone (10, 30, .293, 74 runs, 12 SB's) transfers from Vancouver.[52]

Vincent had at his disposal the speediest outfield in the IL. Dagres swiped 31 bags as recently as 1957 with Knoxville of the Class A Sally League, Fred Valentine managed 28 with Miami the year before, and Dagres had been timed as one of the swiftest runners in the Orioles organization. Dagres remembers impressing the Orioles brass with a demonstration of his speed.

> But the thing that impressed him at the time was when I went to Baltimore they had me run the 60-yard dash. And I did that in 6.2. And then they timed me going down to first base, and I had to do it after I did the 6.2, Harry Brecheen was at one time the Orioles pitching coach.
>
> Yeah, the Cat. A great guy. He took the watch and showed it to Paul Richards and Paul Richards says [laughing], "You better do that again." So I had to do it again. I did a 6.2 something else. It was 6.2. And finally, I had to go down to first base. And they had me do it. And then I went down on a bunt. And they timed me in 3.25.[53]

Fred Valentine summoned up a memory of his swift of foot teammates that had a reputation for their rapidity on the base paths. Valentine was proud to say he was the fastest.

> There was Angelo Dagres, Barry Shetrone, and myself. We were pretty much noted for speed in the organization. Every spring training, they would have races between us down there, and sure enough, that was the big bet every spring. Before the end of spring training, they had us get together and line us

up and we would run 40-yard three times in a row. Barry was fast, but he just had those long legs and he just couldn't get started [chuckling].[54]

Going into spring training, the returning (over 30) veterans list included Johnny Bucha, Harry Byrd, Foster Castleman, Herb Moford, Woody Smith, Jerry Snyder, Vito Valentinetti, and Norm Zauchin. Only Moford, Smith, and Zauchin would see significant action, the remainder eventually drew their releases, or were dealt or sold during the early part of the campaign.[55]

Conspicuously absent as the team broke camp was Bill Durney. The voice of the Marlins from WGBS, and public relations director extraordinaire, continued to fight health issues relating to his blood pressure and heart. Spending extended time at Mercy Hospital, Durney was unable to listen to the Marlins results on opening day.[56] In Big Bill's stead, Program Director Bob Martin, took over mic duties.

Bill Durney Jr. evoked memories of his father and the issues he had with his health starting at an early age.

> My Dad actually, he had his first heart attack at 49, and had one every year, until he had five of them. The last one took him at fifty-four. Yeah, my Dad was a big man. He was 6'2" and about 315 pounds, ex-Marine, and he was a big, big man. I know he got his weight down to about 280. He cut down on his smoking and everything else, but I can remember him always saying that if he had to go any further than what he was doing he might as well be dead.[57]

Despite the absence of their beloved play-by-play man, under Vincent's stern hand, Miami opened the season against the Buffalo Bisons. A much different atmosphere existed in the Marlins dugout compared to the past years. Tommy Fitzgerald of the *Miami News* summed up the new environment well in his March 19 column when he compared the vibe between Pepper Martin versus the dictator-like Vincent.

> His words, delivered clearly, crisply, unequivocally, and reinforced by steely unwavering blue eyes and a granite expression, left no doubt that Mr. Vincent would be the boss, the whole boss, and nothing but the boss of these Marlins, and

that anybody unwilling to work and to work hard wouldn't be around long. It was inconceivable that any ballplayer would tell this man how to run his ball club.

His clubhouse visitor could not help noting a strikingly dissimilarity between Mr. Vincent and his predecessor, the lovable but trusting and soft-hearted Mr. Pepper Martin.[58]

An expected crowd of over 6,500 failed to materialize. Despite heavy downpours, 4,765 attended the game. It was a disappointment for MacDonald upon receiving the news that over 12,000 turned out in Havana and Columbus, and 5,640 at Richmond despite cold weather for their season lid-lifters.[59] After seven frames, an ominous rainstorm returned and doused the Miami Stadium faithful. Despite the exhortations of Mrs. Snoozie MacDonald, a premature ending came resulting in a 6 to 2 loss at the hands of the herd. Archer, who said his ball was sailing all night, took the loss after allowing six runs in two-plus innings of work.[60]

Mr. MacDonald remained hopeful that the crowds would come. Under his watch with Tampa, the Tarpons attracted 8,531 during a grocery store sponsored game. The ambitious owner boldly predicted that he could draw 20,000 in Miami with the exact same promotion.[61]

On May 19, "Food Fair Night" brought in the biggest crowd at Miami Stadium since July 15, 1956, when a similar promotion night drew 11,836. The final gate count reflected 11,214 passing through the gates. A co-operative giveaway ticket arrangement with the Food Fair grocery chain produced an impressive turnout, but less than McDonald had predicted. Much to the dismay of Marlins' fans, the visiting Vees jumped all over Valentinetti for four runs in the first inning. Bunky Stewart and Kay followed, faring little better than their predecessor did until Dick Luebke came in to hurl two scoreless innings. Nevertheless, Richmond coasted to an easy 14 to 4 victory that left the Marlins (12–16) seven games off the pace in seventh place.[62][63]

That same night the Marlins further purged themselves of veterans, Harry Byrd the first casualty sold off to Portland of the Pacific Coast League.[64] Eight days later, Valentinetti followed his teammate to the Rose City.[65] Although uncertain why the Marlins sent him packing, the second year Marlins hurler felt that the decision boiled down to an incident between him and his skipper, and his choice not to follow orders. Valentinetti remembered.

I went to the ballgame one day and he [Vincent] says, "Come on down, I want to talk to you in the runway." He said, "I want you to throw all fastballs. Don't throw anything but a fastball." I said, "It's senseless. I'm trying to win a ballgame." And he wants me to throw fastballs. . . . a little later in the season, not too long after that incident that he asked me to throw all fastballs, I was traded to Portland, Oregon the furtherest point in the United States from Miami . . . They did, I think, just to stick it to me.

Yeah well, later on, I thought about that and I said, "What the hell." I said, "Maybe I should've done it, you know. Maybe I should have followed his orders and seen what happens. Maybe that's what the front office at Baltimore wanted. They don't want to see my curveball and my slider. They wanted to see if could get anyone with my fastball."[66]

Further troubling was the play of many of the regulars. Nicholson, benched at the end of April, after hitting only .207 to start the season and collecting more whiffs at the plate (13) than hits (6), was at the head of the list of several disappointments.[67] Woody Smith was in the midst of his worst season with the bat since breaking into professional baseball in 1946, joined by regulars, Adair, Burke, and Zauchin all struggling to keep their averages above the "Mendoza Line."

Vincent's early assessment of the play of his club was that his faith was in the younger players. He reiterated, "We need some hitting. The boys have been pressing at the plate." Despite the purge of several veterans, Miami reached out and in a move to try to turn around their fortunes signed free-agent veteran major league fly-chaser extraordinaire, Jim Busby.[68] Known for his speed, and ability to cover significant patches of the outfield, the former Texas Christian University star quarterback broke into the big leagues with the White Sox in 1950. In 1951, he batted .283 and stole 26 bags, but in one of many deals pulled off by Frank "Trader" Lane, Busby surprisingly found himself dealt to the Senators. He had his best seasons in the nation's capital in 1953 (6, 82, .312), and 1954 (7, 80, .298).[69] He never again reached those heights, found himself looking for a job on the open market. Hopes were that Busby's presence and leadership would assist some of the young players.[70]

Misery loves company, and so with it came further bad news on May 28, when the Marlins arguably best hitter, Shetrone, batting .314 at the time, went down with a bad shoulder.[71] Shortly after, Zauchin (illness),[72] Valentine (torn leg muscle) joined the injured reserve list.

The increasing tally of the walking wounded compelled GM Ryan to sign another free agent. He found 29-year-old former Indians and long-time minor leaguer sojourner, outfielder Joe Caffie, who made it to the majors with Cleveland as a part-time outfielder in 1956 and 1957.[73]

Typical with life in the minors, Busby's stay was all too brief. On June 14, the Orioles recalled the swift centerfielder to Baltimore and demoted outfielder, Albie Pearson to Miami.[74] Pearson, only two years removed from winning the rookie-of-the-year award while with the Senators in 1958, arrived in town with quite a bit of fanfare. After his freshman season, batting .275 and scoring 63 runs, he struggled mightily with the bat and at the time of his demotion was only hitting at a .244 clip having appeared in 48 games while making 101 plate appearances.[75] In a unique show of salutation, the diminutive outfielder was awarded a June 21, "Welcome Albie Pearson Day," that was soon thereafter canceled due to an airline strike, which left him stranded elsewhere.[76] The postponement of the festivities appeared emblematic of how the season was playing out; nothing was falling into place as planned.

Despite the added veteran presence of Caffie and Pearson, the team's struggles continued. Losing breeds dissatisfaction and frustrations came to a loggerhead in July when Vincent butted heads with the third-string catcher, Roger McCardell, and outfielder, Angelo Dagres. After McCardell had refused to join the club on a road trip at the end of June, he went to GM Ryan complaining about Vincent giving him enough playing time. "Since you have two other catchers (Dick Brown and Gene Green) my services will not be missed," stated the disgruntled backstop.[77] Ryan later obliged him sending him to Charleston of the American Association for sidearm chucking relief pitcher, Dick Hyde.[78]

Within a few short days after that incident, Vincent confronted Dagres about his lackluster effort on a ball hit to the outfield. It seems he turned a single into a double, and committed an error on the play; part of a 4-run rally by Richmond. The strict manager had approached his outfielder before about his lack of hustle and the latest incident drew his especially hard ire when he later reported, "I just know he's through with this club," said Vincent and asked for Dagres' release. He later issued a one-day suspension, only to have it overturned by Orioles management who made it clear he was to stay on the roster. Dagres, who had recently returned to the club after spending time with his wife and seriously ill son, announced that it was just a misunderstanding.[79]

The Orioles brass was showing increasing discontent with the team's play and the job that Vincent was doing. Tommy Devine wrote in his *Miami News* column about Richards expressing his frustration, "I'm afraid Al's rating, like that of the team, must be put down as disappointing."[80] Fans were in agreement with the evaluation and the general feeling was that Vincent lacked fan appeal compared to his predecessor Martin.

Not only was Orioles management frustrated, so was MacDonald who was losing money at an alarming rate. Saddled with an expensive stadium lease deal that cost $50,000 a year, a poor concessionary income arrangement with the Jacob Brothers, and lagging attendance that most nights pulled in less than 2,500 fans, the optimistic owner's patience was waning. He seriously considered relocating the team outside of Miami.

On June 27, a representative from Puerto Rico accompanied GM Ryan to Toronto for the league meetings setting off rumors of a proposed move of the club to the island. When asked by reporters if the Marlins were planning a move, Ryan responded, "Not necessarily."[81]

Further speculation followed on July 13, when IL president, Frank Shaughnessy called a special meeting of league owners. The increasing unstable conditions in Havana due to the political strife in the capital and the uncertain viability of the Cuban capital's franchise necessitated the team's relocation to Jersey City, New Jersey. In the course of the powwow, MacDonald made it known that he was considering other locations where he might move the Marlins, including Jacksonville and Atlanta.[82]

By the end of July, Miami found itself ensconced in a tie for last place with Columbus 25½ games behind Toronto. Despite the return of Shetrone, the consistent play of Valentine, and the emergence of Gene "The Animal" Green, the Marlins continued to struggle to manufacture runs, landing last in the IL in runs scored.

Ryan was not neglectful of the shortages on his pitching staff. He also made a move on July 17, acquiring on option from the Phillies, 32-year-old right-handed screwball artist Ruben Gomez.[83] The 6'0" native of Puerto Rico came with an impressive resumé including being the second pitcher to reach the majors, and the first to pitch in the World Series, from his country. In 1954, he went 17–9 for the New York Giants and won game three of the Fall Classic against the Cleveland Indians that the Giants went on to sweep. Gomez struggled with the Giants going 9–10, and 7–17 in 1955 and 1956 respectively before bouncing back the following season winning 15 games. At the beginning of 1959, he was dealt to Philadelphia where he struggled to find consistency. Soon after, he was demoted to Buffalo.[84] The Marlins faced him when he pitched for the Bisons and felt that he still had some gas left in his tank. Ryan held hopes Gomez would provide a consistent arm in his rotation.

On August 21, the Marlins finished the evening by splitting a twin bill with the visiting Red Wings. A sparse turnout of 1,953 watched the fish take the opener, 4 to 3 as the once dominating starter John Anderson won his second game of the season in relief against eight losses. In the nightcap, Rochester came from behind, scoring four runs in the final two innings that overcame a three-run home run by Burke in the sixth frame. Just for old times' sake, 40-year-old Luke Easter drove in a pair of runs in the top of the ninth frame that proved to be the difference in a 7 to 5 victory. The loss was Anderson's ninth of the season in a season full of disappointments for the one time ace that just the year before, had teamed with Archer as one of the best one-two punches in the IL.[85]

MacDonald, the "glass is half full" guy, frustrated with another low turnout had seen enough. The usually jovial owner made it known while his team was playing in Jersey City, "I've had it." He added, "Let somebody else take a shot at it." Although stating there was a 50–50 chance of remaining in Miami, it was clear after reporting losses of $132,000, and rumors of a proposed move, that the handwriting was on the wall. "I'd be delighted to sell the franchise if somebody else wanted to give it a try," said MacDonald. He added, "Before moving the franchise, I feel the civic thing to do is give somebody in Miami a chance to keep it here." The proclamation spelled out the beginning of the end of the Marlins as an IL member.[86][87]

The Marlins were playing out the string—a sad ending to a franchise that started out with so much promise. On September

11, the season-ending finale found Miami in Richmond. Rudy Arias, the ex-White Sox southpaw, took the mound against Virginians' own lefty, Ed Dick. Showers dampened the grounds, but not enough to force the cancellation of play. With the score tied at four apiece in the fourth inning, Woody Smith caught an offering that was too good to let pass giving the Marlins a one-run lead, and ultimately the game winner, a 5 to 4 Miami triumph. One inning later, heavy rains forced cancellation of proceedings and closed the books on the 1960 season. It proved to be the last appearance for Smith as a Marlins player. It was a fairytale ending for the Marlins icon. Only the author of flight and fancy could have dreamed-up a more fitting ending for the most beloved player that ever graced the diamond in Miami.[88]

At the season's close, MacDonald reiterated, "If I can't move the team to another city, then I will surrender the franchise to the league.[89] Subsequently, he was working behind the scenes with city officials in San Juan to relocate the team to play in antiquated Sixto Escobar Stadium in anticipation of playing in a new ballpark under construction.[90]

A token offer made by the city of Miami to reduce the yearly lease from $50,000 to $40,000 was no match for the San Juan offer that included an agreement for a stadium rental at $1, and broadcasting rights amounting to approximately $75,000. On November 28, the IL formally announced their approval of the relocation of the Marlins to Puerto Rico. Tommy Devine pointed out that the ultimate failure of the Marlins was squarely on the shoulders of Storer and MacDonald, specifically their yearly wrangling over the lease and uncertainty of the future viability of the franchise to stay in Miami, lack of a solid background in the game's administration, and the slipshod and indifferent direcion they held for the club. What started out with such hope, excitement, and optimism under the watchful eye of Bill Veeck, had deteriorated to harsh feelings and fan apathy.[91]

MacDonald's move ultimately proved to be a disaster. A strong affiliation with the St. Louis Cardinals supplied the team with a cornucopia of top-shelf talent, but the team never ingratiated themselves to the fans of Puerto Rico. Attendance at home games averaged only 1,000, the radio deal to broadcast games fell through, and travel costs were staggering. The situation was so bad that ultimately MacDonald pulled up stakes in mid-season and moved the team to Charleston, West Virginia. By then the financial situation was so bad that the team kept the Marlins' uniforms and the name so that they could save the expense of new togs that would have come with an obvious name change. In a bizarre public relations move, the club retained the same nickname associating them with the Marlin hunting rifle, popular with local hunters.[92]

Despite the season labeled as a bust, several of Miami's players made it back to the big leagues. The most significant were Adair, Pearson, and Valentine. Adair, nicknamed, "Casper the Friendly Ghost" for his pale complexion, played 13 years in the majors and was considered a premier defensive second baseman of his era. He went on to share an American League record for fewest errors in a season (5) by a second baseman joined later by luminaries, Roberto Alomar, and Bobby Grich. The Friendly Ghost's greatest accomplishment as a gloveman consisted of an incredible streak of 89 straight games handling 458 chances without a miscue from July 22, 1964, to May 6, 1965.[93]

Valentine made his mark later with the Senators. Following two years of toiling in the minors, he returned to Baltimore for a short stint in 1963. After that season, the Orioles dealt the swift outfielder to Washington where he flourished under the watchful eye of manager Gil Hodges. During his seven-year stay in the majors, his best seasons came in 1966 when he batted .276 and bashed 16 dingers finishing 21st in the AL MVP voting, and 1967 hitting .234 with 11 homers. During his 15 years as a professional, he played both in the U.S., and overseas in Canada, Honolulu (Hawaii), Vancouver, and one season with the Hanshin Tigers of the Japanese Central League.[94] His two seasons in Miami were among his fondest memories. He reminisced with a "smile" in his voice, and said:

> Oh, I had quite an experience there. It was a wide awakening for me. Particularly that level of baseball, you know. I just enjoyed the city itself. The only thing that stands out more than anything is the heat in Miami. I mean it got hot down there . . . And always enjoyed the trip to Cuba, that's when Cuba was part of the International League.[95]

One of the great stories of a player making his comeback to the big leagues was the tale of the diminutive Albie Pearson. Although Vincent's style as a manager may have rubbed a few of the players the wrong way, on the flipside, Pearson appreciated his skipper's attention. The 5'5", 140 lb. dynamo known for his determination and hustle, had a big heart. Through the extra efforts of Vincent, the joint workouts provided Albie with the opportunity to return to the big leagues for six more seasons. Only later did a bad back derail what would have otherwise been a long career.

> I really, when I say I really, enjoyed my time there. It was a time for me to make a comeback and do some things that second year when I hit two or three something [hit .301]. Yeah, that was a time in Miami when if I recall, that during that time the confidence, and I don't know but I'm sure you've heard the term many times through baseball players, really the key to play well is being confident. And my confidence, after having being Rookie of the Year and quote "sophomore jinx," I had about ten ounces of it. When I went down to Miami my confidence returned and I was able to hit the ball and perform well enough where I felt that I could play any place and so at that time, they wanted me to play.
>
> I know that Paul Richards and Al they were very close. In fact, I played golf with them both. They both loved golf but anyway I remember that they wanted me to begin to work with a Willie Mays basket catch. And I worked in the outfield there in Miami. Rather a strong memory of Miami is of being hit fungoes by Al until my eyes were coming out of my head until I could see out of my back.[96]

With the demise of the Marlins as a member of the IL, so went the hopes of possible consideration as a location for a major league baseball expansion. Eventually, to stave off threats of a proposed third major league named the Continental League (CL), an idea hatched by New York attorney, William Shea to return professional baseball to New York, his vision forced major league baseball to expand from 16 to 20 teams. Miami's name had been bantered as a possible location for the CL, but the failure of the Marlins to establish themselves as a successful franchise put that baby to rest. It would take over thirty years before MLB chose to expand into South Florida.

Minor league baseball would make its comeback by 1962. Meanwhile, hardball devotees were left to enjoy their cherished memories of past diamond heroes. The long-suffering Miami baseball fans were resigned to taking a break from the game they loved; at least for a year. For now, without baseball, they had time to reflect under those alluring, swaying palms. The ones that saw so much history unfold beneath them. Perhaps it was true, absence *does* makes the heart grow fonder.

Final Standings

TEAM	W	L	GB
Toronto	100	54	–
Richmond	82	72	17
Rochester	81	73	19
Buffalo	78	75	21.5
Havana / Jersey City	76	77	23.5
Columbus	69	84	30.5
Miami	65	88	34.5
Montreal	62	92	38

NOTES

1. Burns, Jimmy. Martin Named to Put Pepper Into Miami Ball, *Sporting News*, 24 January, 1959, p. 22.
2. Veeck's in Again As Detroit Bidder, *The News Journal* (Wilmington, Delaware), 29 June, 1956, p. 24.
3. Burns, Jimmy. Miami's Storer Seeking Exit in Red Ink Deluge, *Sporting News*, 17 December, 1958, p. 21.
4. Burns, Jimmy. Martin Named to Put Pepper Into Miami Ball, *Sporting News*, 24 January, 1959, p. 22.
5. Ibid.
6. Different Marlins Play Pair, *Miami News*, 16 April, 1959, racing edition.: p. 1-D.
7. Baseball-reference.com.
8. Archer, Jim. Phone interview with author 21 February, 2010.
9. Marlins Go for 'Youth' Cut Paige 52, Sign Trucks, 40, *Sporting News*, 22 April, 1959, p. 30.
10. O'Neil, Ed. Everything Was So Nice . . . Then The Roof Caved In, *Miami News*, 19 May, 1959, final home edition.: p. 2-C.
11. Deals of the Week, *Sporting News*, 17 June, 1959, p. 36.
12. Baseball-reference.com.
13. Ibid.
14. Owens, Bob. Hurrah For Rolf Scheel! He Wronged, But We Won, *Miami News*, 15 April, 1959, racing edition.: p. 1-C.
15. 3 Ex-big Timers On Disabled List, But Marlins Top Loop, *Sporting News*, 6 May, 1959, p. 27.
16. Snyder, Jerry. Phone interview with author, 23 August, 2014.
17. Burns, Jimmy. Red Hot Marlins Complete first Tour With 8–3 Mark, *Sporting News*, 20 May, 1959, p. 29.

18. Nowlin, Bill. Norm Zauchin, retrieved 5 April, 2018 from https://sabr.org/ bioproj/person/048b1058.
19. Baseball-reference.com.
20. INT AVERAGES, *Sporting News*, 27 May, 1959, p. 31.
21. Burns, Jimmy. Fisher of Marlins Wins First Six on Five-Day System, *Sporting News*, 3 June, 1959, p. 29.
22. Burns, Jimmy. Fisher Gets Wedding Gift-Joins Orioles From Miami, *Sporting News*, 1 July, 1959, p. 29.
23. Ibid.
24. Baseball-reference.com.
25. Burns, Jimmy. Bid at First Base Nixed, Anderson Turned to Mound, *Sporting News*, 29 July, 1959, p. 31.
26. Willis, Bobby. Phone interview with author, 26 August, 2011.
27. Zuverink, George. Phone interview with author, 3 May, 2010.
28. Valentinetti, Vito. Phone interview with author, 24 August, 2011.
29. Burke, Leo. Phone interview with author, 23 August, 2011.
30. Korcheck, Steve. Phone interview with author, 11 April, 2010.
31. Mickey Goes Route - - In Beach Jail, *Miami News*, 17 July, 1959, p. 1-C.
32. McDermott, Mickey with Eisenberg, Howard. *A Funny Thing Happened on the Way to Cooperstown* (Chicago: Triumph Books: 2003), p. 142.
33. Burke, Leo. Phone interview with author, 23 August, 2011.
34. Baseball-reference.com.
35. Fitzgerald, Tommy. If You Can't Beat, Pick 'Em, *Miami News,* 15 July, 1959, metropolitan edition.: p. 2-C.
36. *Sporting News*, 2 September, 1959, pgs. 28 and 36.
37. Burns, Jimmy. Player Sales May Erase Red Ink, Keep Marlins in O.B., *Sporting News*, 2 September, 1959, p. 36.
38. Burns, Jimmy. Marlins' Owner Has No Regrets, Lots of Faith, *Miami Herald*, 21 August, 1957, p. 3-D.
39. Kritzer, Cy. All-Stars Pummel Pirates, 14 to 5, *Sporting News*, 9 September, 1959, p. 31. Actual score was 14–6 and was a misprint in the headline.
40. Burns, Jimmy. Wild Hoss Rarin' to Return, But Marlins' Plans Clouded, *Sporting News*, 16 September, 1959, p. 30.
41. *Sporting News*, 16 September, 1955, p. 30.
42. Baseball-reference.com.
43. Burns, Jimmy. Wild Hoss Rarin' to Return, But Marlins' Plans Clouded, *Sporting News*, 16 September, 1959, p. 30.
44. Kritzer, Cy. Al Vincent Lends Color, Prestige To Our Marlins, *Miami News*, 13 December, 1959, final home edition.: 6-C.
45. Baseball-reference.com.
46. Change In NFL By-Laws Needed For Expansion, *Miami News*, 16 December, 1959, final home edition.: p. 2-C.
47. Cox, Paul. Marlins Are Sold, *Miami News*, 3 January, 1960, final home edition.: p. 1-A.
48. Fitzgerald, Tommy. Several Doormen Were His Good Luck Charms, *Miami News*, 24 January, 1960, final home edition.: p. 5-C.
49. Acer, Margaret. Snoozie-Oh What A Gal!, *Miami News,* 18 January, 1960, final home edition.: p. B-1.
50. Fitzgerald, Tommy. Several Doormen Were His Good Luck Charms, *Miami News*, 24 January, 1960, final home edition.: p. 5-C.
51. Ibid.
52. Baseball-reference.com.
53. Dagres, Angelo. Phone interview with author, 24 October, 2010.
54. Valentine, Fred. Phone interview with author, 6 August, 2014.
55. Ibid.

56. Durney In Hospital, To Miss First Game, *Miami News*, 20 April, 1960, final home edition.: p. 2-E.
57. Durney Jr., Bill. Phone interview with author, 21 December, 2010.
58. Fitzgerald, Tommy. Reprieve From The Sky, *Miami News*, 19 March, 1960, metropolitan edition.: p. 1-B.
59. *Sporting News*, 4 May, 1960, p. 31.
60. Fitzgerald, Tommy. Ball Club's Opener Great...For Flotilla, *Miami News*, 21 April, 1960, final home edition.: p. 2-D.
61. *Sporting News*, 4 May, 1960, p. 32.
62. Grocery Night Lures 11,214, Miami's Top Crowd Since '56, *Sporting News*, p. 30.
63. Owens, Bob. 'Summit Meeting On Player Cut', *Miami News*, 20 May, 1960, final home edition.: p. 2-C.
64. Int Items, *Sporting News*, 1 June, 1960, p. 30.
65. Int Items, *Sporting News*, 8 June, 1960, p. 44.
66. Valentinetti, Vito. Phone interview with author, 24 August, 2011.
67. Nicholson Flops With Marlins, *Sporting News*, 11 May, 1960, p. 30.
68. Burns, Jimmy. Miami Inks Busby to Stabilize Kids, *Sporting News*, 25 May, 1960, p. 31.
69. Baseball-reference.com.
70. Burns, Jimmy. Miami Inks Busby to Stabilize Kids, *Sporting News*, 25 May, 1960, p. 31.
71. Shetrone Hurts Shoulder, Lost to Marlins for Month, *Sporting News*, 8 June, 1960, p. 44.
72. *Sporting News*, 15 June, 1960, p. 30.
73. Injuries Jolt Marlin Outfield, *Sporting News*, 15 June, 1960, p. 30.
74. Devine, Tommy. Two Platoon Squeeze Nips Albie, *Miami News*, 14 June, 1960, final home edition.: p. 2-C.
75. Baseball-reference.com.
76. Staggering Marlins Play Two, *Miami News*, 21 June, 1960, final home edition.: p. 2-C.
77. Burns, Jimmy. Miami Catcher Refuses Trip, Miffed Over Lack of Action, *Sporting News*, 6 July, 1960, p. 30.
78. Dick Hyde Purchased By Miami, *Miami News*, 3 July, 1960, early bird edition.: p. C-1.
79. Pilot Fires Miami Slugger-Orioles Order Him Retrained, *Sporting News*, 29 July, 1960, p. 31.
80. Devine, Tommy. Scout May Carry Axe For Vincent, *Miami News*, 4 July, 1960, final home edition.: p. 7-A.
81. Int Items, *Sporting News*, 6 July, 1960, p. 30.
82. Burns, Jimmy. Cubans' Shift to Jersey City Okayed by Int, *Sporting News*, 20 July, 1960, p. 31.
83. Marlins Get Ruben Gomez, *Miami News*, 17 July, 1960, early bird edition.: p. C-1.
84. Baseball-reference.com.
85. Fitzgerald, Tommy. They Won't Forget Luke's Last Wallop, *Miami News*, 21 August, 1960, metropolitan edition.: p. 1-C.
86. Fitzgerald, Tommy. Marlin Owner Declares He's Had It, *Miami News*, 25 August, 1960, metropolitan edition.: p. 4-D.
87. Burns, Jimmy. Miami Owner Wants to Move or Yield Team, *Sporting News*, 21 September, 1960, p. 36.
88. It's All Over Now For Marlins, *Miami News*, 12 September, 1960, metropolitan edition.: p. 4-C.
89. Burns, Jimmy. Miami Owner Wants to Move or Yield Team, *Sporting News*, p. 36.
90. Anderson, Peter. San Juan Has Good Chance for Int Club'-MacDonald, *Sporting News*, p.36.

91. Devine, Tommy. Sad Baseball Era Finished For Marlins, *Miami News*, 29 November, 1960, final home edition.: p.2-C.
92. Burns, Jimmy. Int Fights Mounting Costs With San Juan Switch to Charleston, *Sporting News*, 24 May, 1961, p.32.
93. Baseball-reference.com.
94. Ibid.
95. Valentine, Fred. Phone interview with author, 6 August, 2014.
96. Pearson, Albie. Phone interview with author 17 May, 2010.

Bibliography

Books

Adams, Adam G. *Some Pre-Boom Developers of Dade County*, Tequesta Vol. XVII, 1957.

Barthel, Thomas. *The Fierce Fun of Ducky Medwick*, (Lanham, Maryland, Scarecrow Press, 2003).

———. *Pepper Martin: A Baseball Biography*, (Jefferson, North Carolina & London, McFarland & Company, Inc.).

Bedingfield, Gary. *Baseball's Dead of World War II: A Roster of Professional Players Who Died in Service* (McFarland & Company, Inc. Publishers: Jefferson, North Carolina & London).

Bramson, Seth. *Burdine's: Sunshine Fashions & The Florida Store* (Charleston, South Carolina: The History Press, 2011).

Brown, Scott. *Baseball in Pensacola: America's Pastime and the City of Five Flags* (History Press, Charleston, SC, 2013).

Dickson, Paul, Bill Veeck. *Baseball's Greatest Maverick*, (Walker Brothers, USA, 2012).

Figueredo, Jorge. *Cuban Baseball: A Statistical History 1878-1961*, (Jefferson, North Carolina & London), McFarland & Company, Inc., 2003).

———. *Beisbol Cubano: A un Paso de las Grandes Ligas: 1878-1961*, (Jefferson, North Carolina & London, McFarland & Company, Inc., 2005).

———. *Who's Who in Cuban Baseball, 1878-1961*, (Jefferson, North Carolina and London McFarland & Co., Inc., 2003).

George, Paul. *Miami: One Hundred Years of History*, South Florida History.

Golenbock, Peter. *Wrigleyville: A Magical History Tour of the Chicago Cubs* (St. Martins Griffin: New York, 2007).

Horvitz, Peter S. & Horvitz, Joachim. *The Big Book of Jewish Baseball, 151-152*, (S.P.I. Books: New York, New York, 2001)

James, Bill, Neyer, Rob. *The Neyer/James Guide to Pitchers*, (New York, New York: Fireside Book Published by Simon & Schuster).

Johnson, Lloyd & Wolff, Miles. *Encyclopedia of Minor League Baseball Third Edition* (Durham, NC: Baseball America, 2007).

Llanes, Rolando. *White Elephant: The Rise and Fall of Miami Baseball Stadium*, (Blurb Inc., 2010).

McCarthy, Kevin. *Baseball In Florida* (Sarasota, FL: Pineapple Press Inc., 1996).

McDermott, Mickey with Eisenberg, Howard. *A Funny Thing Happened on the Way to Cooperstown* (Chicago: Triumph Books: 2003).

Neyer, Rob & James, Bill. *The Neyer/James Guide to Pitchers*, (New York, NY: Fireside Books, Simon & Schuster).

Olson, James S. *Historical Dictionary of the 1950s*, (Greenwood Press, Westport, Connecticut, 2000).

Paige, Leroy Satchel (as told to David Lipman). *Maybe I'll Pitch Forever*, (Lincoln: University of Nebraska Press, 1993).

Parks, Arva Moore. *The New Miami The Magic City* (Miami, FL: Community Media, 2008).

Ribowsky, Mark. *Don't Look Back: Satchel Paige in the Shadows of Baseball* (Simon & Schuster: New York).

Spatz, Lyle. *The SABR Baseball List & Record Book*, (New York Scribner a Division of Simon & Schuster: 2007).

Spivey, Donald. *If You Were Only White: The Life of Leroy "Satchel" Paige* (Columbia, MO: University of Missouri Press, 2012).

Standiford, Les. *Last Train to Paradise: Henry Flagler And The Spectacular Rise And Fall Of The Railroad That Crossed An Ocean* (New York, NY: Broadway Books, 2002).

Stirling, Christopher H, O'Dell, Cary & Kieth, Michael. *Biographical Dictionary of American Radio* (New York: Routledge-Taylor & Francis Group, 2011).

Stone, George. *"Muscle" A Minor League Legend* (Infinity Publishing: Haverford, PA, 2003).

Tye, Larry. *Satchel: The Life and Times of an American Legend* (New York: Random House, 2011).

Veeck, Bill & Linn, Ed. *Veeck as in Wreck: The Autobiography of Bill Veeck* (University of Chicago Press, 2001).

Newspapers and Publications

Akron Beacon Journal
Anniston Star
Associated Press
Athens Banner-Herald
Baseball Research Journal
Bedford Gazette
Courier News (Bridgewater, New Jersey)
Daily Metropolis
Democrat and Chronicle (Rochester, New York)
Evening Independent (St. Petersburg, Florida)
Florence Morning News (Florence, South Carolina)
Florida Sun-Sentinel
Fort Lauderdale News
Gadsen Times
Herald Journal (Spartanburg, South Carolina)
Kingsport News
Lansing State Journal
Los Angeles Times
Miami Daily News
Miami Daily News and Metropolis
Miami Herald
Miami Metropolis
Miami News
Miami New Times
Monthly Weather Review
Newark Advocate
News Journal (Wilmington, Delaware)
Palm Beach Post
Palm Beach Post-Times
Panama City News-Herald
Pittsburgh Post-Gazette
Pittsburgh Press
Portsmouth Daily Times
Post-Standard (Syracuse, New York)
Pottstown Mercury
Prologue Magazine
Reading Eagle
Reading Times
Sarasota Herald-Tribune
Shamokin News-Dispatch
South Florida History
Spalding-Reach Official Base Ball Guide
Sporting News
Sporting News Baseball Guide and Record Book
St. Petersburg Times
St. Louis Dispatch
Tallahassee Democrat
Tampa Times
Tropical Sun

Personal Interviews

Family members and Front Office Personnel

Anagnost, Tim (Batboy)
Carr, Elizabeth "Betty"
Conroy Jr., Mike
Darden, Elvie
Durney Jr., Bill
Enos, Anne
Fassbender, Terri
Foye-Cox, Nancy
Kleinberg, Howard
McKenna, Nancy

Nee, John
Rotzell, Ryan
Rotzell, Thomas
Sheridan, Bob
Smith, Jerry
Smith, June

Smith, Reggie
Stammen, Bill
Stammen, Paul
Streza, Dan
Zachritz, Chris

Players

Ackeret, Jim
Archer, Jim
Bowman, Bob
Bunker, Richard "Dick"
Burke, Leo
Clark, Mel
Dagres, Angelo
DeMars, Billy
Didier, Gerald
Enos, Bill
Exter, Dave
Fernandez, Humberto "Chico"
Getter, Dick
Gray, Johnny
Green, Dallas
Gulvas, Joe
Herzog, Dorrel "Whitey"
Hopke, Fred
Hunsinger, Earl
Johnson, Wilbur
Korcheck, Steve
Kuzava, Bob
Kwiatkowski, Joe
Little, Ed
Locklin, Stu

McCord, Clinton "Butch"
McCoy, Richard "Dick"
Micelotta, Bob "Mickey"
Morant, Charles "Pete"
Pearson, Albie
Qualters, Tom
Samford, Ron
Semproch, Ray
Snyder, Jerry
Spring, Jack
Staab, Caryle
Tompkins, Ben
Tripp, Robert
Usher, Bob
Valentine, Fred
Valentinetti, Vito
Van Dusen, Fred
Villamia, Raul
Wade, Archie
Wasconis, George
Willis, Robert
Wills, Maury
Zubrinski, Eugene
Zuverink, George

Umpire
Albury, Charlie

Websites

aagpbl.com
ancestry.com
baseball-almanac.com
baseballhalloffame.ca
baseball-reference.com
baseballsgreatestsacrifice.com
baseballinwartime.com
baseballrevisited.wordpress.com
bedfordcountysportshalloffame.com
californialeague.webs.com
capecodtimes.com
coconutgrove.com
coe.k-state.edu
cooperstownincanada.com

diamondsinthedusk.com
floridamemory.com
fcit.coedu.usf.edu
fldpi.wordpress.com
groups.google.com
hurricanescience.org
legacy.com
luckyshow.org
miamibeachfl.com
milb.com
minorleaguebaseballplayer.blogspot.com
nationalpastimemuseum.com
newspapers.com
news-reporter.com

palm.fcla.edu
redlandsfortnightly.org
retrosheet.org
sabr.org
satchelpaige.com
stlouisco.com

sun-sentinel.com
thestar.com
tributes.com
veteransfuneralcare.com
wikipedia.org
wwiifoundation.com

Index

About the Authors

Sam Zygner is the author of *The Forgotten Marlins: A Tribute to the 1956–1960 Original Miami Marlins*. He has served as the Chairperson for the South Florida Chapter of the Society for American Baseball Research (SABR) since 2006, and been a member since 1997. His written articles have appeared in *The Baseball Research Journal*; *The National Pastime*; *Nine: A Journal of Baseball History and Culture*. Zygner was the sports and travel journalist for *La Prensa de Miami Newspaper* (Miami, Florida). Sam received his MBA from Saint Leo University. He developed a love for baseball at an early age when his great-grandfather John Jones gifted him with his first baseball encyclopedia.

Barbra Cabrera was born into the baseball world. Her father, Emilio, played professional baseball in Cuba, and the United States. As a youngster, she worked with "Los Cubanitos," the first-of-its-kind youth baseball organization. Founded for Cuban exile children by her dad in Miami, it promoted the love of baseball. At the tender age of five, Barbra became a radio star, the youngest announcer in South Florida. As a print journalist, she covered the gamut from interviewing Hollywood movie and television stars, to securing exclusive interviews when covering true crime stories. On Spanish-language radio, she found her calling as an investigative reporter. A life-long Miamian and baseball devotee, Barbra has the knack of locating things and people that are otherwise impossible to find.